DB2 10.5 Fundamentals for LUW
Certification Study Guide (Exam 615)

Roger E. Sanders

MC PRESS

MC Press Online, LLC
Boise, ID 83703 USA

DB2 10.5 Fundamentals for LUW: Certification Study Guide (Exam 615)

Roger E. Sanders

First Edition

MC Press offers excellent discounts on this book when ordered in quantity for bulk purchases or special sales, which may include custom covers and content particular to your business, training goals, marketing focus, and branding interest.

MC Press Online, LLC
Corporate Offices: 3695 W. Quail Heights Court, Boise, ID 83703-3861 USA
Sales and Customer Service: (208) 629-7275 ext. 500;
service@mcpressonline.com
Permissions and Bulk/Special Orders: mcbooks@mcpressonline.com
www.mcpressonline.com • www.mc-store.com

ISBN: 978-1-58347-457-0   WB201603

To my good friend, Paul Zikopoulos.
Thanks for all your support throughout my professional career.

About the Author

Roger E. Sanders is a DB2 for LUW Offering Manager at IBM and the author of 23 books on relational database technology (22 on DB2 for Linux, UNIX, and Windows; one on ODBC). He has worked with DB2 for Linux, UNIX, and Windows—IBM's relational database management product for open systems—since it was first introduced on the IBM PC as part of OS/2 1.3 Extended Edition (1991), and he has been designing and developing databases and database applications for more than 25 years.

Roger authored a regular column ("Distributed DBA") in *IBM Data Magazine* (formerly *DB2 Magazine*) for 10 years, and he has written numerous tutorials and articles for IBM's developerWorks® website as well as for publications like *Certification Magazine* and *IDUG Solutions Journal* (the official magazine of the International DB2 User's Group). He has delivered a variety of educational seminars and presentations at DB2-related conferences and has participated in the development of 23 DB2 certification exams.

From 2008 to 2015, Roger was recognized as an **IBM Champion** for his contributions to the IBM Data Management community; in 2010 he received recognition as an **IBM developerWorks Contributing Author**, in 2011 as an **IBM developerWorks Professional Author**, and in 2012 as an **IBM developerWorks Master Author, Level 2** for his contributions to the IBM developerWorks community. (Only four individuals worldwide have received this last distinction.) Roger lives in Fuquay-Varina, North Carolina.

Acknowledgments

A project of this magnitude requires both a great deal of time and the support of many individuals. I would like to express my gratitude to the following person for her contributions:

Susan Weaver—former WW Certification Program Manager
Information Management
Susan provided me with screen shots of the IBM Certification Exam Testing software. Susan also reviewed the first chapter of the book and offered valuable feedback.

I would also like to thank my wife, Beth, for her help and encouragement, and for once again overlooking all of the things that did not get done while I worked on yet another (my 25th) book.

Contents

Introduction

One of the biggest challenges computer professionals face today is keeping their skill sets current with the latest changes in technology. When the computing industry was in its infancy, it was possible to become an expert in several different areas, because the scope of the field was relatively small. Today, our industry is both widespread and fast paced, and the skills needed to master a single software package can be quite complex. Because of this, many application and hardware vendors have initiated certification programs that are designed to evaluate and validate an individual's knowledge of their technology. Businesses benefit from these programs because professional certification gives them confidence that an individual has the expertise needed to perform a specific job. Computer professionals benefit because professional certification enables them to deliver high levels of service and technical expertise and, more important, can lead to advancement or new job opportunities within the computer industry.

If you have bought this book (or you are thinking about buying this book), chances are you have already decided you want to acquire one or more of the IBM® DB2® Professional Certifications available. As an individual who has helped IBM develop 23 DB2 certification exams, I can assure you that the tests you must pass to become a certified DB2 professional are not easy. IBM prides itself on designing comprehensive certification exams that are relevant to the work environment an individual holding a particular certification will have had some exposure to. As a result, all of IBM's certification exams are designed with the following questions in mind:

- What are the critical tasks an individual must perform to hold a particular certification?
- What skills must an individual possess to perform each critical task identified?

- What are the consequences if an individual is unable to successfully perform each critical task identified?

You will find that to pass a DB2 certification exam, you must possess a solid understanding of DB2—and for some of the more advanced certifications, you must understand many of its nuances as well.

Now for the good news. You are holding in your hands what I consider to be the best tool you can use to prepare for the *DB2 10.5 Fundamentals for LUW* exam (Exam 615). Because IBM considers me a DB2 Subject Matter Expert (SME), I was invited to participate in the Exam 615 development process. In addition to helping define key exam objectives, I authored roughly 36 exam questions, and I provided feedback on many more before the final exams went into publication. Consequently, I have seen every exam question you are likely to encounter, and I know every concept you will be tested on when you take the *DB2 10.5 Fundamentals for LUW* exam.

Armed with this knowledge and copious notes I composed during the exam development process, I created this study guide, which covers not only every concept you will need to know to pass the *DB2 10.5 Fundamentals for LUW* exam (Exam 615) but also the exam process itself and the requirements for each DB2 10.*x* certification role currently available. In addition, you will find, at the end of the book, sample questions that are worded just like the questions on the actual exam. In short, if you see it in this book, count on seeing it on the exam; if you do not see it in this book, chances are it will not be on the exam. Consequently, if you become familiar with the material presented in this book, you should do well on the *DB2 10.5 Fundamentals for LUW* exam.

About This Book

This book is divided into two parts:

- **Part 1: IBM DB2 Certification (Chapter 1)**

  This section consists of one chapter (Chapter 1), which introduces you to the IBM DB2 Professional Certification Program. In this chapter, you will learn about some of the different certification roles available, along with the basic prerequisites and requirements for each role. This chapter also shows you how to prepare for a DB2 certification exam, and it concludes with a discussion on how to navigate the testing software that IBM uses to administer most of their exams.

- **Part 2: DB2 10. Fundamentals (Chapters 2–7)**

    This section consists of six chapters (Chapters 2 through 7), which provide you with the concepts you will need to master before you can pass the *DB2 10.5 Fundamentals for LUW* exam (Exam 615).

    Chapter 2 presents the various DB2 editions and add-on products that are currently available and shows you which editions and products you should use to create a particular type of database environment. In this chapter, you will learn about the products that make up the *DB2 Family*, the characteristics of data warehouse and OLTP databases, and which DB2 products to use to create each type of database environment. You will also learn how to configure a database to take advantage of BLU Acceleration, and you will learn about the compatibility features that are available in DB2 10.5.

    Chapter 3 introduces you to the authorizations and privileges that are available with DB2, and to the tools that are used to give (grant) and take away (revoke) authorizations and privileges to/from individuals, groups, and roles. In this chapter, you will learn about the two mechanisms that DB2 uses to control access to instances, databases, database objects, and data: *authorities* and *privileges*. You will also discover how to grant authorities and privileges to specific users, groups, and roles, as well as how to revoke authorities and privileges when it is appropriate to do so. And you will learn how to utilize tools like Row and Column Access Control (RCAC) and Label-Based Access Control (LBAC) to secure sensitive data in a way that meets the strictest of security requirements or that adheres to rigid government security standards.

    Chapter 4 introduces you to the various objects that are available with a DB2 environment and shows you how to create and connect to DB2 servers and databases, as well as design and create tables. In this chapter, you will learn about servers, instances, and databases, along with many other different, but often related, objects that make up a DB2 database environment. You will also discover how to create new DB2 databases and how to identify and connect to DB2 servers and databases using Type 1 and Type 2 connections. Finally, you will learn about the different types of tables that can be created in a DB2 10.5 for Linux®, UNIX®, and Windows® database.

Chapter 5 introduces you to the SQL statements and XQuery expressions that can be used to store, modify, delete, and retrieve both relational (traditional) and XML data. In this chapter, you will learn how to use INSERT, UPDATE, and DELETE statements to store, change, and remove data, as well as how to use the SELECT statement and its associated clauses to retrieve data and format the results. You will also discover how to create and invoke SQL stored procedures and user-defined functions. Finally, you will learn what transactions are and how transaction boundaries are defined.

Chapter 6 introduces you to the various data types and constraints that are available with DB2 and shows you how to obtain information about existing tables, indexes, and views. In this chapter, you will learn about the various data types that can be used to store data, as well as how to constrain data with NOT NULL, default, UNIQUE, CHECK, and referential integrity constraints. You will also discover how to create base and temporary tables, as well as how to identify the characteristics of tables, views, and indexes. Finally, you will be shown how to create and use triggers to supplement one or more of the data constraints available.

Chapter 7 introduces you to the concept of data consistency and to the two important mechanisms DB2 uses to maintain data consistency in both single and multiuser database environments: *isolation levels* and *locks*. In this chapter, you will learn what isolation levels are, which isolation levels are available, and how to use isolation levels to keep transactions from interfering with each other in a multiuser environment. You will also discover how DB2 provides concurrency control through the use of locking, which types of locks are available, how to acquire locks, and which factors can influence locking performance.

Audience

The book is written primarily for IT professionals who have some experience working with DB2 10.5 for Linux, UNIX, and Windows and want to take (and pass) the *DB2 10.5 Fundamentals for LUW* certification exam (Exam 615). However, any individual who would like to learn the fundamentals of DB2 10.5 for LUW will benefit from the information in this book.

Conventions Used

You will find many examples of DB2 commands and SQL statements throughout this book. The following conventions are used whenever a DB2 command or SQL statement is presented:

[ ]	Parameters or items shown inside brackets are required and must be provided.
< >	Parameters or items shown inside angle brackets are optional and do not have to be provided.
|	Vertical bars indicate that one (and only one) item in the list of items presented can be specified.
, ...	A comma followed by three periods (ellipsis) indicate that multiple instances of the preceding parameter or item can be included in the DB2 command or SQL statement.

The following examples illustrate each of these conventions:

Example 1

```
REFRESH TABLE [TableName, ...]
<INCREMENTAL | NON INCREMENTAL>
```

In this example, you must supply at least one *TableName* value, as the brackets ([ ]) indicate, and you can provide more than one *TableName* value, as the comma and ellipsis (, ...) characters that follow the *TableName* parameter suggest. INCREMENTAL and NON INCREMENTAL are optional, as the angle brackets (< >) signify, and you can specify either one or the other, but not both, as the vertical bar (|) indicates.

Example 2

```
CREATE SEQUENCE [SequenceName]
<AS [SMALLINT | INTEGER | BIGINT | DECIMAL]>
<START WITH [StartingNumber]>
<INCREMENT BY [1 | Increment]>
<NO MINVALUE | MINVALUE [MinValue]>
<NO MAXVALUE | MAXVALUE [MaxValue]>
<NO CYCLE | CYCLE>
```

```
<NO CACHE | CACHE 20 | CACHE [CacheValue]>
<NO ORDER | ORDER>
```

In this example, you must supply a *SequenceName* value, as the brackets ([ ]) indicate. However, everything else is optional, as the angle brackets (< >) signify; in many cases, a list of available option values is provided (for example, NO CYCLE and CYCLE), but you can specify only one, as the vertical bar (|) denotes. In addition, when some options are provided (for example, START WITH, INCREMENT BY, MINVALUE, MAXVALUE, and CACHE), you must supply a corresponding value for each option used, as the brackets ([ ]) that follow the option indicate.

SQL is not a case-sensitive language, but for clarity, the examples shown throughout this book use mixed case—command syntax is presented in upper case, and user-supplied elements such as table names and column names are presented in lower case. (This same format is used with all of the DB2 certification exams.)

Note: Although basic syntax is presented for most of the SQL statements covered in this book, the actual syntax supported can be much more complex. To view the complete syntax for a specific DB2 command or SQL statement or to obtain more information about a particular command or statement, refer to the IBM DB2 Version 10.5 Knowledge Center (*https://www-01.ibm.com/support/ knowledgecenter/#!/SSEPGG_10.5.0/com.ibm.db2.luw.wn.doc/doc/ c0061179.html*).

IBM DB2 for Linux, UNIX, and Windows Certification

Certification has long been a popular trend in the Information Technology (IT) industry. Consequently, many hardware and software vendors—including IBM—have certification programs in place that are designed to evaluate and validate an individual's proficiency with their product offerings.

Recognized throughout the world, the *IBM Professional Certification Program* offers a wide variety of certification options for IT professionals who want to demonstrate their knowledge and expertise with a particular IBM product. And if you regularly use IBM hardware, software, or both, chances are you have heard of this program and have thought about becoming IBM certified. But, are you aware that IBM has more than 275 different certification roles to choose from? More important, do you know which certification role is right for you? And, do you know how to prepare for and take the certification exams that are required for the certification role you wish to pursue?

This chapter is designed to provide you with answers to these and other questions. It begins by introducing you to the certification roles that have been defined for individuals who use IBM's DB2 for Linux, UNIX, and Windows (DB2 for LUW) Information Management software. Then, it shows you how to prepare for the DB2 certification tests, and it concludes with a discussion on how to navigate the testing software that IBM uses to administer most of its exams.

DB2 10.1 and 10.5 for LUW Certification Roles

The *IBM Professional Certification Program* consists of several distinct certification roles that are designed to guide you in your professional development. To obtain a particular certification, you simply select the role you wish to pursue (based on your knowledge and experience working with a particular IBM product), familiarize yourself with the requirements that have been defined for that role, and then take the necessary certification exam(s) for the role you have chosen. This book focuses on the **IBM Certified Database Associate—DB2 10.5 Fundamentals for LUW** role (as well as the exam you must take and pass to obtain this certification); however, two DB2 Version 10.5 and three DB2 Version 10.1 for LUW certification roles are currently available. They are:

- IBM Certified Database Associate—DB2 10.1 Fundamentals
- IBM Certified Database Associate—DB2 10.5 Fundamentals for LUW
- IBM Certified Database Administrator—DB2 10.1 for Linux, UNIX, and Windows
- IBM Certified Database Administrator—DB2 10.5 for LUW Upgrade from DB2 10.1
- IBM Certified Advanced Database Administrator—DB2 10.1 for Linux, UNIX, and Windows

IBM Certified Database Associate—DB2 10.1 Fundamentals

The **IBM Certified Database Associate—DB2 10.1 Fundamentals** certification is intended for entry-level DB2 users who are knowledgeable about the basic concepts of DB2 10.1 for Linux, UNIX, and Windows *and* DB2 10 for z/OS. In addition to having some hands-on experience or training (either formal or informal) on DB2 10 for z/OS or DB2 10.1 for LUW, individuals seeking this certification should:

- ✓ Know which DB2 10 and 10.1 products are available, as well as the function of each product (at a high level)
- ✓ Know which DB2 10 and 10.1 product to use for a given type of database workload (online transaction processing [OLTP], decision support system [DSS], or data warehouse)
- ✓ Know how to store and manipulate nonrelational data, such as large objects (LOBs) and Extensible Markup Language (XML) documents
- ✓ Possess an in-depth knowledge about the authorities and privileges that can be used to protect databases and data against unauthorized access and modification
- ✓ Know how to grant and revoke authorities and privileges

✓ Possess a basic understanding of Row and Column Access Control (RCAC)

✓ Possess a basic understanding of roles and trusted contexts

✓ Know how to create and connect to DB2 servers and databases

✓ Know how to create, access, and manipulate basic DB2 objects, such as tables, indexes, and views

✓ Know how and when to create system-period, application-period, and bitemporal temporal (time-travel) tables

✓ Possess an in-depth knowledge of Structured Query Language (SQL), as well as an understanding of the Data Definition Language (DDL), Data Manipulation Language (DML), and Data Control Language (DCL) statements that are available with DB2

✓ Know how to sort and group data

✓ Possess a strong understanding of transactions and know what constitutes a transaction boundary

✓ Know how to create and invoke SQL procedures and SQL user-defined functions (UDFs), as well as how to pass parameters to and retrieve results from SQL procedures and SQL UDFs

✓ Possess a basic knowledge of XQuery

✓ Know how to query temporal (time-travel) tables

✓ Know how to use the various data types—including the Oracle® compatibility data types—that are available with DB2

✓ Know how and when to create temporary tables

✓ Know how and when to use the different types of constraints (NOT NULL, default, CHECK, UNIQUE, referential integrity, and informational) that are available with DB2

✓ Know how and when to create triggers

✓ Know how to use schemas

✓ Possess a basic understanding of the mechanisms (transactions, isolation levels, and locks) that are used to isolate the effects of transactions from one another in a multiuser environment

✓ Know which factors influence locking

✓ Know how and when to use the LOCK TABLE statement

✓ Be able to identify the characteristics of common DB2 locks that are used on both the Linux, UNIX, and Windows and the z/OS platform

✓ Be able to identify the appropriate isolation level to use for a given situation

✓ Know how and when to use Currently Committed semantics with the Cursor Stability isolation level

To obtain **IBM Certified Database Associate—DB2 10.1 Fundamentals** certification, candidates must take and pass the *DB2 10.1 Fundamentals* exam (Exam 610). Figure 1.1 illustrates the road map for acquiring this certification.

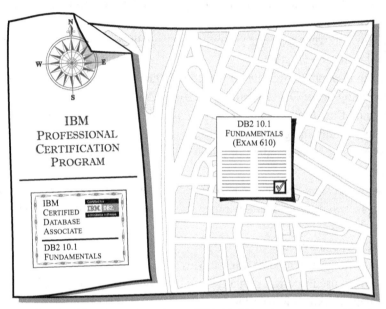

Figure 1.1: IBM Certified Database Associate—DB2 10.1 Fundamentals certification road map

IBM Certified Database Associate—DB2 10.5 Fundamentals for LUW

The **IBM Certified Database Associate—DB2 10.5 Fundamentals for LUW** certification is intended for entry-level DB2 users who are knowledgeable about the basic concepts of DB2 10.5 for Linux, UNIX, and Windows. In addition to having some hands-on experience or training (either formal or informal) on DB2 10.5 for Linux, UNIX, and Windows, individuals seeking this certification should:

- ✓ Know which DB2 10.5 for LUW products are available, as well as the function of each product (at a high level)
- ✓ Know which DB2 10.5 for LUW product to use for a given type of database workload (online transaction processing [OLTP], decision support system [DSS], or data warehouse)
- ✓ Possess an in-depth knowledge about DB2 10.5 BLU Acceleration and when it should be used
- ✓ Know how to configure a DB2 10.5 for LUW database for analytics

✓ Possess a basic understanding of the Oracle compatibility features that are available with DB2 10.5 for LUW

✓ Possess an in-depth knowledge about the authorities and privileges that can be used to protect databases and data against unauthorized access and modification

✓ Know how to grant and revoke authorities and privileges

✓ Possess a basic understanding of Row and Column Access Control (RCAC)

✓ Possess a basic understanding of Label-Based Access Control (LBAC)

✓ Possess a basic understanding of roles and trusted contexts

✓ Know how to create and connect to DB2 servers and databases

✓ Know how to create, access, and manipulate basic DB2 objects, such as tables, indexes, and views

✓ Possess an in-depth knowledge of Structured Query Language (SQL), as well as an understanding of the Data Definition Language (DDL), Data Manipulation Language (DML), and Data Control Language (DCL) statements that are available with DB2 10.5 for LUW

✓ Possess an in-depth knowledge about the different types of tables that are available with DB2 10.5 for LUW

✓ Know how to retrieve data from a table or view

✓ Know how to sort and group data

✓ Possess a strong understanding of transactions and be able to manage transactions using COMMIT, ROLLBACK, and SAVEPOINT statements

✓ Know how to create and invoke SQL procedures and SQL user-defined functions (UDFs), as well as how to pass parameters to and retrieve results from SQL procedures and SQL UDFs

✓ Possess a basic understanding of the SQL compatibility enhancements that were added in DB2 10.5 for LUW

✓ Possess a basic knowledge of XML and XQuery

✓ Know how and when to use the various data types—including the Oracle compatibility data types—that are available with DB2 10.5 for LUW

✓ Be able to identify the characteristics of an existing table, view, or index

✓ Know how and when to create and use temporary tables

✓ Know how and when to create and use triggers

✓ Possess a basic understanding of the mechanisms (isolation levels and locks) that are used to isolate the effects of transactions from one another in a multiuser environment

✓ Know which factors influence locking

✓ Know how and when to use the LOCK TABLE statement

✓ Be able to identify the characteristics of DB2 locks

✓ Be able to identify the appropriate isolation level to use for a given situation
✓ Know how and when to use Currently Committed semantics with the Cursor Stability isolation level

To obtain **IBM Certified Database Associate—DB2 10.5 Fundamentals for LUW** certification, candidates must take and pass the DB2 10.5 Fundamentals for LUW exam (Exam 615). Figure 1.2 illustrates the road map for acquiring this certification.

Figure 1.2: IBM Certified Database Associate—DB2 10.5 Fundamentals for LUW certification road map

IBM Certified Database Administrator—DB2 10.1 DBA for Linux, UNIX, and Windows

The **IBM Certified Database Administrator—DB2 10.1 DBA for Linux, UNIX, and Windows** certification is designed for experienced DB2 users who possess the knowledge and intermediate-to-advanced skills needed to perform the day-to-day administration of DB2 10.1 for Linux, UNIX, and Windows instances and databases. Along with being knowledgeable about DB2 fundamentals and having significant hands-on experience as a DB2 10.1 Database Administrator (DBA), individuals seeking this certification should:

✓ Know how to configure and manage DB2 servers, instances, and databases

✓ Know how to use the autonomic features that are available with DB2 10.1 for Linux, UNIX, and Windows
✓ Know how to perform administrative tasks using Data Studio
✓ Know how to create a new DB2 10.1 for Linux, UNIX, and Windows database
✓ Know how to create, access, modify, and manage DB2 database (data) objects
✓ Be able to convert an existing DB2 for Linux, UNIX, and Windows database to an automatic storage database
✓ Know how to use the ADMIN_MOVE_TABLE() procedure
✓ Possess a basic knowledge of DB2's partitioning capabilities
✓ Know how to store and manage XML data
✓ Be able to describe how classic and adaptive row compression works, as well as know how to enable a table or index for either type of compression
✓ Possess a basic knowledge of the new table features that were introduced in DB2 10.1
✓ Know how and when to use the multi-temperature data feature
✓ Know how and when to create NOT NULL, default, CHECK, UNIQUE, referential integrity, and informational constraints
✓ Know how and when to use the WITH CHECK OPTION clause of the CREATE VIEW statement
✓ Know how and when to create and use triggers
✓ Know how and when to use the SET INTEGRITY command
✓ Know how to use administrative views and SQL functions to monitor a DB2 10.1 database environment
✓ Possess a basic knowledge of the monitoring features available with Workload Manager
✓ Be able to use the auto-monitoring tools that are available with DB2 10.1
✓ Know how to use the DB2 Problem Determination Tool (db2pd)
✓ Know how to capture and analyze Explain information
✓ Know how to use the DB2 data movement utilities (EXPORT, IMPORT, LOAD, and db2move)
✓ Know how and when to use the Ingest utility
✓ Know how and when to use the REORGCHK, REORG, REBIND, RUNSTATS, and FLUSH PACKAGE CACHE commands
✓ Know how and when to use the DB2 Design Advisor
✓ Possess an in-depth knowledge of crash recovery, version recovery, and roll forward recovery
✓ Know how to perform database-level and table space-level backup and recovery operations

✓ Be able to configure and manage a High Availability Disaster Recovery (HADR) environment, as well as enable a standby server for read-only operations

✓ Possess a basic knowledge of the high availability (HA) features DB2 pureScale® provides

✓ Possess an in-depth knowledge of the authorities and privileges that can be used to protect databases and data against unauthorized access and modification

✓ Know which operations someone with Security Administrator (SECADM) authority can perform

✓ Possess a basic understanding of the Audit facility

✓ Possess a basic understanding of trusted contexts

✓ Possess an in-depth knowledge of RCAC

✓ Possess an in-depth knowledge of LBAC

✓ Be able to configure database connectivity

✓ Know how to perform a DB2 Discovery request, as well as how to prevent DB2 Discovery requests from seeing servers, instances, and/or databases

✓ Know how to configure a DB2 server for Lightweight Directory Access Protocol (LDAP) connectivity

Candidates who have taken and passed either the *DB2 9 Family Fundamentals* exam (Exam 730), the *DB2 10.1 Fundamentals* exam (Exam 610), or the *DB2 10.5 Fundamentals for LUW* exam (Exam 615) can obtain **IBM Certified Database Administrator—DB2 10.1 DBA for Linux, UNIX, and Windows** certification by taking (and passing) the *DB2 10.1 DBA for Linux, UNIX, and Windows* exam (Exam 611). All other candidates must take and pass either the *DB2 10.1 Fundamentals* exam (Exam 610) or the *DB2 10.5 Fundamentals for LUW* exam (Exam 615) *and* the *DB2 10.1 DBA for Linux, UNIX, and Windows* exam (Exam 611). Figure 1.3 illustrates the road map for acquiring **IBM Certified Database Administrator—DB2 10.1 DBA for Linux, UNIX, and Windows** certification.

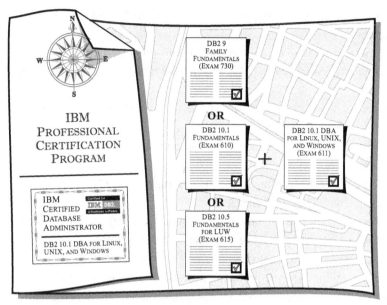

Figure 1.3: IBM Certified Database Administrator—DB2 10.1 DBA for Linux, UNIX, and Windows certification road map

IBM Certified Database Administrator—DB2 10.5 DBA for LUW Upgrade from DB2 10.1

The **IBM Certified Database Administrator—DB2 10.5 DBA for LUW Upgrade from DB2 10.1** certification is designed for experienced DB2 for LUW users who already possess **IBM Certified Database Administrator—DB2 10.1 DBA for Linux, UNIX, and Windows** certification, are knowledgeable about the new features and functions that were introduced with DB2 Version 10.5, and are capable of performing the tasks required to administer DB2 10.5 for LUW instances and databases. Individuals seeking this certification should:

- ✓ Know how to configure a DB2 10.5 for LUW environment for an analytics workload
- ✓ Know which registry variables and configuration parameters are affected when BLU Acceleration is enabled
- ✓ Know how to use the autonomic features that are available with BLU Acceleration
- ✓ Know how automatic space reclamation works with BLU Acceleration
- ✓ Know how to perform administrative tasks using Data Studio 4.1
- ✓ Be able to use automated workload management when a DB2 10.5 for LUW environment has been configured for an analytics workload

✓ Possess a basic understanding of the seven big ideas behind DB2 10.5 BLU Acceleration

✓ Know how and when to create and use column-organized tables

✓ Possess a basic understanding of how synopsis tables are used to facilitate "data skipping"

✓ Know how and when to use static compression, adaptive compression, actionable (Huffman encoding) compression, value compression, and backup compression

✓ Know how and when to use expression-based indexes, as well as how to collect statistics on those indexes

✓ Possess a basic understanding of the Oracle migration and compatibility features that are available with DB2 10.5 for LUW

✓ Know how and when to use unique and primary key informational constraints

✓ Possess a basic understanding of extended row size support

✓ Know how and when to exclude NULL keys from indexes

✓ Be able to monitor dynamic prefetch requests for data in a column-organized table

✓ Be able to measure column data size using appropriate monitoring elements

✓ Be able to measure the time spent in the Columnar Data Engine (CDE) using appropriate monitoring elements

✓ Be able to identify a Column Table Queue (CTQ) operator in Explain output, as well as be able to describe its purpose

✓ Possess a basic understanding of the MON_GET_ROUTINE() monitoring table function

✓ Possess a basic understanding of the HADR monitoring enhancements that were introduced with DB2 10.5 for LUW

✓ Be able to perform an online REORG in a DB2 pureScale environment

✓ Be able to set up HADR in a DB2 pureScale environment

✓ Possess a basic understanding of how HADR standby replay works at a DB2 pureScale standby cluster

✓ Possess a basic understanding of how to make online topology changes to an existing DB2 pureScale cluster

✓ Be able to apply rolling FixPack updates to a DB2 pureScale environment

✓ Be able to use the Self-Tuning Memory Manager (STMM) in a DB2 pureScale environment

✓ Possess a basic understanding of how to use the Explicit Hierarchical Locking Multi-Tenancy Feature in a DB2 pureScale environment

✓ Know how and when to use random ordering for index key columns

✓ Possess a basic understanding of how and when to use DB2 Advanced Copy Services (ACS) customized scripts

✓ Be able to use the IBM Optim Query Workload Tuner
✓ Know how and when to use the IBM Optim Workload Table Organization Advisor
✓ Know how and when to use the db2convert utility
✓ Be able to describe what takes place during the Analyze phase of a Load operation
✓ Be able to describe the default behavior of the Load utility when it is used to populate a column-organized table
✓ Be able to use the IBM Optim Workload Table Organization Advisor to compare "before" and "after" data access plans

Candidates who obtained **IBM Certified Database Administrator—DB2 10.1 for Linux, UNIX, and Windows** certification by taking (and passing) either the *DB2 9 Family Fundamentals* exam (Exam 730), the *DB2 10.1 Fundamentals* exam (Exam 610), or the *DB2 10.5 Fundamentals for LUW* exam (Exam 615) *and* the *DB2 10.1 DBA for Linux, UNIX, and Windows* exam (Exam 611) can acquire **IBM Certified Database Administrator—DB2 10.5 DBA for LUW Upgrade from DB2 10.1** certification by taking (and passing) the *DB2 10.5 DBA for LUW Upgrade from DB2 10.1* exam (Exam 311). Figure 1.4 displays the road map for acquiring **IBM Certified Database Administrator—DB2 10.5 DBA for LUW Upgrade from DB2 10.1** certification.

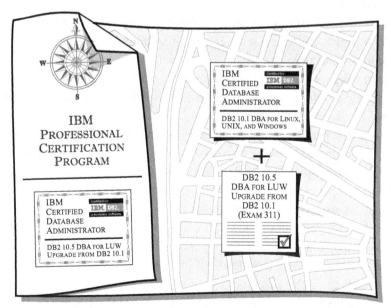

Figure 1.4: IBM Certified Database Administrator—DB2 10.5 DBA for LUW Upgrade from DB2 10.1 certification road map

IBM Certified Advanced Database Administrator—DB2 10.1 for Linux, UNIX, and Windows

The **IBM Certified Advanced Database Administrator—DB2 10.1 for Linux, UNIX, and Windows** certification is designed for individuals who possess extensive knowledge about DB2 10.1 and have significant hands-on experience administering DB2 10.1 databases on Linux, UNIX, or Windows platforms. In addition to being knowledgeable about the more complex concepts of DB2 10.1 and being capable of performing advanced database administration tasks such as monitoring and tuning for optimum performance, planning for high availability, and managing network connectivity, individuals seeking this certification should:

- ✓ Be able to design, create, and manage database storage paths (for automatic storage databases)
- ✓ Be able to design, create, and manage table spaces for automatic storage databases
- ✓ Be able to design, create, and manage buffer pools
- ✓ Be able to design and configure a database for multi-temperature data
- ✓ Be able to use Data Studio to manage database environments
- ✓ Be able to design, create, and manage database partitioning using the Data Partitioning Feature (DPF)
- ✓ Be able to design, create, and manage multidimensional clustered (MDC) tables
- ✓ Be able to design, create, and manage range-partitioned tables
- ✓ Be able to design, create, and manage insert time clustering (ITC) tables
- ✓ Be able to design, create, and manage range clustering tables
- ✓ Know how to develop a logging strategy, as well as be able to use transaction logs for recovery
- ✓ Know how to perform backup and recovery operations, as well as know how to use the advanced backup and recovery features that are available with DB2 10.1 for LUW
- ✓ Know how to configure and use Workload Manager
- ✓ Be able to set up and maintain a HADR environment
- ✓ Know how to use DB2's diagnostic tools
- ✓ Be able to identify the appropriate DB2 diagnostic tool to use for a given situation
- ✓ Possess a strong knowledge of query optimizer concepts
- ✓ Know how to manage and tune database, instance, and application memory in conjunction with database I/O
- ✓ Know how and when to use the different compression methods that are available
- ✓ Be able to correctly analyze, isolate, and resolve database performance problems
- ✓ Know how and when to create indexes to improve query performance

✓ Be able to take advantage of intrapartition and interpartition parallelism
✓ Know how and when to create a federated database environment
✓ Know how and when to use replication
✓ Be able to describe the major components needed in a DB2 pureScale environment, as well as know when DB2 pureScale should be used
✓ Know how and when to use the DB2 Audit facility

Candidates who obtained **IBM Certified Database Administrator—DB2 10.1 DBA for Linux, UNIX, and Windows** certification by taking (and passing) either the *DB2 9 Family Fundamentals* exam (Exam 730), the *DB2 10.1 Fundamentals* exam (Exam 610), or the *DB2 10.5 Fundamentals for LUW* exam (Exam 615) *and* the *DB2 10.1 DBA for Linux, UNIX, and Windows* exam (Exam 611) can acquire **IBM Certified Advanced Database Administrator—DB2 10.1 for Linux, UNIX, and Windows** certification by taking (and passing) the *DB2 10.1 Advanced Database Administrator for Linux UNIX and Windows* exam (Exam 614). Figure 1.5 displays the road map for acquiring **IBM Certified Advanced Database Administrator—DB2 10.1 for Linux, UNIX, and Windows** certification.

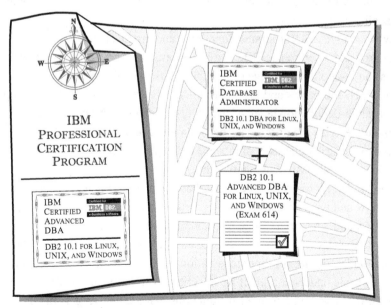

Figure 1.5: IBM Certified Advanced Database Administrator—DB2 10.1 for Linux, UNIX, and Windows certification road map for individuals holding IBM Certified Database Administrator —DB2 10.1 for Linux, UNIX, and Windows certification

Additional DB2 9.7 Certification Roles

In addition to the DB2 Version 10.1 and Version 10.5 for LUW certification roles that are currently available, two additional certification roles exist that are based on DB2 Version 9.7. They are:

- IBM Certified Application Developer—DB2 9.7 for Linux, UNIX, and Windows
- IBM Certified Solution Developer—DB2 9.7 SQL Procedure

IBM Certified Application Developer—DB2 9.7 for Linux, UNIX, and Windows

The **IBM Certified Application Developer—DB2 9.7 for Linux, UNIX, and Windows** certification is intended for intermediate-to-advanced-level application developers who possess the knowledge and skills necessary to design, build, test, and deploy applications that interact with DB2 9.7 databases residing on Linux, UNIX, and Windows platforms. In addition to being knowledgeable about DB2 9.7 and having significant hands-on experience designing and developing applications, individuals seeking this certification should:

- ✓ Be familiar with the naming conventions that are used to identify DB2 objects, such as tables, aliases, and views
- ✓ Know when to use SQL routines, functions, and modules
- ✓ Know how and when to use DB2's built-in functions and stored procedures
- ✓ Possess an in-depth knowledge of the data types that DB2 recognizes
- ✓ Know which authorities and privileges are needed to access data from an application
- ✓ Possess an in-depth knowledge of the SQL statements that DB2 recognizes
- ✓ Be able to describe the differences between static and dynamic SQL
- ✓ Be able to construct queries that retrieve data from multiple tables and views
- ✓ Know how to use DML statements to insert, update, and delete data
- ✓ Be able to identify the types of cursors that can be used in an application
- ✓ Know how and when to use cursors, as well as know what a cursor's scope is
- ✓ Know how and when to use locators to manipulate LOB data
- ✓ Be able to manage transactions using COMMIT, ROLLBACK, and SAVEPOINT statements
- ✓ Be able to identify the appropriate isolation level to use for a given situation
- ✓ Possess a basic understanding of XML schema validation and XML schema evolution
- ✓ Know how to use the built-in XML functions that are provided with DB2
- ✓ Know how to handle white space in XML documents
- ✓ Be able to create an XML document from existing relational data

✓ Be able to execute and evaluate the results of an XQuery expression

✓ Know how to construct queries that retrieve both relational and XML data

✓ Know how to bind and rebind a package

✓ Know how and when to use parameter markers

✓ Know how to connect to a database from an Embedded SQL, Call Level Interface/ Open Database Connectivity (CLI/ODBC), Java® Database Connectivity (JDBC), SQL for Java (SQLJ), ADO.NET, or PHP application

✓ Know how to submit an SQL statement to DB2 for processing from an Embedded SQL, CLI/ODBC, JDBC, SQLJ, ADO.NET, or PHP application

✓ Know how to obtain query results, as well as manipulate data, from an Embedded SQL, CLI/ODBC, JDBC, SQLJ, ADO.NET, or PHP application

✓ Be able to analyze the contents of an SQL Communications Area (SQLCA) data structure

✓ Be able to obtain and analyze ODBC/CLI diagnostic information

✓ Be able to obtain and analyze JDBC trace, SQL exception, and JDBC error log information

✓ Be able to obtain and analyze ADO.NET diagnostic information

✓ Be able to obtain and analyze PHP diagnostic information

✓ Know how to create and register external stored procedures

✓ Know how to create external UDFs, including OLE DB and external table UDFs

✓ Be able to describe what will happen if an application attempts to modify data stored in a table that is part of a referential integrity constraint

✓ Possess a basic understanding of distributed units of work (two-phase commits)

✓ Possess a basic understanding of trusted contexts

✓ Know how to create, access, modify, and manage advanced DB2 database objects, such as sequences, global declared temporary tables, and multidimensional query tables (MQTs)

Candidates who have taken and passed either the *DB2 V8.1 Family Fundamentals* exam (Exam 700), the *DB2 9 Family Fundamentals* exam (Exam 730), or the *DB2 10.1 Fundamentals* exam (Exam 610) can obtain **IBM Certified Application Developer— DB2 9.7 for Linux, UNIX, and Windows** certification by taking (and passing) the *DB2 9.7 Application Development* exam (Exam 543). All other candidates must take and pass both the *DB2 9 Family Fundamentals* exam (Exam 730) or the *DB2 10.1 Fundamentals* exam (Exam 610) *and* the *DB2 9.7 Application Development* exam (Exam 543). Figure 1.6 shows the road map for acquiring **IBM Certified Application Developer—DB2 9.7 for Linux, UNIX, and Windows** certification.

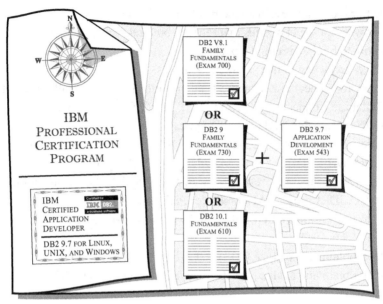

Figure 1.6: IBM Certified Application Developer—DB2 9.7 for Linux, UNIX, and Windows certification road map

IBM Certified Solution Developer—DB2 9.7 SQL Procedure

The **IBM Certified Solution Developer—DB2 9.7 SQL Procedure** certification is intended for intermediate-to-advanced-level developers who possess the knowledge and skills necessary to design, build, test, and deploy stored procedures, UDFs, and triggers that have been written using SQL, SQL Procedural Language (SQL PL), or both. In addition to being knowledgeable about DB2 9.7 and having significant experience programming in SQL and SQL PL (using IBM's development tools), individuals seeking this certification should:

- ✓ Know how to define variables and cursors
- ✓ Be able to code assignment statements
- ✓ Know how to use SQL PL control statements
- ✓ Be familiar with both SQL and SQL PL error handling
- ✓ Know when it is appropriate to use SQL procedures
- ✓ Know how to use the CREATE PROCEDURE statement
- ✓ Know the proper structure of an SQL procedure body
- ✓ Know how to return values and result data sets from SQL procedures
- ✓ Know how to code and use nested SQL procedures

✓ Be able to test and deploy an SQL procedure
✓ Know when it is appropriate to use SQL functions
✓ Know how to use the CREATE FUNCTION statement
✓ Know the proper structure of an SQL function body
✓ Know how to return both values and a table from an SQL function
✓ Know how to invoke an SQL function
✓ Be able to test and deploy an SQL function
✓ Know when it is appropriate to use a trigger (as opposed to an SQL procedure or function)
✓ Know how to use the CREATE TRIGGER statement
✓ Be able to identify the actions of a trigger
✓ Possess an in-depth knowledge of advanced uses of triggers
✓ Be able to test and deploy a trigger
✓ Know how and when to create and use declared global temporary tables
✓ Know how to use the ADMIN_CMD() procedure to execute administrative commands
✓ Know how to take advantage of system features
✓ Know how and when to use arrays and associated arrays
✓ Know how and when to use global variables
✓ Know how and when to use modules
✓ Know how to enable a database to support Oracle PL/SQL procedures
✓ Be familiar with DB2 application development tools such as IBM Data Studio
✓ Be able to debug stored procedures and UDFs using the DB2 development tools available
✓ Know how to capture and analyze Explain information

Candidates who have taken and passed either the *DB2 V8.1 Family Fundamentals* exam (Exam 700), the *DB2 9 Family Fundamentals* exam (Exam 730), or the *DB2 10.1 Fundamentals* exam (Exam 610) can obtain **IBM Certified Solution Developer—DB2 9.7 SQL Procedure** certification by taking (and passing) the *DB2 9.7 SQL Procedure Developer* exam (Exam 545). All other candidates must take and pass both the *DB2 9 Family Fundamentals* exam (Exam 730) or the *DB2 10.1 Fundamentals* exam (Exam 610) **and** the *DB2 9.7 SQL Procedure Developer* exam (Exam 545). Figure 1.7 illustrates the road map for acquiring **IBM Certified Solution Developer—DB2 9.7 SQL Procedure** certification.

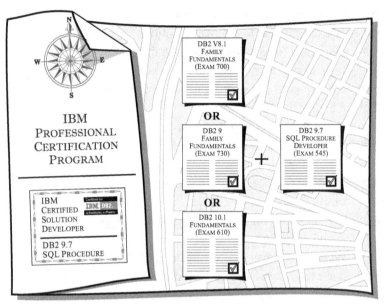

Figure 1.7: IBM Certified Solution Developer—
DB2 9.7 SQL Procedure Developer certification road map

The Certification Process

A quick examination of the road maps just presented reveals that, to obtain a particular certification from IBM, you must take and pass one or more exams that have been designed specifically for that certification role. (Each exam is a software-based test that is neither platform nor product specific.) Therefore, once you have chosen a certification role to pursue and have become familiar with the requirements (objectives) that have been defined for that role, the next step is to prepare for and take the necessary certification exam(s).

Preparing for the Certification Exams

If you have experience using DB2 10.5, 10.1, or 9.7 for LUW in the context of the certification role you have chosen, you might already possess the skills and knowledge needed to pass the exams that have been created for that particular role. However, if your experience with DB2 is limited (or even if it is not), you can prepare for any of the certification exams available by taking advantage of the following resources:

Formal Education

IBM Learning Services offers a wide variety of courses that can help you prepare for certification. The IBM Professional Certification Program website (*www.ibm.com/ certify*) provides a list of recommended courses for each certification exam. Simply locate and select the certification exam of interest and right-click the **Test preparation** tab when information about that exam appears. For more information on courses, schedules, training locations, and pricing, contact IBM Learning Services or visit its website.

Online Tutorials

IBM offers a series of interactive online tutorials to help you prepare for the DB2 10.1 Fundamentals exam (Exam 610) on its developerWorks website. The first tutorial in the series can be found at *www.ibm.com/developerworks/data/tutorials/db2-cert6101/ index.html*.

IBM also offers a series of online tutorials for the DB2 10.1 for Linux, UNIX, and Windows Database Administration certification exam (Exam 611). The first tutorial in this series can be found at *www.ibm.com/developerworks/data/tutorials/db2-cert6111/ index.html*.

Publications

You can find all the information you need to pass any of the DB2 certification exams available in the documentation that is provided with DB2; the product includes a complete set of manuals that you can access online via the IBM Knowledge Center or download from IBM's website in the form of PDF files. (The DB2 Product Family Library, at *www.ibm.com/software/data/db2/library*, contains links to this documentation as well as to DB2 version-specific IBM Knowledge Centers.)

Self-study books (like this one) that focus on one or more DB2 certification roles or specific DB2 certification exams are also available at your local bookstore, or you can order them from many online book retailers. (A list of possible reference materials for a particular certification exam can often be found on the **Test preparation** tab for that exam. And in some cases, ordering information is included with the listing.)

In addition to DB2 product documentation, IBM often produces manuals, known as Redbooks, that cover, among other things, advanced DB2 topics. These manuals are available as downloadable PDF files on IBM's Redbooks® website (*www.redbooks .ibm.com*). Or, if you prefer to have a bound hard copy, you can obtain one for a modest fee by following the appropriate link on the Web page for the Redbook that interests you. (The downloadable Adobe® PDF files are available at no charge.)

Exam Objectives

The IBM Professional Certification Program website (*www.ibm.com/certify*) provides a list of topics that each certification exam is designed to cover. Simply locate and select the certification exam of interest and right-click the **Objectives** tab when information about that exam is presented. To find exam objectives for the *DB2 10.5 Fundamentals for LUW* exam (Exam 615), refer to Appendix A of this book.

Sample Questions and Practice Exams

Sample questions and practice exams offer a glimpse of the topics and the types of questions (as well as the wording) you are likely to encounter on a particular certification exam. More important, they can often help you determine whether you are ready to take a specific exam. (For this reason, sample questions, along with detailed answers, are provided at the back of this book.)

Practice exams for most of IBM's certification exams are available via the IBM Professional Certification Program website (*www.ibm.com/certify*). Simply locate and select the certification exam of interest and right-click the **Sample/Assessment Test** tab when information about that exam appears. Usually, a fee of $30.00 US is charged for each assessment test taken.

It is important to note that IBM's certification exams are designed to be rigorous and extensive. Because of this, and because the range of material covered on a certification exam is usually broader than the knowledge base of many DB2 professionals, you should try to take advantage of as many exam preparation resources as possible. This will help ensure your success in obtaining the certification(s) you desire.

Arranging to Take a Certification Exam

When you are confident that you are ready to take a particular DB2 certification exam, your next step is to contact an IBM-authorized testing vendor and make the necessary arrangements. As of January 2, 2014, Pearson VUE is responsible for administering IBM's DB2 certification exams; however, in some cases IBM might administer them as well. For example, IBM frequently offers certification testing, for a nominal fee, at some of the larger IT conferences, such as the International DB2 User's Group (IDUG) conference and the IBM Insight conference.

Pearson VUE's website (*www.pearsonvue.com/ibm*) offers a list of its testing centers—there are many to choose from throughout the world—and after finding a testing center that is convenient to you, you will need to create an account (or sign in if you already have an account) and make arrangements to take the certification exam desired. (You can also contact the vendor and make the necessary arrangements by phone; contact information for Pearson VUE can be found on their website.)

You must arrange to take a certification exam at least 24 hours in advance, and when you contact Pearson VUE, you should be ready to provide the following information:

- ✓ Your name (as you want it to appear on your certification certificate)
- ✓ Your unique testing identification number, if you have one (if you have taken an IBM certification exam before, this is the number that was assigned to you at that time; if not, Pearson VUE will supply one)
- ✓ A telephone number where you can be reached
- ✓ A fax number
- ✓ The mailing address where you want all hard-copy correspondence to be sent
- ✓ Your billing address, if it is different from your mailing address
- ✓ Your email address
- ✓ The number of the certification exam you wish to take (for example, Exam 615)
- ✓ The method of payment (credit card or debit card) you will use, along with any relevant payment information (such as credit/debit card number, expiration date, and card security code)
- ✓ Your company's name (if applicable)
- ✓ The testing center where you would like to take the exam
- ✓ The date that you would like to take the exam

Before you make arrangements to take a certification exam, you should have paper and pencil or pen handy so you can write down the test applicant identification number the testing center will assign you. You will need this information when you arrive at the testing center. (You should receive a confirmation email containing the number of the certification exam you are scheduled to take, along with corresponding date, time, and location information, at the email address you provided.)

● ●

Note: If you have already taken one or more IBM certification exams, you should make the testing administrator (Pearson VUE or IBM) aware of this and ask them to assign you the same applicant identification number that was used before. This will allow the certification team at IBM to quickly recognize when you have met all the exam requirements for a particular certification role. (If you were assigned a unique applicant identification number each time you took an exam, you can go to the IBM Professional Certification Member website, *www.ibm.com/certify/members*, and select **Member Services** to combine all of your exam results under one ID.)

● ●

With the exception of the *DB2 10.5 DBA for LUW Upgrade from DB2 10.1* exam (Exam 311), each certification exam costs $200.00 US (Exam 311 costs $100.00 US), and you can arrange to take an exam immediately after you provide the appropriate payment information. If, for some reason, you need to reschedule or cancel your testing appointment, you must do so at least 24 hours before your scheduled test time. Otherwise, you will be charged the full price of the exam.

Taking an IBM Certification Exam

On the day you are scheduled to take a certification exam, you should arrive at the testing center at least 15 minutes before the scheduled time, to sign in. As part of the sign-in process, you will be asked to provide the applicant identification number you were assigned when you made arrangements to take the exam, as well as two forms of identification. One form of identification must be a current (not expired) government issued photo ID with your name and signature; the other must feature your name and signature. Examples of valid forms of identification include a driver's license or passport (government issued photo ID with signature) and a credit card (name and signature). The name on both forms of identification presented must match exactly the name that is in the Pearson VUE system.

Once you are signed in, the exam proctor will instruct you to enter the testing area and select an available workstation. The proctor will then enter your name and identification number into the workstation you have chosen, provide you with a pencil and some paper, and instruct you to begin the exam when you are ready. At that point, the Title screen of the IBM Certification Exam testing software should be displayed on the computer monitor in front of you. Figure 1.8 illustrates what this screen looks like.

Figure 1.8: Title screen of the IBM Certification Exam testing software

As you can see in Figure 1.8, the Title screen of the IBM Certification Exam testing software consists of the title "Professional Certification Program from IBM," the IBM logo, and the name of the exam that is about to be administered (for example, the Title screen in Figure 1.8 indicates that the *DB2 10.1 Fundamentals* exam is about to be administered), along with some basic information on how to get started. Before proceeding, you should verify that the exam you are about to take is indeed the exam you expected to take. If the name of the exam that appears on the Title screen is different from the name of the exam you had planned on taking, bring this to the attention of the exam proctor immediately. When you are ready, begin by selecting the **Next** button located in the lower-right corner of the screen (refer to Figure 1.8). To do this, place the mouse pointer over the **Next** button and click the left mouse button.

After you have clicked **Next** on the Title screen, you will be presented with a Proprietary and Confidential Information screen, where you will be asked to agree that you will not disclose the contents of the exam in any manner, to anyone. Figure 1.9 illustrates what this screen looks like.

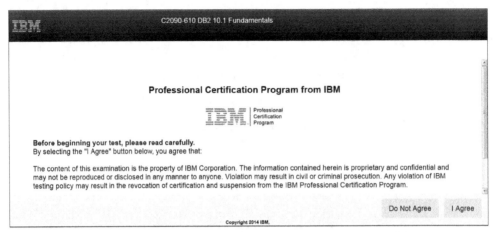

Figure 1.9: Proprietary and Confidential Information screen of the
IBM Certification Exam testing software

If you agree to the terms and conditions outlined on the Proprietary and Confidential
Information screen, click the **I Agree** button located in the lower-right corner of the
screen (refer to Figure 1.9). Once you have clicked **I Agree**, you will be presented
with the Begin Test screen of the IBM Certification Exam testing software. Figure 1.10
illustrates what this screen looks like.

Figure 1.10: Begin Test screen of the IBM Certification Exam testing software

As you can see in Figure 1.10, the Begin Test screen consists of the title "Professional
Certification Program from IBM," the IBM logo, and a welcome message containing

your name and some basic information about the exam you are about to take. Before proceeding, you should verify that your name is spelled correctly. The way your name appears in the welcome message displayed reflects how it has been stored in the IBM Certification database. Consequently, this is how all correspondence to you will be addressed, and, more important, this is how your name will appear on the certification credentials you will receive once you have met all the requirements for a particular certification role.

In addition to telling you which exam is about to be administered, the Begin Test screen lets you know how many questions you can expect to see on the exam, the score you must receive to pass, and the time frame in which the exam must be completed. Most DB2 certification exams contain between 60 and 70 questions, and you are allotted up to 90 minutes to complete them. (The *DB2 10.5 DBA for LUW Upgrade from DB2 10.1* exam contains 30 questions and must be completed within 60 minutes.) However, even though each certification exam must be completed within a predefined time limit, you should never rush through an exam just because the "clock is running"; the time limits imposed are more than adequate for you to work through the questions at a relaxed and steady pace.

When you are ready to start the exam, select the **Begin Test** button located in the lower-right corner of the screen (refer to Figure 1.10). If, instead, you desire a quick refresher course on how to use the IBM Certification Exam testing software, click the **Tutorial** button located in the lower-left corner of the screen.

• •

 Important: If you plan to take a quick refresher course on how to use the IBM Certification Exam testing software, make sure you do so *before* you click Begin Test to begin the exam. Although help is available at any time, the clock does not start running until you select the Begin Test button. Therefore, by viewing help information before the clock has started, you avoid spending what could prove to be valuable testing time reading documentation instead of answering questions.

• •

After you have clicked **Begin Test** on the Begin Test screen, the clock will start running, and the first exam question will be presented in a screen that looks similar to the one shown in Figure 1.11.

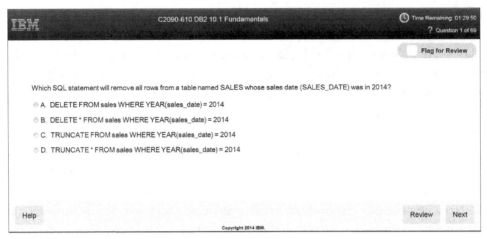

Figure 1.11: Typical question screen of the IBM Certification Exam testing software

Aside from the question itself, one of the first things you might notice if you look closely at the question screen is that the question number appears in the top-right corner of the screen. If you answer each question in the order they are presented, this portion of the screen can act as a progress indicator since it displays both the current question number *and* the total number of questions contained in the exam.

Immediately below the question number, you will find a special check box that is labeled **Flag for Review**. If you want to skip the current question for now and come back to it later, or if you are uncertain about the answer(s) you have chosen and would like to look at this question again after you have completed the rest of the exam, you should mark this check box (by placing the mouse pointer over it and pressing the left mouse button). After you have viewed every question once, you will be given the opportunity to review just the marked (flagged) questions again. At that time, you can answer any unanswered questions remaining and reevaluate any answers you have some reservations about.

Another important feature on the question screen is the **Time Remaining** information, which appears in the top-right corner of the screen, immediately above the question number. This area of the question screen provides continuous feedback on the amount of time you have available in which to complete (and review) the exam.

The most important part of the question screen, however, is the question itself and the corresponding list of possible answers provided. Take time to read each question carefully, and when you have located the correct answer in the list provided, mark it by selecting the answer radio button positioned just to the left of the answer text (by placing the mouse pointer over the desired answer radio button and pressing the left mouse button). After you have selected an answer for the current question (or marked it using the **Flag for Review** check box), you can move to the next question by clicking the **Next** button, located in the lower-right corner of the screen (refer to Figure 1.11).

If at any time you want to return to the previous question, you can do so by clicking the **Previous** button, located just to the left of the **Next** button, at the bottom of the screen (refer to Figure 1.12). And to obtain help on how to use the IBM Certification Exam testing software, click **Help**, located in the lower-left corner of the screen (refer to Figure 1.12).

It is important to note that although you can use the **Next** and **Previous** buttons to navigate through the questions, the navigation process itself is not cyclic in nature—that is, when you are on the first question, you cannot go to the last question by clicking **Previous** (in fact, the **Previous** button will not be displayed if you are on the first question, which is why it is not shown in Figure 1.11). Likewise, when you are on the last question, you cannot go to the first question simply by clicking **Next**. However, you can quickly navigate back to any question from the Item Review screen, which you can get to by clicking **Review**. (We will look at the Item Review screen shortly).

Although in most cases, only one answer in the list provided is the correct answer for the question shown, there are times when multiple answers are valid. On those occasions, the answer radio buttons will be replaced with answer check boxes, and the question will be worded in such a way to make it obvious how many answers are expected. Figure 1.12 shows an example of such a question.

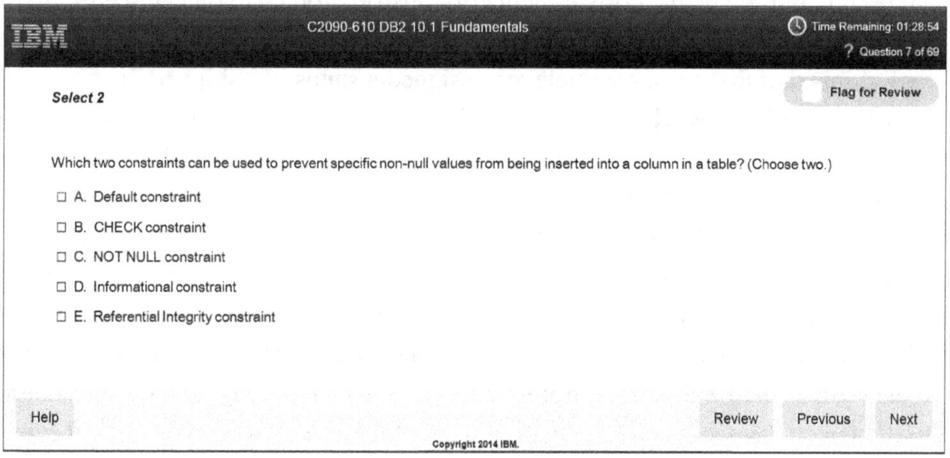

Figure 1.12: Question screen for questions expecting multiple answers

To answer these types of questions, select the answer check box positioned just to the left of the text of every correct answer you find. (Again, to do this, place the mouse pointer over each desired answer check box and press the left mouse button.)

When you have viewed every exam question available (by clicking **Next** on every question screen that appears), an Item Review screen similar to the one shown in Figure 1.13 may be displayed.

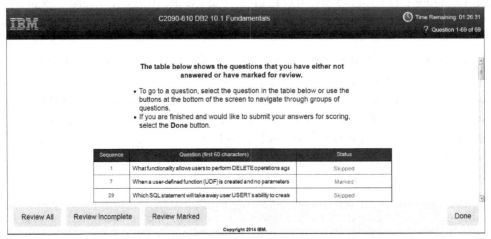

Figure 1.13: Item Review screen of the IBM Certification Exam testing software

The Item Review screen contains a listing of questions from the exam you have just taken that you either marked (by choosing the **Flag for Review** check box) or that you skipped or did not provide the correct number of answers for. (As you can see in Figure 1.13, items that were flagged for review are assigned a status of "Marked," while items that were skipped or that are incomplete are assigned a status of "Skipped.")

By clicking the **Review All** button located in the lower-left corner of the screen (refer to Figure 1.13), you can go back through all the questions on the exam. By clicking the **Review Incomplete** button (located just to the right of the **Review All** button), you can go back through just the questions that have been identified as being incomplete. When you review incomplete items in this manner, each time you click **Next** on a question screen, you proceed to the next incomplete question in the list until you eventually return to the Item Review screen. Likewise, by clicking the **Review Marked** button (located just to the right of the **Review Incomplete** button), you can quickly go back through just the questions you have marked. (Navigation works the same as when you click **Review Incomplete**.)

One of the first things you should do if the Item Review screen appears is resolve any incomplete items found. (When the exam is graded, each incomplete item is marked incorrect, and points are deducted from your final score.) Then, if time permits, you should go back and review the questions that you marked. It is important to note that when you finish reviewing a marked question, you should unmark it (by placing the mouse pointer over the **Flag for Review** check box and pressing the left mouse button) before proceeding to the next marked question or returning to the Item Review screen. This will make it easier for you to keep track of which questions you have reviewed and which you have not.

After you have resolved every incomplete item found, the **Review Incomplete** button will automatically disappear from the Item Review screen; similarly, when no more marked questions exist, the **Review Marked** button will disappear. Consequently, when you have resolved every incomplete and marked item found (or if there were no incomplete or marked items originally), you will be presented with a screen that looks like the one shown in Figure 1.14.

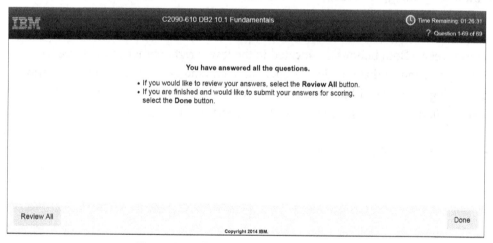

Figure 1.14: Finished with the exam screen

At this point, you can go through all the questions again by selecting the **Review All** button located in the lower-left corner of the screen (refer to Figure 1.14). Or, if you feel comfortable with the answers you have provided, you can end the exam and submit it for grading by clicking the **Done** button, which is located in the lower-right corner of the screen. After you select this button, a screen similar to the one shown in Figure 1.15 will appear.

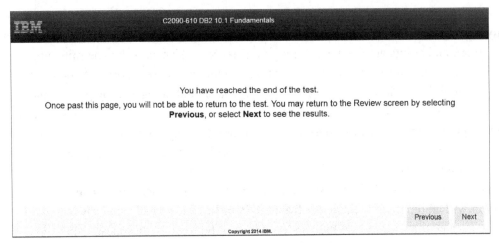

Figure 1.15: End exam session confirmation screen

This screen gives you the opportunity to confirm your decision to end the exam and submit it for grading, or to reconsider and continue resolving or reviewing exam items (questions). If you wish to do the former, click the **Next** button when this screen is displayed; if you wish to do the latter, click the **Previous** button to return to the Item Review screen. (Both buttons are located in the lower-right corner of the screen.)

Once you confirm that you do indeed wish to end the exam, the IBM Certification Exam testing software will evaluate your answers and produce a score report that indicates whether you passed the exam. This report will then be displayed on a Test Results screen similar to the one shown in Figure 1.16. At the same time, a corresponding hard-copy printout will be generated.

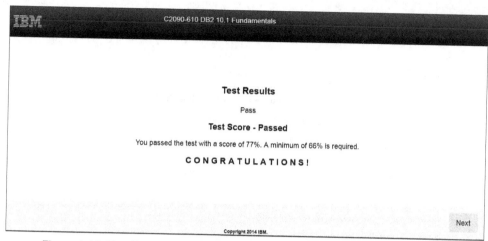

Figure 1.16: Test Results screen of the IBM Certification Exam testing software

As you can see in Figure 1.16, the Exam Results panel shows your test results (Pass or Fail) along with a message that contains the required score and the percentage score you received. If you received a passing score, this message will begin with the word "Congratulations!" However, if you received a score that is below the score needed to pass, the message you see will begin with the words "You did not pass the test."

Each certification exam is broken into sections, and regardless of whether you receive a passing or failing score, you should take a few moments to review the scores you received for each section. This information can help you assess your strengths and weaknesses. And if you failed to pass the exam, this information can help you identify the areas that you should spend more time reviewing before you attempt to take it again. To view the section scores for the exam you just completed, simply click the **Next** button, which is located in the lower-right corner of the screen. You should then see a screen that is similar to the one shown in Figure 1.17.

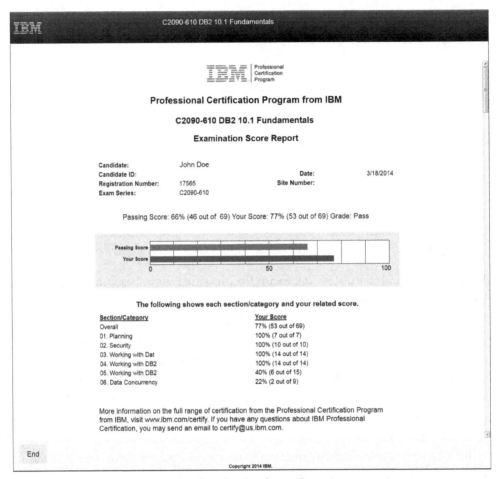

Figure 1.17: Examination Score Report screen

When you have finished reviewing your section scores, you can exit the IBM Certification Exam testing software by clicking the **End** button, which is located at the lower-left corner of the screen.

Shortly after you take a certification exam (usually within five working days), Pearson VUE will send your results, along with your demographic data (for example, name, address, and phone number) to the IBM Certification Group for processing. If you passed the exam, you will receive credit toward the certification role the test was designed for. And if you have met all of the requirements that have been defined for that certification role, you will receive an email (at the email address you provided during registration) directing you to the IBM Certification Members website, where you can download a certificate suitable for framing (in the form of a PDF file), camera-ready artwork of the IBM certification logo, and guidelines for using the "IBM Certified" mark. If desired, you can also receive a printed certificate and/or a wallet-sized certificate via regular mail by going to the appropriate website (referenced in the email) and requesting these materials—you will be asked to provide your Fulfillment ID and Validation Number (also provided in the email) as proof that you have met all the requirements for certification.

Upon receipt of the welcome email, you are officially certified and can begin using the IBM Professional Certification title and trademark. You should receive the IBM Certification Agreement and welcome email within four to six weeks after IBM processes the exam results. If you failed to pass the test and you still wish to become certified, you must arrange to retake the exam (and you must pay the testing fee again). No restrictions apply on the number of times you can take a particular certification exam; however, you cannot take the same exam more than two times within a 30-day period.

2

Planning

Sixteen percent (16%) of the *DB2 10.5 Fundamentals for LUW* certification exam (Exam 615) is designed to test your knowledge of the various DB2 editions and add-on products that are available from IBM. This portion of the exam is also designed to test your ability to identify which edition and products to use to create a specific type of database environment, as well as your knowledge of DB2 10.5 BLU Acceleration. The questions that make up this portion of the exam are intended to evaluate the following:

- Your knowledge of the DB2 10.5 products currently available
- Your ability to identify the characteristics of both data warehouse and online transaction processing (OLTP) workloads
- Your ability to identify which DB2 products should be used to create a particular database environment (data warehouse or OLTP)
- Your knowledge of DB2 10.5 BLU Acceleration, as well as your ability to configure a DB2 database for analytical workloads
- Your knowledge of the compatibility features that are available with DB2 10.5

This chapter introduces you to the various DB2 editions and add-on products that are currently available and shows you which editions and products to use to create a data warehouse or OLTP environment. In this chapter, you will learn about the products that make up the *DB2 Family*, the characteristics of data warehouse and OLTP databases, and which DB2 products to use to create each type of database environment. You will also discover how to configure a database to take advantage of BLU Acceleration, and you will learn about the compatibility features that are available in DB2 10.5.

The DB2 Family

In 1969, while working at IBM's San Jose Research Laboratory in San Jose, California, Edgar Frank "Ted" Codd introduced a relational model for database management in a paper titled "A Relational Model of Data for Large Shared Data Banks." And over the next four years, a variety of research prototypes such as University of California, Berkley's *Ingres* and IBM's *System R* (short for *System Relational*) were developed based on this model. In 1980, as part of an effort to port the System R prototype to their mainframe computer, IBM began work on a new product called *DATABASE 2* (otherwise known as *DB2*), and on June 7, 1983, the company made DB2 available to a limited number of IBM mainframe customers. Then, in 1985, IBM made DB2 generally available to all customers who were using the MVS™ operating system.

In 1987, DB2 arrived on the personal computer (PC) in the form of a product called *Database Manager*, which was one of two special add-on products that were included as part of the Extended Edition version of OS/2 1.3; a year later, a version emerged in the form of *SQL/400* for IBM's new AS/400® server. (IBM developers working on System R created a nonrelational programming language named *SEQUEL*, which was later renamed *SQL*—an acronym for *Structured Query Language*—and the name *SQL/400* was derived by combining this acronym with part of the AS/400 server name.)

By 1992, DB2 had become a standalone product on OS/2 (and was now called *DB2/2*), and in 1993, IBM made DB2 generally available to customers running AIX® on IBM RS/6000® series servers. (Initially, this port was known as *DB2/6000*, but eventually both DB2/2 and DB2/6000 were replaced with a product named *DB2 for Common Servers*.) DB2 for Common Servers arrived on HP-UX and Solaris servers in 1994, on Windows servers in 1995, and on Linux servers in 1999. Along the way the name changed yet again, and DB2 for Common Servers became *DB2 Universal Database™*.

Today, essentially two flavors of DB2 are available: DB2 for Linux, UNIX, and Windows, sometimes referred to as *DB2 for LUW* or *DB2 for distributed platforms*, and DB2 for z/OS. (With the release of DB2 Version 9, the *Universal Database* moniker was replaced with the names of the three most prominent operating systems that the non-z/OS flavor of DB2 runs on.) Several editions of DB2 are available, and each edition has been designed to meet a specific business need. These editions, along with a suite of add-on products that provide additional functionality, are known collectively as the *DB2 Family*. The editions that make up the heart of this family are:

- DB2 Express-C
- DB2 Express Server Edition
- DB2 Workgroup Server Edition
- DB2 Enterprise Server Edition
- DB2 Advanced Workgroup Server Edition
- DB2 Advanced Enterprise Server Edition
- DB2 for z/OS

Figure 2.1 shows all the aforementioned DB2 Family editions, along with the type of computing environment each edition is primarily designed for.

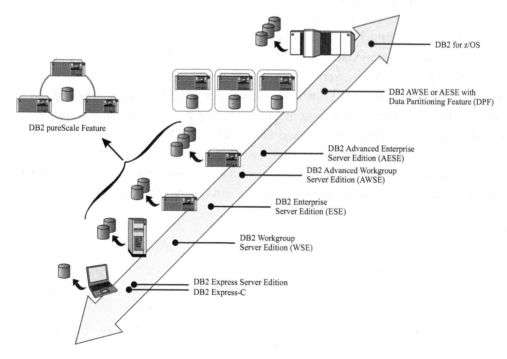

Figure 2.1: The DB2 editions available

• •

Note: Do not confuse DB2 for Linux on System z (also known as zLinux) with DB2 for z/OS. In this case, the DB2 product that runs on zLinux is DB2 for Linux, UNIX, and Windows—and any DB2 client or driver can connect to it, without the need for DB2 Connect™ software (an add-on product that provides connectivity between DB2 for Linux, UNIX, and Windows and DB2 for z/OS databases).

• •

It is important to note that you can easily move from one DB2 edition to another—provided you are not trying to move from an edition of DB2 that has been developed for Linux, UNIX, or Windows to an edition that has been developed for z/OS (or vice versa). That's because on Linux, UNIX, and Windows platforms, approximately 90 percent of the DB2 code base is common, with only 10 percent being slightly different to tightly integrate the software with the underlying operating system (for instance, to leverage huge pages on AIX or the NTFS file system on Windows).

Consequently, if you use DB2 Express-C to create a database and later decide to upgrade to DB2 Enterprise Server Edition, you merely replace the existing DB2 Express-C software with a DB2 Enterprise Server Edition (ESE) image. The end result will be a database environment that looks exactly as it did before, but that can take advantage of additional features and functionality that have been made available to it. This means that any application developed for one edition will work, without modification, with other editions. It also means that any DB2-specific skills that you have learned will remain applicable, regardless of the edition you are using.

DB2 Express-C

DB2 Express-C (also known as *DB2 Express-Community edition*) is a no-charge, entry-level database management system that is ideal for small businesses, IBM business partners, developers, instructors, and students who want to evaluate DB2 or develop applications that interact with DB2 for Linux, UNIX, and Windows databases. DB2 Express-C is simple to set up, easy to use, and contains many of the core features and functionality available with other DB2 editions, including:

- **IBM Data Studio:** An Eclipse-based integrated development environment that can be used to perform instance and database administration; create, deploy, and debug data-centric Java applications; and analyze and provide query-tuning recommendations

Note: IBM Data Studio consists of the *Data Studio client* and the *Data Studio Web console.* For most installations, the Data Studio client component is sufficient; to monitor database health and availability, as well as create and manage jobs, you also need the Data Studio Web console.

- **pureXML®:** Offers a simple, efficient way to store well-formed XML documents while providing the same level of security, integrity, and resiliency that is available for relational data; this allows XML data to be stored in its native, hierarchical format and be manipulated using XQuery, SQL, or a combination of the two
- **Backup compression:** Used to reduce the size of backup images by compressing all of the data in an image, including catalog tables, user tables, index objects, large objects, auxiliary database files, and database metadata, thereby reducing storage space requirements
- **Time-Travel Query:** Lets businesses discover how data looked (or will look) at a specific point in time; (special tables called temporal tables associate time-based, state information with relational data values; data in temporal tables can be valid for a time period that is defined by the database system, user applications, or both)
- **Federation with DB2 for LUW and Informix® data sources:** Makes it possible to access objects like tables and views that reside in other DB2 for Linux, UNIX, Windows, and/or Informix databases as if they were local objects
- **SQL compatibility:** Lets individuals run applications written for Oracle, Sybase, and MySQL databases seamlessly against a DB2 for Linux, UNIX, and Windows database
- **Net Search Extender:** Provides users and application programmers a way to use SQL queries to search full-text documents that are stored in DB2 databases, other databases, and/or file systems
- **DB2 Spatial Extender:** Provides a way to generate and analyze spatial information about geographic features, as well as store and manage the data this information is based upon (a geographic feature is anything in the real world that has an

identifiable location or anything that can be imagined as existing at an identifiable location)

- **Native encryption:** Lets businesses meet security and regulatory requirements by encrypting both the database and any database backup images created

DB2 Express-C is available in more than 16 different languages and can be installed on any server that is running the Linux or Windows operating system (32-bit or 64-bit versions). The server used can contain any number of processors/cores and any amount of memory. However, total resource utilization is limited to two processors/cores and 4 GB of RAM.

Owners of DB2 Express-C can purchase a low-cost, yearly subscription option (known as a *Fixed-Term License* or *FTL*) that provides the following additional benefits and features that are not available with the no-cost version:

- 24/7 customer support, fix packs, and upgrade protection
- Increased resource utilization: eight cores (two sockets) and 8 GB memory
- Failover capabilities with High Availability Disaster Recovery (HADR)
- Enhanced security with both Row and Column Access Control (RCAC) and Label-Based Access Control (LBAC)
- SQL replication

DB2 Express Server Edition

DB2 Express Server Edition is a comprehensive, budget-friendly database management system that is designed to meet the needs of small and midsize businesses, academic institutions, and IBM Business Partners. With support for up to eight processor cores and 8 GB of RAM, DB2 Express Server Edition is ideal for building database environments that are robust, resilient, secure, and cost-efficient. With the exception of native encryption, DB2 Express Server Edition comes with all the features and functionality provided with DB2 Express-C, as well as the following:

- **Advanced Copy Services (ACS):** Enables the use of fast, disk-based replication technology that is available with some storage devices for backup and recovery operations (use of this technology can drastically reduce the amount of time required to back up and restore large databases)
- **Row and Column Access Control (RCAC):** Complements the authorities and privileges security model available with DB2 by controlling access to a table at the

row level, the column level, or both the row and column level; this feature can also be used to mask sensitive information so unauthorized users cannot see it

- **Label-Based Access Control (LBAC):** Provides multilevel data security by controlling who has read access, who has write access, and who has both read and write access to individual rows, individual columns, or individual rows and columns in a table; this feature is implemented by assigning unique labels to users and data and allowing access only when assigned labels match

- **Online reorganization:** Reorganizes tables and rebuilds indexes to eliminate fragmentation and/or compress data; as the name implies, this work can take place while a database remains online and accessible

- **High Availability Disaster Recovery (HADR):** Provides ultrafast hardware and software failover capabilities by replicating data changes made to a source database (called the *primary database*) to one or more target databases (called s*tandby databases*) and failing over to one of the standbys, if for some reason, the primary becomes inaccessible

- **SQL Replication with DB2 for LUW and Informix data sources:** Captures changes made to source tables and views and writes them to staging tables—changes are then read from the staging tables and replicated to corresponding target tables in other DB2 for Linux, UNIX, and Windows or Informix databases

- **IBM Tivoli® System Automation for Multiplatforms:** Provides high availability for critical business applications and middleware through policy-based self-healing that is easily tailored to an individual application environment; it includes plug-and-play automation policy modules for many IBM and non-IBM middleware and applications, such as DB2®, WebSphere®, Apache, and mySAP Business Suite

Like DB2 Express-C, DB2 Express Server Edition is available in multiple languages; unlike DB2 Express-C, DB2 Express Server Edition can be installed on servers that are running 32- or 64-bit versions of the following operating systems:

- Red Hat Enterprise Linux (RHEL) 5, 6, 7, or 7.1
- SUSE Linux Enterprise Server (SLES) 10, 11, or 12
- Ubuntu Linux 12.04 LTS or 14.04 LTS
- Sun Solaris 10
- Microsoft® Windows (Windows 8.1 Enterprise, Windows 8.1 Professional, Windows 8.1 Standard, Windows 8 Enterprise, Windows 8 Professional, Windows 8 Standard, Windows 7 Ultimate, Windows 7 Enterprise, Windows 7 Professional,

Windows Server 2012 Datacenter Edition, Windows Server 2012 Standard Edition, Windows Server 2012 Essentials Edition, Windows Server 2008 Datacenter Edition, Windows Server 2008 Enterprise Edition, Windows Server 2008 Standard Edition)

> **Note:** While native encryption functionality is not provided as part of DB2 Express Server Edition, this functionality can be added by purchasing the **IBM DB2 Encryption Offering** product. With DB2 Version 10.5, FixPack 5 and later, the **IBM Advanced Recovery Feature** and the **IBM DB2 Performance Management Offering** can be added to DB2 Express Server Edition as well.

DB2 Workgroup Server Edition (WSE)

DB2 Workgroup Server Edition (WSE) is a scalable, full-function, high-performance database management system that is ideal for small and midsize businesses, workgroups, and departments that consist of a small number of internal users. In addition to having the power and reliability to handle department-level workloads with ease, DB2 Workgroup Server Edition is packed with all the features that DB2 Express Server Edition offers as well as features that reduce the total cost of ownership (TCO), including:

- **Autonomic features:** Helps lower the cost of data management by automating basic administration tasks, increasing storage efficiency, improving runtime performance, and simplifying the deployment of virtual appliances; the autonomic features available consist of:
  - » **Automatic storage:** Simplifies storage management by allowing DB2 to determine the storage characteristics for table spaces (including the location of containers) and by automatically monitoring and managing table space container growth
  - » **Self-Tuning Memory Manager (STMM):** Responds to significant changes in a database's workload by dynamically distributing available memory resources among several different database memory consumers
  - » **Automatic maintenance:** Simplifies storage management by performing database backup operations automatically, keeping database statistics current, and reorganizing tables and indexes as necessary

» **Self-configuration:** Automatically configures memory allocation, storage management, and business policy maintenance operations for DB2 databases
» **Health monitoring:** Proactively monitors situations or changes in a database environment that can result in performance degradation or potential outages
- **Audit Facility:** Monitors data access and provides information needed for subsequent analysis; auditing can help discover unwanted, unknown, and unacceptable access to data as well as keep historical records of activities performed on a database system
- **Table partitioning:** A data organization scheme in which table data is divided across multiple storage objects (called *data partitions*) according to values stored in one or more columns; each data partition can reside in a different table space, in the same table space, or in a combination of the two

DB2 Workgroup Server Edition is also available in a variety of languages and can be installed on servers that are running 32- and 64-bit versions of the operating systems that DB2 Express Server Edition can be installed on. DB2 Workgroup Server Edition can also be installed on servers that are running 32- or 64-bit versions of the following operating systems:

- IBM AIX 6.1, 7.1, or 7.2
- Sun Solaris 11
- HP-UX 11i v3

One of the main advantages that DB2 Workgroup Server Edition offers over DB2 Express Server Edition (and DB2 Express-C) is that it can leverage more RAM and CPU processing power—DB2 Workgroup Server Edition is restricted to 16 processor cores and 128 GB of memory. Another advantage is that with DB2 Version 10.5, FixPack 5 and later, the following product offerings can be added to DB2 Workgroup Server Edition:

- IBM DB2 BLU Acceleration In-Memory Offering
- IBM DB2 Business Application Continuity Offering
- IBM DB2 Encryption Offering
- IBM Advanced Recovery Feature
- IBM DB2 Performance Management Offering

(We will take a closer look at these product offerings shortly.)

DB2 Enterprise Server Edition (ESE)

Ideal for high-performance, robust enterprise environments, DB2 Enterprise Server Edition (ESE) is designed to meet the data server needs of midsize and large businesses that have hundreds of internal and/or external users. DB2 Enterprise Server Edition can be deployed on Linux, UNIX, and Windows servers (physical or virtual) of any size and, unlike with other DB2 editions, there are no restrictions on the number of processor cores and the amount of memory that can be used.

DB2 Enterprise Server Edition includes all the features and functionality that come with DB2 Workgroup Server Edition, as well as the following additional features:

- **Connection Concentrator:** Improves the performance of applications that require frequent, but relatively transient, simultaneous user connections by allocating host database resources only for the duration of an SQL transaction
- **Federation with DB2 for Linux, UNIX, and Windows and Oracle data sources:** Makes it possible to access objects like tables and views that reside in Oracle databases as if they were local objects
- **Materialized Query Tables (MQTs):** Tables whose definitions are based on the results of a query; MQTs provide a powerful way to improve response time for complex queries, and they are similar to views in that their data comes from one or more base tables—MQT data is generated by executing the query the MQT is based upon, either at regular intervals or at a specific point in time that is dictated by the user; however, unlike with views, MQT data physically resides in the MQT itself
- **Multidimensional Clustering (MDC) Tables:** Offer an elegant way to cluster data along two or more dimensions; MDC tables can significantly improve query performance and drastically reduce the overhead of data maintenance operations— MDC tables are used primarily in data warehouse and large database environments, but they can be used in OLTP environments as well
- **Multi-temperature data management:** Utilizes *storage groups* (a named set of storage paths where data is to be stored) to represent different classes of storage (solid state disks, fibre channel drives, or serial ATA drives) that might be available to a database system—by using multi-temperature data management, it is possible to place frequently or constantly accessed data on faster storage devices and keep infrequently accessed data on slower (and cheaper) disks

- **Query parallelism:** Provides the ability to break a query into multiple parts and process those parts in parallel across multiple partitions of a partitioned database (that spans one or more servers/workstations), thereby improving performance
- **Resource Description Framework (RDF):** A family of World Wide Web Consortium (W3C) specifications that employs Uniform Resource Identifiers (URIs) to create a relationship between data as a triple (for example, in the form of *subject-predicate-object* expressions) or as a quad—(RDF is similar to NoSQL)

As with DB2 Workgroup Server Edition, DB2 Enterprise Server Edition is available in multiple languages and can be installed on servers that are running AIX, Linux, Solaris, HP-UX, and Microsoft Windows (in other words, any operating system that DB2 Workgroup Server Edition can be installed on). Also like DB2 Workgroup Server Edition, with DB2 Version 10.5, FixPack 5 and later, the following product offerings can be added to DB2 Enterprise Server Edition:

- IBM DB2 BLU Acceleration In-Memory Offering
- IBM DB2 Business Application Continuity Offering
- IBM DB2 Encryption Offering
- IBM Advanced Recovery Feature
- IBM DB2 Performance Management Offering

DB2 Advanced Workgroup Server Edition (AWSE)

The second most comprehensive DB2 edition available, DB2 Advanced Workgroup Server Edition (AWSE) is a powerful database management solution that offers all the features and functionality available with DB2 Enterprise Server Edition, as well as the following additional benefits:

- **DB2 Storage Optimization Feature:** Helps decrease disk space utilization and storage infrastructure requirements by transparently compressing data using classic row compression (where data is compressed at the table level), adaptive row compression (where data is compressed dynamically at the page level), or a combination of the two; temporary tables are compressed when DB2 deems it necessary and indexes for compressed tables are compressed by default
- **Column-organized tables:** Adds columnar capabilities to DB2 databases, which includes the ability to store data using column organization and vector processing of column-organized data

- **DB2 Connect™:** Provides fast and robust connectivity to IBM mainframe databases for applications running on Linux, UNIX, and Windows operating systems
- **Data Partitioning Feature (DPF):** Provides the ability to partition a database within a single server or across a cluster of servers, resulting in scalability for very large databases and complex workloads, as well as parallelism for database administration tasks
- **The DB2 pureScale® Feature:** Utilizes a shared-disk, cluster architecture that allows a database to be efficiently scaled across several servers
- **DB2 Workload Manager (WLM):** A comprehensive workload management feature that can help identify, manage, and control database workloads (applications, users, and so forth) to maximize database server throughput and resource utilization; with WLM, it is possible to customize execution environments so that no single workload can control and consume all of the system resources available
- **Continuous Data Ingest (CDI):** A high-speed, client-side DB2 utility that streams preprocessed data from named pipes or output files produced by ETL tools (or some other means) directly into DB2 tables
- **Native encryption:** Lets businesses meet security and regulatory requirements by encrypting both the database and any database backup images created
- **IBM InfoSphere® Optim™:** A family of data life-cycle management tools and solutions that can be used to design, develop, deploy, and manage database applications throughout the data life cycle (from requirements to retirement); the IBM InfoSphere Optim product family consists of:
  - » **IBM InfoSphere Change Data Capture (CDC) for DB2 for LUW:** A log-based replication solution that captures database changes as they happen and delivers them to target databases, Java™ Message Service (JMS) message queues, or extract, transform, and load (ETL) solutions such as InfoSphere DataStage
  - » **IBM InfoSphere CDC Access Server:** Controls all non–command-line access to an IBM InfoSphere CDC for DB2 for LUW replication environment
  - » **IBM InfoSphere CDC Management Console:** Provides a way to configure, monitor, and manage CDC replication on various servers, as well as specify replication parameters, initiate refresh and mirroring operations from a client workstation, and monitor replication operations, latency, event messages, and other statistics supported by the source or target data store

» **IBM InfoSphere Data Architect:** Offers a complete solution for designing, modeling, discovering, relating, and standardizing data assets; used for data modeling, transformation, and Data Definition Language (DDL) generation, as well as to build, debug, and manage database objects such as SQL stored procedures and user-defined functions (UDFs)

» **IBM InfoSphere Optim™ Configuration Manager:** Provides advice on how to change database configurations; also stores states and changes in a repository, making it possible to compare current and historical data, which can be helpful when trying to understand and resolve problems related to configuration changes

» **IBM InfoSphere Optim Performance Manager Extended Edition:** Used to identify, diagnose, solve, and prevent performance problems in DB2 products and associated applications

» **IBM InfoSphere Optim pureQuery® Runtime:** Used to deploy advanced pureQuery applications that use static SQL; bridges the gap between data and Java technology by harnessing the power of SQL within an easy-to-use Java data access platform; and increases security of Java applications, helping to prevent threats like SQL injection

» **IBM InfoSphere Optim Query Tuner:** Often referred to as the *Query Tuner,* used to analyze and make recommendations on ways to tune existing queries, as well as provide expert advice on writing new, efficient, high-quality queries

- **Q Replication:** Technologies within IBM InfoSphere Data Replication that move large volumes of data at high speeds to help businesses connect globally distributed operations, respond quickly to customers, and rapidly recover from problems that affect critical database systems

DB2 Advanced Workgroup Server Edition is also available in a variety of languages and can be installed on servers that are running 32- and 64-bit versions of the operating systems that DB2 Workgroup Server Edition can be installed on. Like DB2 Workgroup Server Edition, DB2 Advanced Workgroup Server Edition is limited to environments that contain up to 16 cores and 128 GB of memory. In DB2 Version 10.5, FixPack 5 and later, the functionality provided by all the DB2 add-on offerings available is included by default with this edition. This edition also comes with a full complement of warehouse tools, Optim tools, and IBM Data Studio; however, these tools must be installed separately.

DB2 Advanced Enterprise Server Edition (AESE)

The most comprehensive DB2 edition available, DB2 Advanced Enterprise Server Edition (AESE) is a powerful database management solution that offers all the features and functionality available with DB2 Advanced Workgroup Server Edition. However, with this edition, there are no processor, memory, or database size limitations, which make it ideal for any size workload.

DB2 Advanced Enterprise Server Edition is also available in a variety of languages and can be installed on servers that are running 32- and 64-bit versions of the operating systems that DB2 Enterprise Server Edition can be installed on. Like DB2 Advanced Workgroup Edition, in DB2 Version 10.5, FixPack 5 and later, the functionality provided by all the available DB2 add-on offerings is included by default with DB2 Advanced Enterprise Server Edition. This edition also comes with a full complement of warehouse tools, Optim tools, and IBM Data Studio; however, these tools must be installed separately.

DB2 for z/OS

DB2 for z/OS is a multiuser, full-function database management system that has been designed specifically for z/OS, IBM's flagship mainframe operating system. Tightly integrated with the IBM mainframe—DB2 for z/OS takes advantage of the latest improvements in System z hardware and software to provide optimum performance and significantly cut IT infrastructure costs, DB2 for z/OS leverages the strengths of System z® 64-bit architecture to provide continuous availability and business resiliency, extraordinary scalability, unmatched security and compliance assurance, and the ability to support complex data warehouses.

Other DB2 Add-on Products

Along with the various editions that make up the bulk of the DB2 family, several add-on products that are designed to expand and enhance the functionality and capabilities of many of the non-advanced editions of DB2 available. As we saw earlier, these products, which make up the remainder of the DB2 family, are:

- IBM DB2 BLU Acceleration In-Memory Offering
- IBM DB2 Business Application Continuity Offering
- IBM DB2 Encryption Offering
- IBM Advanced Recovery Feature
- IBM DB2 Performance Management Offering

IBM DB2 BLU Acceleration In-Memory Offering

Based on the next-generation of in-memory technologies, the IBM DB2 BLU Acceleration In-Memory Offering delivers simple and scalable in-memory acceleration for analytic workloads. Available for DB2 Workgroup Server Edition and DB2 Enterprise Server Edition, the DB2 BLU Acceleration In-Memory Offering:

- Provides the benefits of in-memory columnar processing without the limitations or cost of in-memory only systems
- Provides workload management functionality for in-memory columnar processing
- Leverages Oracle skills with SQL compatibility to enable simple, low-risk migration from Oracle to DB2 with BLU Acceleration
- Reduces risk and improves performance of SAP environments with enhancements to SAP Business Warehouse support
- Offers "load-and-go" simplicity

IBM DB2 Business Application Continuity Offering

The IBM DB2 Business Application Continuity Offering is an affordable, continuous availability solution that is based on DB2 pureScale technology. This two-member DB2 pureScale cluster configuration enables one member to process application workloads, and a second member to perform administrative tasks, as well as provide availability when the first member undergoes a planned or unplanned outage. Available for DB2 Workgroup Server Edition and DB2 Server Enterprise Edition, the DB2 Business Application Continuity Offering helps you to:

- Meet expected or required service level agreements (SLAs)
- Protect your business from planned and unplanned outages
- Optimize resources by offloading administration to a second DB2 pureScale member
- Reduce the costs of high availability

IBM DB2 Encryption Offering

IBM DB2 Encryption Offering provides native data encryption at rest to assist businesses with security and regulatory requirements. Available for DB2 Express Server Edition, DB2 Workgroup Server Edition, and DB2 Enterprise Server Edition, the DB2 Encryption Offering:

- Is simple to enable and deploy
- Is transparent to applications accessing the data
- Applies to both the database and to backup images
- Complies with National Institute of Standards and Technology (NIST) Special Publication (SP) 800-131a requirements for cryptographic algorithms and key lengths
- Utilizes cryptographic libraries that are Federal Information Processing Standard (FIPS) Publication 140-2 certified—FIPS 140-2 is a U.S. government computer security standard that is used to accredit cryptographic modules

IBM Advanced Recovery Feature

The IBM DB2 Advanced Recovery Feature is a suite of advanced database backup, recovery, and data extraction tools that help improve data availability, mitigate risk, and accelerate crucial administrative tasks. Available as a product that can be purchased separately and used with DB2 Express Server Edition and higher, the DB2 Advanced Recovery Feature includes:

- **IBM DB2 Merge Backup for Linux, UNIX, and Windows:** Provides the ability to back up databases more efficiently, lessen impact on production systems, and shorten recovery times
- **IBM DB2 Recovery Expert for Linux, UNIX, and Windows:** Provides the ability to recover with more speed, flexibility, and precise granularity while protecting mission-critical business data and significantly reducing the amount of resources needed; reduces impact on production systems by using remote log analysis; and eliminates the need to resort to full database recovery
- **IBM Optim High Performance Unload for DB2 for Linux, UNIX, and Windows:** Provides the ability to perform high-speed unloads from live databases or backup files; improves regulatory compliance by offering increased data protection during the unload operation; increases data availability, mitigates risk, and accelerates the delivery of full database migrations; and lessens production impact and reduces storage costs by rapidly unloading, extracting and repartitioning data throughout the enterprise

IBM DB2 Performance Management Offering

IBM DB2 Performance Management Offering is a suite of tools that helps businesses monitor, manage, and improve database workload and application performance; it provides users with the information they need to manage performance proactively and prevent problems before they impact the business. Available for DB2 Express Server Edition, DB2 Workgroup Server Edition, and DB2 Enterprise Server Edition, the DB2 Performance Management Offering helps you to:

- Identify emergent problems
- Diagnose the root cause of issues
- Receive notifications of degrading performance or emerging resource bottlenecks
- Isolate problematic components across applications, networks, and databases
- Prevent performance problems by defining and using a more predictable database server execution environment
- Solve performance problems with actionable tuning recommendations for entire workloads

Database Workloads

Operations performed against relational databases are often classified according to the frequency in which they are performed and the volume of data they modify or retrieve. Together, these characteristics identify the type of workloads a particular database supports; most database workloads fall into two distinct categories: *online transaction processing* (OLTP) and *data warehousing*, which includes reporting, online analytical processing (OLAP), and data mining.

What differentiates a data warehousing system from an OLTP system? Data warehousing involves storing and managing large volumes of data (often historical in nature) that is used primarily for analysis. For instance, a data warehouse could be used to summarize a company's sales by region or to identify patterns in products that have been sold over the last five years. Consequently, workloads in a data warehouse environment can vary—they might consist of bulk load operations, short-running simple queries, long-running complex queries involving aggregation, random ad hoc queries, infrequent updates to data, or the execution of online maintenance utilities. To handle these types of workloads, most data warehouse environments have the following requirements:

- **Performance:** This is a system's ability to execute any action within a given time interval. In a data warehouse environment, the system should perform the initial population of tables and any required incremental updates in the shortest amount of time possible. Ad hoc queries should be satisfied, at any time, without degrading the performance of other mission-critical or time-sensitive operations. Similarly, complex and multidimensional queries should handle aggregations, full-table scans, and multiple table joins with little or no performance impact

- **Scalability:** This is a system's ability to be readily enlarged or to handle increases in load without adversely affecting performance. Both the hardware and software components used in building a data warehouse should enable the environment to grow, as needed, without reducing performance
- **Availability:** This relates to the proportion of time that a system is functional and working. A data warehouse should be available 24 hours a day, 7 days a week, 365 days a year. However, a data warehouse may be taken offline at regular intervals, and for a limited amount of time, to be updated or populated with a bulk-load operation
- **Manageability:** This defines how easily administrators can manage a system, usually through tools that are available for monitoring, debugging, and tuning. A data warehouse environment should be flexible and extensible, while minimizing the administrative costs involved in keeping it online and accessible

In contrast, OLTP systems are designed to support day-to-day, mission-critical business activities such as Web-based order entry, stock trading, and inventory management. Consequently, OLTP workloads are often characterized by simple, single-record lookups and by SQL operations (typically inserts, updates, and deletes) that access or modify a small number of records and perform few, if any, input/output (I/O) operations. To better handle these types of workloads, most OLTP environments have the following requirements:

- **High performance:** In an OLTP environment, high throughput, measured in hundreds of transactions per second, is required. And subsecond end-user response time is desired. (Performance of OLTP workloads can often be enhanced by minimizing I/Os, optimizing CPU utilization, eliminating sorts, and improving transaction concurrency.)
- **High volume:** A typical OLTP environment might consist of hundreds to thousands of users issuing millions of transactions per day against databases that vary in size. Consequently, the volume of data affected may be very large, even though each transaction typically makes changes to only a small number of records. (Data tends to be current.)

- **High availability:** Unlike data warehouses, which can be taken offline at regular intervals, OLTP databases typically must be available 24 hours a day, 7 days a week, 365 days a year.

Optimized Solutions for Each Workload Type

Although you can use all the DB2 Editions available *except* DB2 Express-C and DB2 Express Edition to create both data warehouse and OLTP environments, IBM offers two solutions that are tailored specifically for one workload type or the other: the *Data Partitioning Feature* (for data warehousing workloads) and the *DB2 pureScale Feature* (for OLTP workloads).

The Data Partitioning Feature (DPF)

Both DB2 Advanced Workgroup Server Edition and DB2 Advanced Enterprise Server Edition contain data warehouse–enhancing features such as support for Materialized Query Tables (MQTs), the starburst query optimizer, and support for multidimensional clustering (MDC) tables. And when used with either of these editions, the Data Partitioning Feature (DPF) provides the ability to divide very large databases into multiple parts (known as *partitions*) and store them across a cluster of inexpensive servers. (In the past, it was possible to add DPF to DB2 Enterprise Server Edition environments by activating a license key; however, that is no longer the case.)

Sometimes called a *database node* or simply a *node*, each database partition contains its own data, indexes, configuration files, and transaction log files. Because these components—as well as memory and storage—are not shared between partitions, a DB2 database that utilizes DPF is often referred to as a *shared-nothing* environment. Figure 2.2 shows what a simple DB2 with DPF database environment looks like.

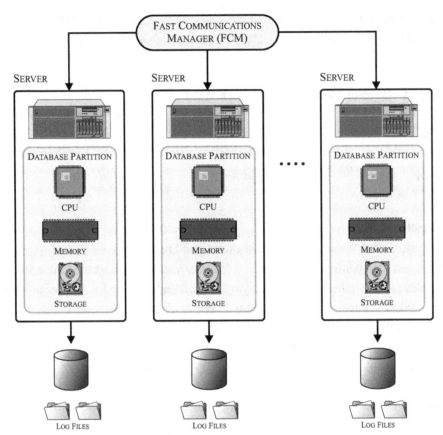

Figure 2.2: A simple DB2 with DPF database environment

When DPF is used, a database can be scaled as an organization's data needs grow simply by adding more database partitions. (The fact that the database is split across multiple partitions is transparent to applications and users.) DPF also enables DB2 to process complex queries more efficiently—data retrieval and update requests are decomposed automatically into subrequests and executed in parallel among all applicable partitions. In addition, DPF can improve data availability by reducing the impact of performing routine maintenance activities and by decreasing the time needed to do so; such activities can be performed on a single partition, one partition at a time rather than against the entire database at once.

The DB2 pureScale Feature

The DB2 pureScale Feature leverages IBM's System z Sysplex technology to bring active-active clustering services to DB2 for LUW database environments. This technology enables a DB2 for LUW database to continuously process incoming requests, even if multiple system components fail simultaneously (which makes it ideal for OLTP workloads where high availability is crucial).

Unlike DPF, the DB2 pureScale Feature is based on a "shared data" architecture. The DB2 engine runs on multiple servers or logical partitions (LPARs) as data "members," each member has its own set of buffer pools and log files (which are accessible to the other members), and each member has equal, shared access to the database's underlying storage. IBM's General Parallel File System (GPFS) makes shared storage access possible; Cluster Caching Facility (CF) software provides global locking and buffer pool management and serves as the center of communication and coordination between all members (synchronous CF duplexing ensures high availability); and integrated Cluster Services (CS) handles failure detection and provides recovery automation.

The DB2 pureScale Feature offers the following key benefits:

- **Practically unlimited capacity:** The DB2 pureScale Feature provides practically unlimited capacity by allowing for the addition and removal of data members, on demand. A DB2 pureScale database is scalable to 128 members and has a highly efficient centralized management facility that allows for very efficient scale-out capabilities. The DB2 pureScale Feature also leverages Remote Direct Memory Access (RDMA) technology to provide a highly efficient internode communication mechanism, which also enhances its scaling capabilities.
- **Application transparency:** Applications that run in a DB2 pureScale environment do not need to know anything about the members in a cluster or be concerned about which member they connect to. Clients see a single, common view of the database and can connect to any member; automatic load balancing and client reroute ensures that application workloads are distributed evenly across all available members. And because the DB2 pureScale Feature provides native support for the SQL syntax used by other database vendors, applications written for other relational database management system products can be run against a DB2 pureScale database with little or no changes.

- **Continuous availability:** The DB2 pureScale Feature provides a fully active-active cluster configuration; the HACMP™ Reliable Services Clustering Technology (RCST) quickly detects failures, while Tivoli® System Automation for Multi-platforms (SA MP) automates recovery. Consequently, if one member goes down, processing is automatically rerouted to and can continue on the remaining active members. During a member failure, only data being modified on the failing member is temporarily unavailable, and data recovery for that member can be completed in a matter of seconds. This is in contrast to other competing solutions in which an entire system freeze might occur as part of the database recovery process.
- **High performance:** The DB2 pureScale Feature uses a low-latency, high-speed interconnect to maximize performance. RDMA-capable interconnects like InfiniBand and 10Gb RoCE Ethernet allow one server to alter the memory contents of another without requiring the CPU in the target server to get involved. Consequently, no interrupt or other message processing is needed to keep changes made by data members synchronized.

Figure 2.3 shows what a DB2 pureScale environment consisting of three data members looks like.

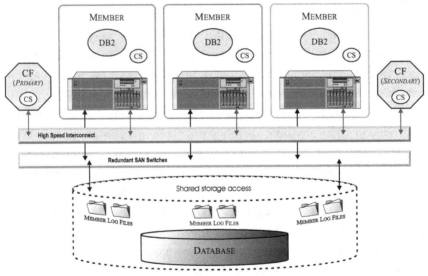

Figure 2.3: A simple DB2 pureScale environment

It is important to note that in DB2 Version 10.5, several enhancements were made to the DB2 pureScale Feature, including:

- The ability to add new members to an existing DB2 pureScale environment while the DB2 instance remains online and accessible
- The ability to apply FixPack updates to a DB2 pureScale environment while the DB2 instance remains available
- Support for in-place (online) table reorganization for tables that use adaptive compression
- The ability to perform extent reclamation operations on insert time clustering (ITC) tables (to consolidate sparsely allocated blocks into a smaller number of blocks)
- The ability to use random ordering for index key columns (to alleviate page contention where pages are shared between multiple DB2 members)
- The ability to isolate application workloads to one or more specific members that have been assigned to a member subset
- The ability to restore an offline database backup image that was taken on a DB2 Enterprise Server Edition instance to a DB2 pureScale instance (and vice versa)
- The ability to restore a database backup image taken on one DB2 pureScale instance to another DB2 pureScale instance that has a different topology
- The ability to restore table space backup images taken on one DB2 pureScale instance to a DB2 pureScale instance with a superset topology
- HADR support (only in asynchronous (ASYNC) and super asynchronous (SUPERASYNC) mode)

DB2 10.5 with BLU Acceleration

IBM BLU Acceleration is a collection of technologies from the IBM Research and Development Labs that accelerate analytics and reporting. It is one of the most significant pieces of technology that has ever been delivered in DB2, and arguably, the database market in general; it delivers unparalleled performance improvements for analytic applications and reporting using dynamic, in-memory optimized, columnar technologies.

"BLU" is not an acronym. Instead, it derives its name from the IBM Research project behind its inception—"Blink Ultra." BLU Acceleration is the second generation of technology that originated in the Blink project. Aimed primarily at mostly-read BI (Business Intelligence) query processing, Blink exploited the scale-out of commodity, multi-core processors and cheap Dynamic Random-Access Memory (DRAM) to keep a copy of a data mart completely in memory. It also used proprietary compression algorithms and techniques that allowed most SQL queries to be performed on the data while it was compressed. Eventually, Blink was incorporated into two IBM products: the *IBM Smart Analytics Optimizer for DB2 for z/OS*, which was released in November 2010, and the *Informix Warehouse accelerator*, which became generally available in March 2011.

Blink Ultra builds on the main-memory efficiencies of the first generation, but is no longer limited to databases that fit in memory. Tables are stored on disk and intermediate results may spill to disk. Blink Ultra was perfected and integrated with DB2 10.5 (as BLU Acceleration) through a collaboration between DB2 Product Development, the IBM Systems Optimization Competency Center, and IBM Research—adding columnar processing, broader SQL support, I/O and CPU efficiencies, and integration with the DB2 SQL compiler, query optimizer, and storage layer. As a result, BLU Acceleration isn't merely an add-on product for DB2; it's tightly integrated with the DB2 kernel.

BLU Acceleration Design Principles

If you've had the opportunity to see a presentation on BLU Acceleration at a DB2-related conference or user's group meeting, chances are you have heard that there were seven "big ideas" that served as guiding principles behind the design and integration of BLU Acceleration with DB2. Those big ideas were:

- Simple to implement and use
- Column store
- Compute-friendly encoding and compression
- CPU acceleration (parallel vector processing)
- Core-friendly parallelism
- Scan-friendly memory caching
- Data skipping

Let's take a closer look at each of these ideas.

Big Idea 1: Simple to implement and use

Arguably, one of the most important design principles of BLU Acceleration was simplicity and ease of use. The goal was to minimize the complexity of deployment while avoiding the creation of additional maintenance tasks. As a result, a significant amount of autonomics and intelligence around BLU Acceleration has been built into the DB2 engine. Basically, all a user needs to do to take advantage of this technology is configure a DB2 10.5 database environment for BLU Acceleration, create the tables needed, load them with data, and then run queries against them. It's that simple. Database administration procedures and the SQL language used remain unchanged, as do system commands, utilities, and the DB2 storage model.

Because of the way in which BLU Acceleration has been designed, there is no need to create indexes, multidimensional clustering (MDC) tables, materialized query tables (MQTs), statistical views, materialized views, or partitioned tables to improve query performance. And without these auxiliary objects, administrative and maintenance efforts are greatly reduced. Furthermore, there is no need to manually reorganize BLU Acceleration tables (using the REORG command) or update their statistics (with RUNSTATS); that work is done behind the scenes, automatically.

The easiest way to configure a DB2 10.5 database environment for BLU Acceleration is to assign the value ANALYTICS to the DB2_WORKLOAD registry variable before any databases are created. This is done by executing a db2set command that looks like this:

```
db2set DB2_WORKLOAD=ANALYTICS
```

When this command is executed, the database system, as a whole, is automatically configured to provide an optimal environment for analytic-type workloads. Specifically:

- The dft_table_org database configuration parameter for newly created databases is set to COLUMN. (This parameter specifies the default table organization method to use when new base tables are created.)
- The dft_degree database configuration parameter for newly created databases is set to ANY. (This parameter specifies the default degree of intrapartition parallelism the optimizer is to use when processing queries; intrapartition parallelism involves breaking an operation into multiple parts and running those parts in parallel, within a single database partition.)
- The pagesize database configuration parameter for newly created databases is set to 32 KB. (This parameter specifies the default page size to use for every newly created database, as well as for every buffer pool and table space that is created in those databases.)

- The dft_extent_sz database configuration parameter for newly created databases is set to 4. (This parameter specifies the default extent size, in pages, that will be used for every newly created table space.)
- The intra_parallel database manager configuration parameter is set to YES. (This parameter indicates whether intrapartition parallelism should be used when certain database operations are performed; *it is important to note that the instance must be stopped and restarted before this change will take effect.*)
- The values of the sortheap and sheapthres_shr database configuration parameters for newly created databases are calculated and set specifically for an analytics workload. (The sortheap parameter defines the maximum number of memory pages that are available for sort operations; the sheapthres_shr parameter represents a soft limit on the total amount of shared sort memory that is available.)
- The util_heap_sz database configuration parameter for newly created databases is set to a value that takes into account the additional memory that is needed to load data into column-organized tables. (This parameter specifies the amount of memory that is to be allocated for use by various DB2 utilities.)
- The auto_reorg database configuration parameter for newly created databases is set to ON. (This parameter indicates whether table and index reorganization operations are to be done automatically.)
- A default space-reclamation policy is installed and automatic table maintenance is configured so that empty extents for column-organized tables are automatically returned to table space storage for reuse.

● ●

Note: Any configuration parameter that is implicitly set when the value ANALYTICS is assigned to the DB2_WORKLOAD registry variable can be explicitly assigned a different value, effectively overriding the default BLU Acceleration configuration.

● ●

Big Idea 2: Column store

The most prominent feature found in BLU Acceleration is a new, in-memory, columnar table type. Unlike row-organized tables, which store data for complete records (rows) in pages and extents, column-organized tables store data *for individual columns* in pages and extents. Figure 2.4 shows how data for a row-organized table is stored; Figure 2.5 illustrates the storage methodology that is used for a column-organized table that has similar characteristics.

EMPLOYEE TABLE

FIRST	LAST	PHONE	ADDRESS	CITY	STATE	ZIP
Rebecca	Geyer	(413) 555-1357	18 Main Street	Springfield	MA	01111
Mark	Hayakawa	(415) 555-2468	1020 Lombard Street	San Francisco	CA	94109
Bryan	Boone	(567) 555-9876	911 Elm Street	Toledo	OH	43601
James	Coleman	(415) 555-5432	2318 Hyde Street	San Francisco	CA	94104
Linda	Bookman	(408) 555-9753	1017 Milton Avenue	San Jose	CA	95141
Robert	Jancer	(971) 555-1357	2009 Elk Lane	Beaverton	OR	97075
Andy	Watson	(408) 555-2468	1017 Chestnut Street	San Jose	CA	95141
Susan	Boodie	(919) 555-1212	5661 Blount Street	Raleigh	NC	27605
Dorian	Naveh	(520) 555-8642	2120 Bank Street	Tucson	AZ	85701
Jane	Esposito	(669) 555-4996	2120 Oak Street	Santa Clara	CA	95051

PAGE ➡

Rebecca	Geyer	(413) 555-1357	18 Main Street	Springfield	MA	01111
Mark	Hayakawa	(415) 555-2468	1020 Lombard Street	San Francisco	CA	94109
Bryan	Boone	(567) 555-9876	911 Elm Street	Toledo	OH	43601

PAGE ➡

James	Coleman	(415) 555-5432	2318 Hyde Street	San Francisco	CA	94104
Linda	Bookman	(408) 555-9753	1017 Milton Avenue	San Jose	CA	95141
Robert	Jancer	(971) 555-1357	2009 Elk Lane	Beaverton	OR	97075

PAGE ➡

Andy	Watson	(408) 555-2468	1017 Chestnut Street	San Jose	CA	95141
Susan	Boodie	(919) 555-1212	5661 Blount Street	Raleigh	NC	27605
Dorian	Naveh	(520) 555-8642	2120 Bank Street	Tucson	AZ	85701

PAGE ➡

Jane	Esposito	(669) 555-4996	2120 Oak Street	Santa Clara	CA	95051

Figure 2.4: How data for a row-organized table is stored

EMPLOYEE TABLE

FIRST	LAST	PHONE	ADDRESS	CITY	STATE	ZIP
Rebecca	Geyer	(413) 555-1357	18 Main Street	Springfield	MA	01111
Mark	Hayakawa	(415) 555-2468	1020 Lombard Street	San Francisco	CA	94109
Bryan	Boone	(567) 555-9876	911 Elm Street	Toledo	OH	43601
James	Coleman	(415) 555-5432	2318 Hyde Street	San Francisco	CA	94104
Linda	Bookman	(408) 555-9753	1017 Milton Avenue	San Jose	CA	95141
Robert	Jancer	(971) 555-1357	2009 Elk Lane	Beaverton	OR	97075
Andy	Watson	(408) 555-2468	1017 Chestnut Street	San Jose	CA	95141
Susan	Boodie	(919) 555-1212	5661 Blount Street	Raleigh	NC	27605
Dorian	Naveh	(520) 555-8642	2120 Bank Street	Tucson	AZ	85701
Jane	Esposito	(669) 555-4996	2120 Oak Street	Santa Clara	CA	95051

Tuple Sequence Number (TSN)

TSN	FIRST	LAST	PHONE	ADDRESS	CITY	STATE	ZIP	
000	Rebecca	Geyer	(413) 555-1357	18 Main Street	Springfield	MA	01111	
001	Mark	Hayakawa	(415) 555-2468	1020 Lombard Street	San Francisco	CA	94109	← PAGE*
002	Bryan	Boone	(567) 555-9876	911 Elm Street	Toledo	OH	43601	
003	James	Coleman	(415) 555-5432	2318 Hyde Street	San Francisco	CA	94104	
004	Linda	Bookman	(408) 555-9753	1017 Milton Avenue	San Jose	CA	95141	
005	Robert	Jancer	(971) 555-1357	2009 Elk Lane	Beaverton	OR	97075	
006	Andy	Watson	(408) 555-2468	1017 Chestnut Street	San Jose	CA	95141	
007	Susan	Boodie	(919) 555-1212	5661 Blount Street	Raleigh	NC	27605	
008	Dorian	Naveh	(520) 555-8642	2120 Bank Street	Tucson	AZ	85701	← PAGE*
009	Jane	Esposito	(669) 555-4996	2120 Oak Street	Santa Clara	CA	95051	
010								
011								
012								
...								

Separate set of pages and extents for each column

Figure 2.5: How data for a column-organized table is stored; the Tuple Sequence Number (TSN) is a logical row identifier that is used to "stitch together" values from the different columns that form a row.

Storing data by column offers several benefits to analytic workloads—that is, workloads that consist primarily of grouping, aggregation, multi-table join, and table scan operations. For one thing, such workloads tend to access a subset of the columns found in one or more tables. So, by storing data using a columnar approach, DB2 only has to move data for the appropriate subset of columns from disk to memory (as opposed to having to move data for an entire row). This ensures that only the data that is needed is retrieved from disk with every I/O operation that's performed. And, because more data values can be stored on a single page, fewer I/O requests are required. Another benefit is that column-organized tables tend to compress very efficiently—the probability of finding repeating patterns on a page is high when the data on that page comes from a single column. This results in significantly faster query performance.

Big Idea 3: Compute-friendly encoding and compression

Another key feature of BLU Acceleration is the way in which data for column-organized tables is encoded and compressed—column-organized tables are compressed automatically, using a technique known as *approximate Huffman encoding*. With this form of compression (sometimes referred to as *actionable compression*), values that appear more frequently are encoded at a higher level than values that don't appear as often. Using a serial stream of zeros (0s) and ones (1s), each value is assigned eight bits. Then, the encoded data is packed as tightly as possible into a collection of bits that equal the register width of the CPU being used. Figure 2.6 illustrates how this type of compression works.

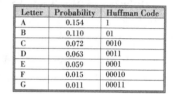

Letter	Probability	Huffman Code
A	0.154	1
B	0.110	01
C	0.072	0010
D	0.063	0011
E	0.059	0001
F	0.015	00010
G	0.011	00011

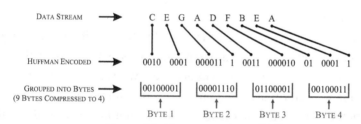

Figure 2.6: How approximate Huffman encoding works

So, if a column contained "city of residence" information for customers who live in the state of Georgia, the city of Atlanta would probably appear more frequently than the city of Brunswick (because the population of Atlanta is significantly greater than that of Brunswick). Consequently, the city of Atlanta would probably be encoded with a single, short bit (1), whereas, the city of Brunswick might be encoded with as many as eight bits (1101 1001), depending upon how frequently records for other cities like Columbus, Savannah, Macon, Marietta, and Decatur occur.

Another compression optimization technique that's used in BLU Acceleration is a process known as *offset coding*. Offset coding is very useful with numeric data; instead of trying to compress a set of numbers like 100, 101, 102, and 103, DB2 will store the first value (100), and then it will store the appropriate offsets from that value (1, 2, 3, and so forth) for the remaining numbers in the set. This technique is very similar to the way DB2 compresses index record IDs (RIDs).

Additional compression may also be performed at the page level to exploit any local clustering of data that might exist, as well as to compress any data values that were untouched by the other compression techniques just described. When it is deemed that page-level compression is beneficial, mini-dictionaries are created and stored within the page to record the compression information produced.

Generally, compression for column-organized tables can be anywhere from three to 10 times better than that of similar row-organized tables (which means the use of column-organized tables can provide, among other things, a significant savings in storage space). More importantly, data stored in column-organized tables does not have to be decompressed before it can be used in many SQL operations—operations that perform predicate evaluations (including range and IN-list predicate evaluations), joins, and data grouping can work directly with encoded data. This enables DB2 to delay the materialization of compressed data for as long as possible, which leads to a more effective use of CPU and memory, along with a reduction in disk I/O.

Big Idea 4: Parallel vector processing

Another important feature of BLU Acceleration is its ability to exploit a leading-edge technology that is found in many of today's modern processors: Single-Instruction, Multiple-Data (SIMD) processing. SIMD instructions are low-level CPU instructions that enable an application to perform the same operation on multiple data points *at the same time*. BLU Acceleration will auto-detect when DB2 is running on a SIMD-enabled CPU (such as a qualifying POWER, AMD, or Intel processor) and automatically exploit SIMD to effectively multiply the power of the processor. (Specifically, DB2 will put 128 bits into a SIMD register and evaluate all of that data with a single instruction.) For example, suppose a query designed to produce a list of all purchases made in December is executed. Without SIMD, the processor must evaluate the query predicate (i.e., does MONTH = 'December'?) one value at a time. Each value for MONTH (for example, September, October, November) would be loaded into its own processor register, and multiple iterations of the instruction would be required. With SIMD, the results for all three months could be obtained with a single instruction, provided the values are loaded into the same register. This results in faster predicate processing. Figure 2.7 illustrates how the scenario just described might be processed by a SIMD-enabled CPU.

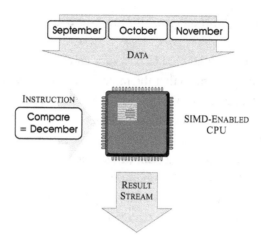

Figure 2.7: SQL query predicate evaluations with a SIMD-enabled CPU

Although the example just presented demonstrates how SIMD helps with predicate evaluation, it's important to note that SIMD exploitation can be used to do scans, joins, grouping, and arithmetic operations. Also, in the previous example, three data values (September, October, and November) were used for display purposes only; the actual number of data elements that can be processed by a single instruction is determined by the size of each element.

DB2 10.5 can still be run on a server that doesn't have SIMD-enabled CPUs; it just won't be able to take advantage of the full benefits BLU Acceleration has to offer. With that said, if a server isn't SIMD capable, BLU Acceleration will emulate SIMD behavior as much as possible using an advanced set of algorithms that rely on bitmasking to achieve some level of parallelism. This is done in an attempt to deliver many of the benefits that SIMD-enabled CPUs provide.

Big Idea 5: Core-friendly parallelism

Core-friendly parallelism refers to BLU Acceleration's ability to take advantage of the growing number of cores found on CPU processors to drive multicore parallelism for queries—without requiring user intervention. (As the name implies, multicore parallelism is the act of breaking an operation into several parts and running those parts, in parallel, across multiple CPU cores.) This is accomplished through the use of several comprehensive algorithms that determine where data that will be revisited should be placed in CPU cache, as well as how work should be shipped across every socket. To maximize parallelization and throughput, all processor cores, memory, and threads available are utilized.

BLU Acceleration is also engineered to pay very careful attention to both cache affinity and memory management so that the majority of memory access occurs in a CPU cache and not by accessing data stored in RAM over and over again. (Compared to CPU cache, access to RAM is slow and something that should be avoided. In fact, a goal of BLU Acceleration is to access data on disk very rarely, access data in RAM only occasionally, and do the overwhelming bulk of its processing using data and instructions that reside in L1, L2, and L3 cache.) By operating almost exclusively on data in a CPU cache, query performance is improved significantly, latency is kept to a minimum, and the power of multiple CPU cores is fully realized.

Big Idea 6: Scan-friendly memory caching

The technique many databases use to cache data in memory (RAM) tends to work well for transaction processing workloads. But that isn't the case for workloads that are analytical in nature. That's because the data access patterns for these two types of workloads are radically different. Transaction processing workloads typically require random access to data, and some data is accessed more frequently than the rest. (Data that is accessed more frequently is referred to as being "hot".) Analytic workloads, on the other hand, tend to have data access patterns that are more sequential and neutral (i.e., that don't contain hot data).

And by design, most databases employ variations of what are known as *Least Recently Used (LRU)* and *Most Recently Used (MRU)* paging algorithms to keep data that was recently accessed in memory and to remove older data when space for new data is needed. But these algorithms do not work well with analytical workloads. That's because analytical workloads are likely to start at the top of a table and scan their way to the bottom. And if the table is large, the LRU algorithm will remove pages that were read at the start of the scan to make room for those read at the end. Consequently, the next time a scan of the same table is initiated (say, to perform an aggregation or join operation), memory will usually be searched for pages that were read from the beginning of the table, and when they are not found, an I/O operation will be performed to retrieve them from disk. Unfortunately, in a large analytic environment, this scenario will play itself out continually, resulting in a significant amount of disk I/O (which will negatively impact query performance.)

To resolve this issue, a special "scan-friendly" memory caching algorithm was developed and incorporated into BLU Acceleration. This algorithm works by detecting "interested" data patterns that are likely to be revisited, and then holding pages with similar data patterns in memory as long as possible. And, when DB2 10.5 accesses column-organized data, it uses this page replacement algorithm automatically; no user intervention is required. However, because use of this algorithm is triggered by some interaction with a column-organized table, it assumes that the data is going to be highly compressed, that columnar access will be required, and that at least 70 to 80 percent of the data is going to be put into memory. (While it is anticipated that most, if not all, of the active data will fit in memory, this is not a requirement.)

Big Idea 7: Data skipping

Another important feature that's available with BLU Acceleration is the ability to skip ranges of data that are not relevant to the current active query. For example, if a query needs to calculate the total dollar amount of every order placed during the month of January, BLU Acceleration can go straight to the data that contains order information for just that month and skip over all nonqualifying data. As operations are performed against column-organized tables, BLU Acceleration generates metadata that describes the minimum and maximum range of the data values found in "chunks" of data. (The ranges are not tied to any particular page or extent boundary; instead, they are associated with approximately 2,000 data records.) This metadata is then stored in a special internal table known as a *synopsis table*, and is updated automatically as INSERT, UPDATE, and DELETE operations are performed. (Synopsis tables use the same storage format as regular column-organized tables and inherit the compression scheme of the user-defined columnar table they are associated with.)

When an analytic query is executed, BLU Acceleration examines the appropriate synopsis table(s) to identify "chunks" that contain data the query is looking for. It then goes straight to those "chunks" and retrieves the data desired. As a result, only data that is needed is actually loaded into system memory. Thus, data skipping results in an order of magnitude of savings across all available compute resources (CPU, memory, and I/O). More importantly, it dramatically increases the speed in which analytic queries are executed.

When to Use BLU Acceleration

As with any technology, there are situations where you'll want to use BLU Acceleration and areas where you won't. BLU Acceleration isn't ideal for every workload and use case. For instance, queries that access a single row or just a few rows (likely by using an index) aren't the best fit for BLU Acceleration. The same is true for workloads that randomly access data, frequently perform insert or update operations, and execute queries that return a small set of values. Basically, any workload that is primarily transactional/ OLTP in nature should avoid the use of column-organized tables. Traditional row-organized tables, together with index access, are generally better suited for these types of workloads.

Likewise, if your environment continually processes fewer than 100 rows per commit, BLU Acceleration isn't the best choice because such a small commit scope compromises the data analysis that needs to be done to achieve optimal compression ratios. And, if Oracle compatibility has been enabled, traditional row-organized tables *must* be used because Oracle compatibility and BLU Acceleration cannot be used together.

BLU Acceleration is designed primarily for analytic and OLAP workloads; that is, workloads that are characterized by activities like grouping, aggregation, range scans, and nonselective data access. Such workloads typically process more than 5 percent of the active data and frequently work with less than 25 percent of a table's columns in a single query. And because the process of inserting data into column-organized tables (or updating previously inserted data) is optimized for large transactions, environments that frequently see these types of workloads will usually benefit from BLU Acceleration. (With column-organized tables, performance is optimal if 100 or more rows are impacted by each insert or update operation performed.)

Keep in mind that the use of BLU Acceleration and traditional row-organized tables is not mutually exclusive; both column-organized tables and row-organized tables can coexist within the same database and, if desired, the same table space. They can also share the same buffer pools. So, for mixed workloads that include a combination of analytic query processing and very selective data access (typically involving less than 2 percent of the data available), a mixture of row-organized tables and column-organized tables might be the best option. This will enable users to take advantage of the features BLU Acceleration has to offer in environments where a combination of OLTP and analytical workloads must be supported.

Note: The db2convert command can be used to convert existing row-organized tables into column-organized tables. This is a manual operation—row-organized tables are not automatically converted when the value ANALYTICS is assigned to the DB2_WORKLOAD registry variable.

The Workload Table Organization Advisor, which is part of the IBM InfoSphere Optim Query Tuner, can be used to examine all the tables that are referenced in a query workload and make recommendations on which row-organized tables should be converted to column-organized tables to improve query performance.

DB2 10.5 Compatibility Features

To allow an application that was written for one relational database management system (RDBMS) product to run against another—unchanged—many obstacles must be overcome. For example, the behavior of the locking mechanisms used must be similar in both RDBMSs, data types that are valid in one RDBMS must be recognized by the other, and the SQL statements and procedural language used must be similar in both syntax and functionality. In an attempt to overcome many of these obstacles, IBM introduced a number of features in DB2 9.7 that were designed to reduce the time and complexity of enabling applications that were written for Oracle, Sybase, and MySQL to run against a DB2 database. And in DB2 10.5, several enhancements were made to this set of features. These enhancements include:

- **Implicit casting (weak typing):** Implicit casting is the automatic conversion of data of one data type to another based on an implied set of conversion rules. If two objects have mismatched types, implicit casting is used to perform comparisons or make assignments provided a reasonable interpretation of the data types can be made. With DB2 10.5, implicit casting is an alternative way to parse character or graphic constants to support applications that expect these constants to be assigned the data types CHAR and GRAPHIC.
- **New built-in scalar functions:** DB2 provides a wide variety of built-in functions that increase the compatibility of applications that were originally written for other databases—a scalar function returns a single value each time it is called. Several new scalar functions were added in DB2 10.5.

- **Improvements to the TIMESTAMP_FORMAT and VARCHAR_FORMAT scalar functions:** The TIMESTAMP_FORMAT function returns a timestamp for an input string, using a specified format; the VARCHAR_FORMAT function returns a string representation of an input expression that has been formatted according to a specified character template.
- **The lifting of several SQL restrictions:** To make the SQL syntax more compatible between products, several restrictions that existed in DB2 9.7 have been removed. Specifically, the use of correlation names in subqueries and table functions is now optional; PL/SQL procedures, functions, triggers, and packages can now be created in a partitioned database environment—but only from the catalog partition; and TYPE declarations are now supported in a function, procedure, trigger, or anonymous block.

  Restrictions that still apply include:

  » The NCLOB data type cannot be used in PL/SQL statements or contexts when the database is not defined as a Unicode database. (In Unicode databases, the NCLOB data type is mapped to a DB2 DBCLOB data type.)
  » The XML data type is not supported.
  » In a partitioned database environment, cursor variables cannot be accessed from remote nodes—they can only be accessed from the coordinator node.
  » The use of nested type data types with PL/SQL package variables is not supported in autonomous routines.
- **New synonyms for SQL syntax:** Several new synonyms were created to mirror the SQL syntax that is used by other database products. For example:

  » TO_DATE and TO_TIMESTAMP are now synonyms for TIMESTAMP_FORMAT
  » TO_CHAR is a synonym for VARCHAR_FORMAT
  » UNIQUE is a synonym for DISTINCT (when used with column functions or in the select list of a query)
  » MINUS is a synonym for the EXCEPT set operator
  » *SequenceName*.NEXTVAL can now be used in place of the SQL syntax NEXT VALUE FOR *SequenceName*
  » *SequenceName*.CURRVAL can now be used in place of the SQL syntax PREVIOUS VALUE FOR *SequenceName*
- **Global variable support:** A global variable is a named memory variable that can be retrieved or modified via SQL statements. Global variables can be used to map package variables, emulate @@nested, @@level, or @errorlevel variables, or pass information from DB2 applications to triggers, functions, or procedures.

- **An ARRAY collection data type:** Many programming techniques use collection types such as arrays, bags, lists, nested tables, sets, and trees; to support these techniques in database applications, PL/SQL provides the data types TABLE and VARRAY, which can be used to declare index-by tables, nested tables, and variable-size arrays. The DB2 ARRAY collection data type is used to map to VARRAY constructs in SQL procedures.

- **Increased identifier length limits:** An identifier is a token that is used to form a name; in DB2 10.5 identifiers used with SQL can be 128 bytes long.

- **A ROWID pseudocolumn:** A pseudocolumn is an assigned value that behaves like a table column, but that is not actually stored in a table; pseudocolumns can be queried, but they cannot be modified or deleted. Oracle provides a pseudocolumn called ROWID that will return a unique identifier for every row found in a table. DB2 10.5 now offers a similar ROWID pseudocolumn.

- **Extended row size support:** With extended row size support, it is possible to create a table whose row length exceeds the maximum record length allowed for the page size used by the table space the table is created in.

- **NULL keys can be excluded from indexes:** It is now possible to tell DB2 not to insert a key into an index object if all the columns in the key contain NULL values.

- **New string unit attributes:** Database columns that hold character data now have a special "string unit" attribute that controls how the length of a data value is determined. This improves the handling of multibyte characters.

While all these compatibility features except extended row size support and the ability to exclude NULL index keys are "always on," there are some additional compatibility features that must be enabled before they can be used. They are:

- Creation of a ROWNUM pseudocolumn
- Creation of a dummy table named DUAL
- Support for outer joins using the plus sign (+) as the outer join operator
- Support for CONNECT BY PRIOR syntax
- Support for the NUMBER data type
- Support for the VARCHAR2 data type
- Use of the DATE data type as TIMESTAMP(0)
- Alternative semantics for the TRUNCATE statement
- Support for assigning the CHAR or GRAPHIC data type to character and graphic string constants whose byte lengths are less than or equal to 254

- Use of collection methods such as FIRST, LAST, NEXT, and PREVIOUS to perform operations on arrays
- Support for creating Oracle data dictionary–compatible views
- Support for compiling and executing PL/SQL statements and other language elements
- Support for insensitive cursors
- Support for INOUT parameters in procedures, along with support for the specification of DEFAULT for INOUT parameter declarations
- Support for the use of MySQL- and PostgreSQL-compatible LIMIT and OFFSET clauses in SELECT, UPDATE, and DELETE statements

These compatibility features are optional and should only be used if they are needed for a specific purpose.

Enabling One or More Optional Compatibility Features

Before applications that have been written for Oracle, Sybase, or MySQL are moved to a DB2 environment, any of the optional compatibility features that are required must be enabled. This is done by assigning a hexadecimal value, where each bit in the value corresponds to one of the optional DB2 compatibility features available, to the DB2_COMPATIBILITY_VECTOR registry variable. (Values are assigned to this variable by executing the db2set command.) Valid hexadecimal bit values, along with the feature each bit represents, include:

- 1 (0x01)   ROWNUM pseudocolumn
- 2 (0x02)   DUAL table
- 3 (0x04)   Outer join operator (+)
- 4 (0x08)   CONNECT BY PRIOR syntax
- 5 (0x10)   NUMBER data type
- 6 (0x20)   VARCHAR2 data type
- 7 (0x40)   DATE as TIMESTAMP(0)
- 8 (0x80)   TRUNCATE statement
- 9 (0x100)   Character literals
- 10 (0x200)   Collection methods
- 11 (0x400)   Oracle data dictionary-compatible views
- 12 (0x800)   PL/SQL compilation
- 13 (0x1000)   Insensitive cursors

- 14 (0x2000)   INOUT parameters
- 15 (0x4000)   LIMIT and OFFSET clauses
- 17 (0x10000)   SQL data-access–level enforcement
- 18 (0x20000)   Oracle database link syntax
- 19 (0x40000)   Synonym usage

If you wish to take advantage of *all* the optional compatibility features that are available for a particular relational database product (or if you want to disable all the available features), you can assign one of the following symbolic values to the DB2_ COMPATIBILITY_VECTOR registry variable instead:

- **NULL:** No optional compatibility features are to be enabled (This is the default)
- **ORA:** Every optional compatibility feature for Oracle applications is to be enabled
- **SYB:** Every optional compatibility feature for Sybase applications is to be enabled
- **MYS:** Every optional compatibility feature for MySQL applications is to be enabled

•••

Note: When one or more optional compatibility features are enabled, some SQL behavior may be different from the way it is documented in the DB2 10.5 Knowledge Center.

•••

CHAPTER 3

Security

Eighteen percent (18%) of the *DB2 10.5 Fundamentals for LUW* certification exam (Exam 615) is designed to test your knowledge of the mechanisms DB2 uses to protect data and database objects against unauthorized access and modification. The questions that make up this portion of the exam are intended to evaluate the following:

- Your ability to identify ways in which access to instances, databases, and user data can be restricted
- Your ability to identify the authorization levels and privileges that are available with DB2 10.5 for LUW
- Your ability to identify how authorizations and privileges are granted and revoked
- Your knowledge of how to define and use roles
- Your knowledge of how and when to use Row and Column Access Control (RCAC)
- Your knowledge of how and when to use Label-Based Access Control (LBAC)
- Your knowledge of how and when to use trusted contexts

This chapter introduces you to the authorizations and privileges that are available with DB2 10.5 for LUW. It also provides you with information about the tools that are used to give (grant) and take away (revoke) authorizations and privileges to/from individuals, groups, and roles.

In this chapter, you will become familiar with the two mechanisms that DB2 uses to control access to instances, databases, data objects, and data: *authorities* and *privileges*. You will also learn how to grant authorities and privileges to specific users, groups, and roles, as well as how to revoke authorities and privileges when it is appropriate to do so. And you will learn how to use tools like RCAC and LBAC to secure sensitive data in ways that meet the strictest of security requirements or that adhere to rigid government security standards.

Controlling Database Access

Identity theft—a crime in which someone wrongfully obtains another person's personal data (such as a Social Security number, bank account number, or credit card number) and uses it in a fraudulent or deceptive manner for economic gain—is the fastest-growing crime in our nation today. Criminals obtain the information needed to steal an identity in a variety of ways: through overheard cell phone conversations; through telephone and email "phishing" scams; by stealing wallets, purses, and personal mail; by taking discarded documents from the trash; and by exploiting careless online shopping and banking habits. If that is not frightening enough, studies show that up to 70 percent of all identity theft cases are "inside jobs"—that is, they are perpetrated by a coworker or by an employee of a business that individuals frequently patronize. In these cases, all that is needed to commit identity theft is access to a company database.

That's why it is essential that a relational database management system be able to protect data against unauthorized access and modification. With DB2, a combination of external security services and internal access controls are used to perform this vital task. Furthermore, three different layers of security are employed: the first controls access to the instance a database was created under, the second controls access to the database itself, and the third controls access to the data and data objects that reside within the database.

Authentication

The first security portal most users must pass through on their way to gaining access to a DB2 instance or database is a process known as *authentication*. The purpose of authentication is to verify that users really are who they say they are. And in most cases, an external security facility that is not part of DB2 is used to perform this task. This facility might be part of the operating system, which is the case when DB2 is deployed on Linux, AIX, Solaris, HP-UX, and recent versions of the Windows operating system.

Or it can be a separate add-on product such as Distributed Computing Environment (DCE) Security Services. In either case, the external security facility used often must be presented with two specific pieces of information before a user can be authenticated: a unique *user ID* and a corresponding *password*. The user ID identifies the user to the security facility, and the password, which is information that is supposedly known only by the user and the security facility, verifies that the user is indeed who he or she claims to be.

Important: Because passwords are an important tool for authenticating users, they should always be required at the operating system level if an operating system will be used to perform authentication. Keep in mind that on most UNIX operating systems, undefined passwords are treated as NULL, and any user who has not been assigned a password will be treated as having a NULL password. Thus, from the operating system's perspective, if no password is provided when a user with a NULL password attempts to log in, authentication will be deemed successful, and the user will be given access to the operating system as well as to DB2.

Where Authentication Takes Place

Because DB2 can be deployed in environments that consist of multiple clients, gateways, and servers (each of which can be running a different operating system), deciding where authentication is to take place can sometimes be challenging. For this reason, DB2 often relies on the security facility that either the client or the server's operating system provides to control how users are authenticated.

With DB2 10.5 for LUW, a parameter in each DB2 Database Manager configuration file (which is a file that is associated with every instance) controls where and how authentication takes place. The value assigned to this parameter, often referred to as the *authentication type*, is set initially when an instance is first created. (On the server side, the authentication type is specified during the instance creation process; on the client side, the authentication type is stipulated when a remote database is cataloged.) Only one authentication type exists for each instance, and it controls access to that instance, as well as to all databases that fall under that instance's control. The following authentication types are available with DB2 10.5 for LUW:

- **CLIENT**: Authentication occurs at the client workstation or database partition where a client application is invoked, using the security facility that the client's operating system provides (assuming one is available). The user ID and password supplied by users wishing to access an instance or database are compared with user ID and password combinations stored at the client or node to determine whether access is permitted.
- **SERVER**: Authentication occurs at the server workstation using the security facility that the server's operating system provides. The user ID and password supplied by users wishing to access an instance or database are compared with user ID and password combinations stored at the server to determine whether access is permitted. Unless otherwise specified, this is the default authentication type used.
- **SERVER_ENCRYPT**: Authentication occurs at the server workstation using the security facility that the server's operating system provides. However, the password supplied by users wishing to access an instance or database is encrypted at the client workstation before it is sent to the server for validation.
- **DATA_ENCRYPT**: Authentication occurs at the server workstation using the SERVER_ENCRYPT authentication method. In addition, all user data is encrypted before it is passed from the client to the server and vice versa.
- **DATA_ENCRYPT_CMP**: Authentication occurs at the server workstation using the SERVER_ENCRYPT authentication method. And all user data is encrypted before it is passed from the client to the server and vice versa. In addition, compatibility for down-level products that do not support the DATA_ENCRYPT authentication type is provided. (Such products connect using the SERVER_ENCRYPT authentication type, and user data is not encrypted.)
- **KERBEROS**: Authentication occurs at the server workstation using a security facility that supports the Kerberos security protocol. This protocol performs authentication as a third-party service by using conventional cryptography to create a shared secret key—the key becomes the credentials used to verify the user's identity whenever local or network services are requested. (This eliminates the need to pass a user ID and password across the network as ASCII text.) If both the client and the server support the Kerberos security protocol, the user ID and password provided by users wishing to access an instance or database are encrypted at the client workstation and sent to the server for validation.
- **KRB_SERVER_ENCRYPT**: Authentication occurs at the server workstation using either the KERBEROS or the SERVER_ENCRYPT authentication method. If the client's

authentication type is set to KERBEROS, authentication takes place at the server using the Kerberos security system; if the client's authentication type is set to anything other than KERBEROS or if the Kerberos authentication service is unavailable, the server acts as if the SERVER_ENCRYPT authentication type was specified, and the rules for that authentication method are applied.

- **GSSPLUGIN**: Authentication occurs at the server workstation using a Generic Security Service Application Program Interface (GSS-API) plug-in. If the client's authentication type is not specified, the server returns a list of server-supported plug-ins to the client. (This list is stored in the *srvcon_gssplugin_list* database manager configuration parameter.) The client selects and uses the first supported plug-in it finds in the list; if no supported plug-in is found, the client is authenticated using the KERBEROS authentication method.

- **GSS_SERVER_ENCRYPT**: Authentication occurs at the server workstation using either the GSSPLUGIN or the SERVER_ENCRYPT authentication method. That is, if client authentication occurs through a GSS-API plug-in, the client is authenticated using the first client-supported plug-in found in the list of server-supported plug-ins supplied. However, if the client does not support any plug-ins in this list, it is authenticated by using the KERBEROS authentication method—if the client does not support the Kerberos security protocol, it is authenticated using the SERVER_ENCRYPT authentication method instead.

It is important to note that if the authentication type a client workstation employs will encrypt user ID and password information before sending it to a server, the server must use an authentication type that can decipher this information. Otherwise, the encrypted data cannot be processed, and an error will result.

Authorities and Privileges

After a user has been authenticated and an attachment to an instance (or a connection to a database) has been established, DB2 evaluates the set of *authorities* and *privileges* that have been assigned to the user to determine which operations, if any, he or she is allowed to perform. Authorities convey the right to perform high-level administrative and maintenance/utility operations on an instance or a database. Privileges, on the other hand, convey the right to perform certain actions against specific database resources (such as tables, indexes, and views). Together, authorities and privileges control access to an instance, to one or more databases under a specific instance's control, to a database, and to a database's objects and data. Users can work only with instances, databases, and objects they have been given appropriate authorities and privileges for.

Administrative Authorities

An *administrative authority* is a set of related privileges that controls which administrative and maintenance operations a user can perform against a DB2 instance or database. Individuals who have been given (granted) administrative authority are responsible both for controlling an instance or database and for ensuring the safety and integrity of any data that might come under that instance/database's control. The following administrative authorities are available:

- **System Administrator (SYSADM) authority:** The highest level of administrative authority available; users who have been granted this authority can run most DB2 utilities, execute most DB2 commands, and perform any SQL or XQuery operation that does not attempt to access data that is protected by RCAC or LBAC. Users with this authority also have the ability to create databases and database objects such as tables, indexes, and views.

  Individuals who hold SYSADM authority are implicitly given all the rights that are granted to users who hold any of the other system-level administrative authorities available.

- **System Control (SYSCTRL) authority:** The highest level of system and instance control authority available; users who have been granted this authority can create and drop DB2 databases, use almost all the DB2 utilities, and execute the majority of the DB2 commands available. However, they cannot access user data directly unless they have been explicitly granted the privileges needed to do so. (SYSCTRL authority is intended to provide select users with nearly complete control of a DB2 system without letting them access sensitive data.) Because a database connection is required to run some of the DB2 utilities available, users who hold SYSCTRL authority for a particular instance automatically receive the privileges needed to connect to any database that falls under that instance's control.

- **System Maintenance (SYSMAINT) authority:** Provides select individuals with the ability to perform maintenance operations (such as forcing users off a server and backing up a database) on an instance and any databases that fall under that instance's control. As with SYSCTRL authority, SYSMAINT authority is intended to let special users maintain a database that contains sensitive data they most likely should not view or modify. Consequently, users who receive this authority cannot access user data unless they have been explicitly granted the privileges needed to do so. Because a database connection is required to run some of DB2's maintenance utilities, users who have SYSMAINT authority for a particular instance automatically receive the privileges needed to connect to any database that falls under that instance's control.

- **System Monitor (SYSMON) authority:** Provides select individuals with the ability to take database system monitor snapshots of an instance and its databases. Users who have been granted this authority can execute the various LIST commands that are available for obtaining information about databases and database objects. However, they are not permitted to access user data directly unless they have been explicitly granted the privileges needed to do so. Because a connection to a database must exist before the DB2 snapshot monitor can be used, users who have SYSMON authority for a particular instance automatically receive the privileges needed to connect to each database under that instance's control.

- **Database Administrator (DBADM) authority:** The highest level of database authority available; users who have been granted this authority can create database objects (such as tables, indexes, and views), issue database-specific DB2 commands, and execute built-in DB2 routines (with the exception of audit routines). Users with DBADM authority also have the ability to access data stored in tables and views, including system catalog tables and views—provided that data is not protected by RCAC or LBAC.

  Users who hold DBADM authority implicitly receive all the rights that are given to users who hold many of the other database-level administrative authorities available.

- **Security Administrator (SECADM) authority:** Provides select individuals with the ability to manage security-related database objects, such as those needed to implement RCAC and LBAC. Users who possess this authority can also grant and revoke database-level authorities and privileges, execute DB2's audit system routines, and access data stored in system catalog tables and views. However, they cannot access or modify user data.

- **Access Control (ACCESSCTRL) authority:** Provides select individuals with the ability to grant and revoke privileges on objects that reside in a specific database. Like users with SECADM authority, individuals with ACCESSCTRL authority can access and modify data stored in system catalog tables and views. However, they cannot access or modify user data.

- **Data Access (DATAACCESS) authority:** Provides select individuals with the ability to access and modify data stored in user tables, views, and materialized query tables. Users with this authority can also execute plans, packages, functions, and stored procedures.
- **SQL Administrator (SQLADM) authority:** Provides select individuals with the ability to monitor and tune SQL statements—that is, to execute EXPLAIN SQL statements, run the RUNSTATS utility, and execute system-defined stored procedures, functions, and packages. Users with this authority can also run the following commands: CREATE EVENT MONITOR, DROP EVENT MONITOR, FLUSH EVENT MONITOR, FLUSH OPTIMIZATION PROFILE CACHE, FLUSH PACKAGE CACHE, PREPARE, REORG, and SET EVENT MONITOR STATE.
- **Workload Management Administrator (WLMADM) authority:** Provides select individuals with the ability to manage workload management objects, such as service classes, work action sets, work class sets, and workloads.

A word about the separation of management and security-related tasks

With earlier versions of DB2, individuals who held the administrative authorities needed to manage instances and databases also had the ability to access the databases they managed, which meant they potentially had access to confidential and/or sensitive information. They also had the ability to grant and revoke authorities and privileges to others. Today, it is possible to separate security administration from system administration, database administration, and data access. Separating management tasks from security administration can simplify system administration and strengthen the security of a database environment.

By default, when a user with SYSADM authority creates a database, that user is automatically granted SECADM authority for that database. To separate SYSADM authority from SECADM authority, a user with SECADM authority must explicitly grant SECADM authority to a user, group, or role; the user who receives SECADM authority must then revoke the authority from everybody else. (Only users with SECADM authority are allowed to grant and revoke SECADM authority to/from others.)

Privileges

As mentioned earlier, *privileges* convey the right to perform certain actions against specific database resources. Two distinct types of privileges exist: *database* and *object*. Database privileges apply to a database as a whole and control which actions a user is allowed to perform against a particular database. With DB2 10.5 for LUW, the following database privileges (also referred to as *database authorities*) are available:

- **BINDADD**: Allows a user to create packages in a certain database (by precompiling Embedded SQL application source code files against the database or by binding application bind files to the database)
- **CONNECT**: Allows a user to establish a connection to a certain database
- **CREATETAB**: Allows a user to create new tables in a certain database
- **CREATE_EXTERNAL_ROUTINE**: Allows a user to register user-defined functions (UDFs) and procedures that are external (for example, that reside in a shared library) with a certain database so other users and applications can execute them
- **CREATE_NOT_FENCED_ROUTINE**: Allows a user to create unfenced UDFs and procedures and store them in a specific database—unfenced UDFs and stored procedures are UDFs/procedures that are considered "safe" enough to be run in the DB2 Database Manager operating environment's process or address space; unless a UDF or procedure is registered as unfenced, the DB2 Database Manager insulates the UDF's or procedure's internal resources such that they cannot be run in DB2 memory space
- **CREATE_SECURE_OBJECT**: Allows a user to create secure triggers and secure functions, as well as alter the secure attribute of such objects
- **EXPLAIN**: Allows a user to explain, prepare, and describe dynamic and static SQL statements without requiring access to data
- **IMPLICIT_SCHEMA**: Allows a user to implicitly create a new schema in a certain database—if a user with this authority attempts to create an object without specifying a schema qualifier, the object will be assigned a schema name that is different from any of the schema names that already exist in the database
- **LOAD**: Allows a user to bulk-load data into one or more existing tables in a certain database
- **QUIESCE_CONNECT**: Allows a user to establish a connection to a certain database while it is in a quiesced state (that is, while access to the database is restricted)

Object privileges, on the other hand, apply to specific database objects (for example, tables, indexes, and views). Because the nature of each database object varies, the individual privileges that exist for each object differ. The remainder of this section describes the various object privileges that are available.

The authorization ID privilege

The authorization ID privilege allows a user to set the session authorization ID to one of a set of specified authorization IDs available (by executing the SET SESSION AUTHORIZATION statement). Only one authorization ID privilege exists—the SETSESSIONUSER privilege.

The table space privilege

The table space privilege controls what users can and cannot do with a particular table space. (Table spaces control where data in a database physically resides.) Only one table space privilege exists—the USE privilege, which, when granted, allows a user to create objects in a certain table space.

• •

Note: The USE privilege cannot be used to give an individual the ability to create tables in the system catalog table space or in any temporary table spaces that might exist.

• •

Schema privileges

Schema privileges control what users can and cannot do with a particular schema. (A schema is an object that is used to logically classify and group other objects in a database; most objects are identified by using a naming convention that consists of a schema name, followed by a period, followed by the object name.) The following schema privileges are available:

- **CREATEIN**: Allows a user to create objects within a certain schema
- **ALTERIN**: Allows a user to change the comment associated with any object in a certain schema or alter any object that resides in the schema
- **DROPIN**: Allows a user to remove (drop) any object within a certain schema

With DB2 10.5 for LUW, the objects that can be manipulated within a schema include tables, views, indexes, packages, data types, functions, triggers, procedures, and aliases.

Table privileges

Table privileges control what users can and cannot do with a particular table in a database. (A table is a logical structure that presents data as a collection of unordered rows with a fixed number of columns.) The following table privileges are available:

- **CONTROL**: Provides a user with all table privileges available; with this privilege, a user can remove (drop) a certain table from the database, execute the RUNSTATS and REORG commands against the table, execute the SET INTEGRITY statement against the table, and grant and revoke individual table privileges (with the exception of the CONTROL privilege) to/from others
- **ALTER**: Allows a user to change a certain table's definition and/or the comment associated with the table, as well as create or drop a table constraint
- **SELECT**: Allows a user to retrieve data from a certain table, as well as create a view that references the table
- **INSERT**: Allows a user to add data to a certain table
- **UPDATE**: Allows a user to modify data in a certain table; this privilege can apply to the entire table or be limited to specific columns within the table
- **DELETE**: Allows a user to remove data from a certain table
- **INDEX**: Allows a user to create an index for a certain table
- **REFERENCES**: Allow a user to create and drop foreign key constraints that reference a certain table in a referential integrity constraint; this privilege can apply to the entire table or be limited to specific columns within the table, in which case a user can only create and drop referential constraints that reference the columns identified

View privileges

View privileges control what users can and cannot do with a particular view. (A view is a virtual table that provides an alternative way of working with data that physically resides in one or more tables; views are frequently used to restrict access to specific columns in a table.) The following view privileges are available:

- **CONTROL**: Provides a user with all view privileges available; with this privilege, a user can remove (drop) a certain view from the database, as well as grant and revoke individual view privileges (with the exception of the CONTROL privilege) to/from others

- **SELECT**: Allows a user to use a certain view to retrieve data from its underlying base table(s)
- **INSERT**: Allows a user to use a certain view to add data to its underlying base table(s)
- **UPDATE**: Allows a user to use a certain view to modify data in its underlying base table(s); this privilege can apply to the entire view or be limited to specific columns within the view
- **DELETE**: Allows a user to use a certain view to remove data from its underlying base table(s)

It is important to note that the owners of a view will receive CONTROL privilege for that view only if they hold CONTROL privilege for every underlying base table the view references.

Note: To create a view, a user must hold, at a minimum, SELECT privilege on each base table the view references.

The index privilege

The index privilege controls what users can and cannot do with a particular index. (An index is an ordered set of pointers that refer to one or more key columns in a base table; indexes are frequently used to improve query performance.) Only one index privilege exists—the CONTROL privilege, which, when granted, allows users to remove a certain index from a database.

Unlike the CONTROL privilege for other objects, the CONTROL privilege for an index does not automatically give users the ability to grant and revoke index privileges to/ from others. That is because the only index privilege available is the CONTROL privilege, and only users with ACCESSCTRL or SECADM authority are allowed to grant and revoke CONTROL privilege.

Sequence privileges

Sequence privileges control what users can and cannot do with a particular sequence. (A sequence is an object that can be used to generate values automatically. Sequences are ideal for producing unique key values because they eliminate the concurrency and performance problems that can occur when unique counters residing outside a database are used for data value generation.) The following sequence privileges are available:

- **USAGE**: Allows a user to use the PREVIOUS VALUE and NEXT VALUE expressions that are associated with a certain sequence (the PREVIOUS VALUE expression returns the most recently generated value for the specified sequence; the NEXT VALUE expression returns the next value for the specified sequence)
- **ALTER**: Allows a user to perform administrative tasks on a certain sequence, such as restarting the sequence or changing the increment value for the sequence

The routine privilege

The routine privilege controls what users can and cannot do with a particular routine. (A routine can be a UDF, a stored procedure, or a method that different users can invoke.) Only one routine privilege exists—the EXECUTE privilege, which, when granted, allows a user to invoke a certain routine, create a function that is sourced from the routine (if the routine is a UDF), and reference the routine in an SQL statement.

Package privileges

Package privileges control what users can and cannot do with a particular package. (A package is an object that contains information that DB2 uses to efficiently process SQL statements embedded in an application.) The following package privileges are available:

- **CONTROL**: Provides a user with all package privileges available; with this privilege, a user can remove (drop) a certain package from the database, as well as grant and revoke individual package privileges (with the exception of the CONTROL privilege) to/from others
- **BIND**: Allows a user to bind or rebind (recreate) a certain package, as well as add new versions of a package that has already been bound, to a database
- **EXECUTE**: Allows a user to execute or run a certain package; because all privileges needed to execute the SQL statements in a package are implicitly granted at run time, users who hold EXECUTE privilege for a particular package can execute that package even if they do not possess the privileges needed to execute the SQL statements stored in it

The server privilege

The server privilege controls whether a user can work with a particular federated server data source. (A federated system is a distributed computing system that consists of a DB2 server, known as a *federated server*, and one or more data sources the federated server sends queries to. Each data source consists of an instance of some supported relational database management system, such as Oracle, plus the database or databases the instance supports.) Only one server privilege exists—the PASSTHRU privilege, which, when granted, allows a user to issue Data Definition Language (DDL) and Data Manipulation Language (DML) SQL statements (as pass-through operations) directly to a data source via a federated database server.

Nickname privileges

Nickname privileges control what users can and cannot do with a particular nickname. (When a client application submits a distributed request to a federated database server, the request is forwarded to the appropriate data source for processing. However, such a request does not identify the data source itself; instead, it references tables and views within the data source by using *nicknames* that map to specific table and view names in the data source. Nicknames are not alternative names for tables and views in the same way that aliases are, but are pointers that a federated server uses to reference external objects.) The following nickname privileges are available:

- **CONTROL**: Provides a user with all nickname privileges available; with this privilege, a user can remove (drop) a certain nickname from the database, as well as grant and revoke individual nickname privileges (with the exception of the CONTROL privilege) to/from others
- **ALTER**: Allows a user to add, reset, or drop a column option for a certain nickname; also lets a user change a nickname's column name or data type, as well as modify the comment associated with the nickname
- **SELECT**: Allows a user to retrieve data from the table or view within a federated data source that a certain nickname refers to
- **INSERT**: Allows a user to retrieve data from the table or view within a federated data source that a certain nickname refers to
- **UPDATE**: Allows a user to modify data in the table or view within a federated data source that a certain nickname refers to; this privilege can apply to the entire table or be limited to specific columns within the table
- **DELETE**: Allows a user to remove rows of data from the table or view within a federated data source that a certain nickname refers to
- **INDEX**: Allows a user to create an index specification for a certain nickname
- **REFERENCES**: Allows a user to create and drop foreign key constraints that reference a certain nickname in a referential integrity constraint

Variable privileges

Variable privileges control what users can and cannot do with a particular global variable. (A global variable is a named memory variable that can be retrieved or modified by using SQL statements; global variables enable applications to share relational data among SQL statements, without the need for additional application logic to support such data transfers.) The following variable privileges are available:

- **READ**: Allows a user to read the value of a certain global variable
- **WRITE**: Allows a user to assign a value to a certain global variable

The XML schema repository (XSR) object privilege

The XML schema repository (XSR) object privilege controls what users can and cannot do with a particular XSR object. (XSR objects are used to validate and process XML instance documents that are stored in an XML column.) Only one XSR object privilege exists—the USAGE privilege, which, when granted, allows a user to use a certain XSR object.

The workload privilege

The workload privilege controls what users can and cannot do with a particular workload. (Workloads are a key part of a DB2 workload management solution and are used to identify a source of work.) Only one workload privilege exists—the USAGE privilege, which, when granted, allows a user to use a certain defined workload.

Note: Users with SYSADM or DBADM authority are implicitly granted the USAGE privilege on all workloads that exist at the current server.

Granting Authorities and Privileges

Individuals can obtain authorities and privileges in a variety of ways:

- **Implicitly:** When a user creates a new database, he or she automatically (implicitly) receives DBADM authority for that database, as well as all database privileges that are currently available. Likewise, when a user creates a database object, he or she automatically receives all privileges that exist for that object, along with the ability to grant any combination of those privileges—with the exception of the CONTROL privilege—to others.

In some cases, a user can implicitly receive authorities and privileges when a higher-level privilege is explicitly granted. For example, if a user is explicitly given CONTROL privilege for a table, he or she will implicitly receive all available table privileges. Implicitly granted privileges are permanent and persist outside the scope in which they are granted.

- **Indirectly:** When a user executes a package that performs operations that require certain privileges (for example, a package that deletes a row of data from a table will require DELETE privilege on the table), he or she is indirectly given those privileges for the express purpose of executing the package. Indirectly granted privileges are temporary and do not exist beyond the scope in which they are granted.

- **Explicitly:** Most authorities and privileges can be explicitly given (granted) to select individuals by someone who has the authority to do so. To explicitly grant authorities and privileges, a user must possess SECADM authority, ACCESSCTRL authority, or CONTROL privilege on the object that privileges are to be granted for. Alternatively, a user can explicitly grant any privilege associated with an object that they have ownership of or any privilege that was granted to them with the WITH GRANT OPTION.

The GRANT Statement

One way to explicitly give authorities and privileges to others is by executing the GRANT statement. Syntax for the GRANT statement varies according to the type of authority or privilege being granted. However, the basic syntax looks something like this:

```
GRANT [Authority | Privilege, ...]
   [ON | OF] [ObjectType] [ObjectName]
   TO [Recipient, ...]
   <WITH GRANT OPTION>
```

or

```
GRANT [ALL <PRIVILEGES> |
   Privilege <(ColumnName, ...)>, ...]
   ON [ObjectType] [ObjectName]
```

```
TO [Recipient, ...]
  <WITH GRANT OPTION>
```

or

```
GRANT <ROLE> [RoleName, ...]
  TO [Recipient, ...]
  <WITH ADMIN OPTION>
```

where:

Authority	Identifies one or more authorities to grant
Privilege	Identifies one or more privileges to grant
Options	Identifies one or more options that are associated with the authority or privilege to be granted; for example, the <[WITH | WITHOUT] DATAACCESS> and <[WITH | WITHOUT] ACCESSCTRL> options can be specified when the DBADM authority/privilege is granted
ColumnName	Identifies, by name, one or more specific columns that the authorities or privileges specified are to be associated with
ObjectType	Identifies the type of object the authorities or privileges specified are to be granted for
ObjectName	Identifies, by name, the object the authorities or privileges specified are to be granted for
RoleName	Identifies, by name, one or more roles that are to be granted
Recipient	Identifies who is to receive the authorities or privileges being granted; the value specified for this parameter can be any combination of the following:

	[*AuthorizationID*]	Identifies a particular user, by authorization ID, whom the authorities or privileges specified are to be granted to
	<<USER> *Name* >	Identifies a particular user, by name, whom the authorities or privileges specified are to be granted to
	<<GROUP> *Name* >	Identifies a particular group, by name, that the authorities or privileges specified are to be granted to

| <<ROLE> *Name* > | Identifies a particular role, by name, that the authorities or privileges specified are to be granted to |
| PUBLIC | Indicates that the authorities or privileges specified are to be granted to the group PUBLIC |

As mentioned earlier, only users with ACCESSCTRL or SECADM authority are allowed to grant and revoke the CONTROL privilege for an object. Consequently, if the ALL PRIVILEGES clause is specified with the GRANT statement used, all privileges for the designated object—*except* the CONTROL privilege—will be granted to each recipient indicated. CONTROL privilege must be granted separately.

If the WITH GRANT OPTION clause is specified with the GRANT statement used, the individual receiving the designated authorities or privileges will receive the ability to grant those authorities or privileges to others. Similarly, if the WITH ADMIN OPTION clause is specified with the GRANT statement used, the individual being granted a role will receive the ability to grant that role to others.

More about roles

A *role* is a database entity that is used to group a combination of authorities and/or privileges together so they can be simultaneously granted or revoked. When roles are used, the assignment of authorities and privileges is greatly simplified. For example, instead of granting the same set of authorities and privileges to every individual in a particular job function, you can assign a set of authorities and privileges to a role that represents the job and then grant membership in that role to every user who performs that particular job. It is important to note that only users with SECADM authority are allowed to create roles (by executing the CREATE ROLE SQL statement).

Roles enable you to control database access in a manner that mirrors the structure of your organization—you can create roles that map directly to specific job functions within your company. And because you can grant users membership in roles that reflect their responsibilities, you can easily move their membership from one role to another as their job responsibilities change.

With the exception of SECADM authority, most of the authorities and privileges available can be granted to a role. And if a role's authorities and privileges are changed, all users who have membership in that role will automatically have their authorities and privileges updated. The authorities and privileges held by each individual user do not have to be altered to reflect the change.

Note: When one role is granted membership in another role, a role hierarchy is formed; in a role hierarchy, the role that is granted membership inherits the authorities and privileges that have been granted to the "parent" role. For example, if the role DOCTOR is granted to the role SURGEON, then the role SURGEON will inherit the authorities and privileges that have been granted to the role DOCTOR.

When role hierarchies are formed, cycles are not allowed. A cycle occurs if one role is granted to another role and then that other role is granted back to the original role. In other words, if the role DOCTOR is granted to the role SURGEON, the role SURGEON cannot be granted back to the role DOCTOR. Any attempt to create a cycle in a role hierarchy will result in an error.

GRANT Statement Examples

Now that we have seen the basic syntax for the GRANT statement, let's look at some examples.

Example 1: Give a user whose authorization ID is USER1 the ability to create a view on a table named SALES:

```
GRANT SELECT ON TABLE sales TO user1
```

Example 2: Give a user whose authorization ID is USER1 the privileges needed to remove records from a table named INVENTORY, as well as the ability to give those privileges to others:

```
GRANT DELETE ON TABLE inventory
   TO USER user1
   WITH GRANT OPTION
```

Example 3: Give a user whose authorization ID is USER1 the privileges required to
run an Embedded SQL application named HR.CALC_BONUS that calls a package named
HR.CALCULATIONS:

```
GRANT EXECUTE ON PACKAGE hr.calculations
  TO user1
```

Example 4: Give a user whose authorization ID is USER1 the ability to assign a
comment to a table named PRODUCT_ID:

```
GRANT ALTER ON TABLE product_id
  TO USER user1
```

Example 5: Give two users (whose authorization IDs are USER1 and USER2) the
privileges needed to use the Import utility to populate a table named DEPARTMENT:

```
GRANT SELECT, INSERT ON department
  TO user1, user2
```

Example 6: Grant all privileges (except CONTROL privilege) for a table named
EMPLOYEES to a role named ADMIN; then, give a user whose authorization ID is USER1
membership in the ADMIN role:

```
GRANT ALL ON TABLE employees TO ROLE admin;
GRANT ROLE admin TO USER user1;
```

Revoking Authorities and Privileges

Just as the GRANT statement can be used to grant authorities and privileges, the REVOKE
statement can be used to remove any authorities and privileges that have been granted.
And as with the GRANT statement, syntax for the REVOKE statement varies according
to the type of authority or privilege being revoked. The basic syntax for the REVOKE
statement looks something like this:

```
REVOKE [ALL PRIVILEGES | Authority | Privilege, ...]
  [ON | OF] [ObjectType] [ObjectName]
  FROM [Forfeiter, ...]
```

or

```
REVOKE <ADMIN OPTION FOR>
  <ROLE> [RoleName, ...]
  FROM [Forfeiter, ...]
```

where:

Authority	Identifies one or more authorities to revoke
Privilege	Identifies one or more privileges to revoke
ObjectType	Identifies the type of object the authorities or privileges specified are to be revoked for
ObjectName	Identifies, by name, the object the authorities or privileges specified are to be revoked for
RoleName	Identifies, by name, one or more roles to revoke
Forfeiter	Identifies who is to lose the authorities or privileges that are being revoked; the value specified for this parameter can be any combination of the following:

	[*AuthorizationID*]	Identifies a particular user, by authorization ID, whom the authorities or privileges specified are to be revoked from
	<<USER> *Name* >	Identifies a particular user, by name, whom the authorities or privileges specified are to be revoked from
	<<GROUP> *Name* >	Identifies a particular group, by name, that the authorities or privileges specified are to be revoked from
	<<ROLE> *Name* >	Identifies a particular role, by name, that the authorities or privileges specified are to be revoked from
	PUBLIC	Indicates that the authorities or privileges specified are to be revoked from the group PUBLIC

If the ALL PRIVILEGES clause is specified with the REVOKE statement used, all
authorities and privileges for the object indicated—*except* the CONTROL privilege—
will be revoked from each forfeiter specified. Therefore, if CONTROL privilege is to
be revoked, it must be revoked separately (by someone with ACCESSCTRL or SECADM
authority).

If the ADMIN OPTION FOR clause is specified with the REVOKE statement used, the
ability to grant the specified role(s) to others will be taken away from the forfeiter(s)
indicated.

REVOKE Statement Examples

Now that we have seen the basic syntax for the REVOKE statement, let us look at some
examples.

Example 1: Remove the ability to create tables in a table space named HR from a user
whose authorization ID is USER1:

```
REVOKE USE OF TABLESPACE hr
    FROM user1
```

Example 2: Remove the ability to use a UDF named MPH_TO_KPH from a user whose
authorization ID is USER1:

```
REVOKE EXECUTE ON FUNCTION mph_to_kph
    FROM USER user1
```

Example 3: Remove the ability to modify information stored in the ADDRESS and
HOME_PHONE columns of a table named EMPLOYEES from a user whose authorization
ID is USER1:

```
REVOKE UPDATE (address, home_phone)
    ON TABLE emp_info
    FROM user1
```

Example 4: Remove the ability to add data to a table named SALES from a user whose authorization ID is USER1:

```
REVOKE INSERT ON TABLE sales
  FROM user1
```

Example 5: Prevent users in the special group PUBLIC from adding, changing, or deleting data stored in a table named EMPLOYEE:

```
REVOKE INSERT, UPDATE, DELETE
  ON TABLE employee
  FROM PUBLIC
```

Example 6: Remove a user whose authorization ID is USER1 from a role named ADMIN role:

```
REVOKE ROLE admin FROM USER user1
```

Row and Column Access Control (RCAC)

Traditionally, if a database administrator needed to restrict access to specific columns or rows in a table, he or she relied on views. For example, if a table containing employee data held sensitive information such as Social Security numbers and salaries, access to that data might be restricted by creating a view that contained only the columns that held nonsensitive data. Then, only authorized users would be given access to the table, while everyone else would be required to work with the view. (This was accomplished by granting appropriate table privileges to select users and the necessary view privileges to everyone else.)

Using views for access control works well when data access rules and restrictions are relatively simple. However, this approach becomes ineffective if several views are needed or if view definitions are complex. And it can be costly, particularly if a large number of views must be manually updated and maintained. Even when data access rules are relatively simple, the use of views for access control has one significant drawback—users with direct access to a database, and users who hold DATAACCESS authority, can often gain access to the sensitive data that one or more views have been designed to protect.

Implemented through SQL and managed by a DB2 security administrator, Row and Column Access Control—sometimes referred to as *fine-grained access control*, or *FGAC*—resolves these issues by stipulating rules and conditions under which a user, group, or role can access rows and columns of a table. With RCAC, all users access the same table (as opposed to accessing alternative views), but access is restricted based on individual user permissions and rules that a DB2 security administrator has specified in a security policy that has been associated with the table. Two sets of RCAC rules exist: one set operates on rows (known as *row permissions*), and the other operates on columns (referred to as *column masks*). These rules can be used together or separately to control how data is accessed.

Row Permissions

A *row permission* is a database entity that describes a specific row access control rule for a certain table. Written in the form of a query search condition, a row permission specifies the conditions under which a user, group, or role can access individual rows of data in a table. Row permissions can be created on all tables except materialized query tables; they are created by executing the CREATE PERMISSION statement. The basic syntax for this statement is:

```
CREATE PERMISSION [PermissionName] ON [TableName]
  FOR ROWS WHERE [SearchCondition]
  ENFORCED FOR ALL ACCESS
  [ENABLE | DISABLE]
```

where:

PermissionName	Identifies the name to assign to the row permission that is to be created
TableName	Identifies, by name, the base table the row permission is to be created for
SearchCondition	Identifies one or more logical conditions that evaluate to TRUE (1) or FALSE (0); the search condition specified must follow the same rules the search condition in a WHERE clause of a query adheres to, with some minor exceptions—notably, the search condition specified cannot contain references to other database objects

If the ENABLE clause is specified with the CREATE PERMISSION statement used, the resulting row permission will be enabled for row access control as soon as it is created. However, because you can use the CREATE PERMISSION statement to create a row permission *before* row access control has been activated for a table, the row permission might not take effect immediately. If row access control is not currently activated for the table specified, the row permission will become effective only after row access control for the table has been activated. (Row access control for a table is activated by executing the ALTER TABLE statement with the ACTIVATE ROW ACCESS CONTROL clause specified.) Activating row access control for the table will make the row permission effective immediately, and all packages and dynamically cached statements that reference the table will be marked as invalid.

Thus, to create a row permission named SREP_ROW_ACCESS that allows only members of the role SREP (which is a role that has been created for sales representatives) to see records stored in a table named SALES, you would execute a CREATE PERMISSION statement that looks something like this:

```
CREATE PERMISSION srep_row_access ON sales
  FOR ROWS WHERE
    VERIFY_ROLE_FOR_USER (SESSION_USER,'SREP') = 1
  ENFORCED FOR ALL ACCESS
  ENABLE
```

Of course, the resulting row permission (SREP_ROW_ACCESS) will not be enforced unless row access control has been activated for the table named SALES.

If multiple row permissions are defined for a single table, the search condition in each row permission is logically ORed together to form the row access control search condition that will be applied whenever users access the table. The final row access control search condition acts as a filter and is processed before any other operations (for example, an ORDER BY operation) are performed. In addition, the final row access control search condition used ensures that any row an authorized user inserts or updates in the table conforms to the definition of all row permissions that have been defined.

Column Masks

A *column mask* is a database entity that describes a specific column access control rule for a certain column in a table. Written in the form of an SQL CASE expression, a column mask indicates the conditions under which a user, group, or role can access values for a column. Depending upon the CASE expression used, a column mask can also control the value that unauthorized users, groups, or roles will receive whenever a protected column is queried.

As with row permissions, column masks can be created on all tables except materialized query tables. Column masks are created by executing the CREATE MASK statement; the basic syntax for this statement is:

```
CREATE MASK [MaskName] ON [TableName]
  FOR COLUMN [ColumnName]
  RETURN [CASEExpression]
  [ENABLE | DISABLE]
```

where:

MaskName	Identifies the name to assign to the column mask that is to be created
TableName	Identifies, by name, the base table the column mask is to be created for
ColumnName	Identifies, by name, the column that the column mask is to be created for
CASEExpression	Identifies a CASE expression that is to be evaluated to determine the appropriate value to return for the column (the result of the CASE expression is returned in place of the column value in a row; therefore, the result data type, NULL attribute, and length attribute of the CASE expression result must be identical to that of the column specified)

If the ENABLE clause is specified with the CREATE MASK statement used, the resulting column mask will be enabled for column access control as soon as it is created—provided column access control has been activated for the table. If column access control has not been activated for the table indicated, the column mask will become effective only after column access control for the table has been activated. (Column access control for a table can be activated by executing the ALTER TABLE statement with the ACTIVATE COLUMN ACCESS CONTROL clause specified.)

Thus, to create a column mask named SSN_MASK that allows only members of the role HR to see Social Security numbers stored in a column named SSN (in a table named EMPLOYEES) and that allows everyone else to see just the last four digits of Social Security numbers, you could execute a CREATE MASK statement that looks something like this:

```
CREATE MASK ssn_mask ON employees
  FOR COLUMN ssn
  RETURN
    CASE
      WHEN (VERIFY_GROUP_FOR_USER (SESSION_USER,'HR') = 1)
        THEN ssn
      ELSE 'XXX-XX-' || SUBSTR(ssn,8,4)
    END
  ENABLE
```

Although multiple columns in a table can have column masks defined, only one column mask can be created per column. When column access control is activated for a table, the CASE expression in the column mask definition is applied to determine the values that will be returned to an application. The application of column masks affects the final output only; it does not affect operations in SQL statements.

Activating Row and Column Access Control

You can activate row and column access control for a table at any time. If row permissions or column masks already exist, activating row and column access control simply makes the permissions or masks become effective—provided they were created with the ENABLE clause specified. If row permissions or column masks do not yet exist, activating row access control for a table will cause DB2 to generate a default row permission that prevents any SQL access to the table from occurring. Activating column access control causes DB2 to wait for column masks to be created.

No database user is inherently exempted from row and column access control rules. Therefore, users with direct access to a database, as well as users who hold DATAACCESS authority, cannot get to sensitive data that row and column access control measures have been defined to protect.

Label-Based Access Control (LBAC)

Label-based access control (LBAC), also known as *multilevel security*, is a security feature that uses one or more security labels to control who has read access, who has write access, and who has both read and write access to individual rows and/or columns in a table. LBAC is implemented by assigning unique labels to users and data and allowing access only when assigned labels match; it is similar, in both form and function, to the security models that the United States and many other governments use to protect important information. Such models may assign hierarchical classification labels like CONFIDENTIAL, SECRET, and TOP SECRET to data based on its sensitivity. Access to data is then restricted to just those users who have been assigned the appropriate label (for example, SECRET) or to users who have been assigned a label that is at a higher level in the classification hierarchy.

To implement an LBAC solution, it is imperative that you have a thorough understanding of the security requirements that need to be enforced. Once the security requirements are known, someone with SECADM authority must define the appropriate *security label components*, *security policies*, and *security labels*. Then, that individual must grant the proper security labels to the appropriate users. Finally, someone with LBAC credentials must create an LBAC-protected table or alter an existing table to add LBAC protection.

Security Label Components

Security label components represent criteria that can be used to determine whether a user should have access to specific data. Three types of security label components can exist:

- **SET**: A set is a collection of elements (character string values) where the order in which each element appears is not important.
- **ARRAY**: An array is an ordered set of elements that represents a simple hierarchy. The order in which the elements appear is important—the first element ranks higher than the second, the second ranks higher than the third, and so on.
- **TREE**: A tree represents a more complex hierarchy that can have multiple nodes and branches.

Security label components are created by executing the CREATE SECURITY LABEL COMPONENT statement. The basic syntax for this statement is:

```
CREATE SECURITY LABEL COMPONENT [ComponentName]
  SET {StringConstant, ...}
```

or

```
CREATE SECURITY LABEL COMPONENT [ComponentName]
  SET [StringConstant, ...]
```

or

```
CREATE SECURITY LABEL COMPONENT [ComponentName]
  TREE (StringConstant ROOT
    <,StringConstant UNDER StringConstant, ...>)
```

where:

ComponentName	Identifies the name to assign to the security label component that is to be created
StringConstant	Identifies one or more string constant values that make up the set, array, or tree of values the security label component will use

Thus, to create a security label component named SEC_COMP1 that contains an array of values listed from highest to lowest order, you could execute a CREATE SECURITY LABEL COMPONENT statement that looks something like this:

```
CREATE SECURITY LABEL COMPONENT sec_comp1
  ARRAY ['MASTER_CRAFTSMAN', 'JOURNEYMAN', 'APPRENTICE']
```

On the other hand, to create a security label component named SEC_COMP2 that consists of a tree of values that describe a company's organizational chart, you would execute a CREATE SECURITY LABEL COMPONENT statement that looks more like this:

```
CREATE SECURITY LABEL COMPONENT sec_comp2
  TREE ('CEO' ROOT,
        'SALES_MGR' UNDER 'CEO',
        'HR_MGR' UNDER 'CEO',
        'ENG_MGR' UNDER 'CEO',
        'SALES_STAFF' UNDER 'SALES_MGR',
        'HR_STAFF' UNDER 'HR_MGR',
        'ENG_STAFF' UNDER 'ENG_MGR')
```

Security Policies

Security policies determine exactly how LBAC is to protect a table. Specifically, a security policy identifies the following:

- The security label components to use in the security labels that will be part of the policy
- The rules to use when security label components are compared (at this time, only one set of rules is supported: DB2LBACRULES)
- Optional behaviors to use when data protected by the policy is accessed

Every LBAC-protected table must have one (and only one) security policy associated with it. Rows and columns in a table can only be protected with security labels that are part of the associated security policy, and all protected data access must adhere to the rules of that policy.

Security policies are created by executing the CREATE SECURITY POLICY statement. The basic syntax for this statement is:

```
CREATE SECURITY POLICY [PolicyName]
  COMPONENTS [ComponentName , ...]
  WITH DB2LBACRULES
  <OVERRIDE NOT AUTHORIZED WRITE SECURITY LABEL |
   RESTRICT NOT AUTHORIZED WRITE SECURITY LABEL>
```

where:

PolicyName	Identifies the name to assign to the security policy that is to be created
ComponentName	Identifies, by name, one or more security label components that are to be part of the security policy

The OVERRIDE NOT AUTHORIZED WRITE SECURITY LABEL/RESTRICT NOT AUTHORIZED WRITE SECURITY LABEL clause specifies the action to take when a user who is not authorized to explicitly provide a security label value for write access attempts to write data to the protected table. By default, the value of a user's security label, rather than an explicitly specified value, is used for write access during insert and update operations (OVERRIDE NOT AUTHORIZED WRITE SECURITY LABEL). However, if the RESTRICT NOT AUTHORIZED WRITE SECURITY LABEL clause is specified with the CREATE SECURITY POLICY statement used, insert and update operations will fail if the user is not authorized to write an explicitly specified security label to the protected table.

So, to create a security policy named SEC_POLICY that is based on the SEC_COMP1 security label component that was created earlier, you would execute a CREATE SECURITY POLICY statement that looks like this:

```
CREATE SECURITY POLICY sec_policy
  COMPONENTS sec_comp1
  WITH DB2LBACRULES
```

Security Labels

Security labels describe a certain set of security criteria and are applied to data to protect it against unauthorized access or modification. When a user attempts to access or modify protected data, his or her assigned security label is compared with the security label that is protecting the data to determine whether access or modification is allowed.

Each security label is part of exactly one security policy, and a security label must exist for every security label component found in that security policy. Security labels are created by executing the CREATE SECURITY LABEL statement. The basic syntax for this statement is:

```
CREATE SECURITY LABEL [LabelName]
    [COMPONENT [ComponentName] [StringConstant, ...]  , ...]
```

where:

LabelName	Identifies the name to assign to the security label that is to be created; the name specified must be qualified with a security policy name and must not match an existing security label for the designated security policy
ComponentName	Identifies, by name, a security label component that is part of the security policy that was specified as the qualifier for the *LabelName* parameter
StringConstant	Identifies one or more string constant values that are valid elements of the security label component that was specified in the *ComponentName* parameter

Thus, to create a set of security labels for the security policy named SEC_POLICY that was created earlier, you could execute a series of CREATE SECURITY LABEL statements that look like this:

```
CREATE SECURITY LABEL sec_policy.master
  COMPONENT sec_comp 'MASTER_CRAFTSMAN'


CREATE SECURITY LABEL sec_policy.journeyman
  COMPONENT sec_comp 'JOURNEYMAN'


CREATE SECURITY LABEL sec_policy.apprentice
  COMPONENT sec_comp 'APPRENTICE'
```

Granting Security Labels to Users

After the security labels needed have been created, you must grant the proper security label to the appropriate users. You must also indicate whether a particular user is to have read access only, write access only, or full access to data that is protected by the security label being granted. A user with SECADM authority can grant security labels to other users by executing a special form of the GRANT SQL statement. The syntax for this form of the GRANT statement is:

```
GRANT SECURITY LABEL [LabelName]
  TO [Recipient]
  FOR [READ | WRITE | ALL] ACCESS
```

where:

LabelName	Identifies, by name, the security label that is to be granted; the label name specified must be qualified with the security policy name that was used when the security label was created
Recipient	Identifies who is to receive the security label being granted; the value specified for this parameter can be any combination of the following:
	[*AuthorizationID*] Identifies a particular user, by authorization ID, to whom the security label specified is to be granted
	<<USER> *Name* > Identifies a particular user, by name, to whom the security label specified is to be granted
	<<GROUP> *Name* > Identifies a particular group, by name, that the security label specified is to be granted to
	<<ROLE> *Name* > Identifies a particular role, by name, that the security label specified is to be granted to

Thus, to give a user named USER1 the ability to only read data that the security label SEC_POLICY.EXEC_STAFF protects, you would execute a GRANT statement that looks like this:

```
GRANT SECURITY LABEL sec_policy.exec_staff
  TO user1 FOR READ ACCESS
```

Implementing Row-Level LBAC Protection

To configure a new table for row-level LBAC protection, you must include a column with the DB2SECURITYLABEL data type in the table's definition and associate a security policy with the table using the SECURITY POLICY clause of the CREATE TABLE statement. For example, to create a table named SALES and configure it for row-level LBAC protection using a security policy named SEC_POLICY, you would execute a CREATE TABLE statement that looks something like this:

```
CREATE TABLE sales
   (po_num     INTEGER NOT NULL,
    date       DATE,
    sales_rep  INTEGER,
    amount     DECIMAL(12,2),
    sec_label  DB2SECURITYLABEL)
   SECURITY POLICY sec_policy
```

Alternatively, you can add a DB2SECURITYLABEL column to an existing table and associate a security policy with it using the ALTER TABLE statement. For instance, to configure an existing table named SALES for row-level LBAC protection using a security policy named SEC_POLICY, you would execute an ALTER TABLE statement that looks like this:

```
ALTER TABLE sales
   ADD COLUMN sec_label DB2SECURITYLABEL
   ADD SECURITY POLICY sec_policy
```

However, to execute either statement, you must have been granted a security label for write access that is part of the SEC_POLICY security policy. Otherwise, the attempt to create the DB2SECURITYLABEL column will fail.

Implementing Column-Level LBAC Protection

Just as you must associate a security policy with a table when configuring it for row-level LBAC protection, you must associate a security policy with the table you want to secure with column-level LBAC protection. However, instead of including a column with the DB2SECURITYLABEL data type in the table's definition, you must configure each of the table's columns for protection using the SECURED WITH clause of the ALTER TABLE statement. For example, to configure a table named EMPLOYEES for column-level LBAC protection using a security policy named SEC_POLICY, you could execute an ALTER TABLE statement that looks something like this:

```
ALTER TABLE employees
  ALTER COLUMN emp_id SECURED WITH confidential
  ALTER COLUMN f_name SECURED WITH unclassified
  ALTER COLUMN l_name SECURED WITH unclassified
  ALTER COLUMN ssn    SECURED WITH confidential
  ALTER COLUMN salary SECURED WITH confidential
  ALTER COLUMN bonus  SECURED WITH confidential
  ADD SECURITY POLICY sec_policy
```

In this case, the security label unclassified will protect data in columns F_NAME and L_NAME, and the security label confidential will protect the data in the remaining columns. It is important to note that if you attempt to execute this ALTER TABLE statement as a user with SYSADM or SECADM authority, the operation will fail. That's because the only user who can secure a column with a security label is a user who has been granted write access to data that is protected by that security label. Consequently, in this example, someone who has been granted write access to data that is protected by the security label unclassified will need to alter the F_NAME and L_NAME columns. And someone who has been granted write access to data that is protected by the security label confidential will need to make the rest of the changes needed. In order for one person to make all the changes shown, he or she must be granted exemptions to the LBAC rules before they will be allowed to make the changes desired.

A Word About Trusted Contexts

Another security enhancement available with DB2 is a feature that is known as a *trusted context*. A trusted context is a database object that describes a trust relationship between a DB2 database and an external entity, such as a Web server or an application client. The following information is used to define a trusted context:

- A system authorization ID that represents the authorization ID that an incoming connection must use to be considered "trusted"
- The IP address, domain name, or security zone name an incoming connection must originate from to be considered "trusted"
- A data stream encryption value that represents the level of encryption that an incoming connection (if any) must use to be considered "trusted"

It is important to note that trusted context objects can only be defined by someone with SECADM authority.

Trusted contexts are designed specifically to address the security concerns involving the use of three-tier (client, gateway, server) configurations. Usually, with such configurations, all interactions with a database server occur through a database connection that the middle tier (gateway) establishes using a combination of an authorization ID and a credential that identifies the middle tier to the server. In other words, the authorities and privileges associated with the middle tier's authorization ID control what clients can and cannot do when working with a database at the server. When trusted contexts are used, each user's authorization ID is used instead, thereby ensuring that each user is only allowed to interact with a database according to the authorities and privileges that he or she has been granted.

So how do trusted contexts work? When a database connection is established, DB2 compares that connection's attributes against the definitions of each trusted context object defined. If the connection attributes match a trusted context object, the connection is treated as a *trusted connection*, and the connection's initiator is allowed to acquire additional capabilities. These capabilities vary depending upon whether the trusted connection is *implicit* or *explicit*.

An implicit trusted connection results from a normal connection request and allows users to inherit a role that is unavailable to them outside the scope of the trusted connection. An explicit trusted connection is established by making a connection request within an application. After an explicit trusted connection is established, an application can switch the connection's user to a different authorization ID. (Switching can occur with or without authenticating the new authorization ID, depending upon the definition of the trusted context object associated with the connection. If a switch request is made using an authorization ID that is not allowed, the explicit trusted connection is placed in an "unconnected" state.)

Creating Trusted Contexts

Trusted contexts are created by executing the CREATE TRUSTED CONTEXT statement. The basic syntax for this statement is:

```
CREATE TRUSTED CONTEXT [TCName]
   BASED UPON CONNECTION USING
   SYSTEM AUTHID [ConnectionAuthID]
   ATTRIBUTES (ADDRESS [IPAddress])
   WITH USE FOR
      [[PUBLIC | UserID <ROLE [RoleName]>]
      [WITH | WITHOUT] AUTHENTICATION ,...]
   [DISABLE | ENABLE]
```

where:

TCName	Identifies the name to assign to the trusted context that is to be created
ConnectionAuthID	Identifies the authorization ID (or user ID) that the trusted context connection is to be established by
IPAddress	Identifies the communication address that is used by the client to communicate with the database server
UserID	Identifies one or more authorization IDs (or user IDs) that are allowed to use the trusted connection associated with the trusted context being created
RoleName	Identifies the role, by name, that is to be used for the *UserID* user when a trusted connection is using the trusted context being created

If the WITH AUTHENTICATION clause is specified with the *UserID* user identified, switching from the current user on a trusted connection to the identified user requires authentication (i.e., a password). If the WITHOUT AUTHENTICATION clause is specified, authentication is not required to switch to the user identified.

If the DISABLE clause is specified with the CREATE TRUSTED CONTEXT statement used, the resulting trusted context will be placed in "disabled" state. A trusted context that is disabled is not considered when a trusted connection is established.

Thus, to create a trusted context that has the following characteristics:

- Is assigned the name APPSERVER
- Establishes a trusted context connection using the authentication ID USER1
- Allows clients to communicate with the database server through the IP address 192.168.1.100
- Allows the current user on a trusted connection associated with the trusted context to be switched to two different user IDs (USER2 and USER3)
- Ensures that when the current user of the connection is switched to user USER2, authentication is not required
- Ensures that when the current user of the connection is switched to user USER3, authentication is required
- Is enabled at the time it is created

you would execute a CREATE TRUSTED CONTEXT statement that looks like this:

```
CREATE TRUSTED CONTEXT appserver
BASED UPON CONNECTION USING
SYSTEM AUTHID user1
ATTRIBUTES (ADDRESS '192.168.1.100')
WITH USE FOR
    user2 WITHOUT AUTHENTICATION,
    user3 WITH AUTHENTICATION
ENABLE
```

A Word About DB2 Native Encryption

Encryption is the process of transforming data into an unintelligible form so that the original data cannot be obtained or can only be obtained by using a special decryption process. Encryption is mandatory for compliance with many government regulations and industry standards because it offers an effective way of protecting sensitive information that is stored on electronic media or transmitted through untrusted communication channels.

Designed to enable users to meet compliance requirements in a cost-effective manner, native encryption (at the database level) was added to DB2 10.5 for LUW, in FixPack 5. This enhancement is easy to implement—it requires no hardware, software, application, or schema changes—and it provides transparent, secure local key management that is based on Public Key Cryptography Standard #12 (PKCS#12).

With DB2's native database encryption, the data requiring protection is transformed into an unreadable form using a cryptographic algorithm and an encryption key. A cryptographic algorithm is a mathematical function that is used in the encryption and decryption process; an encryption key is a sequence that controls the operation of a cryptographic algorithm and enables the reliable encryption and decryption of data. A local or external key manager is typically used to manage encryption keys—a database data encryption key (DEK) is the encryption key with which actual user data is encrypted while a master key that acts as a "key encrypting key" is used to protect the DEK. The DEK is stored and managed by the database itself; the master key is stored and managed outside of the database. In a DB2 10.5 database environment, encrypted master keys are stored in a PKCS#12-compliant keystore, which is a storage object for encryption keys that exists at the operating system level. There is at most one keystore per DB2 instance.

With DB2's native encryption, the database system encrypts the data before it is sent to the underlying file system to be written to disk. This means that not only is current data protected, but that data written to new table space containers or table spaces that might be added in the future is encrypted as well. And, if the appropriate database configuration parameters are set, database backup images are encrypted as well. Consequently, DB2's native database encryption offers protection for "data at rest" that would otherwise be vulnerable to exposure if a theft of physical disk devices were to take place. It also offers a high level of protection against privileged user abuse.

Working with Databases and Database Objects

Sixteen percent (16%) of the *DB2 10.5 Fundamentals for LUW* certification exam (Exam 615) is designed to test your knowledge of the different DB2 objects available and to assess your ability to create and connect to DB2 servers and databases. The questions that make up this portion of the exam are intended to evaluate the following:

- Your ability to identify DB2 objects
- Your ability to create and connect to DB2 servers and databases
- Your ability to identify the results produced when select Data Definition Language (DDL) statements are executed
- Your knowledge of the various types of tables that are available with DB2

This chapter introduces you to the various objects that are available with DB2. It also shows you how to create and connect to DB2 servers and databases, as well as how to create a DB2 database. In this chapter, you will learn about servers, instances, and databases, along with many other objects that make up a DB2 database environment. You will also discover how to create new DB2 databases and how to identify and connect to DB2 servers and databases using Type 1 and Type 2 connections. Finally, you will learn about the various types of tables that can be created in a DB2 10.5 for Linux, UNIX, and Windows database.

Servers, Instances, and Databases

DB2 sees the world as a hierarchy of objects. *Servers* running DB2 software occupy the highest level of this hierarchy, *instances* comprise the second level, and *databases* make up the third. Figure 4.1 shows what this hierarchical relationship looks like in a DB2 for LUW environment.

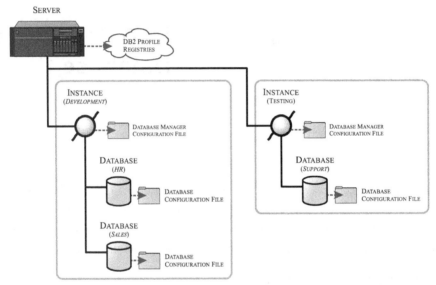

Figure 4.1: Hierarchical relationship between systems, instances, and databases in a DB2 for LUW environment

When DB2 is first installed, program files for a background process known as the *DB2 Database Manager* are physically copied to a server and, typically, an instance of this process is created and initialized as part of the installation process. (This instance is started immediately after creation and, by default, it will be restarted whenever the server is rebooted.)

Instances are responsible for managing system resources and databases that fall under their control. And although only one instance exists initially, multiple instances can be created on a single server. When multiple instances are used, each instance behaves as if it were a separate, standalone DB2 server, even though it might share the same DB2 binary program files with other instances. (If one instance is running a DB2 version that is different from the others, that instance will have its own set of program files that corresponds to the different DB2 version.) In addition, each instance has its own environment, which can be configured by modifying the contents of an associated DB2 Database Manager configuration file.

A database is an entity that contains many physical and logical components, all of which aid in the storage, modification, and retrieval of data. Multiple databases can exist and, like instances, each database has its own environment. To a certain extent, a database's environment is also governed by a set of configuration parameters, which reside in an accompanying database configuration file.

Other DB2 Objects

Although servers, instances, and databases are the primary components that make up a DB2 database environment, many other different, but often related, objects exist. Typically, these objects are classified as being either *system objects* or *data objects* (sometimes referred to as *database objects* or *data structures*).

Data Objects

Data objects control how user data is stored and, in some cases, how data is organized inside a database. Some of the more common data objects available include:

- Schemas
- Tables
- Views
- Indexes
- Aliases
- Sequences
- Triggers
- User-defined data types (UDTs)
- User-defined functions (UDFs)
- Stored procedures
- Packages

Schemas

Schemas provide a way to logically group objects in a database; they are used to organize data objects into sets. When objects that can be qualified by a schema are created, they are given a two-part name—the first (leftmost) part of the name is the *schema name* or *qualifier*, and the second (rightmost) part is the user-supplied object name. Syntactically, these two parts are concatenated and separated by a period (for example, HR.EMPLOYEES).

When select data objects (that is, table spaces, tables, indexes, distinct data types, functions, stored procedures, and triggers) are created, they are automatically assigned to (or defined into) a schema, based on the qualifier that was provided as part of the user-supplied name. Figure 4.2 illustrates how to assign a table named EMPLOYEES to a schema named HR during the table creation process.

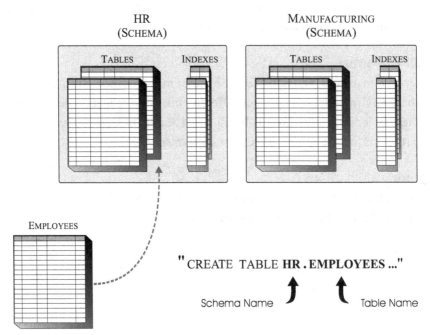

Figure 4.2: Assigning a table object to a specific schema

If a schema name or qualifier is not provided as part of an object's name, the object is automatically assigned to a default schema, which typically has the name of the authorization ID of the individual who created the object.

It is important to note that objects cannot be created in the schemas that are automatically produced when a database is created (that is, in a schema whose name begins with the letters "SYS").

Tables

A *table* is an object that acts as the main repository for data. Tables present data as a collection of unordered *rows* with a fixed number of *columns*. Each column contains values of the same data type, and each row contains a set of values for one or more of the columns available. The storage representation of a row is called a *record*, the storage representation of a column is called a *field*, and each intersection of a row and column is called a *value* (or *cell*). Figure 4.3 shows the structure of a simple table.

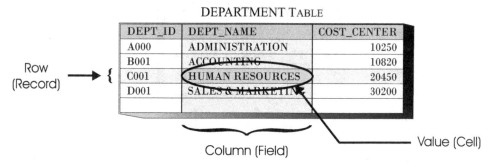

DEPARTMENT TABLE

DEPT_ID	DEPT_NAME	COST_CENTER
A000	ADMINISTRATION	10250
B001	ACCOUNTING	10820
C001	HUMAN RESOURCES	20450
D001	SALES & MARKETING	30200

Row (Record) → { ... Column (Field) ... Value (Cell)

Figure 4.3: Structure of a table

With DB2, the following types of tables are available:

- Base tables
- Synopsis tables
- Partitioned tables
- Range-clustered tables (RCTs)
- Multidimensional clustering (MDC) tables
- Insert time clustering tables (ICTs)
- Materialized query tables (MQTs)
- Shadow tables
- Temporal (time-travel) tables
- History tables
- Temporary tables
- Typed tables

Because tables are the basic data objects used for storing information, many are often created for a single database. (We will look at each of these types of tables in detail a little later.)

Views

Views provide an alternative way of describing and displaying data stored in one or more tables. As with base tables, views can be thought of as having columns and rows. Essentially, a view is a named specification of a result table that is populated each time the view is referenced in an SQL operation. Figure 4.4 shows a simple view that presents data values from two different base tables.

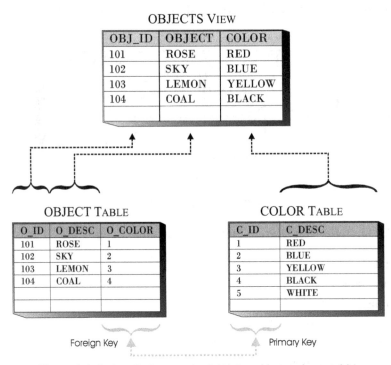

OBJECTS VIEW

OBJ_ID	OBJECT	COLOR
101	ROSE	RED
102	SKY	BLUE
103	LEMON	YELLOW
104	COAL	BLACK

OBJECT TABLE

O_ID	O_DESC	O_COLOR
101	ROSE	1
102	SKY	2
103	LEMON	3
104	COAL	4

COLOR TABLE

C_ID	C_DESC
1	RED
2	BLUE
3	YELLOW
4	BLACK
5	WHITE

Foreign Key   Primary Key

Figure 4.4: A view that presents data stored in two base tables

Although views look similar to base tables, they do not contain data. Instead, they obtain their data from the table(s) or view(s)—views can be derived from other views—they are based upon. Consequently, only a view's definition is stored in a database. Even so, in most cases, views can be referenced in the same way that tables can be referenced. That is, they can be the source of queries as well as the target of insert, update, and delete operations. (Whether a particular view can be used to insert, update, or delete data depends upon how the view was defined—views can be defined as being *insertable*, *updatable*, *deletable*, or *read-only*.)

When a view is the target of an SQL operation, the query that was used to define the view is executed, the results produced are returned in a table-like format, and the operation is then performed on the results. Therefore, when a transaction performs insert, update, and delete operations against a view, those operations are actually executed against the base table(s) the view is based upon. If the view is derived from another view, the operation cascades down through all applicable views and is applied to the appropriate underlying base table(s).

It is important to note that a single base table can serve as the source of multiple views; the SQL query you provide as part of a view's definition determines the data that is to be presented when a particular view is referenced. Because of this, views are often used to control access to sensitive data. For example, if a table contains information about every employee who works for a company (including sensitive information like bank account numbers), managers might access this table via a view that allows them to see only nonsensitive information about employees who report directly to them. Similarly, Human Resources personnel could be given access to the table by means of a view that lets them see only information needed to generate paychecks for every employee. Because each set of users are given access to data through different views, they each see different presentations of data that resides in the same table.

Indexes

An *index* is an object that contains pointers to rows in a table that are logically ordered according to the values of one or more columns (known as *key columns* or *keys*). Figure 4.5 shows the structure of a simple index, along with its relationship to the table it derives its data from.

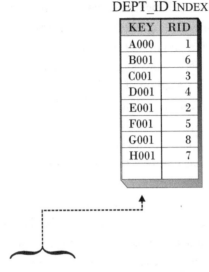

DEPT_ID INDEX

KEY	RID
A000	1
B001	6
C001	3
D001	4
E001	2
F001	5
G001	8
H001	7

DEPARTMENT TABLE

	DEPT_ID	DEPT_NAME	COST_CENTER
Row 1 →	A000	ADMINISTRATION	10250
Row 2 →	E001	ACCOUNTING	10820
Row 3 →	C001	HUMAN RESOURCES	20450
Row 4 →	D001	SALES & MARKETING	30200
Row 5 →	F001	MANUFACTURING	50120
Row 6 →	B001	OPERATIONS	50820
Row 7 →	H001	CUSTOMER SUPPORT	42100
Row 8 →	G001	LEGAL	60680

Figure 4.5: A simple index that has a one-column key

Indexes are important because:

- They provide a fast, efficient method for locating specific rows of data in large tables. (In some cases, the index itself can contain all the information needed to resolve a query, in which case, table data does not have to be retrieved.)
- They provide a logical ordering of the rows in a table. (When indexes are used, the values of one or more columns can be sorted in ascending or descending order; this is beneficial when queries that contain ORDER BY and GROUP BY clauses are executed.)

- They can enforce the uniqueness of records in a table. (If an index is defined as being UNIQUE, rows in the table associated with the index are not allowed to have more than one occurrence of the same value in the set of columns that make up the index key; any attempt to perform an insert or update operation that compromises the uniqueness of the key will result in an error.)
- They can force a table to use *clustering* storage, which causes the rows of a table to be physically arranged according to the ordering of their key column values. Usually, a clustering index will improve query performance by decreasing the I/O needed to access data. When a logical set of rows are physically stored close together, read operations typically require less I/O because adjacent rows are more likely to be found within the same extent (data pages are written in groups called *extents*) instead of being widely distributed across multiple extents.

Although some indexes are created automatically to support a table's definition (for example, to enforce unique and primary key constraints), indexes are typically created explicitly using SQL, Data Studio, or the DB2 Design Advisor. A single table can contain a significant number of indexes (up to 32,767); however, every index comes at a price. Because indexes store key column and row pointer data, additional storage space is needed for every index used. Furthermore, write performance is negatively affected— each time a transaction performs an insert, update, or delete operation against a table with indexes, every index that is affected must be updated to reflect the changes that were made. Because of this, indexes should be created only when there is a clear performance advantage to having them available.

Indexes are typically used to improve query performance. Therefore, tables that are used for data mining, business intelligence, business warehousing, and by applications that execute many (and often complex) queries but that rarely modify data are prime candidates for indexes. Conversely, tables in online transaction processing (OLTP) environments or environments where data throughput is high should use indexes sparingly or avoid them altogether.

Aliases

An *alias* is an alternate name for a module, nickname, sequence, table, view, or other alias. After it is created, an alias can be referenced in the same way its corresponding object can. However, an alias cannot always be used in the same context. For example, an alias cannot be used in the check condition of a check constraint or to reference a user-defined temporary table.

Unlike with tables (but similar to views), aliases can refer to other aliases via a process known as *chaining*. Aliases are publicly referenced names, so no special authority or privilege is required to use them. Still, appropriate authorization *is* needed to access the module, nickname, sequence, table, or view an alias refers to.

So why would you want to create and use an alias? Because by using aliases, you can construct SQL statements in such a way that they are independent of the objects they reference. An SQL statement that references an alias behaves no differently than a similar SQL statement that references the associated object. Therefore, by using an alias, it is possible to create a single SQL statement that works with a variety of objects—the target of the alias can be changed dynamically, and as long as the underlying structure of the new target is similar to that of the old target, SQL statements that reference the alias do not have to be altered.

Sequences

As the name implies, a *sequence* is an object that is used to generate a sequence of numbers, in either ascending or descending order. Unlike identity columns, which produce data values for a specific column in a table, sequences are not tied to any specific column or to any specific table. Instead, sequences behave as unique counters that reside outside of the database. However, because DB2 generates the values that are needed for a given sequence, performance bottlenecks that often occur when an application relies on an external counter are eliminated.

In addition to delivering better performance, sequences offer the following advantages over external counters:

- They are guaranteed to generate unique values (assuming the sequence is never reset and does not allow values to cycle).
- They are guaranteed to produce unique values independently of any running transactions.
- They can be used to generate values of any exact numeric data type that has a scale of zero (that is, SMALLINT, BIGINT, INTEGER, or DECIMAL).
- They can produces consecutive values that differ by any increment value specified (the default value is 1).
- They ensure that the values produced are fully recoverable; if DB2 should fail, the sequence is reconstructed from transaction logs so that unique values will continue to be generated.
- They can cache values to improve performance.

- They provide versatility—one sequence can be used for several tables, or multiple, individual sequences can be created for every table that needs uniquely generated values.

Another benefit of using sequences is that you can use SQL (the ALTER SEQUENCE statement) to dynamically modify many of a sequence's attributes. For instance, you can restart a sequence, change the way in which values are incremented, establish new minimum and maximum values, increase or decrease the number of sequence numbers that are cached, change whether a sequence cycles, and alter whether sequence numbers are required to be generated in their original order *while the sequence remains online and accessible.* It is important to note, however, that if a different data type is needed or desired, a sequence must be dropped and recreated—the data type of an existing sequence cannot be dynamically changed.

Once they are created, sequences can generate values in one of three ways:

- By incrementing (or decrementing) by a specified amount, without bounds
- By incrementing (or decrementing) by a specified amount to a user-defined limit, and then stopping
- By incrementing (or decrementing) by a specified amount to a user-defined limit, and then cycling back to the beginning and starting again

To facilitate the use of sequences in SQL operations, two expressions are available: PREVIOUS VALUE and NEXT VALUE. The PREVIOUS VALUE expression returns the most recently generated value for the sequence specified, while the NEXT VALUE expression returns the next value that a certain sequence will produce.

Triggers

A *trigger* is an object that is used to define a set of actions that are to be executed whenever an insert, update, or delete operation is performed against a table or updatable view. Triggers are often used to enforce data integrity and business rules; however, they can also be used to automatically update other tables, generate or transform values for inserted and updated rows, and invoke functions to perform specific tasks such as issuing errors or alerts.

Before you can create a trigger, you must identify the following components:

- **Subject table/view:** The table or view that the trigger is to be associated with
- **Trigger event:** An SQL operation that, when performed against the subject table or view, will cause the trigger to be activated (*fired*); the trigger event can be an insert operation, an update operation, a delete operation, or a merge operation that inserts, updates, or deletes data
- **Trigger activation time:** A component that indicates whether the trigger should be fired *before*, *after*, or *instead of* the trigger event
- **Set of affected rows:** The rows of the subject table or view that are being added, updated, or removed
- **Triggered action:** An optional search condition and a set of SQL statements that are executed when the trigger is fired—if a search condition is specified, the SQL statements are executed only if the search condition evaluates to TRUE
- **Trigger granularity:** A component that specifies whether the triggered action is to be executed once, when the trigger event takes place, or once for each row the trigger event affects

As was mentioned earlier, a trigger can be fired in three different ways: before the trigger event takes place, after the trigger event completes, or in place of the trigger event. Because of this, triggers are often referred to as being BEFORE triggers, AFTER triggers, or INSTEAD OF triggers. As the name implies, BEFORE triggers are fired before the trigger event occurs and can see new data values that are about to be inserted into the subject table. For this reason, BEFORE triggers are typically used to validate input data, to automatically generate values for newly inserted rows, and to prevent certain types of trigger events from being performed.

AFTER triggers, however, are fired after the trigger event occurs and can see data values that have already been inserted into the subject table. AFTER triggers are frequently used to insert, update, or delete data in the same or in other tables, to check data against other data values (in the same or in other tables), and to invoke UDFs that perform non-database operations.

Unlike BEFORE and AFTER triggers, INSTEAD OF triggers are executed against a subject view, rather than a subject table. Because INSTEAD OF triggers are executed in place of the trigger event, they are typically used to ensure that applications can perform insert, update, delete, and query operations against an updatable view only; INSTEAD OF triggers prevent such operations from being performed against a table.

User-defined data types

As the name implies, *user-defined data types* (*UDTs*) are data types that database users create. Two types of UDTs are available: *distinct* and *structured*.

A *distinct data type* (or simply *distinct type*) is a UDT that is derived from one of the built-in data types that are provided with DB2. Distinct types are useful when it is desirable for DB2 to handle certain data differently from other data of the same type. For example, even though you can use a decimal data type to store currency values, a distinct type will prevent currencies such as Canadian dollars from being compared against United States dollars or United Kingdom pounds.

Such a UDT could be created by executing an SQL statement that looks like this:

```
CREATE DISTINCT TYPE currency AS DECIMAL(10,2)
    WITH STRONG TYPE RULES
```

Although a distinct data type shares a common internal representation with a built-in data type, it is considered a wholly separate type that is different from all other data types available. Furthermore, because DB2 enforces strong data typing, the value of a distinct data type is compatible only with values of the same distinct type. Consequently, distinct types cannot be used as arguments for most built-in functions. (Likewise, built-in data types cannot be used in arguments or parameters that expect distinct data types.) Instead, UDFs that provide similar functionality must be developed if that kind of capability is needed.

When a distinct data type is created, by default, six comparison functions (named =, <>, <, <=, >, and >=) are also created—provided the distinct type is not based on a large object (LOB) data type. (Because LOB values cannot be compared, comparison functions are not created for distinct types that are based on LOB data types.) These functions let you compare two values of the distinct data type in the same manner that you can compare two values of a built-in data type. In addition, two casting functions are generated that allow data to be converted between the distinct type and the built-in data type the distinct type is based upon.

A *structured data type* (or *structured type*) is a UDT that contains multiple attributes, each of which has a name and data type of its own. A structured data type often serves as the data type of a typed table or view, in which case each column of the table or view derives its name and data type from an attribute of the structured type. A structured data type can also be created as a *subtype* of another structured type (referred to as its *supertype*); in this case, the subtype inherits the supertype's attributes and can optionally add additional attributes of its own.

Just as six comparison functions and two casting functions are normally created to support a distinct data type, six comparison functions (also named =, <>, <, <=, >, and >=) and two casting functions can be created for a structured type. However, unlike with distinct data types, these functions are not created automatically.

User-defined data functions

User-defined functions (*UDFs*) are special objects that are used to extend and enhance the support provided by the built-in functions that are supplied with DB2. As with UDTs, UDFs (also called *methods*) are created by database users. Unlike built-in functions, UDFs can exploit system calls and DB2 administrative APIs.

Up to five different types of UDFs can be created:

- **SQL:** A function whose body is written entirely in SQL and SQL Procedural Language (SQL PL). An SQL function can be scalar in nature (scalar functions return a single value and can be specified in an SQL statement wherever a regular expression can be used), or it can return a row or table.
- **Sourced (or Template):** A function that is based on some other function that already exists. Sourced functions can be columnar, scalar, or tabular in nature; they can also be designed to overload a specific operator such as +, −, *, and /. When a sourced function is invoked, all arguments passed to it are converted to the data types that the underlying source function expects, and the source function itself is invoked. Upon completion, the source function performs any conversions necessary on the results produced and returns them to the calling application. Typically, sourced functions are used to provide built-in function capability for distinct UDTs.
- **External Scalar:** A function that is written using a high-level programming language such as C, C++, or Java that returns a single value. The function itself resides in an external library and is registered in the database, along with any related attributes.
- **External Table:** A function (written in a high-level programming language) that returns a result data set in the form of a table. As with external scalar functions, the function itself resides in an external library and is registered in the database, along with any related attributes. External table functions can make almost any data

source appear as a base table. Consequently, the result data set produced can be used in join operations, grouping operations, set operations, or any other operation that can be applied to a read-only view.

- **OLE DB External Table:** A function (written in a high-level programming language) that can access data from an Object Linking and Embedding Database (OLE DB) provider and return a result data set in the form of a table. A generic built-in OLE DB consumer that is available with DB2 for Linux, UNIX, and Windows can be used to interface with any OLE DB provider; simply register an OLE DB table function with a database and refer to the appropriate OLE DB provider as the data source—no additional programming is required.

Once a UDF is created (and registered with a database), it can be used anywhere a comparable built-in function can be used.

Stored procedures

In a basic DB2 client/server environment, each time an SQL statement is executed against a remote database stored on a server workstation, the statement itself is sent through a network from the client to the server. The database at the server then processes the statement, and the results are returned, again through the network, to the client. This means that two messages must go through the network for every SQL statement that is executed.

Breaking an application into separate parts, storing those parts on the appropriate host (that is, the client or the server), and having them communicate with each other as the application executes can minimize network traffic. This can also enable applications to execute faster—code that interacts directly with a database can reside on the database server, where computing power and centralized control can provide quick, coordinated data access. And application logic can be stored at a client, where it can make effective use of all the resources the client has to offer.

If an application contains transactions that perform a relatively large amount of database activity with little or no user interaction, those transactions can be stored separately on a database server in what is known as a *stored procedure*. Stored procedures allow work that is done by one or more transactions to be encapsulated and stored in such a way that they can be executed directly at a server by *any* application or user who has been given the authority needed to use them. And, because only one SQL statement is required to invoke a stored procedure, fewer messages are transmitted across the network—only the data that is actually needed at the client is sent across.

Just as there are different types of UDFs available, there are different types of stored procedures. Two different types of stored procedures can be created:

- **SQL (or Native SQL):** A stored procedure whose body is written entirely in SQL or SQL PL.
- **External:** A stored procedure whose body is written in a high-level programming language such as Assembler, C, C++, COBOL, Java, REXX, or PL/I. Whereas SQL procedures offer rapid application development and considerable flexibility, external stored procedures can be much more powerful because they can exploit system calls and administrative APIs. However, this increase in functionality makes them more difficult to produce. In fact, the following steps are needed to create an external stored procedure:
  1. Create the body of the procedure, using a supported high-level programming language.
  2. Compile and link the procedure to create a shared (dynamic-link) library.
  3. Debug the procedure; repeat steps 1 and 2 until all problems have been resolved.
  4. Physically store the library containing the procedure on the database server.
  5. Modify the system permissions for the library so that all users with the proper authority can execute it.
  6. Register the procedure with the appropriate DB2 database.

It is important to note that when a stored procedure is used to implement a specific business rule, the logic needed to apply that rule can be incorporated into any application simply by invoking the procedure. Thus, the same business rule logic is guaranteed to be enforced across multiple applications. And if business rules change, only the logic in the procedure has to be modified—applications that call the procedure do not have to be altered.

Packages

A *package* is an object that contains the control structures DB2 uses to execute SQL statements that are coded in an application. (A *control structure* can be thought of as the operational form of an SQL statement.) High-level programming language compilers do not recognize, and therefore cannot interpret, SQL statements. So, when SQL statements are embedded in a high-level programming language source code file, they must be converted to source code a compiler can understand. A tool known as an *SQL*

Precompiler, which is included in the DB2 Software Development Kit, is used to perform this conversion.

During the precompile process, a high-level programming language source code file containing SQL statements is converted to source code that a compiler can process. A package containing the control structures needed to execute the statements in the source code file is produced as well. The process of creating and storing a package in a DB2 database is known as *binding*, and by default, binding occurs automatically when the precompile process is complete. However, by specifying appropriate SQL precompiler options at precompile time, it is possible to store the control structures needed to create a package in a file that can be bound to the database later. Another tool, called the *SQL Binder* (or simply the *Binder*), can be used to create and store a package in a DB2 database, using the contents of such a file. (This is referred to as *deferred binding*.)

System Objects

DB2 has a comprehensive infrastructure that is used to provide, among other things, data integrity, exceptional performance, and high availability. And a large part of this infrastructure consists of *system objects*, which unlike data objects, are controlled and accessed primarily by DB2. Some of the system objects available include:

- Buffer pools
- Table spaces
- The system catalog
- Transaction log files

Buffer pools

A *buffer pool* is an object that is used to cache table and index pages. The first time a row of data is accessed, a DB2 agent retrieves the page containing the row from storage and copies it to a buffer pool before passing it on to the user or application that requested it. (If an index was used to locate the row, the index page containing a pointer to the row is copied first; the pointer is then used to locate the data page containing the row, and that page is copied to the buffer pool as well.) And in most cases, when a page of data is retrieved, DB2 uses a set of heuristic algorithms to try to determine which pages will be needed next and those pages are copied from storage, too. (This behavior is known as *prefetching*). Once a page has been copied to a buffer pool, it remains there until the space it occupies is needed or until the database is taken offline. This is done to improve performance—data that resides in a buffer pool can be accessed much faster than data that resides on disk.

As subsequent requests for data are made, DB2 searches every buffer pool available to see whether the data requested already resides in memory. If the data is found, it is forwarded to the user or application that requested it; if not, the process of locating and copying data pages from storage is performed again. If a row is to be updated or deleted, the page containing the row is copied to a buffer pool (if it is not already there) before the update or delete operation is performed. The page is then marked as being "dirty" until it is written back to storage, which typically occurs when the transaction that made the modification is committed. Dirty pages that are written to storage are not automatically removed from the buffer pool they were stored in. Instead, they remain in memory in case they are needed again.

Before a page can be copied into a buffer pool, space for that page must be available. So, if a buffer pool is full, DB2 will selectively remove existing pages (referred to as "victim" pages) to make room for others. DB2 chooses victims by examining when a page was last referenced, by determining whether the page is for a table or an index, by evaluating the likelihood that the page will be referenced again, and by determining whether the page is dirty.

To guarantee data integrity, dirty pages are always written to disk before they are removed from memory. Therefore, if a buffer pool contains a significant number of dirty pages, performance can be adversely affected. That is because transactions may be forced to wait for dirty pages to be written to disk before they can continue. To prevent too many dirty pages from accumulating, DB2 uses special agents called *page cleaners* to periodically scan a buffer pool for dirty pages and asynchronously write them to disk. Page cleaners ensure that some amount of buffer pool space is always available for future read operations.

Table spaces

Table spaces provide a layer of indirection between a data object (such as a table or an index) and the physical storage where that object's data resides. The physical storage for a table space is comprised of one or more *containers*, which can be an operating system directory, an individual file, or a raw logical volume/disk partition. A single table space can span many containers, but each container can belong to only one table space.

Table spaces are divided into equal-sized units, called *pages*, which can be 4, 8, 16, or 32 KB in size. (Unless otherwise specified, a page size of 4 KB is used by default.)

And pages are grouped into contiguous ranges called *extents*. When a table space spans multiple containers, data is written in a round-robin fashion, one extent at a time, to each container used. This is done to evenly distribute data across all of the containers that belong to a given table space. Figure 4.6 shows the relationship between table space containers, pages, and extents.

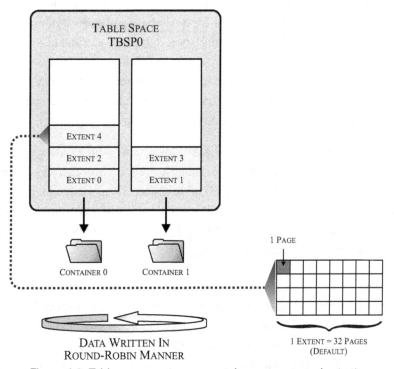

Figure 4.6: Table spaces, storage containers, pages, and extents

The following types of table spaces can exist:

- **System Managed Space (SMS):** SMS table spaces are used to store temporary data. Only directory containers can be used for storage, and the operating system's file manager is responsible for controlling how space is used. The SMS storage model consists of many files (each representing a table, index, or large object data) that reside within the file system space—a DBA specifies the files' location, DB2 assigns the files their names, and the file system is responsible for managing growth.

- **Database Managed Space (DMS):** DMS table spaces are used to store regular, large object, and XML data. Only file, raw device/raw logical volume, or disk partition containers can be used for storage, and the DB2 Database Manager is responsible for controlling how space is used.
- **Automatic Storage (AS):** AS table spaces are used only if a database is configured to use automatic storage. Automatic storage table spaces consume space in the storage paths that have been defined for a database and grow automatically as the table space is filled. Although at first glance, automatic storage table spaces appear to be a third type of table space, they are actually an extension of SMS and DMS table spaces: regular and large table spaces are created as DMS table spaces with one or more file containers; system temporary and user temporary table spaces are created as SMS table spaces with one or more directory containers.

It is important to note that each table space is associated with a buffer pool. One buffer pool is created automatically as part of the database creation process; this buffer pool is named IBMDEFAULTBP, and by default, all table spaces are associated with this buffer pool. You can assign a different buffer pool to a table space at any time; however, before such an assignment can be made, the buffer pool must already exist and both the buffer pool and the table space must have matching page sizes.

The system catalog

The *system catalog* (or *DB2 catalog*, or simply *catalog*) is a set of special tables that contain information about everything that has been defined for a database system that is under DB2's control. DB2 uses the system catalog to keep track of information like object definitions, object dependencies, column data types, constraints, and object relationships (specifically, how one object is related to another). A set of system catalog tables are created and stored in a database as part of the database creation process; several system catalog views are created as well, and it is recommended that you use these views to query the system catalog. You can also use a limited number of these views to modify select system catalog data values.

DB2 updates the information stored in the system catalog whenever any of the following events occur:

- Database objects (such as tables, indexes, and views) are created, altered, or dropped.
- Authorizations and privileges are granted or revoked.

- Statistical information is collected.
- Packages are bound to the database.

In most cases, when an object is first created, its characteristics (also known as its *metadata*) are stored in one or more system catalog tables. However, in some cases, such as when triggers and constraints are defined, the actual SQL used to create the object is stored in the catalog instead.

Transaction log files

Transaction log files (sometimes called *log files* or simply *logs*) are files that DB2 writes data changes and other significant database events to. Using a process called *write-ahead logging*, DB2 keeps track of changes that are made to a database *as those changes occur*. So how does write-ahead logging work? When a transaction adds a new row to a table via an insert operation, that row is first created in the appropriate buffer pool. If the transaction performs an update or delete operation instead, the page containing the record that is to be altered is copied to the appropriate buffer pool, where it is then modified accordingly.

Then, as soon as the desired insert, update, or delete operation is complete, a record reflecting the insertion or modification is written to the *log buffer*, which is simply a designated storage area in memory. (If a transaction performs an insert operation, a record for the new row is written to the log buffer; if it performs a delete operation, a record containing the row's original values is written to the log buffer; and if it performs an update operation, a record containing the row's original data, together with the corresponding new data, is stored in the log buffer.) When the transaction that performed the insert, update, or delete operation is terminated, a record indicating whether the transaction was committed or rolled back is written to the log buffer as well.

As transactions are executed, any time the log buffer becomes full, buffer pool page cleaners are activated, or transactions are terminated, records stored in the log buffer are immediately written to one or more log files on disk. This is done to minimize the number of log records that might be lost in the event a system failure occurs. Eventually, after all log records associated with a particular transaction have been externalized to log files, the effects of the transaction itself are written to the database. Figure 4.7 illustrates this process.

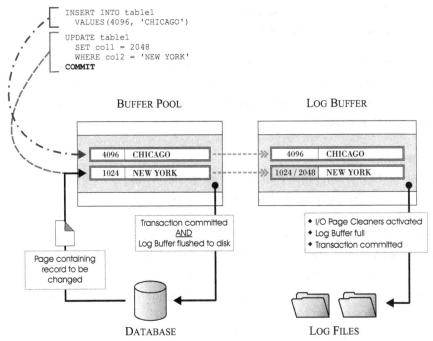

Figure 4.7: The transaction-logging process

Because log files are updated frequently and because changes made by a particular transaction are externalized to the database only when the transaction successfully completes, DB2 can replay changes recorded in log files to return a database to a consistent state after a catastrophic failure occurs. When a database is restarted, log records are analyzed, and each record that corresponds to a transaction that was committed is reapplied to the database. Records for uncommitted transactions, on the other hand, are are either ignored or backed out (which is why "before" and "after" information is recorded for update operations).

Creating a DB2 Database

Of all the objects that make up a DB2 database environment, it is probably safe to say that the most important object is the database itself. Many of the system objects available exist to support one or more databases, and most data objects cannot be created unless a database exists. A DB2 database can be created in one of two ways: with Data Studio and by executing the CREATE DATABASE command. In its simplest form, the syntax for the CREATE DATABASE command looks like this:

```
CREATE DATABASE [DatabaseName]
```

where:

DatabaseName   Identifies a unique name that is to be assigned to the database that
                   is to be created

The only value you must provide when using this form of the CREATE DATABASE
command is a database name. This name:

- Can consist of only the characters "a" through "z", "A" through "Z", "0" through
  "9", "@", "#", "$", and "_" (underscore)
- Cannot begin with a number
- Cannot begin with the letter sequences "SYS", "DBM", or "IBM"
- Cannot match the name of another database that already exists within the same
  instance

When this form of the CREATE DATABASE command is executed, the characteristics of
the database produced, such as page size and location, are specified according to a set of
predefined default values. To change any of these default characteristics, you must use a
more complex form of the CREATE DATABASE command. The basic syntax for this form
of the CREATE DATABASE command is:

```
CREATE [DATABASE | DB] [DatabaseName]
  <AUTOMATIC STORAGE [YES | NO]>
  <ON [StoragePath, ...] <DBPATH [DBPath]>>
  <ALIAS [Alias]>
  <USING CODESET [CodeSet] TERRITORY [Territory]>
  <COLLATE USING [CollateType]>
  <PAGESIZE [4096 | Pagesize <K>]>
  <DFT_EXTENT_SZ [DefaultExtentSize]>
  <RESTRICTIVE>
  <CATALOG TABLESPACE [TS_Definition]>
  <USER TABLESPACE [TS_Definition]>
  <TEMPORARY TABLESPACE [TS_Definition]>
  <WITH "[Description]">
```

where:

DatabaseName	Identifies a unique name that is to be assigned to the database that is to be created
StoragePath	If AUTOMATIC STORAGE NO is specified, identifies one or more locations (drives and/or directories) where both data and metadata files associated with the database are to be physically stored; otherwise, this parameter identifies one or more storage paths that are to be used to hold automatic storage table space containers
DBPath	If AUTOMATIC STORAGE YES is specified (the default), identifies the location where metadata files associated with the database are to be physically stored
Alias	Identifies the alias to be assigned to the database that is to be created
CodeSet	Identifies the code set that is to be used for storing data in the database (with DB2, each single-byte character is represented internally as a unique number between 0 and 255—this number is referred to as the *code point* of the character; assignments of code points to every character in a particular character set is known as a *code page*, and the International Organization for Standardization term for a code page is *code set*)
Territory	Identifies the geographical location that is to be used for storing data in the database
CollateType	Identifies the collating sequence (that is, the sequence in which characters are ordered for the purpose of sorting, merging, and making comparisons) that the database is to use
PageSize	Identifies the page size that is to be used by the default buffer pool (IBMDEFAULTBP) and the default table spaces (SYSCATSPACE, TEMPSPACE1, USERSPACE1) that are to be constructed for the database; this parameter also identifies the default page size to use when new buffer pools/table spaces are created and a page size is not specified with the CREATE BUFFERPOOL and/or CREATE TABLESPACE statements used—if you do not provide a value for this parameter, a page size of 4 KB will be used by default
DefaultExtentSize	Identifies the default extent size that is to be used when a new table space is created and an extent size is not specified with the CREATE TABLESPACE statement used

TS_Definition	Specifies the table space definition that is to be used to create one or more of the default table spaces (SYSCATSPACE, TEMPSPACE1, USERSPACE1) that are automatically constructed for the database
Description	Identifies a comment that is to be used to describe the database; this comment is stored in the database directory and helps identify the database; the description provided cannot be more than 30 characters in length and must be enclosed in double-quotation marks

If the AUTOMATIC STORAGE NO clause is specified with the CREATE DATABASE command used, the resulting database will not be an automatic storage database and cannot use automatic storage table spaces. If, however, the AUTOMATIC STORAGE YES clause is specified (or if neither clause is specified), it is assumed that the database is to be an automatic storage database. (With DB2 10.5, the AUTOMATIC STORAGE NO clause has been deprecated and may be removed in a future release.)

If the RESTRICTIVE clause is specified with the CREATE DATABASE command used, the *restrict_access* database configuration parameter for the database is set to YES and no authorities or privileges will automatically be granted to the group PUBLIC.

Thus, to create a database named SAMPLE that:

- Uses automatic storage
- Uses the paths "/mnt/fsystem1" and "/mnt/fsystem2" (which refer to file systems that have been created on Fibre Channel drives) to store its data and metadata
- Recognizes the United States and Canada code set
- Uses a collating sequence that is based on the United States and Canada code set
- Has a page size of 8 KB

you would execute a CREATE DATABASE statement that looks something like this:

```
CREATE DATABASE sample
  ON /mnt/fsystem1, /mnt/fsystem2
  USING CODESET 1252 TERRITORY US
  COLLATE USING SYSTEM
  PAGESIZE 8192
```

DB2'S Directory Files

Because a database can physically reside anywhere, each DB2 instance must know where databases that fall under its control physically reside, as well how to establish connections to those databases on behalf of users and/or applications. To keep track of this information, DB2 uses a special set of files known as *directory files* (or *directories*). Four types of directories exist; they are:

- The system database directory
- The local database directory
- The node directory
- The Database Connection Services (DCS) directory

The System Database Directory

A system database directory is created automatically the first time a database is created under a particular instance. Information about the new database is then recorded in the system database directory, and as additional databases are created or cataloged, information about those databases is recorded in the system database directory as well. (Databases are implicitly cataloged when they are created; databases can be explicitly cataloged using Data Studio or the CATALOG DATABASE command.) Every entry in the system database directory contains the following information:

- The name assigned to the database when the database was created (or explicitly cataloged)
- The alias assigned to the database (which is the same as the database name, if no alias was specified when the database was created/cataloged)
- Descriptive information about the database (if that information is available)
- The location of the local database directory file that contains additional information about the database
- A database entry type that indicates whether or not the database is *indirect* (i.e., a database that resides on the same workstation as the current DB2 instance) or *remote*
- Other system information, including the code page the database was created under

The contents of the system database directory or a local database directory file can be viewed by executing the LIST DATABASE DIRECTORY command. The syntax for this command is:

```
LIST [DATABASE | DB] DIRECTORY <ON [Location]>
```

where:

Location   Identifies the drive or directory where one or more databases are
                        stored

If no location is specified when this command is executed, the contents of the system database directory file will be displayed. If a location is specified, the contents of the local database directory file at that particular location will displayed instead.

The Local Database Directory

Anytime a DB2 database is created in a new location, a local database directory file is also created at that location. Information about the database is then recorded in the local database directory, and as other databases are created in that location, information about those databases is recorded in the local database directory as well. Thus, while only one system database directory exists for a particular instance, several local database directories can exist, depending upon how databases have been distributed across available storage.

Each entry recorded in a local database directory contains the following information:

- The name assigned to the database when the database was created (or explicitly cataloged)
- The alias assigned to the database (which is the same as the database name, if no alias was specified when the database was created/cataloged)
- Descriptive information about the database (if that information is available)
- The name of the root directory of the hierarchical tree used to store information about the database
- Other system information, including the code page the database was created under

As was mentioned earlier, the contents of a local database directory file can be viewed by executing the LIST DATABASE DIRECTORY command.

The Node Directory

Unlike the system database directory and the local database directory, which are used to keep track of what databases exist and where they are stored, the node directory contains information that identifies how and where remote systems or instances can be found. A node directory file is created on each client workstation the first time a remote server or instance is cataloged there. As other remote instances/servers are cataloged, information about those instances/servers is recorded in the node directory as well. Entries in the node directory are then used in conjunction with entries in the system database directory to make connections and instance attachments to DB2 databases stored on remote servers.

Each entry in the node directory contains, among other things, information about the type of communication protocol that is to be used to communicate between the client workstation and the remote database server. The contents of the node directory file can be viewed by executing the LIST NODE DIRECTORY command; the syntax for this command is

```
LIST <ADMIN> NODE DIRECTORY <SHOW DETAIL>
```

(If the ADMIN option is specified when this command is executed, information about administration servers will be displayed.)

The Database Connection Services (DCS) Directory

The Database Connection Services (DCS) directory is used to provide information about host databases a workstation has access to if DB2 Connect™ has been installed. DB2 Connect gives applications running on LAN-based workstations, personal computers (PCs), and mobile devices the ability to work with data stored in DB2 databases that reside on IBM System z, System i®, and IBM Power Systems™ platforms. An add-on product that must be purchased separately, DB2 Connect is a combination of several industry-standard application programming interfaces (which are implemented as drivers) and a robust, highly scalable, communications infrastructure. DB2 Connect is not actually responsible for connecting workstations to remote databases. Instead, it provides a way for applications to establish connections to databases using a variety of standard interfaces for database access, such as JDBC, SQLJ, ODBC, OLE DB, ADO, ADO.NET, RDO, DB2 CLI, and Embedded SQL.

The contents of the DCS directory file can be viewed by executing the LIST DCS DIRECTORY command. The syntax for this command is:

```
LIST DCS DIRECTORY
```

Cataloging and Uncataloging a DB2 Database

Because a database is implicitly cataloged as soon as it is created, most users never have to concern themselves with the cataloging process. However, if you need to catalog a previously uncataloged database, if you want to set up an alternate name for an existing database, or if you need to access a database stored on a remote server, you will need to become familiar with the tools that can be used to catalog DB2 databases. Fortunately, cataloging a database is a relatively straightforward process that can be done using Data Studio or by executing the CATALOG DATABASE command. The syntax for this command is:

```
CATALOG [DATABASE | DB] [DatabaseName]
<AS [DatabaseAlias]>
<ON [Path] | AT NODE [NodeName]>
<AUTHENTICATION [AuthenticationType]>
<WITH "[Description]">
```

where:

DatabaseName	Identifies the name that has been assigned to the database to be cataloged
DatabaseAlias	Identifies the alias that is to be assigned to the database when it is cataloged
Path	Identifies the location (drive and/or directory) where the files associated with the database to be cataloged are physically stored
NodeName	Identifies the node where the database to be cataloged resides; the node name specified should match an entry in the node directory file (i.e., should correspond to a node that has already been cataloged)
AuthenticationType	Identifies where and how authentication is to take place when a user attempts to access the database; the following values are valid for this parameter: SERVER, CLIENT, SERVER_ENCRYPT, SERVER_ENCRYPT_AES , KERBEROS TARGET PRINCIPAL [*PrincipalName*] (where *PrincipalName* is the fully qualified Kerberos principal name for the target server), DATA_ENCRYPT, and GSSPLUGIN.
Description	A comment that is used to describe the entry that will be made in the database directory for the database being cataloged

Thus, if you wanted to catalog a database named TEST_DB that physically resides in the directory /home/db2data, you could do so by executing a CATALOG DATABASE command that looks something like this:

```
CATALOG DATABASE test_db AS test
ON /home/db2data
AUTHENTICATION SERVER
```

• •

Note: If a DB2 Connect remote client does not specify an authentication type, the client will try to connect using the SERVER_ENCRYPT authentication type first. If the server does not accept this authentication type, the client will try using an appropriate authentication type that is returned by the server. To help optimize performance, always specify the authentication type at the client to avoid this extra network flow.

• •

Since a database must be cataloged before a user or application can connect to it, you're probably wondering why you would ever want to uncatalog a database. Suppose you are running an older version of DB2, and when you upgrade, you decide to completely uninstall the old DB2 software before installing the latest release. To prevent this software upgrade from having an impact on existing databases, you could uncatalog them before you uninstall the old version and then recatalog them after the new version of DB2 has been installed. (Migration may or may not be necessary.) When a database is uncataloged, its entry is removed from both the system and the local database directory; however, the database itself is not destroyed, nor are its table space storage containers made available for other databases to use.

A database can be uncataloged by executing the UNCATALOG DATABASE command. The syntax for this command is:

UNCATALOG [DATABASE | DB] [*DatabaseAlias*]

where:

DatabaseAlias   Identifies the alias assigned to the database to be uncataloged

So, if you wanted to uncatalog a database that has the name and alias TEST_DB, you could do so by executing an UNCATALOG DATABASE command that looks like this:

```
UNCATALOG DATABASE test_db
```

Cataloging and Uncataloging a Node

The process used to catalog nodes (servers) is similar that used to catalog databases. Nodes are typically cataloged by executing the CATALOG ... NODE command that corresponds to the communications protocol that will be used to access the server being cataloged. Several forms of the CATALOG ... NODE command are available, including:

- CATALOG LOCAL NODE
- CATALOG LDAP NODE
- CATALOG NAMED PIPE NODE
- CATALOG TCPIP NODE

The syntax for all of these commands is very similar, the major difference being that many of the options available with each are specific to the communications protocol the command has been tailored for. Because TCP/IP is probably the most common communications protocol in use today, let's take a look at the syntax for that form of the CATALOG ... NODE command.

The syntax for the CATALOG TCPIP NODE command is:

```
CATALOG <ADMIN> [TCPIP | TCPIP4 | TCPIP6] NODE [NodeName]
REMOTE [IPAddress | HostName]
SERVER [ServiceName | PortNumber]
<SECURITY [SOCKS | SSL]>
<REMOTE INSTANCE [InstanceName]>
<SYSTEM [SystemName]>
<OSTYPE [SystemType]>
<WITH "[Description]">
```

where:

NodeName   Identifies the alias to be assigned to the node to be cataloged; this is an arbitrary name created on the user's workstation and is used to identify the node

IPAddress	Identifies the IP address of the server where the remote database you want to communicate with resides
HostName	Identifies the host name, as it is known to the TCP/IP network; this is the name of the server where the remote database you want to communicate with resides
ServiceName	Identifies the service name that the DB2 instance on the server uses to communicate with
PortNumber	Identifies the port number that the DB2 instance on the server uses to communicate with
InstanceName	Identifies the name of the server instance to which an attachment is to be made
SystemName	Identifies the DB2 system name that is used to identify the server
SystemType	Identifies the type of operating system being used on the server; the following values are valid for this parameter: AIX, WIN, HPUX, SUN, OS390, OS400, VM, VSE, and LINUX.
Description	A comment that is used to describe the node entry that will be made in the node directory for the node being cataloged

Thus, if you wanted to catalog a node for an AIX server that has the IPv6 address 1080:0:0:0:8:800:200C:417A and a DB2 instance that listens on port 50000, and assign it the alias RMT_SERVER, you could do so by executing a CATALOG TCPIP NODE command that looks something like this:

```
CATALOG TCPIP6 NODE rmt_server
REMOTE 1080:0:0:0:8:800:200C:417A
SERVER 50000
OSTYPE AIX
```

Regardless of how a node was cataloged, it can be uncataloged at any time by executing the UNCATALOG NODE command. The syntax for this command is:

UNCATALOG NODE [*NodeName*]

where:

NodeName   Identifies the alias assigned to the node to be uncataloged

So if you wanted to uncatalog the node that was cataloged in the previous example, you could do so by executing an UNCATALOG NODE command that looks like this:

```
UNCATALOG NODE rmt_server
```

Cataloging and Uncataloging a DCS Database

The process for cataloging a Database Connection Services (DCS) database is very similar to that used to catalog a regular DB2 database. A DCS database is cataloged by executing the CATALOG DCS DATABASE command. The syntax for this command is:

```
CATALOG DCS [DATABASE | DB] [DatabaseAlias]
<AS [TargetName]>
<AR [LibraryName]>
<PARMS "[ParameterString]">
<WITH "[Description]">
```

where:

DatabaseAlias	Identifies the alias of the target database that is to be cataloged; this name should match an entry in the system database directory associated with the remote node
TargetName	Identifies the name of the target host or System i database to be cataloged
LibraryName	Identifies the name of the Application Requester library that is to be loaded and used to access the remote database listed in the DCS directory
ParameterString	Identifies a parameter string to be passed to the Application Requestor when it is invoked
Description	A comment that is used to describe the database entry that will be made in the DCS directory for the database being cataloged

So, if you wanted catalog information about a DB2® for z/OS® database that has the alias TEST_DB in the DCS directory, you could do so by executing a CATALOG DCS DATABASE command that looks something like this:

```
CATALOG DCS DATABASE test_db
AS dcs_db
```

Keep in mind that an entry for the database TEST_DB would also have to exist in the system database directory before the entry in the DCS database directory could be used to connect to the database.

Entries in the DCS database directory can be removed by executing the UNCATALOG DCS DATABASE command. The syntax for this command is:

```
UNCATALOG DCS [DATABASE | DB] [DatabaseAlias]
```

where:

DatabaseAlias   Identifies the alias assigned to the DCS database to be
                       uncataloged

Thus, if you wanted to uncatalog the DCS database cataloged in the previous example, you could do so by executing an UNCATALOG DCS DATABASE command that looks like this:

```
UNCATALOG DCS DATABASE test_db
```

> **Note:** When queries are run against federated databases, the DB2 optimizer performs what is known as *pushdown analysis* to determine whether a particular operation (such as the execution of a system or user function) can be conducted at a remote data source. By updating local catalog information regularly, the DB2 query compiler is guaranteed to have access to accurate information about SQL support at remote data sources.

Establishing a Database Connection

When a database is first created, it contains only the system catalog; before it can be used to store data, data objects like tables, views, and indexes must first be defined. And before new data objects can be defined (or anything else can be done with the database for that matter), a connection to the database must be established. Usually, a connection to a database is established by executing some form of the CONNECT SQL statement. The basic syntax for this statement is:

```
CONNECT
<TO [ServerName]>
<USER [UserID] USING [Password]>
```

or

```
CONNECT RESET
```

where:

ServerName	Identifies, by name, the application server a connection is to be made to
UserID	Identifies an authorization ID (or user ID) that DB2 is to use to verify that the individual attempting to establish the connection is actually authorized to connect to the server specified
Password	Identifies the password that is associated with the authorization ID provided; it is important to note that passwords are case-sensitive

Therefore, if a user whose authentication ID is db2user and password is ibmdb2 wants to establish a connection to a database named SAMPLE, he or she can do so by executing a CONNECT statement that looks like this:

```
CONNECT TO sample USER db2user USING ibmdb2
```

Note: When the CONNECT statement is executed without a user ID and password specifed, DB2 will either attempt to use the user ID and password that was supplied to gain access to the operating system of the database server, or it will prompt for this information. (The former is referred to as an *implicit connect*, as it is implied that the credentials of the current user are to be used; when a user ID and password are specified, the operation is called an *explicit connect*, because the required user credentials were explicitly provided.

Once a database connection is established, it will remain in effect until it is explicitly terminated or until the application that established the connection ends. You can explicitly terminate a database connection at any time by executing a CONNECT statement with the RESET clause specified. Such a statement looks like this:

```
CONNECT RESET
```

Type 1 and Type 2 Connections

Applications that interact with DB2 databases have the option of using two types of connection semantics. Known simply as Type 1 and Type 2, each connection type supports a very different connection behavior. For instance, Type 1 connections allow a transaction to be connected to only one database at a time. Type 2 connections, however, allow a single transaction to connect to and work with multiple databases simultaneously. Table 4.1 shows other differences between Type 1 and Type 2 connections.

Table 4.1: Differences between Type 1 and Type 2 connections	
Type 1 Connections	**Type 2 Connections**
The current transaction (unit of work) must be committed or rolled back before a connection to another application server can be established.	The current transaction does not have to be committed or rolled back before a connection to another application server can be established.
Establishing a connection to another application server causes the current connection to be terminated. The new connection becomes the current connection.	Establishing a connection to another application server places the current connection into the dormant state. The new connection then becomes the current connection.
The CONNECT statement establishes the current connection. Subsequent SQL requests are forwarded to this connection until another CONNECT statement is executed.	The CONNECT statement establishes the current connection the first time it is executed against a server. If the CONNECT statement is executed against a connection that is in the dormant state, that connection becomes the current connection— provided the SQLRULES precompiler option was set to DB2 when the application was precompiled. Otherwise, an error is returned.
The SET CONNECTION statement is supported, but the only valid target is the current connection.	The SET CONNECTION statement changes the state of a connection from dormant to current.
Connecting with the USER...USING clauses will cause the current connection to be disconnected and a new connection to be established with the given authorization ID and password.	Connecting with the USER...USING clauses is allowed only when there is no dormant or current connection to the same named server.

When a database connection is established from the DB2 Command Line Processor (CLP), Type 1 connections are used by default. However, the connection semantics that Embedded SQL applications use is controlled by the following set of SQL precompiler and Binder options:

- **CONNECT [1 | 2]**: Specifies whether to process CONNECT statements as Type 1 (1) or Type 2 (2)
- **SQLRULES [DB2 | STD]**: Specifies whether to process Type 2 connections according to DB2 rules (DB2), which allow the CONNECT statement to switch to a *dormant* connection, or according to the SQL92 Standard rules (STD), which do not allow this behavior
- **DISCONNECT [EXPLICIT | CONDITIONAL | AUTOMATIC]**: Specifies which database connections are to be disconnected when a COMMIT operation occurs—those that have been explicitly marked for release by the RELEASE statement (EXPLICIT), those that have no open WITH HOLD cursors and that are marked for release (CONDITIONAL), or all connections (AUTOMATIC)

With Call Level Interface (CLI) and Open Database Connectivity (ODBC) applications, the connection semantics used is controlled by assigning the value SQL_CONCURRENT_TRANS (Type 1) or SQL_COORDINATED_TRANS (Type 2) to the SQL_ATTR_CONNECTTYPE connection attribute (using the SQLSetConnectAttr() function).

Tables Revisited

Earlier we saw that a table is a logical database object that acts as the main repository in a database. We also saw that the following types of tables can exist:

- Base tables
- Synopsis tables
- Partitioned tables
- Range-clustered tables (RCTs)
- Multidimensional clustering (MDC) tables
- Insert time clustering tables (ICTs)
- Materialized query tables (MQTs)
- Shadow tables
- Temporal (time-travel) tables
- History tables

- Temporary tables
- Typed tables

The following sections describe each of these types of tables in more detail.

Base Tables

A *base table* (or *regular table*) is a physical data structure that is used to hold persistent user data. Base tables are the most common type of table used in a DB2 database. And beginning with DB2 10.5 for LUW, base tables can be organized by row or by column.

Synopsis Tables

A *synopsis table* is a system-generated, automatically maintained, column-organized table that is used to store metadata for an associated user-defined, column-organized table. The synopsis table for a user-defined table contains the minimum and maximum values for each column in that table (across a range of rows). DB2 uses those values to skip over data that is of no interest to a query during the evaluation of certain types of query predicates—specifically: =, >, >=, <, <=, BETWEEN, NOT BETWEEN, IS NOT NULL, IN, and NOT IN.

Synopsis tables are created in the SYSIBM schema, and the relationship between a user-defined table and its associated synopsis table is recorded in the SYSCAT.TABDEP catalog view. Because synopsis tables are generated and maintained by DB2, the only operation that can be performed against a synopsis table is a SELECT operation.

Partitioned Tables

Partitioned tables (also known to as *range-partitioned tables*) are tables that use a data organization scheme in which data is divided across multiple storage objects, called *data partitions* or *ranges*, according to values found in one or more partitioning key columns. Each data partition is stored separately, and the storage objects used for each partition can reside in different table spaces, the same table space, or a combination of the two. Figure 4.8 illustrates how a partitioned table named SALES whose data resides in four partitions—one for each quarter—might look if the data for each partition was stored in a separate table space.

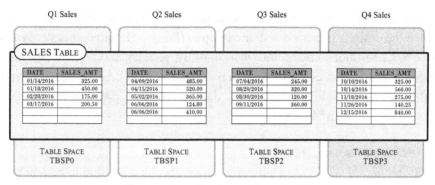

Figure 4.8: A simple partitioned table

Partitioned tables improve performance by eliminating large amounts of I/O. Other advantages include:

- **Easy roll-in and roll-out of data.** A new range of data can be easily added (rolled-in) to an existing partitioned table as a new data partition. Similarly, one or more ranges of data can removed from (rolled-out of) a partitioned table and converted to one or more base tables. Once a data partition has been rolled-out to a separate table, that table can be deleted (dropped), archived, or be rolled-in to another partitioned table. (Data partitions are rolled in and out by executing the ALTER TABLE statement with the ATTACH PARTITION or DETACH PARTITION clause specified.)

- **Easier administration of large tables.** Table-level administration becomes more flexible because administrative tasks can be performed on individual data partitions, as opposed to the entire partitioned table. Likewise, time-consuming maintenance operations can be shortened. For example, backup operations can be performed at the data-partition level when each data partition is placed in a separate table space, making it possible to back up one data partition at a time.

- **Flexible index placement.** With table partitioning, indexes can be placed in different table spaces, allowing for more granular control of index placement. Indexes can also be partitioned, which aids in the rolling-in and rolling-out of data partitions.

- **Faster query processing.** In the process of resolving queries, one or more data partitions may be automatically eliminated based on the query predicates used. This functionality, known as *partition elimination*, improves the performance of many queries because less data has to be analyzed before a result data set can be produced. In addition, queries can be automatically directed to just the partition(s) where the desired data resides. For example, if the SALES table presented earlier were to be partitioned by month (instead of by quarter), and a query designed to calculate the total sales for the month of March were to be executed against the table, the query would only access the data stored in the partition that contained data for the month of March.

Range-Clustered Tables (RCTs)

A *range-clustered table (RCT)* is a table that uses a special algorithm to associate record key values (which are similar to index key values) with specific locations of rows in the table; each record in a RCT table receives a predetermined record identifier or RID, and these RIDs are used to quickly locate individual records in the table. (This provides exceptionally fast access to specific rows.) The algorithm does not use hashing because hashing does not preserve key-value order; by using a algorithm that preserves key-value order, the need to reorganize the table over time is eliminated.

Range-clustered tables are particularly useful when data is tightly clustered across one or more columns. They can bring about significant performance advantages during query processing, because fewer input/output (I/O) operations are required. And, they require less maintenance, less logging, and less buffer pool memory than similarly sized base tables with one or more indexes. That's because there are no secondary objects to maintain; clustering indexes are not required, nor are they supported.

Although no records exist at the time an RCT is created, the entire range of anticipated pages is preallocated and reserved for use at table creation time. (Preallocation is based on the record size and the projected maximum number of records that are to be stored.) Consequently, RCTs have no need for free space control records. However, RCTs do not grow as data is added to them—all RCTs have a fixed size that is specified at the time the table is created.

Multidimensional Clustering (MDC) Tables

A *multidimensional clustering (MDC) table* is a special table that allows its data to be physically clustered on more than one key (dimension), simultaneously. (In contrast, a base table with a clustering index can only cluster data on a single key.) In addition, an MDC table is able to maintain its clustering over the dimensions specified, automatically and continuously, eliminating the need to reorganize the table to maintain its clustering sequence. (A base table with a clustering index will become unclustered over time and will need to be reorganized.) Thus, MDC tables can significantly reduce maintenance overhead when clustering is desired. (It is important to note that deleted rows will result in free extents, which can only be reclaimed by executing the REORG command with the RECLAIM EXTENTS clause specified. Consequently, if a significant amount of delete operations are performed against an MDC table, maintenance overhead may not be reduced as much.) Figure 4.9 depicts how an MDC table named SALES whose data is clustered along three dimensions (CUSTOMER, REGION, and YEAR) would look.

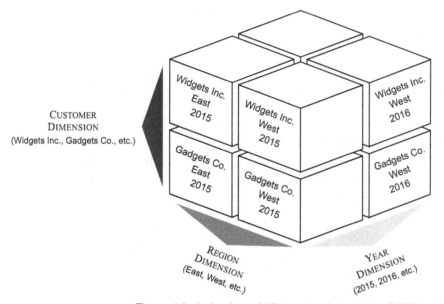

Figure 4.9: A simple multidimensional clustering (MDC) table

One thing you may notice immediately about the MDC table depicted in Figure 4.9 is that an MDC table can be divided into *slices* that contain all the blocks of data that have the same dimension value. For example, the slice that contains all blocks in which the CUSTOMER column contains the value "Widgets Inc." can be seen in Figure 4.10.

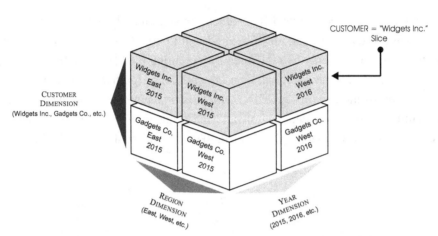

Figure 4.10: The CUSTOMER = "Widgets Inc." slice of the MDC table

Each unique attribute value combination of the dimensions used in an MDC table identifies a possible *cell*. For example, a cell that contains rows where the CUSTOMER dimension (column) contains the value "Widgets Inc.", the REGION dimension contains the value "West", and the YEAR dimension contains the value 2015, can be seen in Figure 4.11. Each cell may have zero or more blocks of data.

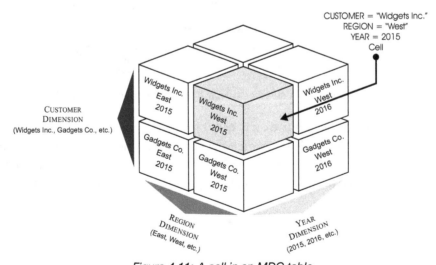

Figure 4.11: A cell in an MDC table

MDC tables are primarily intended to be used with large tables in data warehouse and decision support environments. In terms of query performance, range queries involving any combination of the dimensions specified for the clustered table will benefit most, because they need only to access just those pages that have records with the desired dimension values. (Qualifying pages will be grouped together in extents.)

The dimension key (or keys) along which an MDC table's data is to be clustered is specified at the time the table is created. (Each dimension can consist of one or more columns.) And when an MDC table is created, a dimension block index is created automatically for each dimension specified. This index identifies the list of blocks available for a given key value and is used to quickly and efficiently access data along each of those dimensions. (Dimension block indexes point to extents instead of individual rows and are much smaller than regular indexes; therefore, they can be used to quickly access only those extents that contain specific dimension values.) If the table has more than one dimension, a composite block index containing all dimension key columns is created as well; this index is used to maintain the clustering of the data during insert and update operations, as well as to aid in query processing. Figure 4.12 shows a simple MDC table and its associated indexes.

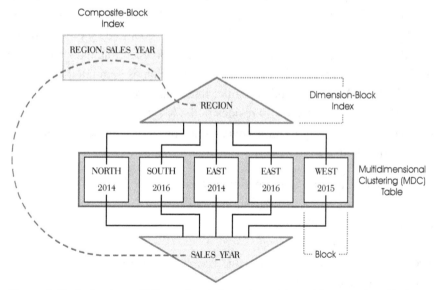

Figure 4.12: A simple multidimensional clustering table and its associated indexes

The best criteria to use for determining which clustering dimensions are ideal for a given table is a set of frequently executed queries that might benefit from clustering at the block level. Columns involved in equality or range predicate queries—especially those with low cardinalities—will show the greatest benefit from, and should be considered as candidates for, clustering dimensions. Foreign keys in a fact table that is involved in star joins with other dimension tables are good candidates for clustering as well.

Insert Time Clustering (ITC) Tables

An *insert time clustering (ITC) table* is a table whose data is physically clustered based on row insert time. ITC tables have similar characteristics to MDC tables; for example, ITC tables use block-based allocation and block indexes. Where ITC and MDC tables differ is in how their data is clustered. ITC tables cluster data using a virtual column that physically stores rows that are inserted at a similar time, together. (MDC tables cluster data according to clustering dimensions that are specified by the table creator.)

Materialized Query Tables (MQTs)

Materialized query tables (MQTs) are tables whose definition is based on the result of a query. MQTs can be thought of as a kind of materialized view because they are typically populated with precomputed results that have been obtained from one or more base tables. How an MQT differs from a view is in the way the data is generated and where the data is physically stored. Usually, data for a view is generated by executing the query upon which the view is based each time the view is referenced; the data itself resides in the underlying base table(s) the view references. MQT data is generated by executing the query upon which the MQT is based at regular intervals or at a user-controlled specific point in time; the data itself physically resides in the MQT.

MQTs offer a powerful way to improve response time for complex queries, particularly queries that:

- Aggregate data over one or more dimensions
- Join and aggregate data over a group of tables
- Perform repeated calculations
- Perform resource-intensive scans
- Access a common subset of data—that is, retrieve data from a "hot" horizontal or vertical database partition
- Retrieve data from a table, or a part of a table, in a partitioned database environment

Two different types of MQTs are available: MQTs that are maintained by the system and MQTs that are maintained by the user. Insert, update, and delete operations cannot be performed against system-maintained MQTs. However, a REFRESH IMMEDIATE system-maintained MQT is updated -automatically, as changes are made to the underlying tables upon which the MQT is based. (REFRESH IMMEDIATE indicates that changes made to underlying tables are to be cascaded to the MQT as they happen; REFRESH DEFERRED means that the data in the MQT will only be refreshed when the REFRESH TABLE statement is executed—often at regular intervals.)

User-maintained MQTs allow insert, update, or delete operations to be executed against them and can be populated with Import and Load operations. However, they cannot be populated by executing the REFRESH TABLE statement. Essentially, a user-defined MQT is a summary table that the user is responsible for populating, but that the DB2 optimizer can utilize to improve query performance.

Shadow Tables

A shadow table is a column-organized copy of a row-organized table that contains all or a subset of the columns found in the row-organized table upon which it is based. Shadow tables are implemented as MQTs that are maintained by replication. They provide the performance benefits of BLU Acceleration to analytic queries that must be executed in online transaction processing (OLTP) environments. (BLU Acceleration enhances the performance of complex queries through the use of, among other things, a column-organized architecture.)

Shadow tables are maintained by IBM® InfoSphere® Change Data Capture for DB2® for Linux, UNIX, and Windows (InfoSphere CDC), which is a component of the InfoSphere Data Replication product. InfoSphere CDC asynchronously replicates DML statements that are performed against the source (row-organized) table to the corresponding shadow table. Queries are automatically routed to the source table or the shadow table according to the results of a latency-based algorithm that prevents shadow table access whenever replication latency exceeds a user-defined limit.

Temporal (Time-Travel) Tables

Temporal tables are tables that are designed to record an appropriate time period for every row that gets stored in them. A *time period* (or *period*) is simply an interval of time that is defined by two specific dates, times, or timestamps—one date/time/timestamp identifies the beginning of the period and the other indicates when the period ends. The beginning value for a period is inclusive and the ending value is exclusive, which means that a row with a period from January 1 to February 1 is actually valid from 12:00 a.m. on January 1 until 11:59 p.m. on January 31. February 1 is not included in the period range.

When it comes to managing temporal data, the term *system period* refers to the period in which a particular row is considered current. And the term *system time* is often associated with tracking when changes are made to the state of a row (record)—for example, when a new bank account is opened or an insurance policy is modified to reflect that a higher premium must be paid.

The term *application period*, however, refers to the period in which a particular row is considered valid. And the term *business time* (sometimes referred to as *valid time* or *application time*) is usually associated with tracking the effective dates of certain business conditions—for example, when a warranty takes effect (and when it expires) or when a particular item goes on sale (and how long it stays at the sale price).

Some organizations need to track both system-period and application-period information for rows stored in a single table. When this is the case, the table is considered to be *bitemporal*.

Consequently, you can create the following types of temporal (also referred to as *time-travel*) tables:

- System-period temporal tables
- Application-period temporal tables
- Bitemporal tables

System-period temporal tables

A *system-period temporal table* is a table that maintains historical versions of its rows. Such tables are used to automatically track and manage multiple versions of data values. For this reason, every system-period temporal table must be associated with a history table—any time a row in a system-period temporal table is modified, DB2 automatically inserts a copy of the original row into the corresponding history table. This storage of original data values enables you to retrieve data from previous points in time.

The table definition for a system-period temporal table must include "system time begin" and "system time end" columns, which are used to track when a row is considered current. DB2 will automatically populate the "system time begin" column with the current timestamp, and it will store the value 12/30/9999 in the "system time end" column as rows are inserted into the table. If a row is subsequently updated or deleted, DB2 will update these columns accordingly, and then write a historical record to the corresponding history table.

Application-period temporal tables

An *application-period temporal table* is a table that maintains "currently in effect" values of application data. Such tables let you manage time-sensitive information by defining the time periods in which specific data values are considered valid. The definition for an application-period temporal table must include "business time begin" and "business time end" columns, which are normally populated with user- or application-supplied values that indicate the time period in which a particular row is considered valid. The "business time begin" column is used to store the date/time/timestamp that indicates the beginning of a row's validity, and the "business time end" column is used to store the date/time/timestamp that designates when a row is no longer considered valid.

Bitemporal tables

A *bitemporal table* combines the historical tracking of a system-period temporal table with the time-specific data storage capabilities of an application-period temporal table. Consequently, bitemporal tables are used when a single table needs to maintain historical versions of its rows *and* keep track of data values that are currently considered valid.

History Tables

As was mentioned earlier, a *history table* is a special table that is used to store historical versions of rows found in a system-period temporal table. (When a row is updated or deleted from a system-period temporal table, DB2 automatically inserts a copy of the original row into its associated history table. This storage of old system-period temporal table data gives you the ability to retrieve data from previous points in time.)

The columns in a history table must have the same names, order, and data types as the system-period temporal table it is associated with. And although history tables are user-defined, when a system-period temporal table is deleted (dropped), its associated history table and any indexes defined on the history table are implicitly dropped as well. To avoid losing historical data when such an event takes place, you can either create the history table with the RESTRICT ON DROP attribute specified, or you can add this attribute to the history table (with the ALTER TABLE statement) before the system-period temporal table is deleted.

Temporary Tables

As the name implies, a *temporary table* is a table that is used to store data temporarily. Two types of temporary tables are available. They are:

- **Declared global temporary tables**: These tables are used to hold nonpersistent data temporarily, on behalf of a single application. Declared global temporary tables are explicitly created by an application when they are needed and implicitly destroyed when the application that created them is terminated.
- **Created global temporary tables**: These tables are used to hold nonpersistent data temporarily, on behalf of one or more applications. Unlike declared global temporary tables, definitions for created global temporary tables are stored in the system catalog, and an empty instance of the table is created the first time it is referenced in an OPEN (cursor), SELECT, INSERT, UPDATE, or DELETE SQL statement. Each connection that references a created global temporary table has its own unique instance of the table and only has access to rows that it inserts or updates. The instance is not persistent beyond the life of the connection.

It is important to note that a user temporary table space must exist before a temporary table can be created. (We will take a closer look at working with temporary tables in Chapter 6, "Working with DB2 Tables, Views, and Indexes.")

Typed Tables

A *typed table* is a table that is defined with a user-defined structured type. Typed tables store instances of structured types as rows, in which each attribute of the type is stored in a separate column. Using typed tables, you can establish a hierarchical data structure (called a *table hierarchy*) by defining a relationship between several different typed tables. A table hierarchy is made up of a single *root table* and one or more *supertables* or *subtables*.

Because typed tables contain objects that can be referenced by other objects, every typed table must have an object identifier column as its first column. The object identifier uniquely identifies a row object in a typed table hierarchy. For every structured user-defined data type you create, DB2 automatically creates a companion type known as a *reference type*. (The structured type to which a reference type refers is called the *referenced type*.) DB2 uses this reference type as the data type for the object identifier column. Reference types are also used to store references to rows in typed tables.

A Word About Compression

As the volume of data increases, the cardinality of that data tends to drop. Consequently, there aren't that many truly unique things in the world. Things may be unique when used in combination, but the basic elements themselves aren't all that varied. Consider the periodic table—everything in our world is made up of combinations of the rather small set of chemical elements that appear in this table. Apply the concept to other things, and you find the same to be true. For instance, according to the last U.S. census, there are about 300 million people in living in the United States. But there are only about 78,800 unique last names, resulting in very low cardinality with huge "clumps" in certain name sets. First names are even worse, coming in at around 6,600 (4,400 unique first names for females and 2,200 for males). The names of cities, streets, and addresses, not to mention product names, descriptions, and attributes, also tend to be highly redundant with low cardinality. DB2's row compression technology is based on this principle.

Row compression was first introduced with Version 9 of DB2 for LUW, and significant improvements have been made to its functionality since then. With DB2 10.5, two different row compression methods are available:

- **Classic (or static) row compression**: Works by searching for repeating patterns in row-organized table data and replacing those patterns with 12-bit symbols, which are stored along with the patterns they represent in a static dictionary, which is kept in the table, along with the compressed data, and loaded into memory whenever data in the table is accessed (to aid in decompression). Only one compression dictionary exists for each table object.
- **Adaptive row compression**: A compression mode that is superior to classic row compression in that it generally achieves better compression and requires less database maintenance to keep the compression ratio near an optimal level. Like classic row compression, adaptive row compression relies on a dictionary-based compression algorithm. The difference is that there can be multiple compression dictionaries for each table object—each dictionary contains a mapping of patterns that frequently occur in rows *throughout a single page*. Adaptive compression not only yields significantly better compression ratios in many cases but can also adapt to changing data characteristics.

With the exception of temporary tables, before data in a row-organized table can be compressed, the table must be "enabled" for compression. This is done by executing either a CREATE TABLE or an ALTER TABLE statement with the COMPRESS YES <ADAPTIVE | STATIC> clause specified. (Temporary tables are automatically enabled for classic row compression at the time they are created; only classic compression is supported.) Similarly, before data in an index can be compressed, it must be enabled for compression; this is done by executing either a CREATE INDEX or an ALTER INDEX statement with the

COMPRESS YES clause specified. When an index is created on a table that has been enabled for compression, the index is enabled for compression, by default.

Note: When index compression is enabled, the on-disk and memory format of index pages are modified according to the compression algorithms used by DB2. The degree of compression achieved will vary based on the type of index used and the data the index contains. For example, DB2 might compress an index with a large number of duplicate keys by storing an abbreviated format of the record identifier (RID) for the duplicate keys. In an index where there is a high degree of commonality in the prefixes of the index keys, DB2 may apply compression based on index key prefix similarities.

In Chapter 2, "Planning," we saw that column-organized tables are automatically compressed using a technique known as *approximate Huffman encoding*. With this form of compression (sometimes referred to as *actionable compression*), values that appear more frequently are compressed at a higher level than values that do not appear as often. And once encoded, data is packed as tightly as possible in a collection of bits that equal the register width of the CPU of the server being used, resulting in fewer I/Os, better memory utilization, and fewer CPU cycles to process.

Aside from reducing storage space requirements, another benefit of actionable compression is that data does not have to be decoded or uncompressed until the DB2 engine is ready to return a result. During query evaluation, predicates (=, >, >=, <, <=, BETWEEN, etc.), joins, and aggregations can be applied directly to encoded values. This results in better query performance since more data can be stored and processed directly in memory.

5

Working with DB2 Data Using SQL and XQuery

Twenty-three percent (23%) of the *DB2 10.5 Fundamentals for LUW* certification exam (Exam 615) is designed to test your knowledge of the various SQL statements and XQuery expressions that are commonly used to store, manipulate, and retrieve data. The questions that make up this portion of the exam are intended to evaluate the following:

- Your ability to perform INSERT, UPDATE, and DELETE operations
- Your ability to retrieve and format data using various forms of the SELECT statement
- Your ability to SORT and GROUP data retrieved by a SELECT statement
- Your ability to access Extensible Markup Language (XML) data using XQuery expressions and the built-in SQL/XML functions that are available with DB2
- Your ability to create and invoke an SQL stored procedure or an SQL user-defined function (UDF)
- Your knowledge of what transactions are, as well as how transactions are initiated and terminated
- Your knowledge of the DB2 10.5 SQL compatibility enhancements that can help applications that were written for other database products work with DB2

This chapter introduces you to the SQL statements and XQuery expressions that are used to store, modify, delete, and retrieve both relational (traditional) and XML data. In this chapter, you will learn how to use INSERT, UPDATE, and DELETE statements to store, change, and remove data, as well as how to use the SELECT statement and its associated clauses to retrieve data and format the results. You will also discover how to query XML documents and how to create and invoke SQL stored procedures and UDFs. Finally, you will learn about transaction management, and you will be introduced to several SQL compatibility enhancements that can reduce the time and complexity of enabling applications that were written for another relational database product to run in a DB2 10.5 for LUW environment.

Structured Query Language (SQL)

Structured Query Language (SQL) is a standardized language that is used to work with database objects and the data they contain. Using SQL, you can define, alter, and delete database objects, as well as add data to, change data in, and retrieve or remove data from any objects you create. One of the strengths of SQL is that it can be used in a variety of ways. For example, you can execute SQL statements interactively using tools such as IBM Data Studio and the DB2 Command Line Processor (CLP). Or you can embed them in high-level programming language source code files. (Because SQL is nonprocedural by design, it is not an actual programming language; therefore, most applications that use SQL are built by combining the decision and sequence control of a high-level programming language with the data storage, manipulation, and retrieval capabilities of SQL.) Like most other languages, SQL has a defined syntax and its own set of language elements.

SQL statements are frequently categorized according to the function they have been designed to perform. As a result, SQL statements typically fall under one of the following categories:

- **Embedded SQL Application Construct statements:** Used for the sole purpose of constructing Embedded SQL applications
- **Data Control Language (DCL) statements:** Used to grant and revoke authorities and privileges
- **Data Definition Language (DDL) statements:** Used to create, alter, and delete database objects
- **Data Manipulation Language (DML) statements:** Used to store data in, manipulate data in, retrieve data from, and remove data from select database objects

- **Transaction Management statements:** Used to establish and terminate database connections and transactions

You may recall that the two primary DCL statements—GRANT and REVOKE—were covered in Chapter 3, "Security," and that many of the objects that can be created with DDL statements were discussed in Chapter 4, "Working with Databases and Database Objects." Some of the DDL statements that are used to create those objects are covered in Chapter 6, "Working with DB2 Tables, Views, and Indexes." So, instead of covering DCL and DML statements here, this chapter begins by examining the DML statements that are available with DB2, and then focuses on transactions and the SQL statements that support them. (Because you do not need to be familiar with the Embedded SQL Application Construct statements to pass the *DB2 10.5 Fundamentals for LUW* certification exam, these statements are not addressed.)

SQL Data Manipulation Language (DML) Statements

In Chapter 4, "Working with Databases and Database Objects," we saw that a table is a logical object that acts as the main repository in a database, and that often many tables are defined. After one or more tables are created, the next step toward building a fully functional database is to populate those tables with data. And after a table is populated, at some point, you might need to retrieve, modify, or in some cases, delete the data that is stored in it.

That's where the DML statements come in to play. DML statements are used exclusively to store, modify, and delete data, as well as to retrieve data from tables, views, or both. Four DML statements are available. They are:

- INSERT
- UPDATE
- DELETE
- SELECT

The INSERT Statement

When a table is first created, it is nothing more than a definition of how a set of data values are to be stored; no data is associated with it. But once created, a table can be populated in a variety of ways. For example, it can be bulk-loaded using utilities like Import and Load, or data can be added to it, one row at a time, using an INSERT statement. The basic syntax for this statement is:

```
INSERT INTO [TableName | ViewName]
  <([ColumnName], ...)>
  VALUES ([Value | NULL | DEFAULT], ...)
```

or

```
INSERT INTO [TableName | ViewName]
  <([ColumnName], ...)>
  [SELECTStatement]
```

where:

TableName	Identifies, by name, the table data is to be added to; this can be any type of table *except* a system catalog table or a system-maintained materialized query table
ViewName	Identifies, by name, the updatable view data is to be added to; this can be any type of view *except* a system catalog view or a read-only view that does not have a corresponding INSTEAD OF trigger associated with it
ColumnName	Identifies, by name, one or more columns that data values are to be assigned to; each column name provided must identify an existing column in the table or updatable view specified, and it must not reference a column that was defined as being GENERATED ALWAYS AS IDENTITY
Value	Identifies one or more data values that are to be added to the table or updatable view specified
SELECTStatement	Identifies a SELECT statement that, when executed, will produce the data values that are to be added to the table or updatable view specified (by retrieving them from other tables, views, or both)

Therefore, to add a record to a base table named DEPARTMENT that has the following characteristics:

Column Name	Data Type
DEPTNO	CHAR(3)
DEPTNAME	CHAR(20)
MGRID	INTEGER

you could execute an INSERT statement that looks something like this:

```
INSERT INTO department
  (deptno, deptname, mgrid)
  VALUES ('A01', 'ADMINISTRATION', 1000)
```

It is important to note that the number of values provided in the VALUES clause must equal the number of column names identified in the column name list. Furthermore, the values provided will be assigned to the specified columns in the order in which they appear—in other words, the first value listed is assigned to the first column identified, the second value is assigned to the second column identified, and so on. Finally, each value supplied must be compatible with the data type of the column it is being assigned to. (For example, a character string value can only be assigned to a column that has character string data type.)

If values are provided (using the VALUES clause) for every column found in the table, the column name list can be omitted. In this case, the first value provided is assigned to the first column in the table, the second value is assigned to the second column, and so on. Thus, the row of data that was added to the DEPARTMENT table in the previous example could just as easily have been added by executing an INSERT statement that looks like this:

```
INSERT INTO department
  VALUES ('A01', 'ADMINISTRATION', 1000)
```

Along with literal values, two special tokens can be used to assign values to individual columns. The first token, DEFAULT, is used to assign a system- or user-supplied value to an identity column or a column that was defined as having a default constraint. The second, the NULL token, is used to assign a NULL value to any nullable column—that is, to any column that was *not* defined as having a NOT NULL constraint. (Identity columns, default constraints, and the NOT NULL constraint are covered in detail in Chapter 6, "Working with DB2 Tables, Views, and Indexes.")

Therefore, you could add a record that contains a NULL value for the MGRID column to the DEPARTMENT table presented earlier by executing an INSERT statement that looks like this:

```
INSERT INTO department
  VALUES ('A01', 'ADMINISTRATION', NULL)
```

By using another form of the INSERT statement (the second syntax version presented), the results of a query can be used to supply values for one or more columns as well. With this form, you supply a SELECT statement (known as a *subselect*) in place of a VALUES clause; this form of the INSERT statement performs a type of cut-and-paste operation in which values are retrieved from one base table or view and copied to another.

As you might imagine, the number of values that the subselect returns must match the number of columns identified in the column name list (or the number of columns found in the target table or view if a column name list is not provided). And the order of assignment is the same as that used when literal values are supplied.

Consequently, you could add a record to the DEPARTMENT table presented earlier, using the results of a subselect, by executing an INSERT statement that looks like this:

```
INSERT INTO department (deptno, deptname)
  SELECT deptno, deptname FROM organization
```

Notice that the INSERT statement in the previous example did not provide values for every column found in the DEPARTMENT table. Just as there are times when you might want to insert complete records into a table or view, there may be times when you want or are forced to insert partial records. On such occasions, you can construct and execute an INSERT statement in which only the columns you have data for are specified in the column names list provided. However, for such an INSERT statement to execute correctly, all columns in the table the record is being inserted into that *do not* appear in the column name list must either accept NULL values or have a defaults constraint associated with them. Otherwise, the INSERT statement will fail and an error will be returned.

The UPDATE Statement

Data in a database is rarely static. Over time, the need to change or remove one or more values stored in a table can, and will, arise. This is where the UPDATE statement comes into play—once a table has been created and populated, you can modify any of the data values stored in it by executing an UPDATE statement. The basic syntax for this statement is:

```
UPDATE [TableName | ViewName]
  SET [ColumnName] = [Value | NULL | DEFAULT], ...]
  <WHERE [Condition] | WHERE CURRENT OF [CursorName]>
```

or

```
UPDATE [TableName | ViewName]
  SET ([ColumnName], ...) =
    ([Value | NULL | DEFAULT], ...)
  <WHERE [Condition] | WHERE CURRENT OF [CursorName]>
```

or

```
UPDATE [TableName | ViewName]
  SET ([ColumnName], ...) = ([SELECTStatement])
  <WHERE [Condition] | WHERE CURRENT OF [CursorName]>
```

where:

TableName	Identifies, by name, the table that contains the data that is to be modified; this can be any type of table *except* a system catalog table or a system-maintained materialized query table
ViewName	Identifies, by name, the updatable view that contains the data that is to be modified; this can be any type of view *except* a system catalog view or a read-only view that does not have a corresponding INSTEAD OF trigger associated with it
ColumnName	Identifies, by name, one or more columns that contain data that is to be modified; each column name provided must identify an existing column in the table or updatable view specified, and it must not reference a column that was defined as being GENERATED ALWAYS AS IDENTITY
Value	Identifies one or more data values that are to be used to replace existing values for the column name(s) specified
SELECTStatement	Identifies a SELECT statement that, when executed, will produce data values that are to be used to replace existing values in the table or updatable view specified (by retrieving them from other tables, views, or both)

Condition	Identifies the search criterion that is to be used to locate one or more specific rows whose data values are to be modified; this condition is coded like the WHERE clause in a SELECT statement—we will look at the SELECT statement, along with the WHERE clause and its predicates, a little later
CursorName	Identifies, by name, the cursor that is currently positioned on the row whose data values are to be modified

⚠ **Important:** In most cases, you should provide an appropriate *Condition* (or use the WHERE CURRENT OF [*CursorName*] clause) when using the UPDATE statement. Otherwise, the update operation specified will be performed on every row found in the table or updatable view referenced.

Thus, if you have a base table named EMPLOYEE that has the following characteristics:

Column Name	Data Type
EMPNO	INTEGER
FNAME	CHAR(10)
LNAME	CHAR(10)
SEX	CHAR(1)
HIREDATE	DATE
TITLE	CHAR(25)
DEPT	CHAR(3)
SALARY	DECIMAL(8,2)

you can modify the records stored in this table such that the salary of every employee who has the title of DATABASE ADMINISTRATOR is increased by 10 percent, by executing an UPDATE statement that looks like this:

```
UPDATE employee SET salary = salary * 1.10
  WHERE title = 'DATABASE ADMINISTRATOR'
```

In addition to providing a way to change existing data values, the UPDATE statement can also be used to remove data stored in one or more columns—provided the columns are nullable. (Such delete operations are performed by changing the existing data value to NULL.) For example, to delete the values assigned to the DEPT column of every record found in the EMPLOYEE table presented earlier, you could execute an UPDATE statement that looks like this:

```
UPDATE employee SET dept = NULL
```

As with an INSERT statement, a subselect can be used with an UPDATE statement to supply values for one or more columns that are to be updated. This form of the UPDATE statement (the third syntax format presented) performs a type of cut-and-paste operation in which values are retrieved from one base table or view and copied over existing values stored in another.

And like the INSERT statement, the number of values the subselect returns must match the number of columns provided in the column name list. However, the subselect used *must not return more than one row*! If the subselect returns multiple rows, the update operation will fail and an error will be generated.

Consequently, to change the value assigned to the DEPT column of each record found in the EMPLOYEE table presented earlier, using the results of a subselect, you might execute an UPDATE statement that looks like this:

```
UPDATE employee SET (dept) =
  (SELECT deptno
     FROM department
     WHERE deptname = 'ADMINISTRATION')
```

It is important to note that update operations can be conducted in one of two ways: by performing what is known as a *searched update* or by performing what is referred to as a *positioned update*. So far, the examples presented have illustrated searched update operations. To perform a positioned update operation, a cursor must be created, opened, and then positioned on the row that is to be updated. (We will look at cursors shortly.) Then, to modify data stored in the row the cursor is currently positioned on, an UPDATE statement that contains a WHERE CURRENT OF [*CursorName*] clause must be executed.

Positioned update operations change data in a single row only, whereas searched update operations can modify several rows at one time. Because of their added complexity, positioned update operations are typically used in custom applications.

The DELETE Statement

While the UPDATE statement can be used to delete individual values from a base table or updatable view (by replacing those values with NULL), it cannot be used to remove entire records/rows. To remove one or more rows of data from a table or updatable view, the DELETE statement must be used instead. The basic syntax for the DELETE statement is:

```
DELETE FROM [TableName | ViewName]
    <WHERE [Condition] | WHERE CURRENT OF [CursorName]>
```

where:

TableName	Identifies, by name, the table that contains the data that is to be deleted; this can be any type of table *except* a system catalog table or a system-maintained materialized query table
ViewName	Identifies, by name, the updatable view that contains the data that is to be deleted; this can be any type of view *except* a system catalog view or a read-only view that does not have a corresponding INSTEAD OF trigger associated with it
Condition	Identifies the search criterion that is to be used to locate one or more specific rows that are to be deleted; this condition is coded like the WHERE clause in a SELECT statement
CursorName	Identifies, by name, the cursor that is currently positioned on the row whose values are to be deleted

••

Important: In most cases, you should provide an appropriate *Condition* (or use the WHERE CURRENT OF [*CursorName*] clause) when using the DELETE statement. Otherwise, every row found in the table or updatable view referenced will be deleted.

••

Thus, to remove every record for company ACME, INC. from a base table named SALES that has the following characteristics:

Column Name	Data Type
ORDERNO	CHAR(10)
COMPANY	CHAR(20)
PURCHASEDATE	DATE
SALESPERSON	INTEGER

you would execute a DELETE statement that looks like this:

```
DELETE FROM sales
  WHERE company = 'ACME, INC.'
```

On the other hand, to remove every record from the SALES table used in the previous example for which no salesperson has been assigned, you would execute a DELETE statement that looks more like this:

```
DELETE FROM sales
  WHERE salesperson IS NULL
```

As with update operations, delete operations can be conducted in one of two ways: by performing a *searched delete* or by performing a *positioned delete*. To perform a positioned delete operation, a cursor must be created, opened, and then positioned on the row that is to be deleted. Then, a DELETE statement that contains a WHERE CURRENT OF [*CursorName*] clause must be executed to remove the row the cursor is currently positioned on. Like positioned update operations, positioned delete operations work with a single row at a time and are typically used in applications.

A word about the TRUNCATE statement

Although the DELETE statement is typically used to delete individual records, it can be used to remove every row in a table. However, such delete operations can have unwanted side effects. For one thing, every time a row is deleted from a table, a record about the deletion is written to a transaction log file. Thus, the removal of every row in a table can cause a large number of log records to be generated, particularly if the table being emptied contains hundreds of thousands of rows.

Consequently, if circular logging is used or you have a limited amount of log space available, the influx of log records that is generated can cause a "log full" condition to occur. This, in turn, can cause the delete operation and any concurrently running transactions or operations to fail. Similarly, if any DELETE triggers have been defined on the table being emptied, those triggers can be fired multiple times. And depending on how the triggers were defined, other tables can be flooded with unnecessary information.

A better alternative to using the DELETE statement to empty a table of its contents is to use the TRUNCATE statement instead. Truncate operations do not generate transaction log records. And they give you more control over any DELETE triggers that may have been defined. The basic syntax for the TRUNCATE statement is:

```
TRUNCATE <TABLE> [TableName]
  <[DROP | REUSE] STORAGE>
  <IGNORE DELETE TRIGGERS | RESTRICT WHEN DELETE TRIGGERS>
```

where:

TableName   Identifies, by name, the table that is to be emptied of its contents

If the DROP STORAGE clause is specified with the TRUNCATE statement used, storage space that has been allocated for the table will be released and made available to the operating system. If the REUSE STORAGE clause is used instead, storage space for the table is merely emptied, and the space remains available for the table's future needs.

If the IGNORE DELETE TRIGGERS clause is specified with the TRUNCATE statement used, DELETE triggers defined on the table will not fire as the data in the table is being deleted. However, if the RESTRICT WHEN DELETE TRIGGERS clause is used, the system catalog will be examined to determine whether DELETE triggers on the table have been created. And if one or more triggers are found, the truncate operation will end and an error will be returned. (In this case, the table's storage remains intact and its records are left untouched.)

So, to remove every record from the SALES table presented earlier without firing any DELETE triggers that might have been created on the table, you could execute a TRUNCATE statement that looks like this:

```
TRUNCATE FROM sales
  IGNORE DELETE TRIGGERS
```

The SELECT Statement

Most databases are not used strictly as a place for archiving data. Therefore, at some point, the need to retrieve specific pieces of information (data) from a database will arise. The operation used to retrieve data from a database is called a *query* (because the database is usually searched to find the answer to some question), and the results returned are typically expressed either as a single data value or as multiple rows of data, otherwise known as a *result data set*, or simply *result set*. (If no values that correspond to the query specification are located, an empty result data set is returned to the user or application.)

All queries begin with a SELECT statement, which is a powerful SQL statement that can be used to construct a wide variety of queries containing an infinite number of variations. And because it is recursive, a single SELECT statement can derive its output from a successive number of nested SELECT statements, known as *subqueries*. (Earlier, you saw how to use a SELECT statement to provide data to INSERT and UPDATE statements. You can use a SELECT statement to provide input to other SELECT statements in a similar manner.) In its simplest form, the syntax for the SELECT statement is:

```
SELECT * FROM [TableName | ViewName]
```

where:

TableName	Identifies, by name, the table to retrieve data from
ViewName	Identifies, by name, the view to retrieve data from

Therefore, to construct a query that will retrieve all values currently stored in the DEPARTMENT table presented earlier, you would create a SELECT statement that looks like this:

```
SELECT * FROM department
```

And assuming the DEPARTMENT table is populated with the data shown in Table 5.1, when this query is executed, you should get a result data set that looks like this:

```
DEPTNO DEPTNAME              MGRID

------ -------------------- -----------

A01    ADMINISTRATION             1000
B01    PLANNING                   1002
C01    DEVELOPMENT                1007
D01    PERSONNEL                  1008
E01    OPERATIONS                    -
F01    SUPPORT                       -


  6 record(s) selected.
```

Table 5.1: Data stored in the DEPARTMENT table		
DEPTNO	**DEPTNAME**	**MGRID**
A01	ADMINISTRATION	1000
B01	PLANNING	1001
C01	DEVELOPMENT	1007
D01	PERSONNEL	1008
E01	OPERATIONS	(NULL)
F01	SUPPORT	(NULL)

A Closer Look at the SELECT Statement and Its Clauses

You just saw how to retrieve every value stored in a table (or the underlying table of a view). But what if you want to retrieve just the values stored in two columns of a table? Or you want to arrange the data retrieved alphabetically in ascending order? (Data is stored in a table in no particular order, and unless otherwise specified, a query will return data in the order in which it is found.) To perform these types of operations, you will need to use a more advanced form of the SELECT statement to construct the query needed. The syntax used to construct more advanced queries looks like this:

```
SELECT <ALL | DISTINCT>
  [* | [[Expression] <<AS> [NewColumnName]>, ...]
  FROM [TableName | ViewName <<AS> [CorrelationName]>, ...]
  <WhereClause>
  <GroupByClause>
  <HavingClause>
  <OrderByClause>
  <FetchFirstClause>
  <IsolationClause>
```

where:

Expression	Identifies one or more valid SQL language elements (such as column names or functions) that values are to be returned for when the SELECT statement is executed
NewColumnName	Identifies a column name to use in place of the column name that will be returned, by default, in the result data set produced by the SELECT statement
TableName	Identifies, by name, one or more tables to retrieve data from
ViewName	Identifies, by name, one or more views to retrieve data from
CorrelationName	Identifies a shorthand name that can be used to reference the table(s) or view(s) specified, in any of the SELECT statement clauses
WhereClause	Specifies a WHERE clause that is to be used with the SELECT statement
GroupByClause	Specifies a GROUP BY clause that is to be used with the SELECT statement
HavingClause	Specifies a HAVING clause that is to be used with the SELECT statement
OrderByClause	Specifies an ORDER BY clause that is to be used with the SELECT statement
FetchFirstClause	Specifies a FETCH FIRST clause that is to be used with the SELECT statement
IsolationClause	Specifies the isolation level under which the SELECT statement is to be run

If the DISTINCT clause is specified with the SELECT statement used, duplicate rows will be eliminated from the result data set returned. (Two rows are considered duplicates of one another if the value of every column of the first row is identical to the value of the corresponding column of the second row. For the purpose of determining whether two rows are identical, NULL values are considered equal.) However, if the ALL clause is specified or if neither clause is specified, duplicate rows will be returned. (If neither clause is specified, the ALL clause is used by default.) It is important to note that you cannot use the DISTINCT clause if you know that the result data set produced will contain BLOB, CLOB, DBCLOB, or XML data.

Thus, to retrieve just the first and last name of all employees found in the EMPLOYEE table presented earlier, you could execute a SELECT statement that looks like this:

```
SELECT fname, lname FROM employee
```

And if the EMPLOYEE table is populated with the data shown in Table 5.2, when this statement is executed you should get a result data set that looks like this:

```
FNAME        LNAME
----------   ----------
JAMES        DEAN
MARILYN      MONROE
HUMPHREY     BOGART
INGRID       BERGMAN
JAMES        CAGNEY
WILLIAM      HOLDEN
JACK         LEMMON
WALTER       MATTHAU
KATHARINE    HEPBURN
AVA          GARDNER

   10 record(s) selected.
```

Table 5.2: Data stored in the EMPLOYEE table							
EMPNO	FNAME	LNAME	SEX	HIREDATE	TITLE	DEPT	SALARY
1000	JAMES	DEAN	M	04/10/2002	PRESIDENT	A01	158096.00
1001	MARILYN	MONROE	F	05/10/2008	SYSTEMS ENGINEER	B01	103675.00
1002	HUMPHREY	BOGART	M	09/10/2006	DATABASE ADMINISTRATOR	C01	88192.00
1003	INGRID	BERGMAN	F	02/14/2001	PROGRAMMER/ ANALYST	C01	79475.00
1004	JAMES	CAGNEY	M	10/01/2004	TECHNICIAN I	E01	105787.00
1005	WILLIAM	HOLDEN	M	01/01/2012	TECHNICIAN I	F01	64428.00
1006	JACK	LEMMON	M	07/04/2007	TECHNICIAN II	E01	51584.00
1007	WALTER	MATTHAU	M	10/12/2003	DATABASE ADMINISTRATOR	F01	66943.00
1008	KATHARINE	HEPBURN	F	03/15/2002	MANAGER	C01	48903.00
1009	AVA	GARDNER	F	06/06/1999	ENGINEER	B01	59081.00

On the other hand, to retrieve just the first and last name of all employees from the EMPLOYEE table, *and* change the names of the FNAME and LNAME columns in the result data set produced to FIRST_NAME and LAST_NAME, respectively, you would need to execute a SELECT statement that looks more like this:

```
SELECT fname AS first_name,
       lname AS last_name
  FROM employee
```

When this statement is executed, you should get a result data set that looks like this:

```
FIRST_NAME LAST_NAME

---------- ----------

JAMES      DEAN
MARILYN    MONROE
HUMPHREY   BOGART
INGRID     BERGMAN
```

Continued

```
JAMES        CAGNEY
WILLIAM      HOLDEN
JACK         LEMMON
WALTER       MATTHAU
KATHARINE    HEPBURN
AVA          GARDNER


  10 record(s) selected.
```

You could produce the same result data set by executing a query that looks almost identical to the previous query, but that uses the correlation name E to refer to columns found in the EMPLOYEE table. The altered the SELECT statement will look something like this:

```
SELECT e.fname AS first_name,
       e.lname AS last_name
  FROM employee AS e
```

As you can see, the columns named FNAME and LNAME are qualified with the correlation name E, which is then assigned to the EMPLOYEE table in the FROM clause of the SELECT statement used. With this particular example, the use of a correlation name and a qualifier is unnecessary because data is being retrieved from a single table (which guarantees that columns have unique names).

However, if data is retrieved from two or more tables *and* if one or more columns in those tables have identical names, a correlation name and qualifier is needed to tell DB2 which table to get data from for a particular column. For example, suppose the DEPTNO column in the DEPARTMENT table presented earlier was named DEPT. To retrieve data from both this table and the EMPLOYEE table presented earlier, *and* to ensure that the DEPT values retrieved came from the EMPLOYEE table (instead of the DEPARTMENT table), you would need to construct a SELECT statement that looks something like this:

```
SELECT e.lname, e.dept, d.deptname
  FROM employee AS e, department AS d
  WHERE e.dept = d.dept
```

Here, the correlation names E and D, along with their corresponding qualifiers, tell DB2 when to retrieve data from the EMPLOYEE (E) table and when to retrieve it from the DEPARTMENT (D) table.

Other SELECT Statement Clauses

If you look at the syntax for the advanced form of the SELECT statement that was presented earlier, you will notice that a single SELECT statement can contain up to eight additional clauses:

- The DISTINCT clause
- The FROM clause
- The WHERE clause
- The GROUP BY clause
- The HAVING clause
- The ORDER BY clause
- The FETCH FIRST clause
- The isolation clause

(Incidentally, DB2 processes these clauses in the order that they are listed.) With the exception of the isolation clause, you can use each of these clauses to further control the size and contents of the result data sets produced in response to a query.

The Where Clause

The WHERE clause is used to tell DB2 *how* to select the rows that are to be returned in the result data set produced. When specified, the WHERE clause is followed by a *search condition*, which is nothing more than a simple test that, when applied to a row of data, will evaluate to TRUE, FALSE, or UNKNOWN. If the test evaluates to TRUE, the row is returned in the result data set produced; if the test evaluates to FALSE or UNKNOWN, the row is ignored.

The search condition itself consists of one or more predicates that are designed to make simple value comparisons. DB2 recognizes six common types of WHERE clause predicates; they are:

- Relational predicates
- BETWEEN
- LIKE

- IN
- EXISTS
- NULL

Each of these predicates can be used alone, or they can be combined, using parentheses or Boolean operators like AND and OR to create a WHERE clause that is quite complex.

Relational predicates

The *relational predicates* (or *comparison operators*) consist of a set of special operators that define a comparison relationship between the contents of a column and a constant value, the contents of two different columns (from the same or from different tables), or the results of some SQL expression and the results of another query (known as a *subquery*). The following comparison operators are available:

- = (Equal to)
- < (Less than)
- > (Greater than)
- <= (Less than or equal to)
- >= (Greater than or equal to)
- <> (Not equal to)

Furthermore, when any of these operators are used to define a comparison relationship between the results of an SQL expression and the results of a subquery, the qualifiers SOME, ANY, and ALL can be used to further control how rows are evaluated. When you use the qualifier SOME or ANY, the result of the comparison is considered TRUE if the relationship specified is true for at least one value returned by the subquery. If you use the qualifier ALL instead, the result of the comparison is considered TRUE only if the relationship is true for *every* value returned by the subquery.

Typically, relational predicates are used to include or exclude specific rows from the result data set produced. Therefore, to retrieve values from the EMPNO and SALARY columns of the EMPLOYEE table presented earlier and display information only for rows in which the value stored in the SALARY column is greater than $80,000.00, you would execute a SELECT statement that looks something like this:

```
SELECT empno, salary
  FROM employee
  WHERE salary > 80000.00
```

When this statement is executed, you should get a result data set that looks like this (provided the EMPLOYEE table is populated as shown in Table 5.2):

```
EMPNO        SALARY
-----------  ----------
       1000  158096.00
       1001  103675.00
       1002   88192.00
       1004  105787.00

 4 record(s) selected.
```

On the other hand, to retrieve values from the EMPNO, TITLE, HIREDATE, and SALARY columns of the EMPLOYEE table and display information only for employees who were hired before January 1, 2005, and whose salary is greater than $80,000.00 *or* who have the title of MANAGER, you would execute a SELECT statement that looks more like this:

```
SELECT empno, title, hiredate, salary
  FROM employee
  WHERE (hiredate < '2005-01-01' AND salary > 80000.00)
    OR (title = 'MANAGER')
```

This time, the result data set produced should look more like this (assuming the EMPLOYEE table is populated as shown in Table 5.2):

```
EMPNO        TITLE                          HIREDATE    SALARY
-----------  -----------------------------  ----------  ----------
       1000  PRESIDENT                      04/10/2002  158096.00
       1004  TECHNICIAN I                   10/01/2004  105787.00
       1008  MANAGER                        03/15/2002   48903.00

  3 record(s) selected.
```

It is important to note that the data types of all items involved in a relational predicate comparison must be compatible or the comparison will fail. However, in many cases, you can use built-in functions provided with DB2 to make any data type conversions needed, as well as to perform other operations that might be necessary or desired. For example, if you wanted to find out how many employees were hired in the month of October, you could query the EMPLOYEE table presented earlier with a SELECT statement that looks like this:

```
SELECT COUNT(*) AS num_employees
  FROM employee
  WHERE MONTHNAME(hiredate) = 'October'
```

Here, the built-in function MONTHNAME() produces a mixed-case character string value (representing the name of the month) for the month portion of each date value stored in the HIREDATE column of the EMPLOYEE table. This string value is then compared with the string 'October' to determine which rows are to be included in the final count—the built-in function COUNT() totals the matching records found. Consequently, if this query is executed against the EMPLOYEE table presented earlier, a result data set that looks like this will be produced (provided the EMPLOYEE table is populated as shown in Table 5.2):

```
NUM_EMPLOYEES
-------------
            2

  1 record(s) selected.
```

The BETWEEN predicate

The BETWEEN predicate is used to define a comparison relationship in which the contents of a column or the results of some SQL expression are checked to determine whether they fall within a specified range of values. As with relational predicates, the BETWEEN predicate is used to include or exclude individual rows from the result data set produced.

Thus, to retrieve values from the LNAME and SALARY columns of the EMPLOYEE table presented earlier and display information only for rows where the value stored in the SALARY column is greater than or equal to $50,000.00 and less than or equal to $90,000.00, you could execute a SELECT statement that looks like this:

```
SELECT lname, salary
  FROM employee
  WHERE salary BETWEEN 50000.00 AND 90000.00
```

And when this statement is executed, you should get a result data set that looks like this (assuming the EMPLOYEE table is populated as shown in Table 5.2):

```
LNAME        SALARY
----------   ----------
BOGART         88192.00
BERGMAN        79475.00
HOLDEN         64428.00
LEMMON         51584.00
MATTHAU        66943.00
GARDNER        59081.00

   6 record(s) selected.
```

Using the NOT (negation) operator with the BETWEEN predicate (or with any predicate, for that matter) reverses the meaning of the predicate. This means that, in the case of the BETWEEN predicate, the contents of a column or the results of an SQL expression are checked, and only values that fall *outside* the range specified are returned in the final result data set produced.

Therefore, to retrieve values from the LNAME and SALARY columns of the EMPLOYEE table presented earlier and display information only for rows where the value stored in the SALARY column is *less than or equal to* $50,000.00 and *greater than or equal to* $90,000.00, you could execute a SELECT statement that looks like this:

```
SELECT lname, salary
  FROM employee
  WHERE salary
    NOT BETWEEN 50000.00 AND 90000.00
```

And when this statement is executed, you should get a result data set that looks like this (provided the EMPLOYEE table is populated as shown in Table 5.2):

```
LNAME         SALARY
----------    ----------
DEAN          158096.00
MONROE        103675.00
CAGNEY        105787.00
HEPBURN        48903.00

    4 record(s) selected.
```

The LIKE predicate

The LIKE predicate is used to define a comparison relationship in which a character string value is checked to determine whether it contains a specific pattern of characters. The pattern of characters specified can consist of regular alphanumeric characters or a combination of alphanumeric characters and one or more of the following special metacharacters:

- The underscore character (_), which is treated as a wildcard character that stands for any single alphanumeric character
- The percent character (%), which is treated as a wildcard character that stands for any sequence of alphanumeric characters

Thus, to retrieve values from the EMPNO and LNAME columns of the EMPLOYEE table presented earlier and display information only for rows in which the value stored in the LNAME column begins with the letter M, you could execute a SELECT statement that looks like this:

```
SELECT empno, lname
  FROM employee
  WHERE lname LIKE 'M%'
```

When this statement is executed, you should get a result data set that looks like this (provided the EMPLOYEE table is populated as shown in Table 5.2):

```
EMPNO        LNAME
----------   ----------
      1001 MONROE
      1007 MATTHAU


  2 record(s) selected.
```

It is important to note that when using wildcard metacharacters, you must take care to ensure that they are placed in the appropriate location in the pattern string specified. For instance, specifying the character string pattern 'M%' (as in the previous example) will return only records for employees whose last name *begins with* the letter M. However, using the character string pattern '%M%' will return records for employees whose last name *contains* the character M (anywhere in the name). Consequently, had this character string pattern been used in the previous query, the result data set produced would have looked like this:

```
EMPNO        LNAME
----------   ----------
      1001 MONROE
      1003 BERGMAN
                                         Continued
```

```
     1006 LEMMON
     1007 MATTHAU


 4 record(s) selected.
```

You must also be careful when using uppercase and lowercase characters in pattern strings. If the data being examined was stored in a case-sensitive manner, the characters used in the pattern string specified must *exactly* match the value being looked for. Otherwise, no matching records will be found.

Important: Although the LIKE predicate provides a relatively easy way to search for character string values, it should be used with caution; the overhead involved in processing a LIKE predicate is very high and can be extremely resource-intensive.

The IN predicate

The IN predicate is used to define a comparison relationship in which a value is checked to determine whether it matches a value found in a finite set of values. This finite set of values can consist of one or more literal values that are coded directly in the IN predicate, or it can comprise a set of non-null values that were produced by a subquery.

Note: A subquery might contain search conditions of its own, and these search conditions might in turn include their own subqueries. When such *nested* subqueries are processed, DB2 executes the innermost query first and uses the results to execute the next outer query and so on until all nested queries have been processed.

Therefore, to retrieve values from the EMPNO and DEPT columns of the EMPLOYEE table presented earlier and display information only for rows in which the value stored in the DEPT column is either 'B01' or 'C01', you could execute a SELECT statement that looks like this:

```
SELECT lname, dept
  FROM employee
  WHERE dept IN ('B01', 'C01')
```

And when this statement is executed, you should get a result data set that looks like this (assuming the EMPLOYEE table is populated as shown in Table 5.2):

```
LNAME       DEPT
----------  ----
MONROE      B01
BOGART      C01
BERGMAN     C01
HEPBURN     C01
GARDNER     B01

  5 record(s) selected.
```

On the other hand, to retrieve values from the LNAME and DEPT columns of the EMPLOYEE table and display information only for rows in which an employee works in a department that currently does not have a manager, you would execute a SELECT statement that looks more like this:

```
SELECT lname, dept
  FROM employee
  WHERE dept IN
    (SELECT deptno FROM department WHERE mgrid IS NULL)
```

And when this statement is executed, you should get a result data set that looks like this (provided the DEPARTMENT table is populated as shown in Table 5.1 and the EMPLOYEE table is populated as shown in Table 5.2):

```
LNAME        DEPT

----------   ----

CAGNEY       E01

HOLDEN       F01

LEMMON       E01

MATTHAU      F01


   4 record(s) selected.
```

In this example, the subquery "SELECT deptno FROM department WHERE mgrid IS NULL"
produces a result data set that contains the values E01 and F01. The main query then checks
each value found in the DEPT column of the EMPLOYEE table against the values returned by
the subquery to see whether there is a match. If a match is found, the record is returned.

The EXISTS predicate

The EXISTS predicate is used to determine whether a particular value exists in a given
result data set. Consequently, the EXISTS predicate is always followed by a subquery, and
this predicate returns either TRUE or FALSE to indicate whether a specific value is found in
the result data set produced by the subquery provided.

Consequently, to find out which values in the DEPTNO column of the DEPARTMENT
table presented earlier are used in the DEPT column of the EMPLOYEE table (also presented
earlier), you could execute a SELECT statement that looks like this:

```
SELECT deptno, deptname
  FROM department
  WHERE EXISTS
    (SELECT dept
        FROM employee
        WHERE dept = deptno)
```

When this statement is executed, you should get a result data set that looks like this
(assuming the DEPARTMENT table is populated as shown in Table 5.1 and the EMPLOYEE
table is populated as shown in Table 5.2):

```
DEPTNO DEPTNAME
------ --------------------
A01    ADMINISTRATION
B01    PLANNING
C01    DEVELOPMENT
E01    OPERATIONS
F01    SUPPORT


   5 record(s) selected.
```

In most situations, the EXISTS predicate is ANDed with other WHERE clause predicates to control final row selection.

The NULL predicate

The NULL predicate is used to determine whether a particular value is NULL. So, to retrieve values from the DEPTNO and DEPTNAME columns of the DEPARTMENT table presented earlier and display information only for rows in which the value stored in the MGRID column is NULL, you could execute a SELECT statement that looks like this:

```
SELECT deptno, deptname
  FROM department
  WHERE mgrid IS NULL
```

And when this statement is executed, you should get a result data set that looks like this (assuming the DEPARTMENT table is populated as shown in Table 5.1):

```
DEPTNO DEPTNAME
------ --------------------
E01    OPERATIONS
F01    SUPPORT


   2 record(s) selected.
```

On the other hand, to retrieve the same information for rows in which the value stored in the MGRID column is *not* NULL, you would execute a SELECT statement that looks more like this:

```
SELECT deptno, deptname
  FROM department
  WHERE mgrid IS NOT NULL
```

Now, when the SELECT statement is executed, you should get a result data set that looks like this:

```
DEPTNO DEPTNAME
------ --------------------
A01    ADMINISTRATION
B01    PLANNING
C01    DEVELOPMENT
D01    PERSONNEL

   4 record(s) selected.
```

When using the NULL predicate, it is important to keep in mind that NULL, zero (0), and blank ("") are three different values. NULL is a special marker that represents missing information, whereas zero and blank (or an empty string) are actual values that can be stored in a column to indicate a specific value or the lack thereof. Moreover, some columns accept NULL values while other columns do not, depending upon how they have been defined. So, before you execute a query that checks for NULL values, make sure a NULL value can be stored in the column(s) being queried.

The GROUP BY Clause

The GROUP BY clause is used to instruct DB2 on how to organize rows of data that are returned in a result data set. In its simplest form, the GROUP BY clause is followed by a *grouping expression*, which usually consists of one or more names that refer to columns in the result data set that is to be organized.

The GROUP BY clause is frequently used to group columns whose values are to be provided as input to aggregate functions such as AVG() and SUM(). For example, to obtain the average salary for each department found in the DEPT column of the EMPLOYEE table presented earlier (using salary information stored in the SALARY column), round the average salaries to two decimal points, and organize the information retrieved by department, you would execute a SELECT statement that looks like this:

```
SELECT dept,
        DECIMAL(AVG(salary),9,2) AS avg_salary
  FROM employee
  GROUP BY dept
```

And when this statement is executed, you should get a result data set that looks like this (provided the EMPLOYEE table is populated as shown in Table 5.2):

```
DEPT AVG_SALARY
---- -----------
A01    158096.00
B01     81378.00
C01     72190.00
E01     78685.50
F01     65685.50

  5 record(s) selected.
```

Here, each row returned in the result data set produced contains the department code for a particular department, along with the average salary for individuals who work in that department.

●●

 Important: A common mistake that is often made with the GROUP BY clause is the addition of nonaggregate columns to the list of columns that are supplied as the grouping expression for the clause. Grouping is performed by combining all columns specified into a single concatenated key and breaking whenever that key value changes. Consequently, extraneous columns can cause unexpected breaks to occur.

●●

The GROUP BY ROLLUP Clause

The GROUP BY ROLLUP clause is used to analyze a collection of data in a single dimension, but at more than one level of detail. For example, you might group data by successively larger organizational units (such as team, department, and division) or by successively larger geographical units (such as city, county, state or province, and country).

Thus, if you were to change the GROUP BY clause used in the previous example to a GROUP BY ROLLUP clause, you would end up with a SELECT statement that looks like this:

```
SELECT dept,
       DECIMAL(AVG(salary),9,2) AS avg_salary
   FROM employee
   GROUP BY ROLLUP (dept)
```

And when this statement is executed, you should get a result data set that looks like this (assuming the EMPLOYEE table is populated as shown in Table 5.2):

```
DEPT AVG_SALARY

---- -----------
-        82616.40
A01     158096.00
B01      81378.00
C01      72190.00
                                        Continued
```

```
E01      78685.50
F01      65685.50


   6 record(s) selected.
```

Now, the result data set produced contains average salary information for all employees found in the EMPLOYEE table, regardless of which department they work in (the line in the result data set produced that has a NULL value for the DEPT column), as well as average salary information for each department found, rounded to two decimal points and organized by department.

This example contains only one grouping expression (the DEPT column) in the GROUP BY ROLLUP clause. However, multiple grouping expressions can be specified—for example, GROUP BY ROLLUP (dept, division). When multiple grouping expressions are supplied, DB2 groups the data by all expressions used, then by all but the last expression used, and so on until all grouping expressions have been processed. Then, it makes one final grouping that consists of the entire contents of the table or view. Consequently, when specifying multiple grouping expressions, it is important to ensure that the expressions provided are listed in the appropriate order; if one kind of group is logically contained inside another (for example, departments within a division), that group should be listed *after* the group it is logically contained in—for example, GROUP BY ROLLUP (city, state)—not before.

The GROUP BY CUBE Clause

The GROUP BY CUBE clause is used to analyze a collection of data by organizing it into groups, in multiple dimensions. For example, if you were to execute a SELECT statement that looks like this:

```
SELECT dept,
       sex,
       DECIMAL(AVG(salary),9,2) AS avg_salary
  FROM employee
  GROUP BY CUBE (dept, sex)
```

Assuming the EMPLOYEE table is populated as shown in Table 5.2 when this statement is executed, you should get a result data set that looks like this:

```
DEPT SEX AVG_SALARY
---- --- -----------
  -   F      72783.50
  -   M      89171.66
  -   -      82616.40
 A01  -     158096.00
 B01  -      81378.00
 C01  -      72190.00
 E01  -      78685.50
 F01  -      65685.50
 A01  M     158096.00
 B01  F      81378.00
 C01  F      64189.00
 C01  M      88192.00
 E01  M      78685.50
 F01  M      65685.50

  14 record(s) selected.
```

Here, the result data set produced contains:

- Average salary information for all employees, regardless of the department they work in (the lines in the result data set that have a NULL value for both the DEPT and the SEX columns)
- Average salary information for both male and female employees, regardless of the department they work in (lines in the result data set that have a NULL value for the DEPT column only)
- Average salary information for each department (lines in the result data set that have a NULL value for the SEX column only)
- Average salary information for both male and female employees, by department (lines in the result data set that have a value for every column)

In other words, the data in the result data set produced is grouped:

- By sex only
- By department only
- By sex and department
- As a single group that contains all sexes and all departments

In addition, the average salary information provided is rounded to two decimal points and the records returned are organized by department.

The term CUBE is intended to suggest that data is being analyzed in more than one dimension. In the previous example, you can see that data analysis was performed in two dimensions, which resulted in four types of groupings.

Suppose the following SELECT statement is executed:

```
SELECT dept,
       sex,
       title,
       DECIMAL(AVG(salary),9,2) AS avg_salary
  FROM employee
  GROUP BY CUBE (dept, sex, title)
```

In this case, data analysis will be performed in three dimensions (DEPT, SEX, and TITLE), and the data will be broken into eight types of groupings. In fact, you can determine the number of types of groupings a GROUP BY CUBE operation will produce by using the calculation 2^n, where n is the number of grouping expressions used in the GROUP BY CUBE clause.

The HAVING Clause

The HAVING clause is used to apply further selection criteria to columns that are referenced in a GROUP BY clause. Similar to the WHERE clause, the HAVING clause instructs DB2 on how to select rows that are to be returned in a result data set *from rows that have already been selected and grouped.*

Like the WHERE clause, the HAVING clause is followed by a search condition that acts as a simple test that, when applied to a row of data, evaluates to TRUE, FALSE, or UNKNOWN. If the test evaluates to TRUE, the row is returned in the result data set produced; if the test evaluates to FALSE or UNKNOWN, the row is ignored. Similarly, the search condition of a HAVING clause can utilize the same set of predicates that the WHERE clause recognizes.

Therefore, to obtain the average salary for each department in the DEPT column of the EMPLOYEE table presented earlier (using salary information stored in the SALARY column), round the average salaries to two decimal points and organize the information retrieved by department, and *display information only for rows in which the average salary is greater than $75,000.00*, you would execute a SELECT statement that looks like this:

```
SELECT dept,
       DECIMAL(AVG(salary),9,2) AS avg_salary
  FROM employee
  GROUP BY dept
  HAVING AVG(salary) > 75000
```

And when this statement is executed, you should get a result data set that looks like this (provided the EMPLOYEE table is populated as shown in Table 5.2):

```
DEPT AVG_SALARY

---- -----------
A01    158096.00
B01     81378.00
E01     78685.50

  3 record(s) selected.
```

The ORDER BY Clause

The ORDER BY clause is used to instruct DB2 on how to sort (order) the rows that are returned in a result data set. When specified, this clause is followed by the name (or position number) of one or more columns whose data values are to be sorted and a keyword that indicates whether the data is to be sorted in ascending (ASC) or descending (DESC) order. If no sort order is specified, data is sorted in ascending order by default. Multiple columns can be used, and each column can be ordered in ascending or descending order, independently of the others. However, when multiple columns are specified, the order in which the columns are listed determines the order in which the requested sorts are performed. First, data is sorted for the first column specified (the *primary sort*), then the sorted data is sorted again for the next column specified, and so on until the data has been sorted for every column identified.

> **Note:** Columns that have a data type of BLOB, CLOB, DBCLOB, XML, a structured data type, or a user-defined data type that is based on one of these data types cannot be specified in an ORDER BY clause.

Thus, to retrieve values from the LNAME and DEPT columns of the EMPLOYEE table presented earlier and sort the information returned by department (DEPT) in ascending order, followed by last name (LNAME) in descending order, you could execute a SELECT statement that looks like this:

```
SELECT lname, dept
  FROM employee
  ORDER BY dept ASC, lname DESC
```

When this statement is executed, you should get a result data set that looks like this (assuming the EMPLOYEE table is populated as shown in Table 5.2):

```
LNAME        DEPT
----------   ----
DEAN         A01
MONROE       B01
GARDNER      B01
HEPBURN      C01
BOGART       C01
BERGMAN      C01
LEMMON       E01
                                            Continued
```

```
CAGNEY      E01
MATTHAU     F01
HOLDEN      F01


   10 record(s) selected.
```

Using the ORDER BY clause is relatively easy if the result data set produced consists only of named columns. But what if you need to order the result data set according to data found in a column that cannot be specified by name (such as summary column)? In these situations, an integer value representing the column's position, as it appears in the result data set produced, can be used instead. (The first or leftmost column in a result data set is considered column 1, the next is column 2, and so on.) Consequently, the previous query could just have easily have been written as:

```
SELECT lname, dept
   FROM employee
   ORDER BY 2 ASC, 1 DESC
```

It is important to note that even though integer values are used primarily to refer to columns that cannot be specified by name, you can use them in place of any column, including columns you can reference by name.

The FETCH FIRST Clause

The FETCH FIRST clause is used to limit the number of rows that are returned in a result data set. When used, the FETCH FIRST clause must be followed by a positive integer value, which in turn must be followed by the words ROWS ONLY. This informs DB2 that the user or application executing the query does not want to see more than *n* number of rows, regardless of how many rows might be returned if the FETCH FIRST clause were not specified.

Therefore, to retrieve just the first five values from the EMPNO, LNAME, and DEPT columns of the EMPLOYEE table presented earlier, you would execute a SELECT statement that looks like this:

```
SELECT empno, lname, dept
  FROM employee
  FETCH FIRST 5 ROWS ONLY
```

And when this statement is executed, you should get a result data set that looks like this (provided the EMPLOYEE table is populated as shown in Table 5.2):

```
EMPNO        LNAME       DEPT
----------- ----------- ----

       1000 DEAN        A01
       1001 MONROE      B01
       1002 BOGART      C01
       1003 BERGMAN     C01
       1004 CAGNEY      E01


  5 record(s) selected.
```

If you use other clauses to control the size and contents of the result data set produced *before* returning a specified number of rows, the actual values returned can differ, depending on where the FETCH FIRST clause appears. For example, if an ORDER BY clause were added to the query just executed, making it look like this:

```
SELECT empno, lname, dept
  FROM employee
  ORDER BY lname DESC
  FETCH FIRST 5 ROWS ONLY
```

The result data set produced would look something like this:

```
EMPNO        LNAME       DEPT
-----------  ----------  ----
      1001 MONROE       B01
      1007 MATTHAU      F01
      1006 LEMMON       E01
      1005 HOLDEN       F01
      1008 HEPBURN      C01

  5 record(s) selected.
```

Consequently, the FETCH FIRST clause can be used in conjunction with other clauses to control which rows are processed by other operations, such as updates and deletes, that obtain their values from a subquery.

The Isolation Clause

The isolation clause is used to specify the isolation level a query is to be run under, and in some cases, to suggest the type of lock DB2 should acquire and hold on the data being queried. (Isolation levels and locks are discussed in great detail in Chapter 7, "Data Concurrency.") The basic syntax for the isolation clause is:

```
WITH [RR <USE AND KEEP [SHARE | UPDATE | EXCLUSIVE] LOCKS> |
      RS <USE AND KEEP [SHARE | UPDATE | EXCLUSIVE] LOCKS> |
      CS |
      UR]
```

where:

RR	Indicates the query is to be run under the Repeatable Read isolation level
RS	Indicates the query is to be run under the Read Stability isolation level
CS	Indicates the query is to be run under the Cursor Stability isolation level
UR	Indicates the query is to be run under the Uncommitted Read isolation level

If the USE AND KEEP SHARE LOCKS clause is specified (along with RR or RS), concurrent processes will be allowed to acquire Share (S) or Update (U) locks on the data being queried; if the USE AND KEEP UPDATE LOCKS clause is specified, concurrent processes can obtain Share (S) locks on the data, but will be prevented from acquiring Update (U) or Exclusive (X) locks; and if the USE AND KEEP EXCLUSIVE LOCKS clause is specified, concurrent processes will not be allowed to acquire locks of any kind.

Thus, to retrieve values from the EMPNO, FNAME, and LNAME columns of the EMPLOYEE table presented earlier while running under the Repeatable Read (RR) isolation level, you could execute a SELECT statement that looks like this:

```
SELECT empno, fname, lname
  FROM employee
  WITH RR
```

A Word About Common Table Expressions

Common table expressions are used to construct temporary tables that reside in memory and that exist only for the life of the SQL statements that define them. (In fact, the table that is created for a common table expression can be referenced only by the SQL statement that created it.) Common table expressions are typically used:

- In place of a view when the creation of a view is undesirable, when the general use of a view is not required, or when positioned update or delete operations are not desired
- To enable grouping by a column that is derived from either a subquery or a scalar function that performs some external action
- When the desired result data set is based on host variables
- When the same result data set is to be used by several different queries
- When the results of a query must be derived using recursion

The syntax used to construct a common table expression is:

```
WITH [TableName]
  <([ColumnName], ...)>
  AS ([SELECTStatement])
```

where:

TableName	Identifies a unique name that is to be assigned to the temporary table that is to be created
ColumnName	Identifies one or more names that are to be assigned to columns that are to be part of the temporary table—each column name provided must be unique and unqualified; if you do not provide values for this parameter, names derived from the result data set produced by the *SELECTStatement* specified will be used by default; if you provide a list of column names, the number of column names supplied must match the number of columns that will be returned by the SELECT statement used to create the temporary table (if a common table expression is recursive, or if the result data set produced by the SELECT statement contains duplicate column names, column names *must* be specified)
SELECTStatement	Identifies a SELECT statement that, when executed, will produce the data values that are to be stored in the temporary table that is to be created (by retrieving them from other tables, views, or both)

So, if you wanted to create a common table expression that retrieves values from the LNAME, HIREDATE, and SEX columns of the EMPLOYEE table presented earlier, stores them in a temporary table (named EMP_INFO), and then queries the temporary table to obtain last name and hire date information for female employees, you could execute an SQL statement that looks like this:

```
WITH
    emp_info (lname, hiredate, sex)
      AS (SELECT lname, hiredate, sex FROM employee)
    SELECT lname, hiredate FROM emp_info WHERE sex = 'F'
```

And when this statement is executed, you should get a result data set that looks like this (provided the EMPLOYEE table is populated as shown in Table 5.2):

```
LNAME        HIREDATE

----------   ----------
MONROE       05/10/2008
BERGMAN      02/14/2001
HEPBURN      03/15/2002
GARDNER      06/06/1999


  4 record(s) selected.
```

Multiple common table expressions can be specified with a single WITH keyword/ statement, and each expression specified can be referenced, by name, in the FROM clause of subsequent common table expressions. However, if multiple table expressions are defined using a single WITH keyword/statement, the name you assign to each temporary table must be unique from all other table names used.

It is also important to note that the name assigned to any temporary table created by a WITH keyword/statement will take precedence over any existing base tables, views, or aliases that have the same qualified name. In this case, if a SELECT statement in the common table expression attempts to reference a table, view, or alias that exists outside the expression, it will actually be working with the temporary table that was created in the expression. (Existing tables, views, and aliases whose names match that of the temporary table are not altered but are simply inaccessible.)

A Word About CASE Expressions

One concise and efficient way to display compared values in a readable format is to use one or more SQL CASE expressions in the selection list of a query. Each CASE operation evaluates an expression and supplies a value, if a certain condition is met. CASE expressions can take one of two forms: *simple* or *searched.*

The basic syntax used to create a simple CASE expression is:

```
CASE [Expression1]
  [WHEN [Expression2] THEN [Result1], ...]
ELSE [Result2]
<END>
```

where:

Expression1	Identifies an expression or value that is to be compared against one or more *Expression2* expressions or values
Expression2	Identifies one or more expressions or values that, when compared with *Expression1*, evaluate to TRUE or FALSE
Result1	Identifies a value to use when a search condition evaluates to TRUE
Result2	Identifies a value to use when a search condition evaluates to FALSE

Thus, if you wanted to retrieve values from the EMPNO, LNAME, and DEPT columns of the EMPLOYEE table presented earlier, and you knew that the first character of each department code corresponds to a specific pay grade, you could use a simple CASE expression to convert the department codes found into a description of the pay grade that each employee has been assigned by executing a SELECT statement that looks like this:

```
SELECT empno, lname,
  CASE SUBSTR(dept,1,1)
    WHEN 'A' THEN 'GRADE-60'
    WHEN 'B' THEN 'GRADE-58'
    WHEN 'C' THEN 'GRADE-40'
    ELSE 'UNKNOWN GRADE'
  END AS pay_grade
  FROM employee
```

When this statement is executed, you should get a result data set that looks like this (assuming the EMPLOYEE table is populated as shown in Table 5.2):

```
EMPNO        LNAME        PAY_GRADE

-----------  -----------  --------------
      1000 DEAN           GRADE-60
      1001 MONROE         GRADE-58
      1002 BOGART         GRADE-40
                                         Continued
```

```
1003  BERGMAN     GRADE-40
1004  CAGNEY      UNKNOWN GRADE
1005  HOLDEN      UNKNOWN GRADE
1006  LEMMON      UNKNOWN GRADE
1007  MATTHAU     UNKNOWN GRADE
1008  HEPBURN     GRADE-40
1009  GARDNER     GRADE-58


 10 record(s) selected.
```

On the other hand, the basic syntax used to create a searched CASE expression is:

```
CASE
   [WHEN [SearchCondition] THEN [Result1], ...]
ELSE [Result2]
<END>
```

where:

SearchCondition	Identifies one or more logical conditions that evaluate to TRUE or FALSE
Result1	Identifies a value to use when the search condition specified evaluates to TRUE
Result2	Identifies a value to use when the search condition specified evaluates to FALSE

Therefore, to retrieve values from the TITLE and SALARY columns of the EMPLOYEE table presented earlier and calculate salary increases based on the job each employee performs, you could execute a SELECT statement that looks something like this:

```
SELECT title, salary AS old_salary,
  CASE
    WHEN title = 'PRESIDENT' THEN salary * 1.15
    WHEN title LIKE 'DATABASE%' THEN salary * 1.10
```
Continued

```
    WHEN title LIKE 'TECH%' THEN salary * 1.08
    ELSE salary * 1.05
  END AS new_salary
  FROM employee
```

And when this statement is executed, you should get a result data set that looks like this (provided the EMPLOYEE table is populated as shown in Table 5.2):

```
  TITLE                          OLD_SALARY NEW_SALARY
  ---------------------------    ---------- -------------

  PRESIDENT                       158096.00  181810.4000
  SYSTEMS ENGINEER                103675.00  108858.7500
  DATABASE ADMINISTRATOR           88192.00   97011.2000
  PROGRAMMER/ANALYST               79475.00   83448.7500
  TECHNICIAN I                    105787.00  114249.9600
  TECHNICIAN I                     64428.00   69582.2400
  TECHNICIAN II                    51584.00   55710.7200
  DATABASE ADMINISTRATOR           66943.00   73637.3000
  MANAGER                          48903.00   51348.1500
  ENGINEER                         59081.00   62035.0500

    10 record(s) selected.
```

In this example, a searched CASE expression was used to perform the necessary calculations.

As you can see from the two previous examples, the value returned by a CASE expression is the value of the result-expression (*Result1*) that follows a condition that evaluates to TRUE. If no condition evaluates to TRUE and the ELSE keyword is provided, the CASE expression returns the value of the second result-expression (*Result2*). If, however, no condition evaluates to TRUE and the ELSE keyword is not provided, the result is assumed to be NULL.

It is important to note that when a condition evaluates to UNKNOWN (because a NULL value was returned), the CASE expression is considered not TRUE and therefore is treated the same as a CASE expression that evaluates to FALSE. It is also important to note that the data type of the search condition specified must be compatible with the data type of each result-expression returned.

Joining Tables

So far, the majority of the examples we have looked at have been focused on retrieving data from a single table. However, one of the more powerful features of the SELECT statement (and the feature that makes data normalization possible) is its ability to retrieve data from two or more tables by performing what is known as a *join operation*. In its simplest form, the syntax for a SELECT statement that performs a join operation is:

```
SELECT * FROM [TableName, ...]
```

where:

TableName   Identifies, by name, at least two tables that data is to be retrieved from

Thus, to retrieve values from all columns found in the EMPLOYEE and DEPARTMENT tables presented earlier, you would execute a SELECT statement that looks like this:

```
SELECT * FROM employee, department
```

When this statement is executed, the result data set produced will contain every possible combination of the rows found in both tables. This type of result data set is referred to as a *Cartesian product*. With Cartesian products, every row in the result data set produced consists of a row from the first table referenced concatenated with a row from the second table referenced, in turn concatenated with a row from the third table referenced, and so on. Therefore, the total number of rows returned is always the product of the number of rows in all tables referenced. For example, if the DEPARTMENT table is populated as shown in Table 5.1 (with 6 rows) and the EMPLOYEE table is populated as shown in Table 5.2 (with 10 rows), the query just presented will produce a result data set that consists of 60 rows (6 × 10 = 60).

• •

 Important: Cartesian product joins should be used with extreme caution when working with large tables; a significant amount of resources can be required to perform such operations, and the operation itself can have a negative impact on performance.

• •

Because Cartesian products can generate large result data sets, they typically are not used very often. Instead, most join operations involve collecting data from two or more tables that have a specific column in common, and combining the results. This type of join is referred to as an *inner join*, and by far, inner joins are the simplest type of join operation to perform. Aside from Cartesian products and inner joins, one other type of join operation is possible—an *outer join*. And just as there is a difference between Cartesian products and inner joins, there is a difference between inner and outer joins.

Inner Joins

An inner join can be thought of as the cross product of two tables, in which every row in one table is paired with rows in another table that have matching values in one or more columns. Figure 5.1 depicts a conceptual view of an inner join operation; the shaded area in this illustration represents matching data found in both tables that was used to link the two tables together.

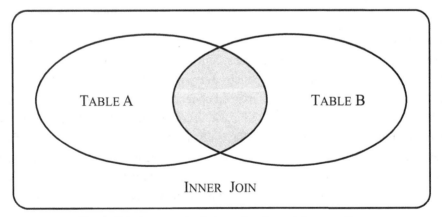

Figure 5.1: A conceptual view of an inner join operation

One way to perform an inner join is by executing a SELECT statement that looks like this:

```
SELECT
  [* | [[Expression] <<AS> [NewColumnName]>, ...]
  FROM [TableName <<AS> [CorrelationName]>, ...]
  [JoinCondition]
```

where:

Expression	Identifies one or more valid SQL language elements (typically column names) that values are to be returned for when the SELECT statement is executed
NewColumnName	Identifies a column name to use in place of the column name that will be returned, by default, in the result data set produced by the SELECT statement
TableName	Identifies, by name, two or more tables to retrieve data from
CorrelationName	Identifies a shorthand name that can be used to reference the tables specified in the *JoinCondition* provided
JoinCondition	Identifies the condition that is to be used to join the tables specified; typically, this is a WHERE clause in which the values of a column in one table are compared with the values of a similar column in another table

Therefore, to retrieve values from the LNAME and DEPTNAME columns of the EMPLOYEE and DEPARTMENT tables presented earlier, using a simple inner join operation, you could execute a SELECT statement that looks like this:

```
SELECT e.lname, d.deptname
  FROM employee AS e, department AS d
  WHERE e.dept = d.deptno
```

And when this statement is executed, you should get a result data set that looks like this (assuming the DEPARTMENT table is populated as shown in Table 5.1 and the EMPLOYEE table is populated as shown in Table 5.2):

```
LNAME       DEPTNAME

----------  --------------------

DEAN        ADMINISTRATION
MONROE      PLANNING
GARDNER     PLANNING
BOGART      DEVELOPMENT
HEPBURN     DEVELOPMENT
BERGMAN     DEVELOPMENT
CAGNEY      OPERATIONS
LEMMON      OPERATIONS
HOLDEN      SUPPORT
MATTHAU     SUPPORT


   10 record(s) selected.
```

The following SELECT statement syntax can be used to perform inner join operations as well:

```
SELECT
  [* | [[Expression] <<AS> [NewColumnName]>, ...]
  FROM [TableName1] <<AS> [CorrelationName1]>
  <INNER> JOIN
  [TableName2] <<AS> [CorrelationName2]>]
  ON [JoinCondition]
```

where:

Expression	Identifies one or more valid SQL language elements (typically column names) that values are to be returned for when the SELECT statement is executed
NewColumnName	Identifies a column name to use in place of the column name that will be returned, by default, in the result data set produced by the SELECT statement
TableName1	Identifies, by name, the first table to retrieve data from

CorrelationName1	Identifies a shorthand name that can be used to reference the first table specified (via the *TableName1* parameter) in the *JoinCondition* provided
TableName2	Identifies, by name, the second table to retrieve data from
CorrelationName2	Identifies a shorthand name that can be used to reference the second table specified (via the *TableName2* parameter) in the *JoinCondition* provided
JoinCondition	Identifies the condition that is to be used to join the two tables specified; typically, this is a WHERE clause in which the values of a column in one table are compared with the values of a similar column in the other table

Therefore, the inner join operation that was performed in the previous example could just as easily have been performed by executing a SELECT statement that looks like this:

```
SELECT e.lname, d.deptname
  FROM employee AS e INNER JOIN department AS d
  ON e.dept = d.deptno
```

Figure 5.2 illustrates how this inner join operation will look if the tables used (EMPLOYEE and DEPARTMENT) are defined and populated as depicted.

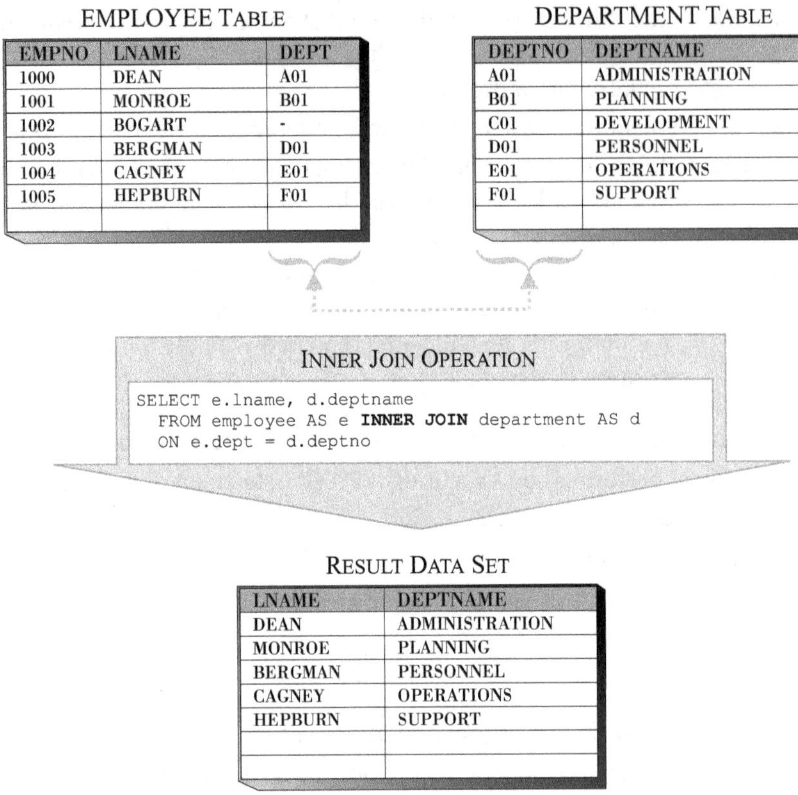

EMPLOYEE TABLE

EMPNO	LNAME	DEPT
1000	DEAN	A01
1001	MONROE	B01
1002	BOGART	-
1003	BERGMAN	D01
1004	CAGNEY	E01
1005	HEPBURN	F01

DEPARTMENT TABLE

DEPTNO	DEPTNAME
A01	ADMINISTRATION
B01	PLANNING
C01	DEVELOPMENT
D01	PERSONNEL
E01	OPERATIONS
F01	SUPPORT

INNER JOIN OPERATION

```
SELECT e.lname, d.deptname
  FROM employee AS e INNER JOIN department AS d
  ON e.dept = d.deptno
```

RESULT DATA SET

LNAME	DEPTNAME
DEAN	ADMINISTRATION
MONROE	PLANNING
BERGMAN	PERSONNEL
CAGNEY	OPERATIONS
HEPBURN	SUPPORT

Figure 5.2: A simple inner join operation

Inner joins work well as long as every row found in the first table has a corresponding row in the second table referenced. But when that is not the case, the result data set produced may be missing rows that exist in one or both of the tables being joined. For example, the result data set in Figure 5.2 does not contain records for BOGART (found in the EMPLOYEE table) and DEVELOPMENT (found in the DEPARTMENT table). That's because the value in the DEPT column of the BOGART record does not have a matching value in the DEPTNO column of the DEPARTMENT table. Similarly, the value in the DEPTNO column of the DEVELOPMENT table does not have a matching value in the DEPT column of the EMPLOYEE table. Consequently, to generate a result data set that contains one or both of these records, you will need to perform an outer join operation.

Outer joins

Outer join operations are used when a join operation is desired and rows that would normally be eliminated by an inner join operation must be preserved. With DB2, three types of outer join operations are available. They are:

- **Left outer join:** With a left outer join operation, rows that an inner join operation would have returned, together with rows stored in the leftmost table of the join operation (that is, the table listed *first* in the OUTER JOIN clause) that the inner join operation would have eliminated, are returned in the result data set produced.
- **Right outer join:** With a right outer join operation, rows that an inner join operation would have returned, together with rows stored in the rightmost table of the join operation (that is, the table listed *last* in the OUTER JOIN clause) that the inner join operation would have eliminated, are returned in the result data set produced.
- **Full outer join:** With a full outer join operation, rows that an inner join operation would have returned, together with rows stored in both tables of the join operation that the inner join operation would have eliminated, are returned in the result data set produced.

To understand the basic principles behind an outer join operation, it helps to look at an example. Suppose Table A and Table B are joined by an inner join operation. Any row in either table that does not have a matching row in the other table (based on the rules of the join condition) is eliminated from the result data set produced.

In contrast, if Table A and Table B are joined with an outer join, any row in either table that does not contain a matching row in the other table can be included in the result data set produced (exactly once). Thus, an outer join operation adds nonmatching rows to the final result data set produced, whereas an inner join operation excludes them. A left outer join of Table A with Table B preserves all nonmatching rows found in Table A; a right outer join of Table A with Table B preserves all nonmatching rows found in Table B; and a full outer join preserves all nonmatching rows found in both Table A *and* Table B. Figure 5.3 depicts a conceptual view of each of these join operations. The shaded areas represent the data that will be returned in the result data set produced by each type of outer join.

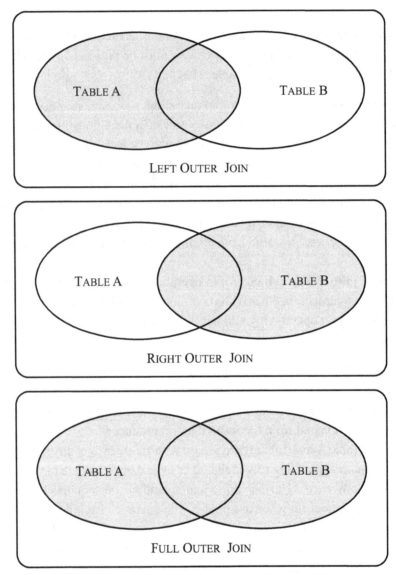

Figure 5.3: A conceptual view of outer join operations

The following syntax is used to perform an outer join operation:

```
SELECT
  [* | [[Expression] <<AS> [NewColumnName]>, ...]
  FROM [TableName1] <<AS> [CorrelationName1]>
  [LEFT | RIGHT | FULL] OUTER JOIN
  [TableName2] <<AS> [CorrelationName2]>]
  ON [JoinCondition]
```

where:

Expression	Identifies one or more valid SQL language elements (typically column names) that values are to be returned for when the SELECT statement is executed
NewColumnName	Identifies a column name to use in place of the column name that will be returned, by default, in the result data set produced by the SELECT statement
TableName1	Identifies, by name, the first table to retrieve data from; this table is considered the *leftmost* table in the outer join operation
CorrelationName1	Identifies a shorthand name that can be used to reference the first table specified (via the *TableName1* parameter), in the JoinCondition provided
TableName2	Identifies, by name, the second table to retrieve data from; this table is considered the *rightmost* table in the outer join operation
CorrelationName2	Identifies a shorthand name that can be used to reference the second table specified (via the *TableName2* parameter), in the JoinCondition provided
JoinCondition	Identifies the condition that is to be used to join the two tables specified; typically, this is a WHERE clause in which the values of a column in one table are compared with the values of a similar column in the other table

Thus, you can perform a simple left outer join operation by executing a SELECT statement that looks like this:

```
SELECT e.lname, d.deptname
  FROM employee AS e LEFT OUTER JOIN department AS d
  ON e.dept = d.deptno
```

Figure 5.4 illustrates how such a join operation will look if the tables used (EMPLOYEE and DEPARTMENT) are defined and populated as depicted.

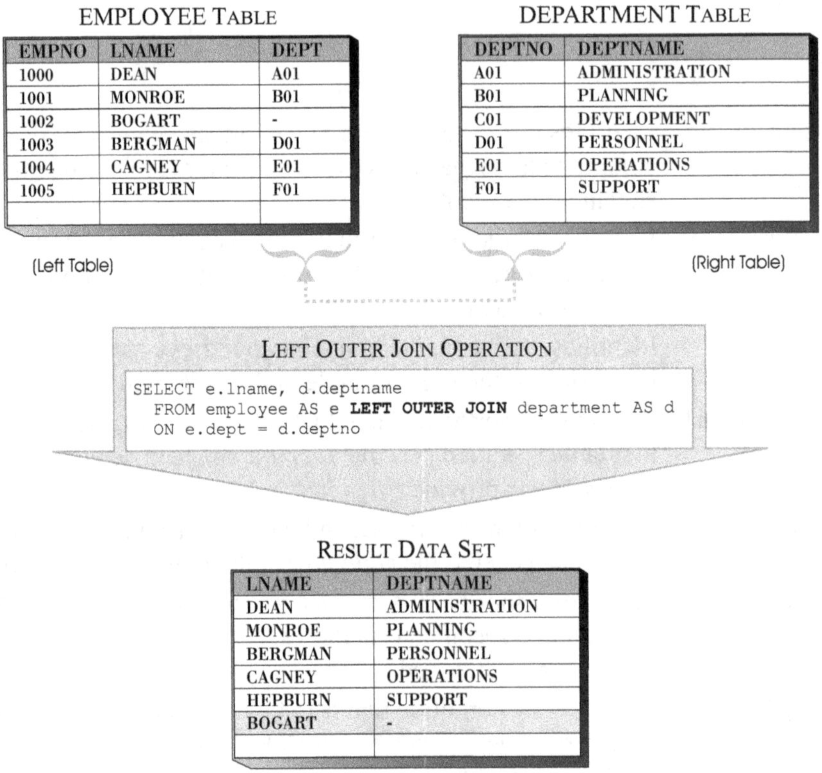

EMPLOYEE TABLE

EMPNO	LNAME	DEPT
1000	DEAN	A01
1001	MONROE	B01
1002	BOGART	-
1003	BERGMAN	D01
1004	CAGNEY	E01
1005	HEPBURN	F01

(Left Table)

DEPARTMENT TABLE

DEPTNO	DEPTNAME
A01	ADMINISTRATION
B01	PLANNING
C01	DEVELOPMENT
D01	PERSONNEL
E01	OPERATIONS
F01	SUPPORT

(Right Table)

LEFT OUTER JOIN OPERATION

```
SELECT e.lname, d.deptname
  FROM employee AS e LEFT OUTER JOIN department AS d
  ON e.dept = d.deptno
```

RESULT DATA SET

LNAME	DEPTNAME
DEAN	ADMINISTRATION
MONROE	PLANNING
BERGMAN	PERSONNEL
CAGNEY	OPERATIONS
HEPBURN	SUPPORT
BOGART	-

Figure 5.4: A simple left outer join operation

Here, the employee record for BOGART is included in the result data set produced, even though the DEPT column value for this record does not have a matching value in the DEPTNO column of the DEPARTMENT table. However, the record for the DEVELOPMENT department is excluded because the DEPTNO column of this record does not have a matching value in the DEPT column of the EMPLOYEE table.

In contrast, you can conduct a simple right outer join operation by executing a SELECT statement that looks like this:

```
SELECT e.lname, d.deptname
  FROM employee AS e RIGHT OUTER JOIN department AS d
  ON e.dept = d.deptno
```

Figure 5.5 illustrates how this type of a join operation will look if the tables used (EMPLOYEE and DEPARTMENT) are defined and populated as depicted.

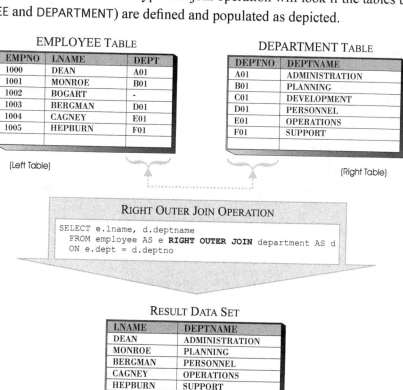

Figure 5.5: A simple right outer join operation

Now, the result data set produced includes the record for the DEVELOPMENT department, even though the value in the DEPTNO column for this record does not have a matching value in the DEPT column of the EMPLOYEE table. However, the employee record for BOGART is excluded because the DEPT column of this record does not have a matching value in the DEPTNO column of the DEPARTMENT table.

Finally, a simple full outer join operation can be conducted by executing a SELECT statement that looks like this:

```
SELECT e.lname, d.deptname
  FROM employee AS e FULL OUTER JOIN department AS d
  ON e.dept = d.deptno
```

Figure 5.6 illustrates how such a join operation will look if the tables used (EMPLOYEE and DEPARTMENT) are defined and populated as depicted.

EMPLOYEE TABLE

EMPNO	LNAME	DEPT
1000	DEAN	A01
1001	MONROE	B01
1002	BOGART	-
1003	BERGMAN	D01
1004	CAGNEY	E01
1005	HEPBURN	F01

(Left Table)

DEPARTMENT TABLE

DEPTNO	DEPTNAME
A01	ADMINISTRATION
B01	PLANNING
C01	DEVELOPMENT
D01	PERSONNEL
E01	OPERATIONS
F01	SUPPORT

(Right Table)

FULL OUTER JOIN OPERATION

```
SELECT e.lname, d.deptname
  FROM employee AS e FULL OUTER JOIN department AS d
  ON e.dept = d.deptno
```

RESULT DATA SET

LNAME	DEPTNAME
DEAN	ADMINISTRATION
MONROE	PLANNING
BERGMAN	PERSONNEL
CAGNEY	OPERATIONS
HEPBURN	SUPPORT
-	DEVELOPMENT
BOGART	-

Figure 5.6: A simple full outer join operation

Here, the result data set produced includes records for both BOGART and DEVELOPMENT, even though the DEPT column value for the BOGART record does not have a matching value in the DEPTNO column of the DEPARTMENT table, and the value in the DEPTNO column for the DEVELOPMENT record does not have a matching value in the DEPT column of the EMPLOYEE table.

Using a Set Operator to Combine the Results of Two or More Queries

While a join operation can be used to retrieve data from two or more dissimilar tables, a special operator known as a *set operator* can be used to query two tables that have similar definitions. Essentially, a set operator combines the output from two or more individual queries to produce a single result data set. Consequently, set operators require that the tables being queried have the same number of columns, and that each of these columns have the same data types assigned to them.

The following set operators are available with DB2:

- **UNION**: The UNION set operator combines the result data sets produced by two individual queries and removes any duplicate rows found. Figure 5.7 illustrates how a simple UNION operation works.

CAKES TABLE

TYPE	INGREDIENT
CHOCOLATE	SUGAR
CHEESECAKE	SUGAR
CHOCOLATE	FLOUR
POUND	SALT
FRUIT	BUTTER
POUND	BUTTER

COOKIES TABLE

TYPE	INGREDIENT
SUGAR	SUGAR
GINGER SNAP	SUGAR
OATMEAL	SALT
SUGAR	VANILLA
OATMEAL	FLOUR

UNION OPERATION

```
SELECT ingredient FROM cakes
UNION
SELECT ingredient FROM cookies
ORDER BY ingredient
```

RESULT DATA SET

INGREDIENT
BUTTER
FLOUR
SALT
SUGAR
VANILLA

Figure 5.7: A simple UNION *operation*

- **UNION ALL**: The UNION ALL set operator combines the result data sets produced by two individual queries, while retaining all duplicate records found. Figure 5.8 illustrates how a simple UNION ALL operation works.

CAKES TABLE

TYPE	INGREDIENT
CHOCOLATE	SUGAR
CHEESECAKE	SUGAR
CHOCOLATE	FLOUR
POUND	SALT
FRUIT	BUTTER
POUND	BUTTER

COOKIES TABLE

TYPE	INGREDIENT
SUGAR	SUGAR
GINGER SNAP	SUGAR
OATMEAL	SALT
SUGAR	VANILLA
OATMEAL	FLOUR

UNION ALL OPERATION

```
SELECT ingredient FROM cakes
UNION ALL
SELECT ingredient FROM cookies
ORDER BY ingredient
```

RESULT DATA SET

INGREDIENT
BUTTER
BUTTER
FLOUR
FLOUR
SALT
SALT
SUGAR
SUGAR
SUGAR
SUGAR
VANILLA

Figure 5.8: A simple UNION ALL *operation*

- **INTERSECT**: The INTERSECT set operator combines the result data sets produced by two individual queries, removes all duplicate rows found, and then removes all records in the first result data set that do not have a matching record in the second result data set, leaving just the records that are found in both result data sets. Figure 5.9 illustrates how a simple INTERSECT operation works.

CAKES TABLE

TYPE	INGREDIENT
CHOCOLATE	SUGAR
CHEESECAKE	SUGAR
CHOCOLATE	FLOUR
POUND	SALT
FRUIT	BUTTER
POUND	BUTTER

COOKIES TABLE

TYPE	INGREDIENT
SUGAR	SUGAR
GINGER SNAP	SUGAR
OATMEAL	SALT
SUGAR	VANILLA
OATMEAL	FLOUR

INTERSECT OPERATION

```
SELECT ingredient FROM cakes
INTERSECT
SELECT ingredient FROM cookies
ORDER BY ingredient
```

RESULT DATA SET

INGREDIENT
FLOUR
SALT
SUGAR

Figure 5.9: A simple INTERSECT operation

- **INTERSECT ALL**: The INTERSECT ALL set operator combines the result data sets produced by two individual queries (retaining all duplicate rows found), and removes all records in the first result data set that do not have a matching record in the second result data set, leaving just the records that are found in both result data sets. Figure 5.10 illustrates how a simple INTERSECT ALL operation works.

CAKES TABLE

TYPE	INGREDIENT
CHOCOLATE	SUGAR
CHEESECAKE	SUGAR
CHOCOLATE	FLOUR
POUND	SALT
FRUIT	BUTTER
POUND	BUTTER

COOKIES TABLE

TYPE	INGREDIENT
SUGAR	SUGAR
GINGER SNAP	SUGAR
OATMEAL	SALT
SUGAR	VANILLA
OATMEAL	FLOUR

INTERSECT ALL OPERATION

```
SELECT ingredient FROM cakes
INTERSECT ALL
SELECT ingredient FROM cookies
ORDER BY ingredient
```

RESULT DATA SET

INGREDIENT
FLOUR
SALT
SUGAR
SUGAR

Figure 5.10: A simple INTERSECT ALL *operation*

- **EXCEPT**: The EXCEPT set operator combines the result data sets produced by two individual queries, removes all duplicate rows found, and then removes all records in the first result data set that have a matching record in the second result data set, leaving just the records not found in both result data sets. Figure 5.11 illustrates how a simple EXCEPT operation works.

CAKES TABLE

TYPE	INGREDIENT
CHOCOLATE	SUGAR
CHEESECAKE	SUGAR
CHOCOLATE	FLOUR
POUND	SALT
FRUIT	BUTTER
POUND	BUTTER

COOKIES TABLE

TYPE	INGREDIENT
SUGAR	SUGAR
GINGER SNAP	SUGAR
OATMEAL	SALT
SUGAR	VANILLA
OATMEAL	FLOUR

EXCEPT OPERATION

```
SELECT ingredient FROM cakes
EXCEPT
SELECT ingredient FROM cookies
ORDER BY ingredient
```

RESULT DATA SET

INGREDIENT
BUTTER

Figure 5.11: A simple EXCEPT operation

- **EXCEPT ALL**: The EXCEPT ALL set operator combines the result data sets produced by two individual queries (retaining all duplicate rows found), and removes all records in the first result data set that have a matching record in the second result data set, leaving just the records not found in both result data sets. Figure 5.12 illustrates how a simple EXCEPT ALL operation works.

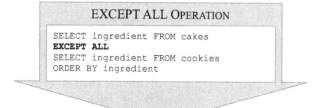

CAKES TABLE

TYPE	INGREDIENT
CHOCOLATE	SUGAR
CHEESECAKE	SUGAR
CHOCOLATE	FLOUR
POUND	SALT
FRUIT	BUTTER
POUND	BUTTER

COOKIES TABLE

TYPE	INGREDIENT
SUGAR	SUGAR
GINGER SNAP	SUGAR
OATMEAL	SALT
SUGAR	VANILLA
OATMEAL	FLOUR

EXCEPT ALL OPERATION

```
SELECT ingredient FROM cakes
EXCEPT ALL
SELECT ingredient FROM cookies
ORDER BY ingredient
```

RESULT DATA SET

INGREDIENT
BUTTER
BUTTER

Figure 5.12: A simple EXCEPT ALL *operation*

It is important to note that, unlike when the UNION, UNION ALL, INTERSECT, and INTERSECT ALL set operators are used, the order in which queries are combined when the EXCEPT or EXCEPT ALL set operators are used is essential. Reversing the order of the queries when using the EXCEPT or EXCEPT ALL set operators will produce a very different result data set. Figure 5.13 illustrates how the EXCEPT operation presented earlier will produce a completely different result data set if the order of the queries specified are reversed.

COOKIES TABLE

TYPE	INGREDIENT
SUGAR	SUGAR
GINGER SNAP	SUGAR
OATMEAL	SALT
SUGAR	VANILLA
OATMEAL	FLOUR

CAKES TABLE

TYPE	INGREDIENT
CHOCOLATE	SUGAR
CHEESECAKE	SUGAR
CHOCOLATE	FLOUR
POUND	SALT
FRUIT	BUTTER
POUND	BUTTER

EXCEPT OPERATION

```
SELECT ingredient FROM cookies
EXCEPT
SELECT ingredient FROM cakes
ORDER BY ingredient
```

RESULT DATA SET

INGREDIENT
VANILLA

Figure 5.13: A simple EXCEPT operation with the order of the queries reversed

So, when might you want to combine the results of two queries using a set operator? Suppose your company keeps employee expense account information in a table whose contents are archived at the end of each fiscal year. (When a new fiscal year begins, expenditures for that year are recorded in a new table.) Now suppose, for tax purposes, you need a record of all employees' expenses for the past two years.

To obtain this information, each archived table must be queried, and the results must be combined. You can do this in a number of ways, but the easiest way by far is to query both archived tables and combine the results using the UNION set operator.

Using a Cursor to Obtain Results from a Result Data Set

It was mentioned earlier that you can execute SQL statements interactively using tools such as Data Studio and the DB2 CLP. It was also pointed out that SQL statements can be embedded in high-level programming language source code files. However, the way in which a query is executed from within an application program is significantly different from the way in which it is executed from Data Studio or the CLP.

When a SELECT statement is executed from within an application program, DB2 uses a mechanism known as a *cursor* to retrieve data values from the result data set produced. The name *cursor* probably originated from the blinking cursor found on early computer screens. And just as that cursor indicated the current position on the screen, a DB2 cursor points to the current position in a result data set (that is, the current row). Depending upon how it is defined, a cursor can fall under one of the following categories:

- **Read-only:** Cursors that have been constructed in such a way that rows in the result data set they are associated with can be read but not modified or deleted; a cursor is considered read-only if it is based on a read-only SELECT statement (the statement "SELECT deptno FROM department" is an example of a SELECT statement that is considered read-only)
- **Updatable:** Cursors that have been constructed in such a way that rows in the result data set they are associated with can be modified or deleted; a cursor is considered updatable if the FOR UPDATE clause was specified when the cursor was created and if only one table was referenced in the SELECT statement that was used to create it
- **Ambiguous:** Cursors that have been constructed in such a way that it is impossible to tell whether they are meant to be read-only or updatable (ambiguous cursors are treated as read-only cursors if the BLOCKING ALL option was specified at the time the application that created the cursor was precompiled or bound to a database; otherwise, they are considered updatable)

Regardless of which type of cursor you use, to incorporate a cursor into an application program, you must perform the following steps, in the order shown:

1. Declare (define) the cursor along with its type and associate it with a query (that is, a SELECT or VALUES statement). (This is done by executing a DECLARE CURSOR statement.)
2. Open the cursor. (This is done by executing an OPEN statement.) This will cause the corresponding query to be executed and a result data set to be produced.

3. Retrieve (fetch) each row in the result data set, one by one, until an "End of data" condition occurs. (This is done by repeatedly executing a FETCH statement.) Each time a row is retrieved (fetched), the cursor is automatically moved to the next row.

4. If appropriate, alter or delete the current row by executing an UPDATE ... WHERE CURRENT OF or a DELETE ... WHERE CURRENT OF statement (but only if the cursor is updatable).

5. Close the cursor. (This is done by executing a CLOSE statement.) This will delete the result data set that was produced when the cursor was first opened.

Once a cursor that has been declared is opened, it can be in one of three positions: "Before a Row of Data," "On a Row of Data," or "After the Last Row of Data." A cursor positioned "Before a Row of Data" is placed immediately before the first row of data in the result data set, and data values stored in that row will be assigned to the appropriate host variables when a FETCH statement is executed.

When a FETCH statement is executed, the cursor will be positioned "On a Row of Data," and subsequent executions of the FETCH statement will cause the cursor to move to the next row in the result data set (if one exists). Each time the cursor moves, data values stored in the new row are automatically transferred to the appropriate host variables. If a cursor is positioned on the last row of the result data set when the FETCH statement is executed, it is moved to the "After the Last Row of Data" position, the value +100 (which means NOT FOUND) is assigned to the *sqlcode* field of the current SQLCA data structure variable, and the value 02000 is assigned to the *sqlstate* field of the same variable. No data is copied to the associated host variables because the cursor no longer sits on a valid row.

Keep in mind that an application can use several cursors concurrently. However, each cursor used must have a unique name, along with its own set of DECLARE CURSOR, OPEN, FETCH, and CLOSE SQL statements.

A Word About Working with Temporal (Time-Travel) Tables

In Chapter 4, "Working with Databases and Database Objects," we saw how temporal tables can be used to manage multiple versions of data, as well as track effective dates for data that is subject to changing business conditions. We also saw that three different types of temporal tables are available: system-period, application-period, and bitemporal (which is a combination of the other two).

For the most part, the syntax and semantics of the INSERT, UPDATE, and DELETE statements presented earlier remain the same when used in conjunction with temporal tables. Thus, to add a record to a system-period temporal table named POLICY that has the following characteristics:

Column Name	Data Type
POLICYNUM	INTEGER
TYPE	CHAR(10)
COVERAGE	INTEGER
DEDUCTIBLE	INTEGER
SYS_START	TIMESTAMP(12)
SYS_END	TIMESTAMP(12)
TRANS_START	TIMESTAMP(12)

you could execute an INSERT statement that looks like this:

```
INSERT INTO policy (policynum, type, coverage, deductible)
    VALUES (1001, 'HOME', 350000, 500)
```

And if you wanted to change a record stored in the POLICY table such that the deductible for policy number 1001 is increased from $500.00 to $2,000.00, you could execute an UPDATE statement that looks like this:

```
UPDATE policy
    SET deductible = 2000
    WHERE policynum = 1001
```

Similarly, to add a record to an application-period temporal table named LOAN that has the following characteristics:

Column Name	Data Type
ACCTNUM	INTEGER
PRINCIPAL	INTEGER
RATE	DOUBLE
BUS_START	DATE
BUS_END	DATE

you could execute an INSERT statement that looks like this:

```
INSERT INTO loan
    VALUES (1000, 30000, 6.25, '14-07-01', '18-07-01')
```

And to remove the record for account number 5000 from the LOAN table, you would execute a DELETE statement that looks like this:

```
DELETE FROM loan
    WHERE acctnum = 5000
```

One significant difference between performing update and delete operations on traditional tables and performing similar operations on application-period and bitemporal temporal tables is that with these types of temporal tables, you have the ability to change the values of one or more columns *for a specific period of time*. This is done by including the FOR PORTION OF BUSINESS_TIME FROM ... TO ... clause with the UPDATE or DELETE statement used. For example, to modify the record for account number 1000 that is stored in the LOAN table presented earlier in such a way that the interest rate is reduced from 6.25 percent to 5 percent *for the first six months of the loan*, you would execute an UPDATE statement that looks like this:

```
UPDATE loan
    FOR PORTION OF BUSINESS_TIME
        FROM '2016-01-01' TO '2016-06-30'
    SET rate = 5.0
    WHERE policynum = 1000
```

(Notice that the FOR PORTION OF BUSINESS_TIME FROM ... TO ... clause in this example—otherwise known as the *temporal restriction*—appears after the table name and not as part of the WHERE clause.)

Querying System-Period Temporal Tables

As with the other DML statements, when the SELECT statement is used to query temporal tables, the syntax and semantics remains essentially the same. One significant difference, however, is that SELECT statements that query system-period temporal tables can contain one of the following system time-period specifications:

- **FOR SYSTEM_TIME AS OF [*Timestamp*]**: Lets you query data as of a specific point in time
- **FOR SYSTEM_TIME FROM [*Timestamp*] TO [*Timestamp*]**: Lets you query data from one point in time to another—DB2 uses an *inclusive-exclusive* approach for this time-period specification, which means that the period specified begins at the start time provided and ends just prior to the end time provided; thus, a time-period specification of January 1, 2016 to February 1, 2016 would indicate a range from 12:00 a.m. on January 1, 2016 until 11:59 p.m. on January 31, 2016; February 1, 2016 is not included in the range
- **FOR SYSTEM_TIME BETWEEN [*Timestamp*] AND [*Timestamp*]**: Lets you query data between a start time and an end time—DB2 uses an *inclusive-inclusive* approach for this time-period specification, which means that the period begins at the start time provided and ends at the end time provided

To see only data that is current, simply construct a SELECT statement that does not contain one of these time-period specifications. For example, to find out what the deductible is for policy number 1001 *right now*, you could query the POLICY table presented earlier with a SELECT statement that looks like this:

```
SELECT deductible
  FROM policy
  WHERE policynum = 1001
```

However, to see historical data, you will need to include an appropriate system time-period specification in your query. For example, to determine what the deductible *was* for policy number 1001 *at 12:30 a.m. on July 24, 2014*, you would need to query the POLICY table presented earlier with a SELECT statement that looks like this:

```
SELECT deductible
  FROM policy
  FOR SYSTEM_TIME AS OF TIMESTAMP('2014-07-24-12.30.00')
  WHERE policynum = 1001
```

To resolve this query, DB2 will transparently access the POLICY table's history table to retrieve the information requested. Note that the history table itself is not referenced in the query; the FOR SYSTEM_TIME AS OF time-period specification causes DB2 to automatically look in the associated history table for the information being sought.

Querying Application-Period Temporal Tables

Querying application-period temporal tables is also relatively straightforward—if you are not concerned with obtaining temporal information, the syntax and semantics of the SELECT statement used remains essentially the same. However, if you want to retrieve past, current, or future data values, you will need to construct a SELECT statement that contains one of the following business time-period specifications:

- **FOR BUSINESS_TIME AS OF [*Timestamp*]**: Lets you query data as of a specific point in time
- **FOR BUSINESS_TIME FROM [*Timestamp*] TO [*Timestamp*]**: Lets you query data from one point in time to another—DB2 uses an *inclusive-exclusive* approach for this time-period specification, which means that the period specified begins at the start time provided and ends just prior to the end time provided
- **FOR BUSINESS_TIME BETWEEN [*Timestamp*] AND [*Timestamp*]**: Lets you query data between a start time and an end time—DB2 uses an *inclusive-inclusive* approach for this time-period specification, which means that the period begins at the start time provided and ends at the end time provided

For example, to retrieve information about the loan for account number 1000 *as it will be structured on November 18, 2016*, you could query the LOAN table presented earlier using a SELECT statement that looks something like this:

```
SELECT principal, DECIMAL(rate, 4, 2) AS rate
  FROM loan
  FOR BUSINESS_TIME AS OF '2016-11-18'
  WHERE acctnum = 1000
```

Querying Bitemporal Temporal Tables

If you want to query a bitemporal temporal table, you have the option of constructing a SELECT statement that:

- Does not contain any time-period specifications
- Contains a system time-period specification only
- Contains a business time-period specification only
- Contains both a system time-period specification *and* a business time-period specification

Regardless of the option you choose, the syntax and semantics of the SELECT statement used will be the same as that used to query the other types of temporal tables. If appropriate, you can construct a SELECT statement that contains both a system time-period specification and a business time-period specification.

Working with XML Data

DB2's pureXML technology unlocks the latent potential of XML by providing simple, efficient access to XML data, while offering the same levels of security, integrity, and resiliency that has always been available for relational data. With pureXML, XML data is stored in a hierarchical structure that naturally reflects the structure of XML documents. The ability to store XML data in its native structure, along with innovative indexing techniques, means that DB2 can efficiently manage XML documents while eliminating the complex and time-consuming parsing that is typically required to store XML data in a relational database.

To facilitate the storing of XML data in its native format, a new data type—the XML data type—was introduced in DB2 for LUW, Version 9. As the name implies, this data type is used to define columns that will be used to store well-formed XML documents, which typically look something like this:

```
<?xml version="1.0" encoding="UTF-8" ?>
<customerinfo>
  <name>John Doe</name>
  <addr country="United States">
    <street>25 East Creek Drive</street>
    <city>Raleigh</city>
                                              Continued
```

```
    <state-prov>North Carolina</state-prov>
    <zip-pcode>27603</zip-pcode>
  </addr>
  <phone type="work">919-555-1212</phone>
  <email>john.doe@xyz.com</email>
</customerinfo>
```

Most XML documents begin with an XML and version encoding declaration. In the preceding XML document, the XML version and encoding declaration is the line that looks like this:

```
<?xml version="1.0" encoding="UTF-8" ?>
```

This is normally followed by one or more *elements* and *attributes*. XML elements are enclosed with opening and closing tags and look something like this:

```
<name>John Doe</name>
<email>john.doe@xyz.com</email>
```

Important: Opening and closing tags are case-sensitive—the tag <Letter> is different from the tag <letter>. Therefore, opening and closing tags must be written using the same case.

Similar to XML elements, XML attributes describe XML elements or provide additional information about a particular element. XML attributes are always contained within the opening tag of an element, and attribute values are always enclosed with double quotation marks (""). The attributes found in the XML document just presented are:

```
<addr country="United States">
<phone type="work">919-555-1212</phone>
```

As with relational data, DML statements can be used to store, alter, and delete XML data, as well as retrieve XML data values from tables and views. Thus, to add a record containing the XML document presented earlier to a table named CUSTOMER that has the following characteristics:

Column Name	Data Type
CUSTID	INTEGER
CUSTINFO	XML

you could execute an INSERT statement that looks something like this:

```
INSERT INTO customer
  VALUES (10,
      '<?xml version="1.0" encoding="UTF-8" ?>
      <customerinfo>
      <name>John Doe</name>
      <addr country="United States">
        <street>25 East Creek Drive</street>
        <city>Raleigh</city>
        <state-prov>North Carolina</state-prov>
        <zip-pcode>27603</zip-pcode>
      </addr>
      <phone type="work">919-555-1212</phone>
      <email>john.doe@xyz.com</email>
    </customerinfo>')
```

And to update only the XML data portion of this record, you could execute an UPDATE statement that looks like this:

```
UPDATE customer
  SET custinfo =
      '<?xml version="1.0" encoding="UTF-8" ?>
      <customerinfo>
        <name>Jane Doe</name>
```

Continued

```
            <addr country="Canada">
              <street>8200 Warden Avenue</street>
              <city>Markham</city>
              <state-prov>Ontario</state-prov>
              <zip-pcode> L6G 1C7</zip-pcode>
            </addr>
            <phone type="work">905-555-3434</phone>
            <email>jane.doe@xyz.com</email>
          </customerinfo>'
    WHERE CUSTID = 10
```

Finally, to delete this record from the CUSTOMER table, you would execute a DELETE
statement that looks something like this:

```
DELETE FROM customer
WHERE
    XMLEXISTS('$info/customerinfo[name/text()="Jane Doe"]'
    PASSING custinfo AS "info")
```

So how do you retrieve XML data after it has been stored in a table? One way is
by using SQL. The SQL:2003 and SQL:2006 language standards include a variety of
functions and features for working with XML data. This functionality is commonly
referred to as SQL/XML and some of the SQL/XML functions that are frequently used
with DB2 are:

- **XMLPARSE()**: Parses a character string value and returns a well-formed XML
  document
- **XMLSERIALIZE()**: Converts a well-formed XML document into a character string or
  large object value
- **XMLTEXT()**: Returns an XML value with a single XQuery text node
- **XMLTABLE()**: Returns a result data set, in the form of a table, from an XQuery
  expression—the table returned can contain columns of any SQL data type,
  including XML; the structure of the table is defined by the COLUMNS clause of the

XMLTABLE() function, and the data in the table can be used to populate other base tables
- **XMLVALIDATE()**: Performs an XML schema validation operation

Using one or more of these SQL/XML functions, you can combine XPath expressions (a query language for selecting nodes from an XML document) with familiar SQL statements to retrieve information stored in XML columns. You can also retrieve XML data using *XQuery*—a functional programming language designed by the World Wide Web Consortium (W3C) to meet specific requirements for querying XML data. XQuery consists of several different kinds of expressions, which can be combined to create more sophisticated expressions than are available with XPath alone. Some of the most important XQuery expressions available include:

- **Path:** Expressions that are used to locate nodes, such as elements and attributes, from the tree structure of an XML document
- **FLWOR:** Expressions that are used to iterate over the items in a sequence and bind variables to intermediate query results (the acronym FLWOR—pronounced *flower*—is based on the keywords for, let, where, order by, and return)
- **Constructor:** Expressions that are used to create nodes, such as elements and attributes, which can then be used to build new XML documents within a query
- **Cast:** Expressions that are used to convert values from one data type to another
- **Arithmetic:** Expressions that are used to perform addition (+), subtraction (-), multiplication (*), division (div), integer division (idiv), and modulus (mod) operations
- **Comparison, logical, and conditional:** Expressions that are used to formulate predicates to search for specific information
- **Sequence:** Expressions that are used to construct and combine sequences
- **Transform:** Expressions that are used to update or transform existing XML documents

Of these, the FLWOR expression is one of the most powerful and therefore the most frequently used. (This expression is comparable to the SELECT-FROM-WHERE statement/ clause combination available with SQL.) The basic syntax for a FLWOR expression is:

```
XQUERY
    for $Variable1 IN Expression1
```

```
let $Variable2 := Expression2
where Expression3
order by Expression4 [ASCENDING | DESCENDING]
return Expression3
```

Thus, to retrieve customer names for all customers who reside in North Carolina from XML documents stored in the CUSTINFO column of the table named CUSTOMER presented earlier, you could execute an XQuery expression that looks something like this:

```
XQUERY
  for $info
  in db2-fn:xmlcolumn('CUSTOMER.CUSTINFO')/customerinfo
  where $info/addr/state-prov="North Carolina"
  return $info/name
```

Assuming the CUSTOMER table was populated by using the INSERT statement shown earlier, you should get a result data set that looks like this:

```
1
----------------------------------------------------
<name>John Doe</name>
```

To remove the XML tags and return only the customer name, you would need to execute an XQuery expression that looks like this instead:

```
XQUERY
  for $info
  in db2-fn:xmlcolumn('CUSTOMER.CUSTINFO')/customerinfo
  where $info/addr/state-prov="North Carolina"
  return $info/name/text()
```

Consequently, the result data set produced when this XQuery expression is executed will look like this:

```
1
--------
John Doe
```

Working with User-Defined Functions (UDFs)

In Chapter 4, "Working with Databases and Database Objects," we saw that UDFs are special objects that can extend and enhance the built-in functions that are available with DB2. Unlike DB2's built-in functions, UDFs can take advantage of system calls and DB2's administrative APIs (depending upon how they are constructed) to provide more synergy between applications, operating systems, and database environments. We also saw that several different types of UDFs can be created:

- **Sourced (or Template):** This function is based on another function (referred to as the *source function*) that already exists. Sourced functions can be columnar, scalar, or tabular in nature; they can also be designed to overload a specific operator such as +, -, *, and /. When a sourced function is invoked, all arguments passed to it are converted to the data types that the underlying source function expects, and the source function itself is invoked. Upon completion, the source function performs any conversions necessary on the results produced and returns them to the calling application.
- **SQL scalar:** This function's body is written entirely in SQL; an SQL scalar function returns a single value each time it is called.
- **SQL table:** This function's body is written entirely in SQL and SQL Procedural Language (SQL PL); an SQL table function returns a result data set, in the form of a table, each time it is called.
- **External Scalar:** This function—written in a high-level programming language such as C, C++, or Java—returns a single value each time it is called. The function itself resides in an external library and is registered in the database, along with any related attributes.
- **External Table:** This function—written in a high-level programming language—returns a result data set, in the form of a table, each time it is called. As with external scalar functions, the function itself resides in an external library and is registered in the database, along with any related attributes. External table functions can make almost any data source appear as a base table. Consequently,

the result data set produced can be used in join operations, grouping operations, set operations, or any other operation that can be applied to a read-only view.

- **OLE DB External Table:** This function—written in a high-level programming language—can access data from an Object Linking and Embedding, Database (OLE DB) provider and return a result data set, in the form of a table, each time it is called. A generic built-in OLE DB consumer that is available with DB2 for Linux, UNIX, and Windows can be used to interface with any OLE DB provider; simply register an OLE DB table function with a database and refer to the appropriate OLE DB provider as the data source—no additional programming is required.

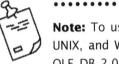

Note: To use OLE DB table functions with a DB2 for Linux, UNIX, and Windows database environment, you must install OLE DB 2.0 or later—which is available from Microsoft—on your database server. (Refer to your data source documentation for more information about the system requirements and OLE DB providers that are available for that data source.)

Creating SQL Scalar and SQL Table User-Defined Functions

UDFs are created (and registered with a database) with the CREATE FUNCTION statement. Several forms of this statement are available; the appropriate form to use is determined by the type of function you wish to create. The basic syntax for the form that is used to create an SQL function (either scalar or tabular) is:

```
CREATE FUNCTION [FunctionName]
    (<<ParameterType> [ParameterName] [DataType], ...>)
    RETURNS [[OutputDataType]
    <LANGUAGE SQL>
    <SPECIFIC [SpecificName]>
    <DETERMINISTIC | NOT DETERMINISTIC>
    <EXTERNAL ACTION | NO EXTERNAL ACTION>
    <READS SQL DATA | CONTAINS SQL | MODIFIES SQL DATA>
    [SQLStatements] | RETURN [ReturnStatement]
```

or

```
CREATE FUNCTION [FunctionName]
  (<<ParameterType> [ParameterName] [DataType], ...>)
  RETURNS TABLE ([ColumnName] [ColumnDataType], ...)
  <LANGUAGE SQL>
  <SPECIFIC [SpecificName]>
  <DETERMINISTIC | NOT DETERMINISTIC>
  <EXTERNAL ACTION | NO EXTERNAL ACTION>
  <CONTAINS SQL | READS SQL DATA | MODIFIES SQL DATA>
  [SQLStatements] | RETURN [ReturnStatement]
```

where:

FunctionName	Identifies the name to assign to the function that is to be created
ParameterType	Indicates whether the parameter specified (in the *ParameterName* parameter) is an input parameter (IN), an output parameter (OUT), or both an input and an output parameter (INOUT)
ParameterName	Identifies the name to assign to one or more function input parameters
DataType	Identifies the data type of the parameter specified (in the *ParameterName* parameter)
OutputDataType	Identifies the data type the function is expected to return
ColumnName	Identifies one or more names to assign to the column(s) the function is expected to return (if the function is designed to return a table)
ColumnDataType	Identifies the data type the function expects to return for each column specified (in the *ColumnName* parameter)
SpecificName	Identifies a specific name to assign to the function that is to be created; you can use this name to reference or delete (drop) the function, but not to invoke it
SQLStatements	Identifies one or more SQL statements that are to be executed when the function is invoked; together, these statements act as a single dynamic compound SQL statement—if two or more statements are used, they should be enclosed with the keywords BEGIN ATOMIC and END, and each statement must be terminated with a semicolon (;)

ReturnStatement   Identifies a RETURN statement that is to be used to return data to the user/application/statement that invoked the function

If the DETERMINISTIC clause is specified with the CREATE FUNCTION statement used, it is implied that the function will always return the same scalar value or table when it is called with the same parameter values. By contrast, if the NOT DETERMINISTIC clause is specified (or if neither clause is specified), it is assumed that the function can return different results each time it is called with the same set of values.

If the EXTERNAL ACTION clause is specified with the CREATE FUNCTION statement used, it is implied that the function will perform some type of action that will change the state of an object that DB2 does not manage (for example, appending data to an external file). If, however, the NO EXTERNAL ACTION clause is specified (or if neither clause is specified), it is assumed that no such actions will be performed.

The <CONTAINS SQL | READS SQL DATA | MODIFIES SQL DATA> clause identifies the types of SQL statements that can be coded in the body of the function. If you specify the CONTAINS SQL clause, the function cannot contain SQL statements that read or modify data. If you specify the READS SQL DATA clause, the function cannot contain SQL statements that modify data. And if you specify the MODIFIES SQL DATA clause, the function can contain SQL statements that both read and modify data.

Therefore, to create an SQL scalar function named CONVERT_CTOF() that accepts a temperature value in degrees Celsius as input and returns a corresponding temperature value in degrees Fahrenheit, you could execute a CREATE FUNCTION statement that looks something like this:

```
CREATE FUNCTION convert_ctof (temp_c FLOAT)
  RETURNS INTEGER
  SPECIFIC convert_temp
  DETERMINISTIC
  RETURN INT((temp_c * 1.8) + 32)
```

On the other hand, to create an SQL table function named DEPT_EMPLOYEES() that accepts a department code as input and returns a result data set, in the form of a table, that contains basic information about each employee who works in the department specified, you would execute a CREATE FUNCTION statement that looks more like this:

```
CREATE FUNCTION dept_employees (deptno CHAR(3))
  RETURNS TABLE (empno CHAR(6),
                fname CHAR(10),
                lname CHAR(10))
  LANGUAGE SQL
  SPECIFIC dept_employees
  DETERMINISTIC
  NO EXTERNAL ACTION
  READS SQL DATA
  BEGIN ATOMIC
    RETURN
      SELECT empno, fname, lname
        FROM employee AS e
          WHERE e.dept = dept_employees.deptno;
  END
```

It is important to note that when a UDF is created, the name (including the implicitly or explicitly provided qualifier), together with the number of parameters specified and the data type of each parameter make up what is know as the function's *signature*. The same name can be assigned to more than one function, but every function's signature must be unique—for the purpose of comparing function signatures, parameter names and data type length, precision, scale, and FOR BIT DATA attributes are ignored.

Thus, if an SQL scalar function named GET_LENGTH() that accepts a 10-byte character string as input and returns a corresponding integer value that represents the length of the string provided is created by executing a CREATE FUNCTION statement that looks like this:

```
CREATE FUNCTION get_length (in_string CHAR(10))
RETURNS INTEGER
LANGUAGE SQL
RETURN LENGTH(in_string)
```

The following CREATE FUNCTION statement will fail because its signature matches that of the GET_LENGTH() function just created:

```
CREATE FUNCTION get_length (string CHAR(100) FOR BIT DATA)
RETURNS INTEGER
LANGUAGE SQL
RETURN LENGTH(string)
```

Invoking SQL Scalar and SQL Table User-Defined Functions

How a UDF is invoked depends, in part, on what it is designed to do. Scalar UDFs are typically invoked as an expression in the select list of a query, whereas table functions must be referenced in the FROM clause of a SELECT statement. For example, suppose you have a base table named CLIMATE that has the following characteristics:

Column Name	Data Type
REGION	CHAR(15)
AVG_TEMP_C	FLOAT

To use the SQL scalar function named CONVERT_CTOF() that was created earlier to convert values found in the AVG_TEMP_C column of this table from degrees Celsius to degrees Fahrenheit, you would execute a SELECT statement that looks like this:

```
SELECT region, convert_ctof(avg_temp_c) AS avg_temp_f
   FROM climate
```

When this statement is executed, the result data set produced should look something like this (assuming the values for AVG_TEMP_C were originally –11 and 36 degrees Celsius, respectively):

```
REGION          AVG_TEMP_F
--------------- -----------
North                    12
South                    96

  2 record(s) selected.
```

Or, if you want use the SQL table function named DEPT_EMPLOYEES() that was created earlier to obtain a list of employees who work in development (the department that has been assigned the code 'C01'), you would execute a SELECT statement that looks like this:

```
SELECT empno, fname, lname
  FROM TABLE(dept_employees('C01')) AS results
```

And when this statement is executed, you should get a result data set that looks like this (provided the EMPLOYEE table—which the DEPT_EMPLOYEES() function queries—is populated as shown in Table 5.2):

```
EMPNO  FNAME       LNAME
------ ----------- -----------
1002   HUMPHREY    BOGART
1003   INGRID      BERGMAN
1008   KATHARINE   HEPBURN

  3 record(s) selected.
```

Working with Stored Procedures

In Chapter 4, "Working with Databases and Database Objects," we saw that if an application contains transactions that perform a relatively large amount of database activity with little or no user interaction, those transactions can be stored separately on a database server in what are known as *stored procedures*. Stored procedures allow work that is done by one or more transactions to be encapsulated and stored in such a way that it can be executed directly at a server by *any* application or user who has been given the necessary authority.

Client/server applications that use stored procedures have the following advantages over client/server applications that do not:

- **Reduced network traffic:** Messages are not sent across the network for SQL statements coded in a stored procedure. Instead, only data that the client application requests is transferred.
- **Improved performance of server-intensive work:** Because less data must be sent across the network, and because processing occurs directly at the server, complex queries and other server-intensive work executes faster.
- **Ability to separate and reuse business logic:** When business rules are incorporated into stored procedures, the logic can be reused multiple times, simply by calling the procedure as needed. Consequently, the same business rule logic will be enforced across all applications. And because the logic used in a stored procedure can be modified independently, you can avoid having to recode applications when business rules change.
- **Ability to access features that exist only on the server:** Because stored procedures run directly on the database server workstation, they can exploit any extra memory, faster processors, and so forth that the database server might have. (Typically, database servers have more memory and multiple or faster processors than client workstations.) Additionally, stored procedures can take advantage of DB2's set of administrative APIs, which can only be run at the server. And, because stored procedures are not restricted to performing database-only activities, they can take advantage of any additional software that has been installed on the server.

Developing and Registering SQL Stored Procedures

Two different types of stored procedures can be created. They are:

- **SQL (or Native SQL):** A stored procedure whose body is written entirely in SQL or SQL PL
- **External:** A stored procedure that is written in a high-level programming language such as Assembler, C, C++, COBOL, Java, REXX, or PL/I that resides in an external library that is accessible to DB2; external stored procedures must be registered in a database, along with all their related attributes, before they can be invoked

Regardless of whether stored procedures are written using SQL or a high-level programming language, they must perform the following tasks, in the order shown:

1. Accept any input parameter values the calling application supplies.
2. Perform whatever processing is appropriate (typically, this involves executing one or more SQL statements within a single transaction).
3. Return output data (if data is to be returned) to the calling application—at a minimum, a stored procedure should return a value that indicates whether it executed successfully.

Stored procedures are created by executing the CREATE PROCEDURE statement. Two forms of this statement are available, and the appropriate form to use is determined by the type of procedure that is to be created. The basic syntax for the form of the CREATE PROCEDURE statement that is used to create an SQL stored procedure looks something like this:

```
CREATE PROCEDURE [ProcedureName]
   <([ParameterType] [ParameterName] [DataType], ...)>
   <LANGUAGE SQL>
   <DYNAMIC RESULT SETS [0 | NumResultSets]>
   <DETERMINISTIC | NOT DETERMINISTIC>
   <CONTAINS SQL | READS SQL DATA | MODIFIES SQL DATA>
   [SQLStatements]
```

where:

ProcedureName	Identifies the name to assign to the procedure that is to be created
ParameterType	Indicates whether the parameter specified (in the *ParameterName* parameter) is an input parameter (IN), an output parameter (OUT), or both an input and an output parameter (INOUT)
ParameterName	Identifies the name to assign to one or more procedure parameters
DataType	Identifies the data type of the parameter specified (in the *ParameterName* parameter)
NumResultSets	Identifies the number of result data sets the procedure returns (if any)
SQLStatements	Identifies one or more SQL statements (or SQL PL statements) that are to be executed when the function is invoked; together,

these statements act as a single dynamic compound SQL statement—if two or more statements are used, they should be enclosed with the keywords BEGIN ATOMIC and END, and each statement must be terminated with a semicolon (;)

Many of the clauses that are used with this form of the CREATE PROCEDURE statement are similar to the clauses that are available with the CREATE FUNCTION statement. For instance, the DETERMINISTIC clause indicates that the procedure will always return the same value (or table) when it is called with the same parameter values. And the <CONTAINS SQL | READS SQL DATA | MODIFIES SQL DATA> clause identifies the types of SQL statements that can be coded in the body of the procedure. (If you specify the CONTAINS SQL clause, the procedure cannot contain SQL statements that read or modify data; if you designate the READS SQL DATA clause, the procedure cannot contain SQL statements that modify data; and if you specify the MODIFIES SQL DATA clause, the procedure can contain SQL statements that both read and modify data.)

Thus, to create an SQL procedure named HIGH_EARNERS() that returns a list of employees whose salary exceeds the average salary, along with the average employee salary (in the form of a result data set), you could execute a CREATE PROCEDURE statement that looks something like this:

```
CREATE PROCEDURE high_earners
    (OUT avgSalary INTEGER)
LANGUAGE SQL
DYNAMIC RESULT SETS 1
READS SQL DATA
BEGIN
   DECLARE c1 CURSOR WITH RETURN FOR
      SELECT fname, lname, salary
         FROM employee
         WHERE salary > avgSalary
         ORDER BY salary DESC;

                                        Continued
```

```
    DECLARE EXIT HANDLER FOR NOT FOUND
      SET avgSalary = 9999;


    SET avgSalary = 0;
    SELECT AVG(salary) INTO avgSalary
      FROM employee;


    OPEN c1;
  END
```

When this particular CREATE PROCEDURE statement is executed, the SQL procedure produced will return an integer value (in an output parameter called AVGSALARY) and a result data set that contains the first name, last name, and salary of each employee whose salary is higher than the average salary. This is done by:

1. Specifying the DYNAMIC RESULT SETS 1 clause with the CREATE PROCEDURE statement used to indicate that the SQL procedure being created is to return a single result data set
2. Defining a cursor within the procedure body (and specifying the WITH RETURN FOR clause in the DECLARE CURSOR statement used) so a result data set can be returned
3. Querying the EMPLOYEE table using the AVG() scalar function to obtain average salary information
4. Opening the cursor (which causes the query that obtains employee salary information to be executed and a result data set to be produced)
5. Returning the average salary to the calling statement (in the output parameter named AVGSALARY) and leaving the cursor that was created open so the data in the result data set produced can be accessed by the calling application

Calling a Stored Procedure

Once a stored procedure has been created and registered with a database (via the CREATE PROCEDURE statement), it can be invoked from an interactive utility such as the DB2 CLP, from an application, or from another stored procedure. Stored procedures are invoked by executing the CALL statement; the basic syntax for this statement is:

```
CALL ()
```

or

```
CALL [ProcedureName]
    ([InputParameter] | [OutputParameter] | DEFAULT | NULL, ...)
```

where:

ProcedureName	Identifies, by name, the stored procedure that is to be invoked
InputParameter	Identifies one or more values (or host variables containing values) that are to be passed to the stored procedure as input parameters
OutputParameter	Identifies one or more host variables or parameter markers that are to receive values that will be returned as output from the stored procedure

Like other dynamic SQL statements that can be prepared and executed at runtime, CALL statements can contain parameter markers in place of constants and expressions. Parameter markers are represented by the question mark character (?) and indicate the position in an SQL statement where the current value of one or more host variables (or elements of an SQLDA data structure variable) are to be substituted when the statement is executed. Parameter markers are typically used where a host variable would be referenced if the SQL statement being executed were static.

Thus, you can invoke the SQL procedure named HIGH_EARNERS() that was created earlier, by connecting to the appropriate database and executing a CALL statement, from the DB2 CLP, that looks something like this:

```
CALL high_earners(?)
```

And when this statement is executed, you should get a result data set that looks like this (provided the EMPLOYEE table—which is queried by the HIGH_EARNERS procedure—is populated as shown in Table 5.2):

```
Value of output parameters
--------------------------

Parameter Name  : AVGSALARY
Parameter Value : 82616




Result set 1
------------


FNAME       LNAME       SALARY
----------  ----------  ----------
JAMES       DEAN         158096.00
JAMES       CAGNEY       105787.00
MARILYN     MONROE       103675.00
HUMPHREY    BOGART        88192.00

4 record(s) selected.
Return Status = 0
```

To invoke the same procedure from an Embedded SQL application, you could execute a static CALL statement that looks more like this:

```
CALL high_earners(:avgSalary)
```

Here, :avgSalary is the name of a host variable that has been defined with an appropriate data type (for example, double avgSalary = 0;).

And finally, the HIGH_EARNERS() SQL procedure could be invoked from within another SQL procedure by coding a DECLARE statement and a CALL statement in the body of the procedure that looks something like this:

```
DECLARE v_avgsalary INTEGER;
...
CALL high_earners(v_avgsalary);
```

Transactions and Transaction Boundaries

A *transaction* (also known as a *unit of work*) is a sequence of one or more SQL operations that are grouped as a single unit, usually within an application process. Such a unit is considered *atomic* (from the Greek word meaning "not able to be cut") because it is indivisible—either all of a transaction's work is carried out, or none of its work is carried out.

A given transaction can perform any number of SQL operations, depending upon what is considered a single step within a company's business logic. With that said, it is important to note that the longer a transaction is—that is, the more SQL operations a transaction performs—the more problematic it can be to manage. This is especially true if multiple transactions must run concurrently.

The initiation and termination of a single transaction defines points of consistency within a database (we will take a closer look at data consistency in Chapter 7, "Data Concurrency"). Consequently, either the effects of all operations performed within a transaction are applied to the database and made permanent (committed), or they are backed out (rolled back) and the database is returned to the state it was in immediately before the transaction was initiated. (Any data pages that were copied to a buffer pool on behalf of a transaction will remain in the buffer pool until their storage space is needed— at that time, they will be removed.)

Normally, a transaction is initiated the first time an SQL statement is executed after a connection to a database has been established, or when a new SQL statement is executed after a running transaction ends. Once transactions are initiated, they can be implicitly committed using a feature known as *automatic commit* (in which case, each executable SQL statement is treated as a single transaction, and changes made by that statement are automatically applied to the database unless the statement failed to execute successfully). Transactions can also be explicitly terminated by executing either the COMMIT or the ROLLBACK statement. The basic syntax for these two statements is:

```
COMMIT <WORK>
```

and

```
ROLLBACK <WORK>
```

When the COMMIT statement is used to terminate a transaction, all changes made to the database since the transaction began are made permanent. When the ROLLBACK statement is used instead, all changes made are backed out, and the database is returned to the state it was in just before the transaction was started. Figure 5.14 shows what happens when a COMMIT statement is used to terminate a transaction. Figure 5.15 illustrates what happens when a ROLLBACK statement is used to end a transaction instead.

EMPLOYEE TABLE

(Before the transaction)

EMPNO	LNAME	DEPT
1000	DEAN	A01
1001	MONROE	B01
1002	BOGART	-
1003	BERGMAN	D01

BEGIN TRANSACTION

```
INSERT INTO employee
    VALUES(1005, 'CAGNEY', 'E01')


COMMIT
```

EMPNO	LNAME	DEPT
1000	DEAN	A01
1001	MONROE	B01
1002	BOGART	-
1003	BERGMAN	D01
1004	CAGNEY	E01

END TRANSACTION

EMPLOYEE TABLE

(After the transaction)

EMPNO	LNAME	DEPT
1000	DEAN	A01
1001	MONROE	B01
1002	BOGART	-
1003	BERGMAN	D01
1004	CAGNEY	E01

Figure 5.14: What happens when the COMMIT statement is used to terminate a transaction

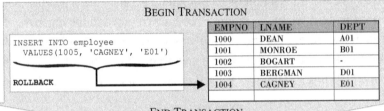

EMPLOYEE TABLE

(Before the transaction)

EMPNO	LNAME	DEPT
1000	DEAN	A01
1001	MONROE	B01
1002	BOGART	-
1003	BERGMAN	D01

BEGIN TRANSACTION

```
INSERT INTO employee
  VALUES(1005, 'CAGNEY', 'E01')


ROLLBACK
```

EMPNO	LNAME	DEPT
1000	DEAN	A01
1001	MONROE	B01
1002	BOGART	-
1003	BERGMAN	D01
1004	CAGNEY	E01

END TRANSACTION

EMPLOYEE TABLE

(After the transaction)

EMPNO	LNAME	DEPT
1000	DEAN	A01
1001	MONROE	B01
1002	BOGART	-
1003	BERGMAN	D01

Figure 5.15: What happens when the ROLLBACK statement is used to terminate a transaction

Note: The following SQL statements and operations are not under transaction control, and therefore are not affected by the execution of COMMIT and ROLLBACK statements:

- SET CONNECTION
- SET SERVER OPTION
- SET PASSTHRU (although the session for submitting native SQL directly to an external data source that is opened by the execution of this statement is under transaction control)
- Assignments made to updatable special registers with the SET statement

It is important to remember that commit and rollback operations have an effect only on the changes that are made within the transaction they terminate. So to evaluate the effects of a series of transactions, you must be able to identify where each transaction begins, as well as when and how each transaction ends. The effects of a series of transactions can be seen in Figure 5.16.

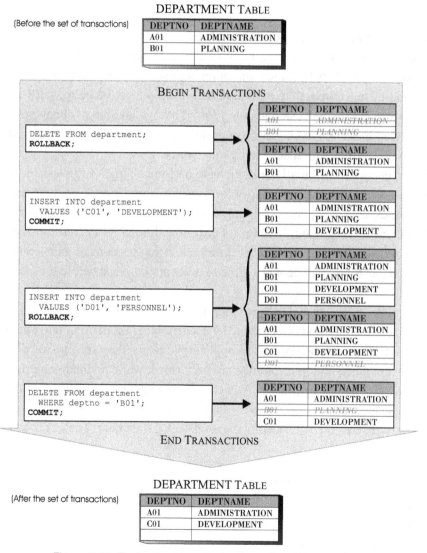

Figure 5.16: Evaluating the effects of a series of transactions

Uncommitted changes made by a transaction are usually inaccessible to other users and applications (there are exceptions, which we will look at in Chapter 7, "Data Concurrency") and can be backed out at any time. However, once a transaction's changes have been committed, they become accessible to all other users and applications— the only way to remove such changes is by performing an update, delete, or truncate operation.

Transaction Management with Savepoints

Often, it is desirable to limit the amount of work performed within a single transaction so that locks acquired on behalf of the transaction are released in a timely manner. (When locks are held by one transaction, other transactions might be forced to wait for those locks to be freed before they can continue.) And if a large number of changes are made within a single transaction, it can take a considerable amount of time to back out those changes should the transaction need to be rolled back.

However, using several small transactions to perform a single large task has its drawbacks as well. First, the opportunity for data to become inconsistent increases if business rules have to cross several transaction boundaries. Second, each time a COMMIT statement is executed, DB2 must perform additional work to commit the current transaction and start a new one. Another drawback is that portions of an operation might be committed and therefore become visible to other applications before the operation can complete.

To get around these issues, DB2 provides a mechanism known as a *savepoint* that can be used to break the work being done by a single large transaction into one or more smaller subsets. By using savepoints, an application avoids the exposure to "dirty data" that might occur when multiple commits are performed, while maintaining granular control over long-running operations. You can use as many savepoints as you desire within a single transaction, provided you do not nest them.

Savepoints are created by executing the SAVEPOINT statement. The basic syntax for this statement is:

```
SAVEPOINT [SavepointName]
  <UNIQUE>
  ON ROLLBACK RETAIN CURSORS
  <ON ROLLBACK RETAIN LOCKS>
```

where:

SavepointName   Identifies the name to assign to the savepoint that is to be created

If the UNIQUE clause is specified with the SAVEPOINT statement used, the name assigned to the savepoint will be unique and cannot be reused as long as the savepoint remains active. If the ON ROLLBACK RETAIN LOCKS clause is specified with the SAVEPOINT statement used, any locks that are acquired after the savepoint is created are not tracked and, therefore, will not be released if the transaction is rolled back to the savepoint. The ON ROLLBACK RETAIN CURSORS clause indicates that any cursors that are opened after the savepoint is created will not be tracked and, therefore, will not be closed if the transaction is rolled back to the savepoint.

Thus, to create a savepoint named MY_SP, you would execute a SAVEPOINT statement that looks like this:

```
SAVEPOINT my_sp ON ROLLBACK RETAIN CURSORS
```

Once created, a savepoint can be used in conjunction with a special form of the ROLLBACK statement to return a database to the state it was in at the time the savepoint was created. The syntax for this form of the ROLLBACK statement is:

```
ROLLBACK <WORK> TO SAVEPOINT <SavepointName>
```

where:

SavepointName   Specifies, by name, the savepoint to roll back operations performed against the database to

Figure 5.17 shows an example of how this form of the ROLLBACK statement is used, together with the SAVEPOINT statement, to break the work being performed by a single transaction into one or more subsets.

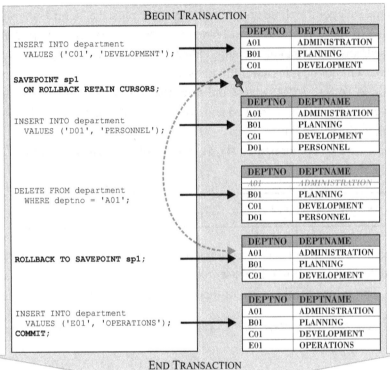

Figure 5.17: Using savepoints with the ROLLBACK statement to provide granular control over a long-running transaction

When a savepoint is no longer needed, you can delete (release) it by executing the RELEASE statement. The syntax for this statement is:

```
RELEASE <TO> SAVEPOINT <SavepointName>
```

where:

SavepointName   Identifies, by name, the savepoint that is to be deleted (released)

So, to delete a savepoint named MY_SP, you would execute a RELEASE statement that looks like this:

```
RELEASE SAVEPOINT my_sp
```

Once a savepoint is created, all subsequent SQL statements that are executed in a transaction are automatically associated with that savepoint until it is deleted—either explicitly by executing the RELEASE statement or implicitly by terminating the transaction the savepoint was created in. However, when a ROLLBACK TO SAVEPOINT statement is executed, the savepoint specified is not automatically deleted as part of the rollback operation.

Consequently, you can use multiple ROLLBACK statements to return a database to the state it was in at the time a particular savepoint was established. And if multiple savepoints are created, it is possible to roll back to any one of those savepoints, regardless of the order in which they were defined. (In other words, you are not required to roll back to every savepoint that exists, successively, in the opposite order in which they were created.)

A Word about DB2 10.5's SQL Compatibility Enhancements

DB2 10.5 for LUW contains three new SQL compatibility enhancements that make DB2 more familiar to individuals who work with relational database products other than DB2. These enhancements are designed to reduce the time and complexity of enabling applications that were written for other relational database products to run in DB2 environments. They are:

- Extended row-size support
- The ability to exclude NULL index keys
- String unit attributes that improve the handling of multibyte characters

Extended Row Size Support

In Chapter 4, "Working with Databases and Database Objects," we saw that records (rows) in a row-organized table are arranged into blocks called pages, which can be up to 4, 8, 16, or 32 KB in length, depending upon the page size of the table space the table is stored in. In previous releases of DB2, the maximum number of bytes allowed in a single row was limited by table space page size—any attempt to create a table whose row length exceeded the maximum length allowed would result in an error. In other words, if you attempted to execute a CREATE TABLE statement that looked like this:

```
CREATE TABLE tab1(col1 INTEGER, col2 VARCHAR(5000))
```

and the default table space used to store user tables (USERSPACE1) had a page size of 4 KB, the statement would fail because of the table's large row size. (The CREATE TABLE statement is discussed in great detail in Chapter 6, "Working with DB2 Tables, Views, and Indexes.")

Extended row size support enables tables that contain rows that exceed the maximum record length allowed by a particular table space to be constructed in that table space. With extended row size support enabled, the CREATE TABLE statement shown earlier will execute successfully in a DB2 10.5 database. (The maximum row size allowed becomes 1,048,319 bytes, regardless of the table space page size used.)

Extended row size support offers several benefits:

- It simplifies the migration of tables (to DB2) that were created with another database vendor's product that have row sizes exceeding 32 KB.
- It can help improve the performance of applications where the majority of data rows can fit on a smaller page but the table definition itself requires a larger page size.
- It allows the creation of tables with more VARCHAR or VARGRAPHIC columns. (The maximum number of columns supported has not changed, but the ability to exceed the maximum record length for the page size used allows for more columns per row.)

With the exception of range-clustered tables (RCTs), any row–organized table can take advantage of extended row size support. However, to do so, the *extended_row_sz* database configuration parameter must be set to ENABLE and the table must contain at least one column that uses the varying-length character string (VARCHAR) or the varying-length double-byte character string (VARGRAPHIC) data type. That's because when a data row whose length exceeds the maximum record length allowed for a table space is placed into a table that has been configured for extended row size support, a subset of the VARCHAR or VARGRAPHIC column's data is stored as large object (LOB) data, outside of the data row. (When this happens the column's data type is not altered; that is the VARCHAR or VARGRAPHIC column is not converted to a column with a LOB data type.)

Ability to Exclude NULL Index Keys

In previous releases of DB2, data for columns that participated in an index key were written to the index, even if that data consisted primarily of NULL values. But, starting with DB2 10.5, the EXCLUDE NULL KEYS clause can be used with the CREATE INDEX statement to reduce the size of such indexes. (The CREATE INDEX statement is discussed in more detail in Chapter 6, "Working with DB2 Tables, Views, and Indexes.")

Indexes that that are created with the EXCLUDE NULL KEYS clause specified do not insert a key into the index object if all the columns in the key contain NULL values. This exclusion of NULL keys can help optimize storage, as well as reduce the overhead involved in maintaining indexes. It can also improve performance in situations where you want queries to avoid accessing data that is associated with a NULL key.

● ●

Note: With unique indexes, the enforcement of the uniqueness of table data causes rows with NULL index keys to be ignored.

● ●

String Unit Attributes Improve Handling of Multibyte Characters

Historically, table columns that hold character data have been defined as being able to store x number of bytes. With single-byte character sets, x is equivalent to the number of characters that are allowed in the column; with double-byte character sets, x is typically half that number. Unfortunately, this can cause problems when moving from a single-byte character set to a multibyte character set because the number of characters that can actually be stored in a column is dependent upon how those characters have been encoded.

Starting with DB2 10.5, FixPack 4, columns that hold character data— that is, columns that have been defined as having a CHAR, VARCHAR, CLOB, GRAPHIC,

VARGRAPHIC, or DBCLOB data type—have a special "string unit" attribute that controls how the length of a data value for that column is determined. (Data types are discussed in great detail in Chapter 6, "Working with DB2 Tables, Views, and Indexes.") This string unit attribute can be set to any of the following values:

- **OCTETS**: Indicates that the units for the length attribute are bytes. This unit of length applies to all character string data types in a non-Unicode database. In a Unicode database, you can explicitly specify this unit of length, or it can be determined based on an environment setting.
- **CODEUNITS16**: Indicates that the units for the length attribute are Unicode UTF-16 code units (which are the same as double-byte). This unit of length can only be used with graphic string data types in a Unicode database. It does not affect the underlying code page of the data type.
- **CODEUNITS32**: Indicates that the units for the length attribute are Unicode UTF-32 code units, which approximates counting in characters. The actual length of a data value is determined by counting the UTF-32 code units that would apply if the data were converted to UTF-32. This unit of length can only be used in a Unicode database. It does not affect the underlying code page of the data type.

Thus, a column that has been defined as having a VARCHAR(5 OCTETS) data type could hold five bytes of characters; a column with a VARCHAR(5 CODEUNITS16) data type could hold five 2-byte characters; and a column with a VARCHAR(5 CODEUNITS32) data type could hold five 4-byte characters.

The units for length attribute is supported in the definition of table columns, routine arguments, array types, distinct types, row types, and variables. It can also be used in the target data type of a CAST specification.

6

CHAPTER

Working with DB2 Tables, Views, and Indexes

Thirteen percent (13%) of the *DB2 10.5 Fundamentals for LUW* certification exam (Exam 615) is designed to test your ability to identify the data types and constraints that are available with DB2, as well as your ability to identify the characteristics of schemas, tables, indexes, and views. The questions that make up this portion of the exam are intended to evaluate the following:

- Your knowledge of the built-in data types that are available with DB2 (including Oracle compatibility data types)
- Your ability to identify the appropriate data type to use for a given situation
- Your ability to create and modify both a base table and a temporary table
- Your ability to identify the characteristics of a table, view, or index
- Your ability to identify how triggers are created and when they should be used

This chapter introduces you to the various data types and constraints that are available with DB2, and it shows you how to work with tables, views, and indexes. In this chapter, you will learn about the built-in data types that can be used to store different kinds of information in a DB2 database, and you will be shown how NOT NULL, default, UNIQUE, CHECK, and referential integrity constraints can be used to provide the logic needed to enforce certain business rules. You will also discover how to create and modify tables, as well as how to identify the characteristics of tables, views, and indexes. Finally, you will learn how to create and use triggers to both automate data processing and supplement any constraints that may exist.

DB2's Data Types

If you stop to think about it, most "data" you encounter on a daily basis falls into several distinct categories. For example, the money you buy coffee with and the change you get back are numerical in nature; the email messages you receive and the replies you send consist of strings of alphanumeric characters; and many things you do such as waking up, going to the office, returning home, and going to bed revolve around time. This holds true for database data as well. Consequently, data stored in a database can be categorized according to its *data type*.

To ensure that data is stored as efficiently as possible, DB2 comes equipped with a wide variety of built-in data types, which are classified according to the kind of data they have been designed to hold:

- Numeric values
- Characters and character strings
- Dates and times
- Large objects
- Extensible Markup Language (XML) documents

In the event that none of the built-in data types meet your needs, DB2 also gives you the ability to create your own "user-defined" data types, which in turn can be used to store complex, nontraditional data that might be found in an intricate computing environment.

Numeric Data Types

As the name implies, numeric data types are used to store numerical values—specifically, numerical values that have a *sign* and a *precision*. The sign is considered positive if the value is greater than or equal to zero and negative if the value is anything else; the precision is the actual number of digits needed to properly display the value. Numeric data is stored by using a fixed amount of storage space, and the amount of space required increases as the precision of the number rises. The numeric data types that are available with DB2 include:

- **Small integer:** This data type is used to store numeric values that have a precision of five or fewer digits. The range for small integer values is –32,768 to 32,767, and 2 bytes of space is needed for every small integer value stored. (Positive numbers have one less value in their range because they start at the value 0; negative numbers start at –1.) The keyword SMALLINT denotes the small integer data type.
- **Integer:** This data type is used to store numeric values that have a precision of 10 digits. The range for integer values is –2,147,483,648 to 2,147,483,647, and 4 bytes of space is required for every integer value stored. The keywords INTEGER and INT denote the integer data type.
- **Big integer:** This data type is used to store numeric values that have a precision of 19 digits. The range for big integer values is –9,223,372,036,854,775,808 to 9,223,372,036,854,775,807, and 8 bytes of space is needed for every big integer value stored. The keyword BIGINT denotes the big integer data type. (This data type is typically used on systems that provide native support for 64-bit integers. On such systems, processing large numbers that have been stored as big integers is much more efficient and results in more precise calculations.)
- **Decimal:** This data type is used to store numeric values that contain both whole and fractional parts separated by a decimal point. Both the precision and the *scale* of the value determine the exact location of the decimal point. (The scale is the number of digits used by the fractional part of the number). The keywords DECIMAL, DEC, NUMERIC, and NUM denote the decimal data type.

  The amount of space required to store a decimal value can be determined by solving the following equation: *Precision* ÷ 2 (truncated) + 1 = *Bytes required.* (For example, the value 67.12345 has a precision of 7, 7 ÷ 2 = 3, and 3 + 1 = 4; therefore, 4 bytes are required to store the value 67.12345.) The maximum precision allowed for decimal values is 31 digits, and the scale must be a positive number that is less than the precision. If no scale or precision is specified, a scale of 5 and a precision of 0 are used by default—in other words, DECIMAL(5,0).
- **Single-precision floating-point:** This data type is used to store a 32-bit approximation of a real number. This number can be zero, or it can fall within the range of $-3.402E^{+38}$ to $-1.175E^{-37}$ or $1.175E^{-37}$ to $3.402E^{+38}$. Each single-precision floating-point value can be up to 24 digits in length, and 4 bytes of space are needed for every value stored. The keywords REAL and FLOAT (with a range of 1 to 24) denote the single-precision floating-point data type.

- **Double-precision floating-point:** This data type is used to store a 64-bit approximation of a real number. This number can be zero, or it can fall within the range of $-1.79769E^{+308}$ to $-2.225E^{-307}$ or $2.225E^{-307}$ to $1.79769E^{+308}$. Each double-precision floating-point value can be up to 53 digits in length, and 8 bytes of space are needed for each value stored. The terms DOUBLE, DOUBLE PRECISION, and FLOAT (with a range of 25 to 53) denote the double-precision floating-point data type.

- **Decimal floating-point:** This data type is used to store floating-point numbers with a decimal point (as defined in the IEEE 754-2008 Standard for Binary Floating-Point Arithmetic) that have a precision of 16 or 34 digits and an exponent range of $10E^{-383}$ to $10E^{+384}$ or $10E^{-6143}$ to $10E^{+6144}$, respectively.

  In addition to finite numbers, the decimal floating-point data type can be used to store any of the following named decimal floating-point special values:

  » *Infinity*—a value that represents a number whose magnitude is infinitely large

  » *Quiet NaN*—a value that represents undefined results and does not cause an invalid number warning (NaN stand for *Not a Number*)

  » *Signaling NaN*—a value that represents undefined results and causes an invalid number warning if used in any numeric operation

  When a number has one of these special values, its coefficient and exponent are undefined—the sign of an infinity value is significant because it is possible to have positive or negative infinity. The sign of a NaN value has no meaning for arithmetic operations. The term DECFLOAT is used to denote the decimal floating-point data type.

Character String Data Types

Character string data types are used to store values composed of one or more alphanumeric characters—together, these characters can form a word, a sentence, a paragraph, or a complete document. A variety of character string data types are available, and deciding which type to use for a given situation depends primarily upon the length and storage requirements of the data value to be stored. Character string data types include:

- **Fixed-length character string:** This data type is used to store character string values that are between 1 and 254 characters in length. The amount of space required to store a fixed-length character string value can be determined by solving the following equation: *(Number of characters × 1) = Bytes required*. A fixed amount of storage space is allocated, even if all the space is not needed—short strings are padded with blanks. The keywords CHARACTER and CHAR denote the fixed-length character string data type.

- **Varying-length character string:** This data type is used to store character string values that are up to 32,672 characters in length—the table space page size used governs the actual length allowed. For tables residing in table spaces that use 4 KB pages, varying-length character string values can be no more than 4,092 characters in length; for tables in table spaces that use 8 KB pages, varying-length character string values can be no more than 8,188 characters in length; and so on. The amount of space required to store a varying-length character string value can be determined by solving the following equation: (*Number of characters* × *1*) + *4* = *Bytes required*. Only the amount of storage space actually needed, plus 4 bytes for an *"end-of-string"* marker, is allocated—short strings are not padded with blanks. The keywords CHARACTER VARYING, CHAR VARYING, and VARCHAR denote the varying-length character string data type.

- **Fixed-length double-byte character string:** This data type is used to store double-byte character set (DBCS) character string values that are up to 127 characters in length. (Most Asian character sets are double-byte character sets.) The amount of space required to store a fixed-length double-byte character string value can be determined by solving the following equation: (*Number of characters* × *2*) = *Bytes required*. A fixed amount of storage space is allocated, even if all the space is not needed—short strings are padded with blanks. The term GRAPHIC denotes the fixed-length double-byte character string data type.

- **Varying-length double-byte character string:** This data type is used to store DBCS character string values that are up to 16,336 characters in length. Again, the table space page size used governs the actual length allowed. For tables residing in table spaces that use 4 KB pages, varying-length double-byte character string values can be no more than 2,046 characters in length; for tables that reside in a table spaces that use 8 KB pages, varying-length double-byte character string values can be no more than 4,094 characters in length; and so on. The amount of space required to store a varying-length double-byte character string value can be determined by solving the following equation: (*Number of characters* × *2*) + *4* = *Bytes required*. The keyword VARGRAPHIC denotes the varying-length double-byte character string data type.

- **National fixed-length character string:** This data type is used to store a sequence of bytes, up to 127 bytes in length, in a Unicode database that uses UTF-16BE encoding. The amount of space required to store a national fixed-length character string value can be determined by solving the following equation: (*Number of characters* × 2) = *Bytes required*. The keywords NATIONAL CHARACTER, NATIONAL CHAR, and NCHAR denote the national fixed-length character string data type.

- **National varying-length character string:** This data type is used to store a sequence of bytes, up to 16,336 bytes in length, in a Unicode database that uses UTF-16BE encoding. Once again, the table space page size used governs the actual length allowed. For tables that reside in table spaces that use 4 KB pages, national varying-length character string values cannot be more than 2,046 characters in length; for tables that reside in a table spaces that use 8 KB pages, national varying-length character string values cannot be more than 4,094 characters in length; and so on. The amount of space required to store a national varying-length character string value can be determined by solving the following equation: (*Number of characters* × 2) + 4 = *Bytes required*. The keywords NATIONAL CHARACTER VARYING, NATIONAL CHAR VARYING, NCHAR VARYING, and NVARCHAR denote the national varying-length character string data type.

Date and Time Data Types

As the name implies, date and time data types are used to store values that represent dates and times. From a user perspective, such values appear to be character strings; however, they are actually stored as binary packed strings. Date/time data types include:

- **Date:** This data type is used to store three-part values (year, month, and day) that represent calendar dates. The range for the year portion is 0001 to 9999; the month portion is 1 to 12; and the day portion is 1 to 28, 29, 30, or 31, depending upon the month value specified and whether the year value corresponds to a leap year. Externally, date values appear to be fixed-length character string values that are 10 characters in length. However, only 4 bytes of space are needed for each date value stored. The keyword DATE denotes the date data type.
- **Time:** This data type is used to store three-part values (hours, minutes, and seconds) that represent time based on a 24-hour clock. The range for the hours portion is 0 to 24, the minutes portion is 0 to 59, and the seconds portion is 0 to 59. Externally, time values appear to be fixed-length character string values that are eight characters in length. However, only 3 bytes of space are required for each time value stored. The keyword TIME denotes the time data type.

- **Timestamp:** This data type is used to store six- or seven-part values (year, month, day, hours, minutes, seconds, and microseconds) that represent a specific calendar date and time (again, using a 24-hour clock). The range for the year portion is 0001 to 9999; the month portion is 1 to 12; the day portion is 1 to 28, 29, 30, or 31, depending upon the month value specified and whether the year specified is a leap year; the hours portion is 0 to 24; the minutes portion is 0 to 59; the seconds portion is 0 to 59; and the microseconds portion is 0 to 999,999,999,999. The number of digits used in the fractional seconds portion can be anywhere from 0 to 12; however, the default is 6 (microseconds).

  Externally, timestamp values appear to be fixed-length character string values that are up to 32 characters in length, and in the United States, this string is normally displayed using the format *YYYY-MM-DD-HH.MM.SS.NNNNNN*, which translates to Year-Month-Day-Hour.Minute.Second.Microseconds, where four digits are used to present the year, six digits are used to present the microseconds (by default), and two digits are used to present each of the remaining elements. However, the internal representation of a timestamp requires between 7 and 13 bytes of storage. The keyword TIMESTAMP denotes the timestamp data type.

Because the representation of date and time values varies throughout the world, the actual string format used to present a date or time value is dependent upon the territory code that has been assigned to the database being used. Table 6.1 shows the date and time string formats that are currently available with DB2.

Table 6.1: Date and time formats currently available with DB2			
Format Name	**Abbreviation**	**Date String Format**	**Time String Format**
International Standards Organization	ISO	YYYY-MM-DD*	HH.MM.SS†
IBM USA Standard	USA	MM/DD/YYYY*	HH:MM AM or PM†
IBM European Standard	EUR	DD.MM.YYYY*	HH.MM.SS†
Japanese Industrial Standard	JIS	YYYY-MM-DD*	HH:MM:SS†
Site Specific	LOC	Based on database territory and the application's country code	Based on database territory and the application's country code
* For date formats: YYYY = Year, MM = Month, and DD = Day † For time formats: HH = Hour, MM = Minute, and SS = Seconds Adapted from Tables 1 and 2, found under **Datetime values** in the IBM DB2 10.5 Knowledge Center (*www-01.ibm.com/support/knowledgecenter/?lang=en#!/SSEPGG_10.5.0/com.ibm.db2.luw.sql.ref.doc/doc/r0008474.html?cp=SSEPGG_10.5.0%2F2-12-2-3-0-6*).			

Large Object Data Types

Large object (LOB) data types are used to store large, unstructured data values. LOB data types include:

- **Binary large object:** This data type is used to store binary data values (such as documents, graphic images, pictures, audio, and video) that are up to 2 GB in size—the actual amount of space set aside to store a binary large object value is determined by the length specification provided when a column with this data type is defined. For example, 800 bytes of storage space will be allocated for a column that is given a BINARY LARGE OBJECT(800) definition. The keywords BINARY LARGE OBJECT and BLOB denote the binary large object data type.

- **Character large object:** This data type is used to store single-byte character set (SBCS) or multibyte character set (MBCS) character string values that are between 32,700 and 2,147,483,647 characters in length—the actual amount of space set aside to store a character large object value is determined by the length specification provided when a column with this data type is defined. For example, 800 bytes of storage space will be allocated for a column that is given a CHARACTER LARGE OBJECT(800) definition. The keywords CHARACTER LARGE OBJECT, CHAR LARGE OBJECT, and CLOB denote the character large object data type.

- **Double-byte character large object:** This data type is used to store DBCS character string values that are between 16,350 and 1,073,741,823 characters in length—the actual amount of space set aside to store a double-byte character large object value is determined by the length specification provided when a column with this data type is defined. For example, 800 bytes of storage space will be allocated for a column that is given a DBCLOB(400) definition. The keyword DBCLOB denotes the double-byte character large object data type.

- **National character large object:** This data type is used to store a sequence of characters—between 16,350 and 1,073,741,823 bytes in length—in a Unicode database that uses UTF-16BE encoding. The actual amount of space set aside to store a national character large object value is determined by the length specification provided when a column with this data type is defined. For example, 800 bytes of storage space will be allocated for a column that is given a NATIONAL CHARACTER LARGE OBJECT(400) definition. The keyword NATIONAL CHARACTER LARGE OBJECT, NCHAR LARGE OBJECT, and NCLOB denote the national character large object data type.

From an application perspective, the LOB data type used determines how LOB data is accessed. For instance, because BLOB data is usually indecipherable, applications have to know the format of a BLOB value and be customized to work with such values.

A word about inline LOBs

Some applications make extensive use of LOBs, and in some cases the LOB data they work with is relatively small—at most, just a few kilobytes. When this is the case, query performance can often be increased by storing LOB data in the same data pages as the rest of a table's rows, rather than in a separate LOB storage object, which is where LOB data is stored by default. Such LOBs are referred to as *inline LOBs*, and they are created by appending the INLINE LENGTH clause to a LOB column's definition; the inline length specified indicates the maximum size, in bytes (including four bytes for overhead), that LOB values stored in the column can be.

Inline LOBs improve the performance of queries that access LOB data because no additional I/O is needed to store and access this type of data. Moreover, inline LOB data is eligible for compression, whereas traditional LOB data is not. However, when a table contains one or more inline LOB columns, fewer rows will fit on a page. Consequently, the performance of queries that return only non-LOB data can be adversely affected (because such queries have to retrieve more pages). In addition, operations against inline LOBs are always logged; therefore, their use can increase logging overhead.

The Extensible Markup Language (XML) Data Type

XML is a simple, yet flexible text-based format that provides a neutral way to exchange data between different devices, systems, and applications—XML data is maintained in a self-describing format that is hierarchical in nature. As the name implies, the **Extensible Markup Language Document** data type is used to store XML documents *in their native format*. In fact, only well-formed XML documents can be stored in columns that have been assigned the Extensible Markup Language data type. (XML values are processed in an internal representation that is not comparable to any string value; however, you can use the XMLSERIALIZE() function to transform an XML value into a serialized string that represents an XML document. Similarly, you can use the XMLPARSE() function to transform a string value that represents an XML document into an XML value.) The amount of space needed to store an XML document varies and is determined, in part, by the size and characteristics of the XML document being stored. (By default, XML data is stored in an XML storage object that is separate from the table's relational storage location.) The keyword XML denotes the Extensible Markup Language Document data type.

A Word About the Oracle Compatibility Data Types

DB2 10.5 for Linux, UNIX, and Windows contains a number of features that can greatly reduce the time and effort required to enable existing applications that were written for other relational database products, such as Oracle and Sybase, to execute in a DB2 environment. Some of these features are enabled by default, and others must be explicitly "turned on" (by assigning the appropriate value to the DB2_COMPATIBILITY_VECTOR registry variable). For instance, to use the DB2 compatibility features that exist for applications that have been developed for an Oracle database, you must assign the value ORA to the DB2_COMPATIBILITY_VECTOR registry variable *before a database is created*. And in the case of Oracle, when features that provide compatibility are explicitly enabled, some additional Oracle-specific data types are made available for use. These data types are:

- **DATE as TIMESTAMP(0)**: This data type provides support for applications that use the Oracle DATE data type. (The Oracle DATE data type is a datetime data type that is used to store date values that contain both date and time information—for example, '2016-07-04-10.45.05'.)
- **NUMBER**: This data type provides support for applications that use the Oracle NUMBER data type. (The Oracle NUMBER data type is a numeric data type that is used to store both fixed and floating-point numbers with up to 38 significant digits—the numeric value stored in a NUMBER data type can be zero, or it can fall within the range of $-1.0E^{-130}$ to $9.99E^{+125}$ or $1.0E^{-130}$ to $9.99E^{+125}$.)
- **VARCHAR2**: This data type provides support for applications that use the Oracle VARCHAR2 data type. (The Oracle VARCHAR2 data type is a variable-length character string data type that is used to store character string values that are up to 4,000 characters in length.) **NVARCHAR2**: This data type provides support for applications that use the Oracle NVARCHAR2 data type. (The Oracle NVARCHAR2 data type is a national variable-length character string data type that is used to store a sequence of bytes, up to 4,000 bytes in length, in a Unicode database that uses AL16UTF16 or UTF8 encoding.)

User-Defined Data Types

In Chapter 4, "Working with Databases and Database Objects," we saw that user-defined data types (UDTs) are data types that are explicitly created by a database user. Two different types of UDTs are available: *distinct* and *structured*. A distinct data type is a UDT that shares a common representation with one of the built-in data types available with DB2. A structured data type is a UDT that consists of a sequence of named attributes, each of which has a name and data type of its own.

UDTs are subject to strong data typing, which means that even though they might share the same representation as other built-in or user-defined data types, the value of one UDT is compatible only with values of that same data type (or of other user-defined data types within the same structured data type hierarchy). As a result, you cannot use UDTs as arguments for most built-in functions. However, as we saw in Chapter 4, "Working with Databases and Database Objects," it is possible to create UDFs and operators that duplicate the functionality provided by many of the built-in functions available.

Understanding Data Constraints

Often, data must adhere to a set of business rules and restrictions. (For example, many companies have a specific format and numbering sequence they use when generating purchase order numbers.) And, in many cases, the logic required to enforce these rules and restrictions is woven into applications that interact with one or more databases. However, the logic needed to enforce business rules can often be placed directly in a database by means of one or more *data constraints*. Data constraints are special rules that govern how new data values can be added to a table, as well as how existing values can be altered once they have been stored. The following types of data constraints are available with DB2:

- NOT NULL constraints
- Default constraints
- UNIQUE constraints
- CHECK constraints
- Referential integrity constraints
- Informational constraints

Any of these constraints can be defined during the table creation process. Or they can be added to existing tables by using various forms of the ALTER TABLE statement.

NOT NULL *Constraints*

With DB2, NULL values (not to be confused with empty strings) represent missing or unknown data and states. Consequently, by default, every column in a table will accept a NULL value—this allows records to be added to a table when all the information associated with a particular record is not known. However, there may be times when this behavior is unacceptable. For example, people hired in the United States usually must provide their Social Security number for state and federal tax purposes. Therefore, you probably do not want to allow NULL Social Security number values to be entered in a table that is used to keep track of employee information.

In these situations, the NOT NULL constraint can be used to ensure that a particular column in a table is never assigned a NULL value. Once a NOT NULL constraint has been defined for a column, any operation that attempts to place a NULL value in that column will fail. Figure 6.1 illustrates how the NOT NULL constraint is enforced.

Default Constraints

Just as there may be times when you want to prevent NULL values from being stored, there might be instances when you would like the system to provide a default value for you. For example, you may want to automatically assign the current date to a particular column each time a new record is added to a table. This is where default constraints come in.

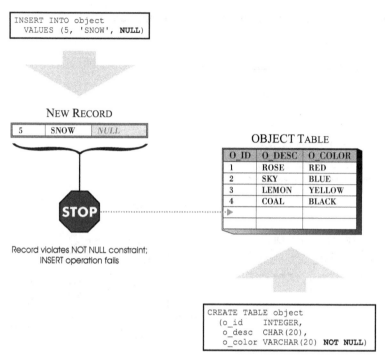

```
INSERT INTO object
    VALUES (5, 'SNOW', NULL)
```

NEW RECORD

| 5 | SNOW | NULL |

OBJECT TABLE

O_ID	O_DESC	O_COLOR
1	ROSE	RED
2	SKY	BLUE
3	LEMON	YELLOW
4	COAL	BLACK

STOP

Record violates NOT NULL constraint;
INSERT operation fails

```
CREATE TABLE object
    (o_id    INTEGER,
     o_desc  CHAR(20),
     o_color VARCHAR(20) NOT NULL)
```

Figure 6.1: How the NOT NULL constraint is enforced

A default constraint ensures that a particular column in a table will be assigned a predefined default value if no value for that column is provided when a new record is added to the table. This default value can be NULL (provided a NOT NULL constraint has not been defined for the column), a user-supplied value that is compatible with the column's data type, or a value that DB2 supplies.

Figure 6.2 illustrates how a default constraint is applied.

```
INSERT INTO object (o_id, o_desc)
   VALUES (5, 'SNOW')
```

NEW RECORD (MISSING VALUES)

5	SNOW	*NULL*

Record is missing a value for a column;
A predefined value is provided by the default constraint

NEW RECORD (WITH DEFAULT)

5	SNOW	Unknown

OBJECT TABLE

O_ID	O_DESC	O_COLOR
1	ROSE	RED
2	SKY	BLUE
3	LEMON	YELLOW
4	COAL	BLACK
5	SNOW	Unknown

```
CREATE TABLE object
   (o_id    INTEGER,
    o_desc  CHAR(20),
    o_color VARCHAR(20) WITH DEFAULT 'Unknown')
```

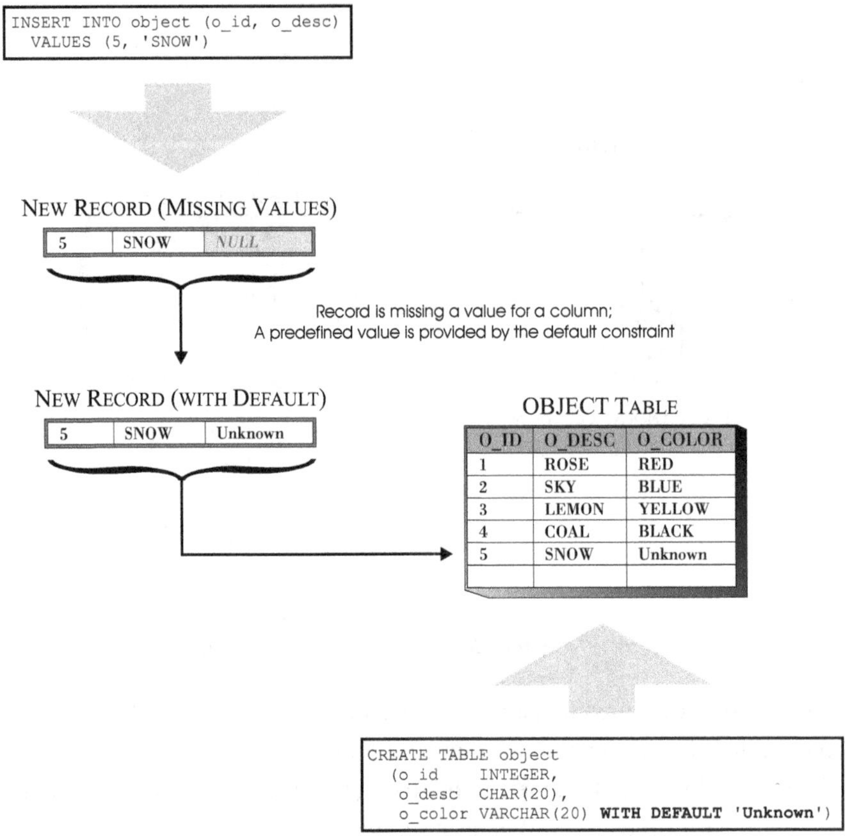

Figure 6.2: How a default constraint is applied

UNIQUE Constraints

By default, records that are added to a table can have the same value assigned to any of their columns, any number of times. And, as long as the records stored in the table do not contain information that should never be duplicated, this kind of behavior is acceptable. However, sometimes certain pieces of information that are stored in a record should be unique. For example, if an employee identification number is assigned to every individual who works for a particular company, each number should probably be used only once— all sorts of problems can arise if two or more employees are assigned the same employee identification number.

In these types of situations, a UNIQUE constraint can be used to ensure that values assigned to one or more columns of a table are always unique. After a UNIQUE constraint has been defined for one or more columns, any operation that attempts to place duplicate values in those columns will fail. Figure 6.3 illustrates how a UNIQUE constraint is enforced.

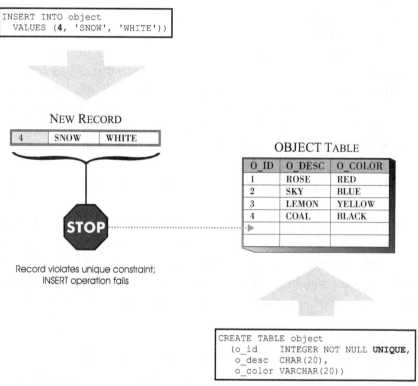

Figure 6.3: How a UNIQUE *constraint can prevent the duplication of data values*

Unlike NOT NULL and default constraints, which can only be associated with single columns, UNIQUE constraints can be associated with individual columns *or* a group of columns. However, each column in a table can participate in only one UNIQUE constraint, regardless of how the columns are grouped. As with the other constraints, a table can have any number of UNIQUE constraints defined, but *a table cannot have more than one UNIQUE constraint defined on the same set of columns.*

When a UNIQUE constraint is defined, the DB2 Database Manager checks to see whether an index for the columns the UNIQUE constraint refers to already exists. If it finds an appropriate index, that index is marked as being "unique and system-required"; if not, a new index is created and given similar characteristics (unique and system-required). In either case, the index is then used to enforce uniqueness in the columns the constraint was defined for.

● ●

Note: Although a unique, system-required index is used to enforce a UNIQUE constraint, a distinction exists between defining a UNIQUE constraint and creating a unique index. While both enforce uniqueness, a unique index will accept one (and only one) NULL value and generally cannot be used in a referential integrity constraint. A UNIQUE constraint, however, does not allow NULL values (thus, every column that is part of a UNIQUE constraint must also be assigned a NOT NULL constraint) and can participate in a referential integrity constraint.

● ●

A *primary key* is a special form of a UNIQUE constraint that uniquely defines the characteristics of each row in a table. The most significant difference between a primary key and a UNIQUE constraint is that only one primary key is allowed per table, whereas a single table can contain multiple UNIQUE constraints. In addition, primary keys can be used to define a referential integrity constraint (which we will look at shortly).

Check Constraints

Sometimes, it is desirable to control which values will be accepted for a particular column (and which values will be denied). For instance, a company might decide that the lowest salary a nonexempt employee can receive is the federal minimum wage; consequently, salary values that are stored in the company's payroll database can never be lower than the current federal minimum wage. In such situations, the logic needed to determine whether a particular value is acceptable can be incorporated into the application that is used to add data to the database. Or, that logic can be included in the definition of the column that is to hold the data using what is known as a CHECK constraint. A CHECK constraint (also referred to as a *table check constraint*) can be used to ensure that a particular column in a table is never assigned an unacceptable value. After a CHECK constraint has been defined for a particular column, any operation that attempts to place a value into that column that does not meet a specific set of criteria will fail.

CHECK constraints consist of one or more predicates (connected by the keywords AND or OR) that collectively are known as a *check condition*. Each time an operation inserts a value into (or changes a value in) a column that has CHECK constraint defined for it, that value is compared with the corresponding check condition, and the result of the comparison is returned as TRUE, FALSE, or Unknown. If the result returned is TRUE, the value is deemed acceptable and is added to the database; if the result returned is FALSE or Unknown, the operation fails and changes made by the operation are backed out (rolled back). Unlike with other roll-back situations, the transaction that initiated the operation is not terminated, and other operations within that transaction are not affected. Figure 6.4 illustrates just one example of how a CHECK constraint can be used.

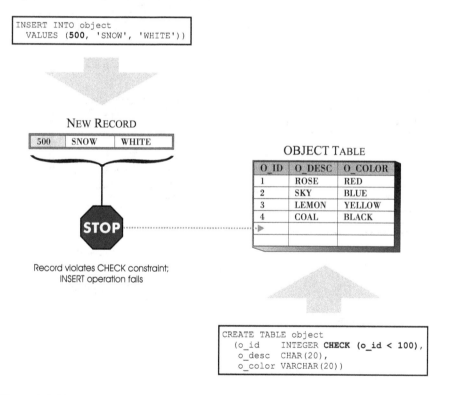

Figure 6.4: How to use a CHECK *constraint to control which values a column accepts*

Referential Integrity Constraints

If you have had the opportunity to work with any relational database management system in the past, you are probably aware that data normalization is a technique that is used to ensure that the same data values are not stored in multiple locations—that there is only one way to get to a single fact. Data normalization is possible because two or more individual tables can have some type of relationship with one another, and as we saw in Chapter 5, "Working with DB2 Data Using SQL and XQuery," information stored in related tables can be combined by using a join operation. And when data is normalized, referential integrity constraints (also known as *referential constraints* and *foreign key constraints*) can be used to define *required* relationships between select columns and tables. Figure 6.5 shows a simple referential integrity constraint (and how such a constraint might be enforced).

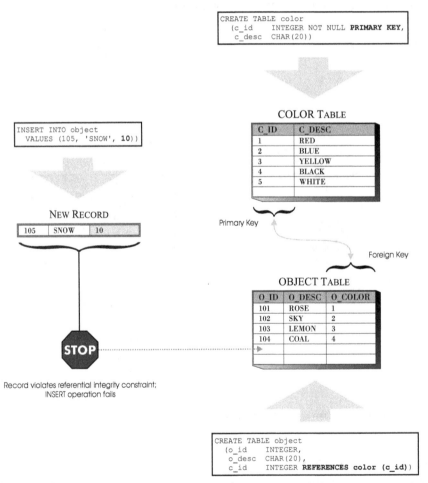

Figure 6.5: How a referential integrity constraint is used to define a relationship between two tables

In this example, a table named COLOR is used to store a numerical code and a corresponding description for several different colors, and a table named OBJECT is used to store predominant color information for a few basic objects. Because every object must be assigned a color value, a referential constraint can be used to ensure that every record that resides in the OBJECT table has a corresponding record in the COLOR table. The relationship between these two tables is established by comparing values that are to be added to the C_ID column of the OBJECT table (known as the *foreign key* of the *child table*) with values that currently exist for the C_ID column of the COLOR table (known as the *parent key* of the *parent table*).

In this scenario, a single column defines the parent and foreign keys of the referential integrity constraint. However, as with UNIQUE constraints, multiple columns can be used to define both parent and foreign keys.

Note: The names of the columns used to create the foreign key of a referential constraint do not have to be the same as the names of the columns that were used to create the primary key. Nevertheless, the data types of the columns that make up the primary and foreign keys of a referential constraint must be identical, and the number of columns used in both keys must be the same.

As you can see, referential constraints are much more complex than the other constraints we have looked at. In fact, referential constraints can be so complex that a set of special terms is used to identify the individual components that can make up a single referential constraint. You have already seen some of them; Table 6.2 contains the complete list.

Table 6.2: Referential integrity constraint terminology	
Term	**Meaning**
Unique key	A column or set of columns in which every row of values is different from the values of all other rows
Primary key	A special key that that uniquely defines the characteristics of each row in a table (and does not accept NULL values); a single primary key can be used in multiple referential constraints
Parent key	A primary key or unique key in a parent table that is referenced by a foreign key in a referential constraint

Table 6.2: Referential integrity constraint terminology (continued)	
Term	**Meaning**
Parent table	A table that contains a parent key of a referential constraint; a table can be both a parent table and a child table of any number of referential constraints
Parent row	A row in a parent table that has at least one matching row in a child (dependent) table
Foreign key	A column or set of columns in a child table whose values must match those of a parent key in a parent table; a foreign key must reference a primary key, but only one primary key can be referenced
Child (or dependent) table	A table containing at least one foreign key that references a parent key in a referential constraint; a table can be both a child table and a parent table of any number of referential constraints
Child (or dependent) row	A row in a child table that has at least one matching row in a parent table
Descendant table	A child table or a descendant of a child table
Descendant row	A child row or a descendant of a child row
Referential cycle	A set of referential constraints defined in such a way that each table in the set is a descendent of itself
Self-referencing table	A table that is both a parent and a child in the same referential constraint; such a constraint is known as a self-referencing constraint
Self-referencing row	A row that is a parent of itself

The primary reason for using referential constraints is to guarantee that data integrity is maintained whenever one table references another. As long as a referential constraint is in place, DB2 ensures that for every row in a child table that has a value in a foreign key column, a corresponding row in the associated parent table exists. So what happens when someone attempts to manipulate data in a way that will violate a referential constraint? To answer this question, let us first look at what can compromise data integrity if the checks and balances a referential constraint provides are not in place:

- An insert operation can add a value to a column in a child table that does not have a matching value in the associated parent table. (For instance, using the example in Figure 6.5, a value could be added to the O_COLOR column of the OBJECT table that does not exist in the C_ID column of the COLOR table.)
- An update operation can change an existing value in a child table such that it no longer has a matching value in the associated parent table. (For example, a value could be changed in the O_COLOR column of the OBJECT table in such a way that it no longer has a corresponding value in the C_ID column of the COLOR table.)

- An update operation can change an existing value in a parent table, leaving rows in a child table with values that no longer match those in the parent table. (For example, a value could be changed in the C_ID column of the COLOR table, leaving records in the OBJECT table with values in the O_COLOR column that no longer have a matching value in the COLOR table.)
- A delete operation can remove a value from a parent table, leaving rows in a child table with values that no longer match those in the parent table. (For example, a record could be removed from the COLOR table, leaving records in the OBJECT table with values in the O_COLOR column that no longer have a matching value in the C_ID column of the COLOR table.)

DB2 can prevent these types of operations from being performed on tables that are part of a referential constraint. Or it can attempt to carry out these actions in a way that will safeguard data integrity by using a special set of rules—an *Insert Rule*, an *Update Rule*, and a *Delete Rule*—to control the behavior. Each referential constraint has its own Insert, Update, and Delete Rule, and the way in which two of these rules will be enforced can be controlled during the referential constraint creation process.

The Insert Rule for referential constraints

The Insert Rule for referential constraints guarantees that a value can never be inserted into the foreign key of a child table unless a matching value exists in the parent key of the associated parent table. Consequently, any attempt to insert a record into a child table that violates this rule will result in an error. In contrast, no checking is performed when records are inserted into the parent key of the parent table. Figure 6.6 illustrates how a row that conforms to the Insert Rule for a referential constraint is successfully added to a child table. Figure 6.7 shows how a row that violates the Insert Rule will cause an insert operation to fail.

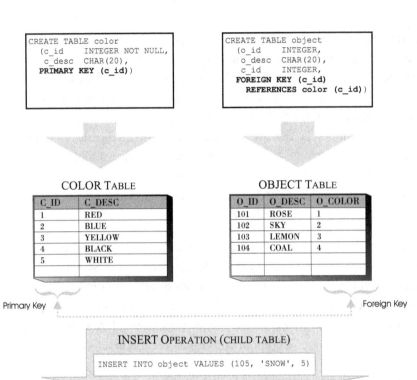

Figure 6.6: An insert operation that conforms to the Insert Rule of a referential constraint

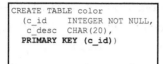

```
CREATE TABLE color
   (c_id    INTEGER NOT NULL,
   c_desc CHAR(20),
   PRIMARY KEY (c_id))
```

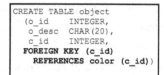

```
CREATE TABLE object
   (o_id    INTEGER,
   o_desc  CHAR(20),
   c_id    INTEGER,
   FOREIGN KEY (c_id)
     REFERENCES color (c_id))
```

COLOR TABLE

C_ID	C_DESC
1	RED
2	BLUE
3	YELLOW
4	BLACK
5	WHITE

OBJECT TABLE

O_ID	O_DESC	O_COLOR
101	ROSE	1
102	SKY	2
103	LEMON	3
104	COAL	4

Primary Key   Foreign Key

INSERT OPERATION (CHILD TABLE)

```
INSERT INTO object VALUES (105, 'SNOW', 8)
```

The value **8** does not exist in the primary key;
INSERT operation fails

COLOR TABLE

C_ID	C_DESC
1	RED
2	BLUE
3	YELLOW
4	BLACK
5	WHITE

OBJECT TABLE

O_ID	O_DESC	O_COLOR
101	ROSE	1
102	SKY	2
103	LEMON	3
104	COAL	4

Figure 6.7: An insert operation that violates the Insert Rule of a referential constraint

An Insert Rule for a referential constraint is automatically created whenever a referential constraint is created, *and its behavior cannot be altered*. Therefore, once a referential constraint has been defined, records must be inserted into the parent key of the parent table *before* records that reference the parent key can be inserted into the foreign key of the child table. (For example, when populating the COLOR and OBJECT tables depicted in Figures 6.6 and 6.7, you must first add a record for a new color to the COLOR table before you can add a record that references the new color to the OBJECT table.)

The Update Rule for Referential Constraints

The Update Rule for referential constraints controls how update operations performed against either table (parent or child) participating in a referential constraint are to be processed. As with the Insert Rule, an Update Rule is automatically created when a referential constraint is created. However, unlike with the Insert Rule, *how* a particular Update Rule is evaluated depends upon how the rule has been defined. Two different definitions are possible:

- **ON UPDATE NO ACTION**: Ensures that whenever an update operation is performed on either table participating in a referential constraint, the value for the foreign key of each row in the child table will have a matching value in the parent key of the associated parent table. *However, the value may or may not be the same as it was before the update operation was performed.* This type of Update Rule is enforced only after all other constraints, including other referential constraints, have been enforced.
- **ON UPDATE RESTRICT**: Ensures that whenever an update operation is performed on the parent table of a referential constraint, the value for the foreign key of each row in the child table will have the same matching value in the parent key of the parent table that it had before the update operation was performed. This type of Update Rule is enforced before all other constraints, including other referential constraints, are enforced.

Figure 6.8 illustrates how the Update Rule is enforced when the ON UPDATE NO ACTION definition is used. Figure 6.9 shows how the Update Rule is enforced when the ON UPDATE RESTRICT definition is used instead.

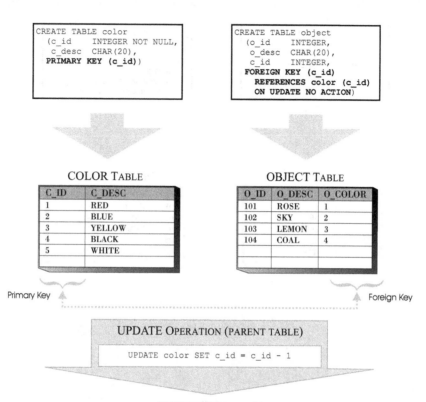

```
CREATE TABLE color
  (c_id    INTEGER NOT NULL,
   c_desc CHAR(20),
   PRIMARY KEY (c_id))
```

```
CREATE TABLE object
  (o_id    INTEGER,
   o_desc CHAR(20),
   c_id    INTEGER,
   FOREIGN KEY (c_id)
     REFERENCES color (c_id)
     ON UPDATE NO ACTION)
```

COLOR TABLE

C_ID	C_DESC
1	RED
2	BLUE
3	YELLOW
4	BLACK
5	WHITE

OBJECT TABLE

O_ID	O_DESC	O_COLOR
101	ROSE	1
102	SKY	2
103	LEMON	3
104	COAL	4

Primary Key   Foreign Key

UPDATE OPERATION (PARENT TABLE)

```
UPDATE color SET c_id = c_id - 1
```

INSERT operation successful

COLOR TABLE

C_ID	C_DESC
0	RED
1	BLUE
2	YELLOW
3	BLACK
4	WHITE

OBJECT TABLE

O_ID	O_DESC	O_COLOR
101	ROSE	1
102	SKY	2
103	LEMON	3
104	COAL	4

Figure 6.8: How an ON UPDATE NO ACTION *Update Rule of a referential constraint is enforced*

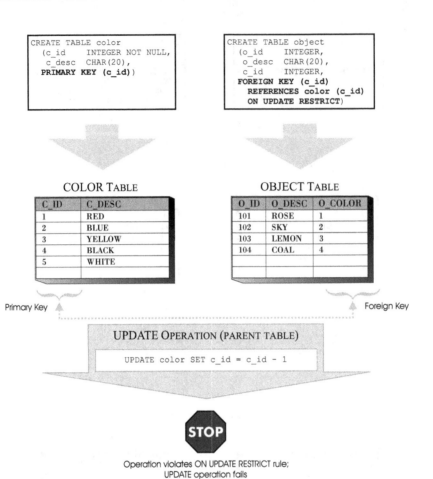

Figure 6.9: How an ON UPDATE RESTRICT *Update Rule of a referential constraint is enforced*

If you do not provide an Update Rule definition when you create a referential constraint, the ON UPDATE NO ACTION definition is used by default. Regardless of which definition is used, if an update operation violates the Update Rule's condition, the operation will fail, an error will be returned, and any changes that you made to either table participating in the referential constraint will be backed out of the database.

The Delete Rule for referential constraints

The Delete Rule for referential constraints controls how delete operations performed against the parent table in a referential constraint are to be processed. As with the Update Rule, *how* a particular Delete Rule is evaluated depends upon the way in which the rule has been defined. Four different definitions are possible:

- **ON DELETE CASCADE**: Ensures that whenever a row is deleted from the parent table of a referential constraint, all records in the child table with matching foreign key values are deleted as well
- **ON DELETE SET NULL**: Ensures that whenever a row is deleted from the parent table of a referential constraint, all records in the child table with matching foreign key values are altered such that the foreign key columns are set to NULL—provided the columns that make up the foreign key are nullable (that is, they do not have a NOT NULL constraint associated with them); other values for the dependent row are not affected
- **ON DELETE NO ACTION**: Ensures that whenever a delete operation is performed on the parent table of a referential constraint, each row in the child table will have the same value for its foreign key that it had before the delete operation was performed; this type of Delete Rule is enforced only after all other constraints, including other referential constraints, have been enforced
- **ON DELETE RESTRICT**: Ensures that whenever a delete operation is performed on the parent table of a referential constraint, each row in the child table will have the same value for its foreign key that it had before the delete operation was performed; this type of Delete Rule is enforced before all other constraints, including other referential constraints, are enforced

Figure 6.10 illustrates how the Delete Rule is enforced when the ON DELETE CASCADE definition is used. Figure 6.11 shows how the Delete Rule is enforced when the ON DELETE SET NULL definition is used instead.

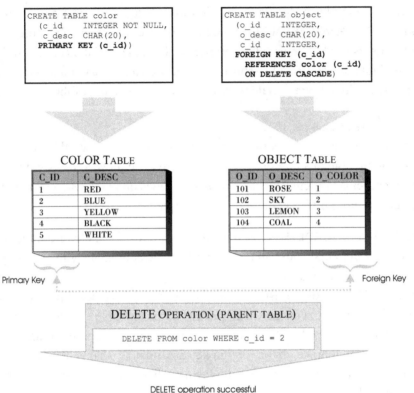

Figure 6.10: How an ON DELETE CASCADE *Delete Rule of a referential constraint is enforced*

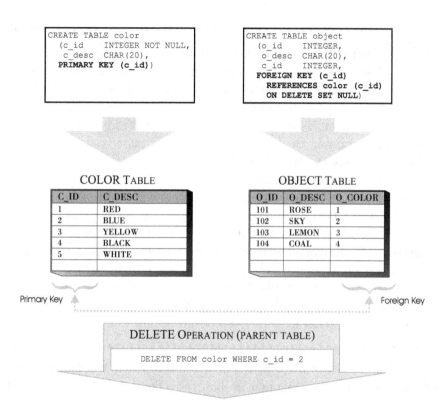

Figure 6.11: How an ON DELETE SET NULL *Delete Rule of a referential constraint is enforced*

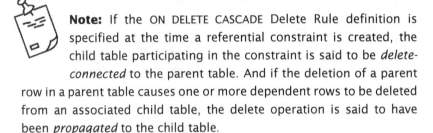

Note: If the ON DELETE CASCADE Delete Rule definition is specified at the time a referential constraint is created, the child table participating in the constraint is said to be *delete-connected* to the parent table. And if the deletion of a parent row in a parent table causes one or more dependent rows to be deleted from an associated child table, the delete operation is said to have been *propagated* to the child table.

Because a delete-connected child table can also be the parent table in another referential constraint, a delete operation that is propagated to one child table can, in turn, be propagated to another child table, and so on. Thus, the deletion of a single parent row can result in the deletion of several hundred rows from any number of tables, depending upon how tables in a database are delete-connected. Consequently, you should use the ON DELETE CASCADE Delete Rule definition with extreme caution when a hierarchy of referential constraints is spread throughout a database.

Figure 6.12 illustrates how the Delete Rule is enforced when the ON DELETE NO ACTION definition is used. And Figure 6.13 shows how the Delete Rule is enforced when the ON DELETE RESTRICT definition is used.

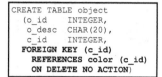

```
CREATE TABLE color
   (c_id    INTEGER NOT NULL,
    c_desc  CHAR(20),
    PRIMARY KEY (c_id))
```

```
CREATE TABLE object
   (o_id    INTEGER,
    o_desc  CHAR(20),
    c_id    INTEGER,
    FOREIGN KEY (c_id)
      REFERENCES color (c_id)
      ON DELETE NO ACTION)
```

COLOR TABLE

C_ID	C_DESC
1	RED
2	BLUE
3	YELLOW
4	BLACK
5	WHITE

OBJECT TABLE

O_ID	O_DESC	O_COLOR
101	ROSE	1
102	SKY	2
103	LEMON	3
104	COAL	4

Primary Key

Foreign Key

DELETE OPERATION (PARENT TABLE)

```
DELETE FROM color WHERE c_id = 2
```

Operation violates ON DELETE NO ACTION rule;
DELETE operation fails

COLOR TABLE

C_ID	C_DESC
1	RED
2	BLUE
3	YELLOW
4	BLACK
5	WHITE

OBJECT TABLE

O_ID	O_DESC	O_COLOR
101	ROSE	1
102	SKY	2
103	LEMON	3
104	COAL	4

Figure 6.12: How an ON DELETE NO ACTION *Delete Rule of a referential constraint is enforced*

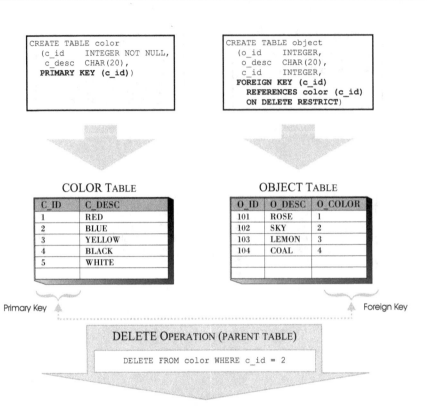

```
CREATE TABLE color
    (c_id     INTEGER NOT NULL,
     c_desc CHAR(20),
     PRIMARY KEY (c_id))
```

```
CREATE TABLE object
    (o_id     INTEGER,
     o_desc CHAR(20),
     c_id     INTEGER,
     FOREIGN KEY (c_id)
        REFERENCES color (c_id)
        ON DELETE RESTRICT)
```

COLOR TABLE

C_ID	C_DESC
1	RED
2	BLUE
3	YELLOW
4	BLACK
5	WHITE

OBJECT TABLE

O_ID	O_DESC	O_COLOR
101	ROSE	1
102	SKY	2
103	LEMON	3
104	COAL	4

Primary Key

Foreign Key

DELETE OPERATION (PARENT TABLE)

```
DELETE FROM color WHERE c_id = 2
```

Operation violates ON DELETE RESTRICT rule;
DELETE operation fails

COLOR TABLE

C_ID	C_DESC
1	RED
2	BLUE
3	YELLOW
4	BLACK
5	WHITE

OBJECT TABLE

O_ID	O_DESC	O_COLOR
101	ROSE	1
102	SKY	2
103	LEMON	3
104	COAL	4

Figure 6.13: How an ON DELETE RESTRICT *Delete Rule of a referential constraint is enforced*

If a table participates in only one referential constraint (as in the previous examples), the behavior of the ON DELETE NO ACTION and the ON DELETE RESTRICT definition is essentially the same—delete operations that violate either Delete Rule will fail, and data will remain unchanged because there are no other constraints to consider. However, that is not the case when a table participates in multiple referential constraints; here, the behavior can differ because of *when* each Delete Rule is enforced. For example, the scenario depicted in Figure 6.14 illustrates how the ON DELETE NO ACTION Delete Rule will allow a delete operation to be performed.

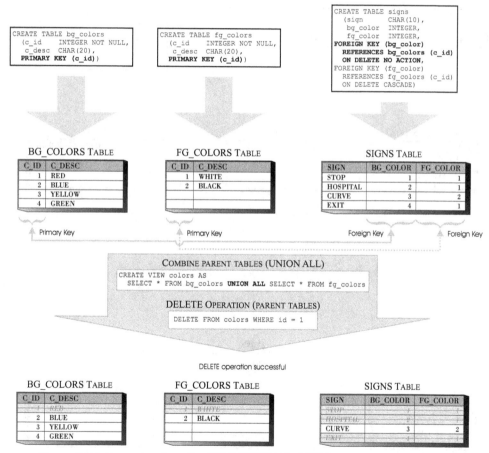

Figure 6.14: Example where the ON DELETE NO ACTION Delete Rule definition allows data in tables to be deleted

In this example, the referential constraint with the ON DELETE NO ACTION Delete Rule definition is enforced only *after* the referential constraint with the ON DELETE CASCADE Delete Rule is processed, allowing the deletion of records from all tables participating in both referential constraints. Had the ON DELETE RESTRICT Delete Rule definition been used in the previous example instead, the referential constraint with that Delete Rule would have been enforced first and the second delete operation would have failed. Figure 6.15 illustrates this behavior.

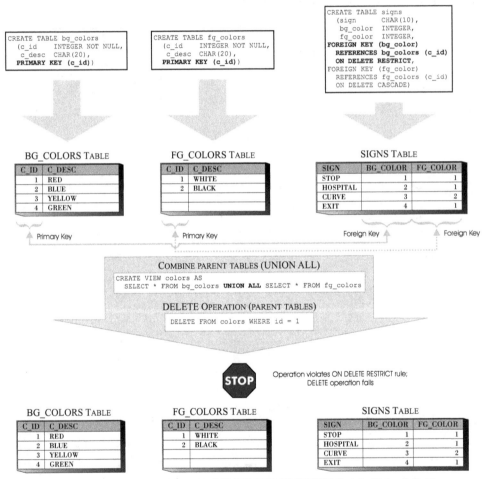

Figure 6.15: Example where the ON DELETE RESTRICT *Delete Rule definition prevents data in tables from being deleted*

As with Insert and Update Rules, a Delete Rule is automatically created when a referential constraint is created. If you do not provide a Delete Rule definition, the ON DELETE NO ACTION definition is used by default.

Informational Constraints

By default, whenever you add, modify, and in some cases delete data from a DB2 database, the DB2 Database Manager automatically enforces any constraints that have been defined. Consequently, if a large number of constraints have been defined, a significant amount of overhead may be required to enforce those constraints, especially when large amounts of data are bulk-loaded into a table that participates in several different constraints. Therefore, if an application already contains the logic needed to apply the business rules and restrictions required, there may not be any advantage to creating a set of similar data constraints that do essentially the same thing. There is, however, a very good reason to create a set of similar *informational constraints*—such constraints can often improve query performance.

Informational constraints tell DB2 which business rules data conforms to, but unlike other constraints, they are not enforced. So why is it important that DB2 know this information? Because if DB2 is aware of constraints that are being enforced at the application level, the DB2 Optimizer can use this information to choose an optimum access plan to use when retrieving data from the database.

Informational constraints are defined by appending the keywords NOT ENFORCED ENABLE QUERY OPTIMIZATION to a CHECK or referential constraint definition. Figure 6.16 illustrates how to create a simple informational constraint, as well as how a record that violates an informational constraint will be inserted into a table because such a constraint is not enforced.

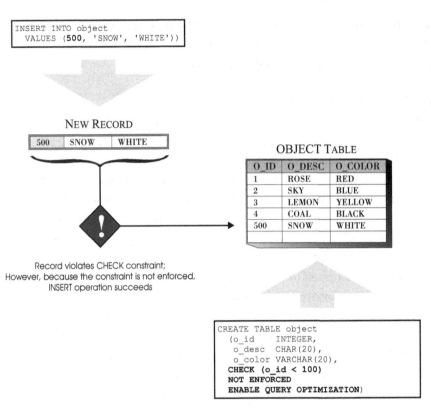

Figure 6.16: A simple informational constraint

Note: With DB2 10.5, the keywords NOT ENFORCED ENABLE QUERY OPTIMIZATION can be added to UNIQUE, primary key, CHECK, and referential constraint definitions.

It is important to note that because the DB2 Optimizer evaluates informational constraints when selecting an access plan to use to resolve a query, records that have been inserted into a table that violate an informational constraint may not be returned by some queries.

Creating Tables

In Chapter 4, "Working with Databases and Database Objects," we saw that tables act as the main repository in a DB2 database. We also saw that tables present data as a collection of unordered rows with a fixed number of columns, that each column contains values of the same data type, and that each row contains a set of values for one or more of the columns available. As with many of the other database objects available, tables can be created from within Data Studio. Tables can also be created by executing the CREATE TABLE statement. However, this statement is probably the most complex SQL statement available. Consequently, its syntax can be very intimidating.

In its simplest form, the syntax for the CREATE TABLE statement looks like this:

```
CREATE TABLE [TableName] ( [Element], ...)
  <ORGANIZE BY [ROW | COLUMN]>
  <IN [TablespaceName]>
```

where:

TableName	Identifies the name to assign to the table that is to be created; the table name specified must be unique within the schema the table is to be defined in
Element	Identifies one or more columns, UNIQUE constraints, CHECK constraints, referential constraints, informational constraints, and/or a primary key constraint to include in the table definition; the syntax used to define each of these elements varies according to the element specified
TablespaceName	Identifies, by name, the table space the table is to be stored in

The basic syntax used to define a column element is:

```
[ColumnName] [DataType]
<NOT NULL>
<WITH DEFAULT <[DefaultValue] | NULL>>
<UniqueConstraint>
<CheckConstraint>
<RIConstraint>
```

where:

ColumnName	Identifies the name to assign to the column; the name specified must be unique
DataType	Identifies the data type (built-in or user-defined) to assign to the column; the data type specified determines the kind of data values that can be stored in the column—Table 6.3 contains a list of valid built-in data type definitions
DefaultValue	Identifies the default value to provide for the column if no value for the column is supplied when a new record is inserted into the table
UniqueConstraint	Identifies a UNIQUE or primary key constraint that is to be associated with the column
CheckConstraint	Identifies a CHECK constraint that is to be associated with the column
RIConstraint	Identifies a referential integrity constraint that is to be associated with the column

Table 6.3: Built-in data type definitions to use with the CREATE TABLE statement

Data Type	Definition(s)
Small integer	SMALLINT
Integer	INTEGER INT
Big integer	BIGINT
Decimal	DECIMAL(*Precision, Scale*) DEC(*Precision, Scale*) NUMERIC(*Precision, Scale*) NUM(*Precision, Scale*) where *Precision* is any number between 1 and 31, and *Scale* is any number between 0 and *Precision*
Single-precision floating-point	REAL FLOAT(*Precision*) where *Precision* is any number between 1 and 24
Double-precision floating-point	DOUBLE DOUBLE PRECISION FLOAT(*Precision*) where *Precision* is any number between 25 and 53
Decimal floating-point	DECFLOAT(*Precision*) where *Precision* is either 16 or 34

Table 6.3: Built-in data type definitions to use with the CREATE TABLE statement (continued)	
Data Type	**Definition(s)**
Fixed-length character string	CHARACTER(*Length*) <FOR BIT DATA> CHAR(*Length*) <FOR BIT DATA> where *Length* is any number between 1 and 254 (see footnote for the meaning of the FOR BIT DATA clause)
Varying-length character string	CHARACTER VARYING(*MaxLength*) <FOR BIT DATA> CHAR VARYING(*MaxLength*) <FOR BIT DATA> VARCHAR(*MaxLength*) <FOR BIT DATA> where *MaxLength* is any number between 1 and 32,672 (see footnote for the meaning of the FOR BIT DATA clause)
Fixed-length double-byte character string	GRAPHIC(*Length*) where *Length* is any number between 1 and 127
Varying-length double-byte character string	VARGRAPHIC(*MaxLength*) where *MaxLength* is any number between 1 and 16,336
National fixed-length character string	NATIONAL CHARACTER(*Length*) NATIONAL CHAR(*Length*) NCHAR(*Length*) where *Length* is any number between 1 and 127
National varying-length character string	NATIONAL CHARACTER VARYING(*MaxLength*) NATIONAL CHAR VARYING(*MaxLength*) NCHAR VARYING(*MaxLength*) NVARCHAR(*MaxLength*) where *MaxLength* is any number between 1 and 16,336
Date	DATE
Time	TIME
Timestamp	TIMESTAMP TIMESTAMP(*Precision*) where *Precision* is any number between 0 and 12
Binary large object	BINARY LARGE OBJECT(*Length* <K | M | G>) BLOB(*Length* <K | M | G>) where *Length* is any number between 1 and 2,147,483,647; if K (for kilobyte) is specified, *Length* is any number between 1 and 2,097,152; if M (for megabyte) is specified, *Length* is any number between 1 and 2,048; and if G (for gigabyte) is specified, *Length* is any number between 1 and 2
Character large object	CHARACTER LARGE OBJECT(*Length* <K | M | G>) CHAR LARGE OBJECT(*Length* <K | M | G>) CLOB(*Length* <K | M | G>) where *Length* is any number between 1 and 2,147,483,647; if K (for kilobyte) is specified, *Length* is any number between 1 and 2,097,152; if M (for megabyte) is specified, *Length* is any number between 1 and 2,048; and if G (for gigabyte) is specified, *Length* is any number between 1 and 2

Table 6.3: Built-in data type definitions to use with the CREATE TABLE statement (continued)	
Data Type	**Definition(s)**
Double-byte character large object	DBCLOB(*Length* <K | M | G>) where *Length* is any number between 1 and 1,073,741,823; if K (for kilobyte) is specified, *Length* is any number between 1 and 1,048,576; if M (for megabyte) is specified, *Length* is any number between 1 and 1,024; and if G (for gigabyte) is specified, *Length* is must be 1
National character large object	NATIONAL CHARACTER LARGE OBJECT(*Length* <K | M | G>) NCHAR LARGE OBJECT(*Length* <K | M | G>) NCLOB(*Length* <K | M | G>) where *Length* is any number between 1 and 1,073,741,823; if K (for kilobyte) is specified, *Length* is any number between 1 and 1,048,576; if M (for megabyte) is specified, *Length* is any number between 1 and 1,024; and if G (for gigabyte) is specified, *Length* is must be 1
XML document	XML
Note: If the FOR BIT DATA option is used with a character string data type definition, the contents of the column the data type is assigned to will be treated as binary data. This means that code page conversions are not performed if data in the column is exchanged between other systems, and that all comparisons are done in binary, regardless of the collating sequence used.	

The syntax used to create a UNIQUE or primary key constraint as part of a column definition is:

```
<CONSTRAINT [ConstraintName]> [UNIQUE | PRIMARY KEY]
```

where:

ConstraintName   Identifies the name to assign to the constraint; the name specified must be unique

The syntax used to create a CHECK constraint as part of a column definition is:

```
<CONSTRAINT [ConstraintName]> CHECK ([CheckCondition])
```

where:

ConstraintName   Identifies the name to assign to the constraint; the name specified must be unique

CheckCondition   Identifies a condition or test that must evaluate to TRUE before a value can be stored in the associated column

And finally, the syntax used to create a referential constraint as part of a column definition is:

```
<CONSTRAINT [ConstraintName]>
REFERENCES [PKTableName] <([PKColumnName], ...)>
<ON UPDATE [NO ACTION | RESTRICT]>
<ON DELETE [CASCADE | SET NULL | NO ACTION | RESTRICT]>
<ENFORCED | NOT ENFORCED>
<[ENABLE | DISABLE] QUERY OPTIMIZATION>
```

where:

ConstraintName	Identifies the name to assign to the constraint; the name specified must be unique
PKTableName	Identifies, by name, the parent table that is to participate in the referential constraint
PKColumnName	Identifies one or more columns that comprise the parent key of the parent table that is to participate in the referential constraint

As mentioned earlier, if the NOT ENFORCED clause is specified as part of a constraint's definition, the constraint will not be enforced—it will become an informational constraint instead. If the ENABLE QUERY OPTIMIZATION clause is specified, the DB2 Optimizer will evaluate the information the constraint provides when deciding which data access plan to use to resolve a query.

Therefore, to create a table named EMPLOYEES that contains three columns, two of which are named EMPID and NAME that will be used to store integer data and one that is named DEPT that will be used to store fixed-length character string data, you could execute a CREATE TABLE statement that looks something like this:

```
CREATE TABLE employees
  (empid  INTEGER,
   name   CHAR(50),
   dept   INTEGER)
```

On the other hand, to create a table named EMPLOYEES that has the same columns, but that also has both a NOT NULL constraint and a primary key constraint associated with the EMPID column, you would execute a CREATE TABLE statement that looks more like this:

```
CREATE TABLE employees
  (empid  INTEGER NOT NULL PRIMARY KEY,
   name   CHAR(50),
   dept   INTEGER)
```

Or, to create a similar table, but have the DEPT column participate in a referential constraint with a column named DEPTID that resides in another table named DEPARTMENT, you would execute a CREATE TABLE statement that looks like this:

```
CREATE TABLE employees
  (empid INTEGER,
   name  CHAR(50),
   dept  INTEGER REFERENCES department (deptid))
```

And finally, to create a similar table that has an informational constraint associated with the DEPT column, you would execute a CREATE TABLE statement that looks like this:

```
CREATE TABLE employees
  (empid INTEGER,
   name  CHAR(50),
   dept  INTEGER REFERENCES department (deptid)
          NOT ENFORCED
          ENABLE QUERY OPTIMIZATION)
```

As these examples show, a UNIQUE constraint, CHECK constraint, referential constraint, or informational constraint can be associated with a particular column as part of that column's definition. But what if you need to define a referential constraint that encompasses more than one column? Or you want to separate constraint definitions from column definitions? In both cases, you can define a constraint as separate element, rather than as an extension to a column definition.

The syntax used to define a UNIQUE or primary key constraint as an individual element is:

```
<CONSTRAINT [ConstraintName]> [UNIQUE | PRIMARY KEY]
  ([ColumnName], ...)
```

where:

ConstraintName	Identifies the name to assign to the constraint; the name specified must be unique
ColumnName	Identifies one or more columns that are to be part of the UNIQUE or primary key constraint

The syntax used to create a CHECK constraint as an individual element is identical to the syntax that is used to create a CHECK constraint as part of a column definition:

```
<CONSTRAINT [ConstraintName]> CHECK ( [CheckCondition] )
```

where:

ConstraintName	Identifies the name to assign to the constraint; the name specified must be unique
CheckCondition	Identifies a condition or test that must evaluate to TRUE before a value can be stored in the associated column

And finally, the syntax used to create a referential constraint as an individual element is:

```
<CONSTRAINT [ConstraintName]>
FOREIGN KEY ([ColumnName], ...)
REFERENCES [PKTableName] <([PKColumnName], ...)>
<ON UPDATE [NO ACTION | RESTRICT]>
```

```
<ON DELETE [CASCADE | SET NULL | NO ACTION | RESTRICT]>
<ENFORCED | NOT ENFORCED>
<[ENABLE | DISABLE] QUERY OPTIMIZATION>
```

where:

ConstraintName	Identifies the name to assign to the constraint; the name specified must be unique
ColumnName	Identifies one or more columns that are to be part of the foreign key of the referential constraint
PKTableName	Identifies, by name, the parent table that is to participate in the referential constraint
PKColumnName	Identifies one or more columns that comprise the parent key of the parent table that is to participate in the referential constraint

Thus, a table that was created by executing a CREATE TABLE statement that looks like this:

```
CREATE TABLE employees
  (empid INTEGER,
   name  CHAR(50),
   dept  INTEGER REFERENCES department (deptid))
```

could also be created by executing a CREATE TABLE statement that looks like this:

```
CREATE TABLE employees
  (empid INTEGER,
   name  CHAR(50),
   dept  INTEGER,
   FOREIGN KEY (dept) REFERENCES department (deptid))
```

Creating Tables with Identity Columns

Often, base tables are designed in such a way that a single column is used to store a unique identifier that represents an individual record (or row). And frequently, this identifier is a number that is sequentially incremented each time a new record is added to the table. You can generate numbers for these types of columns by using a trigger (which we looked at in Chapter 4, "Working with Databases and Database Objects"), or DB2 can generate them automatically—provided the column is defined as an *identity column.*

Identity columns are created by specifying the GENERATED...AS IDENTITY clause, along with one or more identity column attributes, as part of a column's definition. The syntax used to create an identity column is:

```
[ColumnName] [DataType]
GENERATED <ALWAYS | BY DEFAULT> AS IDENTITY
<(
   <START WITH [1 | StartingValue]>
   <INCREMENT BY [1 | IncrementValue]>
   <NO MINVALUE | MINVALUE [MinValue]>
   <NO MAXVALUE | MAXVALUE [MaxValue]>
   <NO CYCLE | CYCLE>
   <CACHE 20 | NO CACHE | CACHE [CacheSize]>
   <NO ORDER | ORDER>
)>
```

where:

ColumnName	Identifies the name to assign to the column; the name specified must be unique
DataType	Identifies the data type (built-in or user-defined) to assign to the identity column; the data type specified must be a numeric data type with a scale of 0; therefore, only the following values are valid: SMALLINT, INTEGER, BIGINT, DECIMAL, NUMERIC, or a user-defined data type that is based on one of these data types
StartingValue	Identifies the first value that is to be assigned to the identity column
IncrementValue	Identifies the interval that is to be used to calculate each consecutive value that is to be assigned to the identity column
MinValue	Identifies the smallest value that can be assigned to the identity column
MaxValue	Identifies the largest value that can be assigned to the identity column

CacheSize   Identifies the number of values of the identity sequence that are to be generated at one time and kept in memory

If the CYCLE clause is specified as part of an identity column's definition, values will continue to be generated for the column after any minimum or maximum value specified has been reached. (After an ascending identity column reaches the maximum value allowed, a new minimum value is generated and the cycle begins again; after a descending identity column reaches the minimum value allowed, a new maximum value is generated and the cycle repeats itself.)

Thus, to create a table named EMPLOYEES that contains a simple identity column that DB2 will always generate a value for, you could execute a CREATE TABLE statement that looks something like this:

```
CREATE TABLE employees
   (empid INTEGER GENERATED ALWAYS AS IDENTITY,
    name   CHAR(50),
    dept   INTEGER)
```

It is important to note that after this table is created, if you attempt to execute an SQL statement that looks like this:

```
INSERT INTO employees VALUES (1, 'SCHIEFER', 50)
```

you will receive an error message that looks like this:

```
SQL0798N  A value cannot be specified for column "EMPID" which
is defined as GENERATED ALWAYS. SQLSTATE=428C9
```

That's because the GENERATED ALWAYS AS IDENTITY clause implies that DB2 will always be responsible for providing values for the EMPID column of the EMPLOYEES table.

On the other hand, to create a table named EMPLOYEES that contains an identity column that DB2 will generate a value for *if no value is explicitly provided*, you would execute a CREATE TABLE statement that looks more like this:

```
CREATE TABLE employees
  (empid INTEGER GENERATED BY DEFAULT AS IDENTITY,
   name  CHAR(50),
   dept  INTEGER)
```

Here, the INSERT statement shown in the previous example will succeed because the GENERATED BY DEFAULT AS IDENTITY clause instructs DB2 to supply a value for the EMPID column only when no value is explicitly provided for that column.

● ●

Note: A table can have only one identity column, all identity columns are implicitly assigned a NOT NULL constraint, and identity columns are not allowed to have a default constraint assigned to them.

● ●

Creating Tables That Are Similar to Existing Tables

At times, it might be desirable to create a new, empty table that has the same attributes as an existing table (for example, when a history table for a system-period temporal table is needed). One way to create a new, empty table that is similar to another is by executing a CREATE TABLE statement that is identical to the statement that was used to create the original table. (Of course, the name assigned to new table will have to be changed.) Another way is to execute a special form of CREATE TABLE that was designed specifically with this purpose in mind. The syntax for this form of the CREATE TABLE statement is:

```
CREATE TABLE [TableName] LIKE [SourceTable]
<[INCLUDING | EXCLUDING] COLUMN DEFAULTS>
<[INCLUDING | EXCLUDING] IDENTITY COLUMN ATTRIBUTES>
```

where:

TableName   Identifies the name to assign to the table that is to be created; the table name specified must be unique within the schema the table is to be defined in

SourceTable   Identifies, by name, an existing table whose structure and attributes are to be used to define the table that is to be created

Thus, to create an empty table named 2ND_QTR_SALES that has the exact same structure as an existing table named 1ST_QTR_SALES, you would execute a CREATE TABLE statement that looks like this:

```
CREATE TABLE 2nd_qtr_sales LIKE 1st_qtr_sales
```

When this form of the CREATE TABLE statement is executed, the table that is created will have the same number of columns as the source table used, and these columns will have the same names, data types, and nullability characteristics as those of the source table. If the EXCLUDING COLUMN DEFAULTS clause is not specified, any default constraints that have been defined for the source table will be copied to the new table as well. Similarly, if the EXCLUDING IDENTITY COLUMN ATTRIBUTES clause is not specified, any identity column attributes that have been defined for the source will be copied to the target table. However, no other attributes of the source table will be duplicated. Thus, the target table will not contain any UNIQUE constraints, CHECK constraints, referential integrity constraints, triggers, or indexes that have been defined for the source table. (If the target table needs these characteristics, you must create them separately after the target table has been created.)

A Quick Reminder About Schemas

In Chapter 4, "Working with Databases and Database Objects," we saw that schemas are objects that are used to logically classify and group other objects (such as tables, indexes, and views) in a database. Schemas also make it possible to create a large number of objects in a database without encountering namespace collisions. Many of the objects in a DB2 database are named using a two-part naming convention—the first (leftmost) part of the name is the *schema name* or *qualifier*, and the second (rightmost) part is the user-supplied object name. Syntactically, these two parts are concatenated and separated by a period (for example, HR.EMPLOYEES).

When select data objects (that is, table spaces, tables, indexes, distinct data types, functions, stored procedures, and triggers) are created, they are automatically assigned to a schema, based upon the qualifier that was provided as part of the user-supplied object name. If a schema name or qualifier is not provided as part of an object's name, the object is automatically assigned to a default schema, which is determined by examining the value found in the CURRENT SCHEMA (or CURRENT_SCHEMA) special register.

By default, the value assigned to this special register is the authorization ID of the current session user. (However, this value can be changed using the SET SCHEMA statement.) Thus, if you were to log on to a DB2 server with the user ID "db2inst1" and execute a CREATE TABLE statement that looks like this:

```
CREATE TABLE employees
  (empid INTEGER GENERATED BY DEFAULT AS IDENTITY,
   name  CHAR(50),
   dept  INTEGER)
```

a table named DB2INST1.EMPLOYEES will be created—because a qualifier was not provided with the table name specified, the authentication ID that the CREATE TABLE statement was executed under (which in this case is "db2inst1"), is used as the qualifier by default.

Examples of the CREATE TABLE Statement

Now that you have seen the basic syntax for the CREATE TABLE statement and some very simple examples of how this statement can be used, let us look at some more-complex CREATE TABLE statement examples and examine the characteristics of the tables that would be produced if each of these statements were to be executed.

Example 1

If the following CREATE TABLE statement is executed:

```
CREATE TABLE project
  (projno   CHAR(6) NOT NULL,
   projname VARCHAR(24) NOT NULL,
   deptno   SMALLINT,
   budget   DECIMAL(6,2),
   startdate DATE,
   enddate  DATE)
```

a table named PROJECT will be created as follows:

- The first column will be named PROJNO and can be used to store fixed-length character string data that is six characters in length (for example, 'PROJ01' or 'PROJ02').
- The second column will be named PROJNAME and can be used to store variable-length character string data up to 24 characters in length (for example, 'DB2 Benchmarks Tool' or 'Auto-Configuration Tool').
- The third column will be named DEPTNO and can be used to store numeric values in the range of –32,768 to +32,767.
- The fourth column will be named BUDGET and can be used to store numerical values that contain both whole and fractional parts. Up to six numbers—four for the whole number part and two for the fractional part—can be stored (for example, 1500.00 or 2000.50).
- The fifth column will be named STARTDATE and can be used to store date values.
- The sixth column will be named ENDDATE and can also be used to store date values.
- The table will be created in a schema that has the name of the authorization ID of the individual who created it (because a schema name was not provided and this is the default schema name used).
- The table will be created in the table space USERSPACE1 (because a table space was not specified and this is the default table space used).
- Whenever data is added to the table, values must be provided for both the PROJNO and the PROJNAME columns. (NULL values are not allowed because a NOT NULL constraint was defined for both of these columns.)

Example 2

If the following CREATE TABLE statement is executed:

```
CREATE TABLE central.sales
  (po_number INTEGER NOT NULL CONSTRAINT uc1 UNIQUE,
   date      DATE NOT NULL WITH DEFAULT),
   office    CHAR(128) NOT NULL WITH DEFAULT 'Dallas',
   amt       DECIMAL(10,2) NOT NULL CHECK (amt > 99.99)
   IN my_space
```

a table named SALES will be created as follows:

- The first column will be named PO_NUMBER (for Purchase Order Number) and can be used to store numeric values in the range of –2,147,483,648 to 2,147,483,647.
- The second column will be named DATE and can be used to store date values.
- The third column will be named OFFICE and can be used to store fixed-length character string data up to 128 characters in length (for example, 'Kansas City' or 'Dallas').
- The fourth column will be named AMT (for Amount) and can be used to store numerical values that contain both whole and fractional parts. Up to 10 numbers— eight for the whole number part and two for the fractional part—can be stored (for example, 20000000.50).
- The table will be created in a schema named CENTRAL.
- The table will be created in a table space named MY_SPACE.
- Whenever data is added to the table, values must be provided for the PO_NUMBER and the AMT columns. (NULL values are not allowed in any column because a NOT NULL constraint was defined for every column; however, because default values can be provided by DB2 for the DATE and OFFICE columns, values do not have to be supplied for those two columns.)
- Every value provided for the PO_NUMBER column must be unique (because a UNIQUE constraint named UC1 was defined for this column).
- An index was automatically created for the PO_NUMBER column (because a UNIQUE constraint named UC1 was defined for this column). As data is added to the table, values provided for the PO_NUMBER column are added to the index, and the entries in the index are sorted in ascending order.
- If a value is not provided for the DATE column when a row is inserted into the table, the system date at the time the row is inserted will be written to the column by default (because a default constraint was defined for this column).
- If a value is not provided for the OFFICE column, the value 'Dallas' will be written to the column by default (because a default constraint was defined for this column).
- Every value provided for the AMT column must be greater than or equal to 100.00 (because a CHECK constraint was defined for this column).

Example 3

If the following CREATE TABLE statements are executed in the order shown:

```
CREATE TABLE payroll.employees
  (empid      INTEGER NOT NULL PRIMARY KEY,
   emp_fname CHAR(30),
   emp_lname CHAR(30))



CREATE TABLE payroll.paychecks
  (empid      INTEGER,
   weeknumber CHAR(2),
   pay_amt    DECIMAL(6,2),
   CONSTRAINT fkconst FOREIGN KEY (empid)
     REFERENCES employee(empid) ON DELETE CASCADE,
   CONSTRAINT chk1 CHECK (pay_amt > 0 AND weeknumber
     BETWEEN 1 AND 52))
```

first, a table named EMPLOYEES will be created as follows:

- The first column will be named EMPID (for Employee ID) and can be used to store numeric values in the range of –2,147,483,648 to 2,147,483,647.
- The second column will be named EMP_FNAME (for Employee First Name) and can be used to store fixed-length character string data up to 30 characters in length (for example, 'Bob' or 'Mark').
- The third column will be named EMP_LNAME (for Employee Last Name) and can be used to store fixed-length character string data up to 30 characters in length (for example, 'Jancer' or 'Hayakawa').
- The table will be created in a schema named PAYROLL.
- The table will be created in the table space USERSPACE1 (because a table space was not specified and this is the default table space used).
- Whenever data is added to the table, values must be provided for the EMPID column. (NULL values are not allowed because a NOT NULL constraint was defined for this column.)

- Every value provided for the EMPID column must be unique (because a primary key constraint was defined for this column).
- An index was automatically created for the EMPID column (because a primary key constraint was defined for this column). As data is added to the table, values provided for the EMPID column are added to the index, and the entries in the index are sorted in ascending order.

Then, a table named PAYCHECKS will be created, as follows:

- The first column will be named EMPID and can be used to store numeric values in the range of –2,147,483,648 to 2,147,483,647.
- The second column will be named WEEKNUMBER and can be used to store fixed-length character string data up to two characters in length (for example, '1' or '35').
- The third column will be named PAY_AMT and can be used to store numerical values that contain both whole and fractional parts. Up to six numbers—four for the whole number part and two for the fractional part—can be stored (for example, 2000.50).
- The table will be created in a schema named PAYROLL.
- The table will be created in the table space USERSPACE1 (because a table space was not specified and this is the default table space used).
- Every value entered in the EMPID column must have a matching value in the EMPID column of the EMPLOYEES table (because a referential constraint has been defined in which the EMPID column of the EMPLOYEES table is the parent key and the EMPID column of the PAYCHECKS table is the foreign key—this referential constraint is named FKCONST).
- Whenever a row is deleted from the EMPLOYEES table, rows in the PAYCHECKS table that have a value in the EMPID column that matches the primary key value of the deleted row are also removed (because the ON DELETE CASCADE Delete Rule was specified for the FKCONST referential constraint).
- Every value provided for the PAY_AMT column must be greater than 0 (because a CHECK constraint named CHK1 was defined for both the PAY_AMT and WEEKNUMBER columns). Every value provided for the WEEKNUMBER column must be greater than or equal to 1 and less than or equal to 52 (again, because a CHECK constraint named CHK1 was defined for both the PAY_AMT and WEEKNUMBER columns).

Example 4

If the following CREATE TABLE statement is executed:

```
CREATE TABLE employees
  (empid     SMALLINT NOT NULL
                GENERATED BY DEFAULT AS IDENTITY,
   firstname VARCHAR(30) NOT NULL,
   lastname  VARCHAR(30) NOT NULL,
   deptid    CHAR(3),
   edlevel   CHAR(1) CHECK (edlevel IN ('C', 'H', 'N')),
   CONSTRAINT emp_pk PRIMARY KEY (empid),
   CONSTRAINT emp_dept_fk FOREIGN KEY (deptid)
     REFERENCES department (deptno))
```

a table named EMPLOYEES will be created as follows:

- The first column will be named EMPID (for Employee ID) and can be used to store numeric values in the range of –32,768 to +32,767.
- The second column will be named FIRSTNAME and can be used to store variable length character string data up to 30 characters in length (for example, 'Melanie' or 'Susan').
- The third column will be named LASTNAME and can be used to store variable length character string data up to 30 characters in length (for example, 'Stopfer' or 'Weaver').
- The fourth column will be named DEPTID and can be used to store fixed-length character string data up to three characters in length (for example, '1' or '352').
- The fifth column will be named EDLEVEL and can be used to store fixed-length character string data that is only one character in length (for example, 'C' or 'H').
- The table will be created in a schema that has the name of the authorization ID of the individual who created it (because a schema name was not provided and this is the default schema name used).
- The table will be created in the table space USERSPACE1 (because a table space was not specified and this is the default table space used).

- Whenever data is added to the table, DB2 will automatically assign a unique numeric value to the EMPID column, unless the user provides a value for this column (because the EMPID column is an identity column that was defined with the GENERATED BY DEFAULT AS IDENTITY clause). If the user does provide a value for the EMPID column, it cannot be the value NULL. (NULL values are not allowed because a NOT NULL constraint was defined for this column.)
- Whenever data is added to the table, values must be provided for both the FIRSTNAME and the LASTNAME columns. (NULL values are not allowed because a NOT NULL constraint was defined for both of these columns.)
- Only the values 'C', 'H', or 'N' can be stored in the EDLEVEL column (because a CHECK constraint was defined for this column).
- Every value provided for the EMPID column must be unique (because a primary key constraint named EMP_PK was defined for this column).
- An index was automatically created for the EMPID column (because a primary key constraint named EMP_PK was defined for this column). As data is added to the table, values provided for the EMPID column are added to the index, and the entries in the index are sorted in ascending order.
- Every value entered in the DEPTID column must have a matching value in the DEPTNO column of a table named DEPARTMENT (because a referential constraint has been defined in which the DEPTNO column of the DEPARTMENT table is the parent key and the DEPTID column of the EMPLOYEES table is the foreign key—this referential constraint is named EMP_DEPT_FK).

Altering Tables

Over time, it may become necessary for a table to hold additional data values either that did not exist or that were not considered at the time the table was created. Or, character data that was originally thought to be one size may have turned out to be larger than anticipated. These are just a couple of reasons why it can become necessary to modify an existing table's definition. When only a small amount of data is stored in a table and the table has few or no dependencies, it can be relatively easy to save the associated data, drop the existing table, create a new table with the appropriate modifications, populate it with the previously saved data, and redefine any necessary dependencies. But how can you make such modifications to a table that holds a large volume of data or has numerous dependency relationships?

Select properties of an existing table can be modified and additional columns and constraints can be added or removed by executing the ALTER TABLE statement. Like the CREATE TABLE statement, the ALTER TABLE statement can be quite complex. However, in its simplest form, the syntax for the ALTER TABLE statement looks like this:

```
ALTER TABLE [TableName] ADD ([Element], ...)
```

or

```
ALTER TABLE [TableName]
  ALTER COLUMN [ColumnName]
  SET DATA TYPE [DataType]
```

or

```
ALTER TABLE [TableName]
  DROP [COLUMN [ColumnName] <CASCADE | RESTRICT> |
    PRIMARY KEY |
    UNIQUE [ConstraintName] |
    CHECK [ConstraintName] |
    FOREIGN KEY [ConstraintName]]
```

where:

TableName	Identifies, by name, the table whose definition is to be altered
Element	Identifies one or more columns, UNIQUE constraints, CHECK constraints, referential integrity constraints, and/or a primary key constraint that are to be added to the existing table's definition; the syntax used to define each of these elements varies according to the element specified
ColumnName	Identifies, by name, an existing column whose data type is to be changed *or* that is to be removed from the table's definition
DataType	Identifies the new data type (built-in or user-defined) that is to be assigned to the column—Table 6.3 contains a list of valid built-in data type definitions
ConstraintName	Identifies, by name, an existing UNIQUE, CHECK, referential integrity, or primary key constraint that is to be removed from the table's definition

The syntax used to define a column element is the same as that used to define a column element with the CREATE TABLE statement. Likewise, the syntax used to define UNIQUE constraints, CHECK constraints, referential integrity constraints, informational constraints, and primary key constraints as individual elements is the same as that used to define each of these constraints.

Therefore, if a table named EMPLOYEES was created with a CREATE TABLE statement that looks something this:

```
CREATE TABLE employees
  (empid  INTEGER,
   name   CHAR(50),
   dept   INTEGER)
```

you could add a column named HIRE_DATE that will be used to store date values to this table by executing an ALTER TABLE statement that looks like this:

```
ALTER TABLE employees
  ADD COLUMN hire_date  DATE
```

On the other hand, to change the size of the column named NAME (in the same EMPLOYEES table) from a fixed-length character string data type that can hold up to 50 bytes (CHAR(50)) to a fixed-length character string data type that can hold up to 100 bytes (CHAR(100)), you would execute an ALTER TABLE statement that looks more like this:

```
ALTER TABLE employees
  ALTER COLUMN name SET DATA TYPE CHAR(100)
```

As we saw in Chapter 3, "Security," the ALTER TABLE statement can also be used to activate row access control and column access control for a given table. In these cases, the ALTER TABLE statement must be executed with either the ACTIVATE ROW ACCESS CONTROL or the ACTIVATE COLUMN ACCESS CONTROL clause specified.

A Closer Look at Temporary Tables

In Chapter 4, "Working with Databases and Database Objects," we saw that, along with base tables, another type of table that is commonly used is a *temporary table*. Unlike base tables, which act as a long-term repository for data, temporary tables serve as temporary work areas. Temporary tables are often used for recording the results of data manipulation or for storing intermediate results of a subquery (when this information will not fit in the memory available). With DB2 10.5, two types of temporary tables are available: *declared temporary tables* and *created temporary tables.*

Unlike base tables, whose definitions are stored in the system catalog of the database they belong to, declared temporary tables are not persistent and can only be used by the application that creates them—and only for the life of that application. When the application that creates a declared temporary table disconnects from the database (or is terminated, either on purpose or prematurely), the table's rows are deleted, and the table is implicitly dropped. Another significant difference centers around naming conventions: base table names must be unique within a schema, but because each application that defines a temporary table has its own instance of that table, multiple applications can create declared temporary tables that have the same name. Similar to declared temporary tables, created temporary tables are used by applications to temporarily store the results of data manipulation. But whereas information about declared temporary tables is not stored in the system catalog, information about created temporary tables *is*. Thus, created temporary tables are persistent and can be shared with other applications, across different connections, and across transaction boundaries. However, each session that queries a created temporary table will only be able to retrieve the rows that were inserted by that session. (Only the created temporary table's definition is shared—not its data.) Table 6.4 lists other important distinctions between base tables, declared temporary tables, and created temporary tables.

Table 6.4: Important distinctions between base tables, declared temporary tables, and created temporary tables			
Area of Distinction	**Base Tables**	**Declared Temporary Tables**	**Created Temporary Tables**
Creation	Created with the CREATE TABLE statement.	Created with the DECLARE GLOBAL TEMPORARY TABLE statement.	Created with the CREATE GLOBAL TEMPORARY TABLE statement.

Table 6.4: Important distinctions between base tables, declared temporary tables, and created temporary tables (continued)			
Area of Distinction	**Base Tables**	**Declared Temporary Tables**	**Created Temporary Tables**
Schema qualifier	The name of the table can be qualified. If the table name is not explicitly qualified, it is implicitly qualified using the current value of the CURRENT SCHEMA special register.	The name of the table can be qualified. If the table name is explicitly qualified, the name SESSION must be used as the qualifier; if the table name is not explicitly qualified, SESSION is implicitly used as the qualifier.	The name of the table can be qualified; if the table name is not explicitly qualified, it is implicitly qualified using the current value of the CURRENT SCHEMA special register.
System catalog storage	A description of the table is stored in the system catalog.	A description of the table is not stored in the system catalog.	A description of the table is stored in the system catalog.
Persistence/ability to share table description	The table description is persistent and shareable across different connections.	The table description is not persistent beyond the life of the connection that was used to declare the table. Furthermore, the description is known only to that connection. Thus, each connection can have its own description of the same declared temporary table.	The table description is persistent and shareable across different connections.
Table instantiation	The CREATE TABLE statement creates one empty instance of the table, and all connections use that instance of the table.	The DECLARE GLOBAL TEMPORARY TABLE statement creates an empty instance of the table for the connection. Each connection that declares the table has its own unique instance of the table, and the instance is not persistent beyond the life of the connection.	The CREATE GLOBAL TEMPORARY TABLE statement does not create an instance of the table. The first implicit or explicit reference to the table in an OPEN, SELECT, INSERT, UPDATE, or DELETE statement that is executed by any program using the connection creates an empty instance of the given table. Each connection that references the table has its own unique instance of the table, and the instance is not persistent beyond the life of the connection.

Area of Distinction	Base Tables	Declared Temporary Tables	Created Temporary Tables
	Table 6.4: Important distinctions between base tables, declared temporary tables, and created temporary tables (continued)		
Ability to share data	The table and data are persistent.	The table and its data are not persistent beyond the life of the connection it was created under.	The table and its data are not persistent beyond the life of the connection it was created under.
References to the table during connections	References to the table name in multiple connections refer to the same single persistent table description and to the same instance at the current server.	References to the table name in multiple connections refer to a distinct description and instance of the table for each connection at the current server.	References to the table name in multiple connections refer to the same single persistent table description, but to a distinct instance of the table for each connection at the current server.
Table privileges and authorization	The owner implicitly has all table privileges on the table and the authority to drop the table. The owner's table privileges can be granted and revoked, either individually or with the ALL clause. Another authorization ID can access the table only if it has been granted appropriate privileges for the table.	PUBLIC implicitly has all table privileges on the table without GRANT authority and also has the authority to drop the table. These table privileges cannot be granted or revoked. Any authorization ID can access the table without requiring a grant of any privileges for the table.	The owner implicitly has all table privileges on the table and the authority to drop the table. The owner's table privileges can be granted and revoked, either individually or with the ALL clause. Another authorization ID can access the table only if it has been granted appropriate privileges for the table.
Indexes and other SQL statement support	Indexes and SQL statements that modify data (INSERT, UPDATE, DELETE, and so on) are supported.	Indexes and SQL statements that modify data (INSERT, UPDATE, DELETE, and so on) are supported.	Indexes and SQL statements that modify data (INSERT, UPDATE, DELETE, and so on) are supported.
Locking, logging, and recovery	Locking, logging, and recovery apply.	Locking and recovery do not apply; logging applies only when LOGGED is explicitly or implicitly specified. The ability to undo recovery (rolling back changes to a savepoint or the most recent commit point) is supported when LOGGED is explicitly or implicitly specified.	Locking and recovery do not apply; logging applies when LOGGED is explicitly specified. The ability to undo recovery (rolling back changes to a savepoint or the most recent commit point) is supported when LOGGED is explicitly or implicitly specified.

Adapted from Table 1 found under **Distinctions between DB2 base tables and temporary tables** in the IBM DB2 10.5 Knowledge Center (*www-01.ibm.com/support/knowledgecenter/?lang=en#!/SSEPGG_10.5.0/com.ibm.db2.luw.admin.dbobj.doc/doc/r0054491.html*)

It is important to note that to construct a declared or created temporary table, you must first create a user temporary table space. That is because declared and created temporary tables can only be stored in user temporary table spaces. And a user temporary table space is not created by default as part of the database creation process.

A Closer Look at Views

In Chapter 4, "Working with Databases and Database Objects," we saw that views can provide a different way of describing and looking at data stored in one or more base tables. Essentially, a view is a named specification of a result table that is populated whenever the view is referenced in an SQL statement. (Each time a view is referenced, a query is executed, and the results are retrieved from the underlying table and returned in a table-like format.)

Like base tables, views can be thought of as having columns and rows. And in most cases, data can be manipulated using a view just as it can be manipulated using a table. (In other words, you can use views to insert, update, and delete data values.)

As with tables, views can be created via Data Studio or by executing the CREATE VIEW statement. The basic syntax for this statement is:

```
CREATE VIEW [ViewName]
  <([ColumnName], ...)>
  AS [SELECTStatement]
  <WITH <LOCAL | CASCADED> CHECK OPTION>
```

where:

ViewName	Identifies the name to assign to the view that is to be created; the view name specified must be unique within the schema the view is to be defined in
ColumnName	Identifies, by name, one or more columns that are to be included in the view—if a list of column names is provided, the number of column names supplied must match the number of columns that will be returned by the SELECT statement used to create the view; if a list of column names is not provided, the view will inherit the names that are assigned to the columns returned by the SELECT statement used
SELECTStatement	Identifies a SELECT statement that, when executed, will produce the data values that are to be used to populate the view (by retrieving them from other tables, views, or both)

Therefore, to create a view named DEPT_VIEW that references specific data values stored in a table named DEPARTMENT, you could execute a CREATE VIEW statement that looks something like this:

```
CREATE VIEW dept_view
  AS SELECT (dept_no, dept_name, dept_size)
  FROM department
  WHERE dept_size > 25
```

The resulting view will contain department number (DEPT_NO), department name (DEPT_NAME), and department size (DEPT_SIZE) information for every department that has more than 25 people assigned to it.

If the WITH <LOCAL> CHECK OPTION clause is specified with the CREATE VIEW statement used, all insert and update operations that are performed against the resulting view will be checked to ensure that the rows being added or modified conform to the view's definition. What does that mean? Suppose you created a view named CHOICE_OBJECTS (that is based on the OBJECTS table that was used in some of the earlier examples) by executing a CREATE VIEW statement that looks like this:

```
CREATE VIEW choice_objects
  AS SELECT * FROM object
  WHERE o_id < 100
  WITH LOCAL CHECK OPTION
```

Now, suppose a user tries to add a new record to this view, using an INSERT statement that looks like this:

```
INSERT INTO choice_objects
  VALUES (500, 'SNOW', 'WHITE')
```

The insert operation will fail because the record violates the view's definition. (The value specified for the O_ID column is greater than 100.) Figure 6.17 illustrates this behavior.

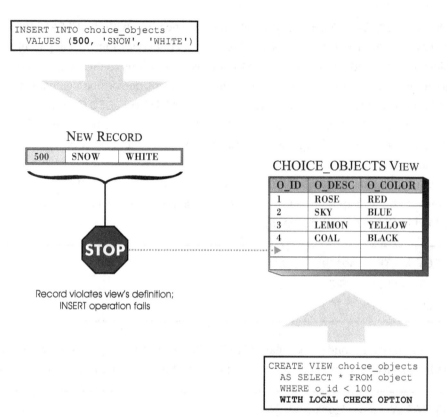

Figure 6.17: How the WITH LOCAL CHECK OPTION *clause ensures that rows being added or modified via a view conform to the view's definition*

Had the WITH LOCAL CHECK OPTION clause not been specified when the CHOICE_ OBJECTS view was created, the insert operation would have been successful. However, the record that was added would not have been visible to the view. So essentially, the WITH LOCAL CHECK OPTION clause guarantees that an insert or update operation performed against a view will not create a record that the view will never see.

Note: Views created with the WITH LOCAL CHECK OPTION clause are referred to as *symmetric views* because every record that can be inserted into them can also be retrieved from them.

If the WITH CASCADED CHECK OPTION clause is specified with the CREATE VIEW statement used, the resulting view will inherit the search conditions of the parent view (that the view is based upon), and it will treat those conditions as one or more constraints that are to be used to validate insert and update operations performed against the view. Any child view of the view that is created with the WITH CASCADED CHECK OPTION clause specified will inherit those constraints as well; the search conditions of both parent and child views are ANDed together to form the complete set of constraints that data must adhere to.

To better understand how the WITH CASCADED CHECK OPTION clause works, let's look at another example. Suppose a view named CHOICE_OBJECTS was created by executing the following CREATE VIEW statement:

```
CREATE VIEW choice_objects
  AS SELECT * FROM object
  WHERE o_id < 100
```

Now, suppose a second a view named RED_OBJECTS (which happens to be a child of the CHOICE_OBJECTS view) is created with a CREATE VIEW statement that looks like this:

```
CREATE VIEW red_objects
  AS SELECT * FROM choice_objects
  WHERE o_color = 'RED'
  WITH CASCADED CHECK OPTION
```

If a user attempts to add a new record to the RED_OBJECTS view using an INSERT statement that looks like this:

```
INSERT INTO red_objects
  VALUES (500, 'CHERRY', 'RED')
```

the insert operation will fail because the record violates the *parent* view's definition— the value specified for the O_ID column is greater than 100. Figure 6.18 illustrates this scenario.

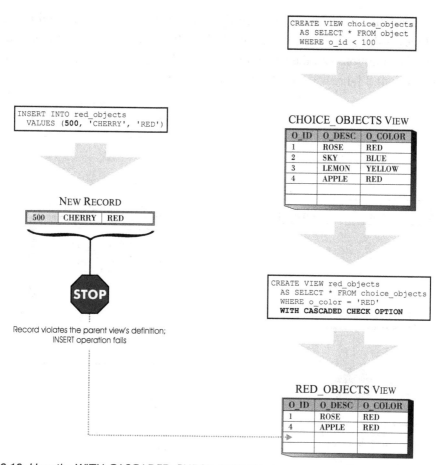

```
CREATE VIEW choice_objects
  AS SELECT * FROM object
  WHERE o_id < 100
```

```
INSERT INTO red_objects
  VALUES (500, 'CHERRY', 'RED')
```

CHOICE_OBJECTS VIEW

O_ID	O_DESC	O_COLOR
1	ROSE	RED
2	SKY	BLUE
3	LEMON	YELLOW
4	APPLE	RED

NEW RECORD

| 500 | CHERRY | RED |

STOP

Record violates the parent view's definition;
INSERT operation fails

```
CREATE VIEW red_objects
  AS SELECT * FROM choice_objects
  WHERE o_color = 'RED'
  WITH CASCADED CHECK OPTION
```

RED_OBJECTS VIEW

O_ID	O_DESC	O_COLOR
1	ROSE	RED
4	APPLE	RED

Figure 6.18: How the WITH CASCADED CHECK OPTION *clause ensures that rows being added or modified via a child view conform to the parent view's definition*

It is important to note that when a view is created with the WITH CASCADED CHECK OPTION clause, all insert and update operations performed against the view will be checked to ensure that the rows being added or modified conform to both the view's definition *and the parent view's definition*. Consequently, if a user tries to add a new record to the RED_OBJECTS view that was created in the previous example using an INSERT statement that looks like this:

```
INSERT INTO red_objects
  VALUES (500, 'SNOW', 'WHITE')
```

the insert operation will fail because the record violates both the view's definition and the parent view's definition—the value specified for the O_ID column is greater than 100 (parent view's definition) and the value provided for the O_COLOR column is not 'RED' (view's definition). Figure 6.19 illustrates this behavior.

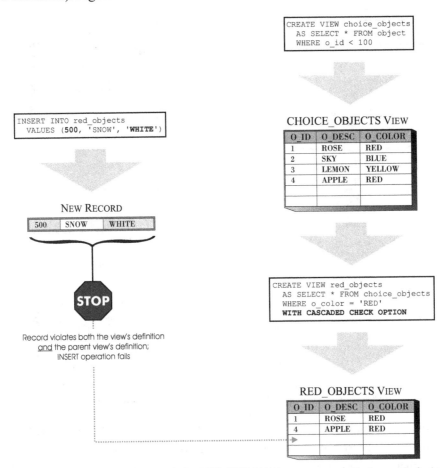

Figure 6.19: How the WITH CASCADED CHECK OPTION *clause ensures that rows being added or modified via a child view conform to both the child and the parent view's definition*

A Closer Look at Indexes

In Chapter 4, "Working with Databases and Database Objects," we saw that an index is an object that contains pointers to rows (in a table) that are logically ordered according to the values of one or more columns (known as *key columns* or *keys*). Indexes are important because:

- They provide a fast, efficient method for locating specific rows of data in large tables
- They provide a logical ordering of the rows in a table
- They can enforce the uniqueness of records in a table
- They can force a table to use *clustering* storage, which causes the rows of a table to be physically arranged according to the ordering of their key column values

Although some indexes are created implicitly to provide support for a unique constraint or primary key, most indexes are explicitly created using either Data Studio or the CREATE INDEX statement. The basic syntax for the CREATE INDEX statement is:

```
CREATE <UNIQUE> INDEX [IndexName]
ON [TableName] ([PriColumnName] <ASC | DESC>, ...)
<INCLUDE ([SecColumnName], ... )>
<CLUSTER>
<PCTFREE [10 | PercentFree]>
```

where:

IndexName	Identifies the name to assign to the index that is to be created; the index name specified must be unique within the schema the index is to be defined in
TableName	Identifies, by name, the table that the index is to be created for (and associated with)
PriColumnName	Identifies, by name, one or more primary columns that are to be part of the key for the index—if the index is a unique index, the combined values of each primary column specified will be used to enforce data uniqueness in the associated base table
SecColumnName	Identifies, by name, one or more secondary columns whose values are to be stored with the values of the primary columns, but that are not part of the index key—if the index is a unique index, the values of each secondary column specified will not be used to enforce data uniqueness
PercentFree	Specifies the percentage of each index page to leave as free space as the index is populated

If the INCLUDE clause is specified with the CREATE INDEX statement used, data from the secondary columns specified will be appended to the index's key values. By storing this information in the index (along with key values), you can improve the performance of some queries—if all the data needed to resolve a particular query can be obtained by accessing the index only, data does not have to be retrieved from the associated base table. (If the data needed to resolve a particular query does not reside solely in an index, both the index and the associated table must be accessed.)

Thus, to create an index named EMPNO_IDX for a base table named EMPLOYEES whose key consists of a column named EMPNO and that includes data from a column named LASTNAME, you would execute a CREATE INDEX statement that looks something like this:

```
CREATE UNIQUE INDEX empno_idx
  ON employees(empno) INCLUDE (lastname)
```

If the UNIQUE clause is specified with the CREATE INDEX statement used, the resulting index will be a *unique index* and, as we saw earlier, it will be used to ensure that the associated table does not contain duplicate occurrences of the same values in the columns that make up the index key. If the base table the index is to be created for already contains data, uniqueness is checked and enforced at the time DB2 attempts to create the index, and if records with duplicate index key values are found, the index will not be created. On the other hand, if no duplicates exist, the index will be created and uniqueness will be enforced whenever insert and update operations are performed against the associated table. (Any time uniqueness of the index key is compromised, the insert or update operation will fail and an error will be generated.)

 Important: If the INCLUDE clause is specified with the CREATE INDEX statement used, the UNIQUE clause must be provided.

Thus, to create a unique index named EMPNO_IDX for a base table named EMPLOYEES whose key consists of a column named EMPNO, you would execute a CREATE INDEX statement that looks like this:

```
CREATE UNIQUE INDEX empno_idx
  ON employees(empno)
```

If the CLUSTER clause is specified with the CREATE INDEX statement used, the resulting index will be a *clustering index*, which as we saw in Chapter 4, "Working with Databases and Database Objects," is a special index that attempts to physically store records for a table on a page that contains other records with similar index key values. (If no space is available on that page, DB2 will attempt to store the record in a nearby page.) A clustering index usually increases performance by decreasing the amount of I/O that is needed to access data. *It's important to note that a table can have only one clustering index.*

Therefore, to create a clustering index named EMPNO_CIDX for a base table named EMPLOYEES whose key consists of a column named EMPNO, you would execute a CREATE INDEX statement that looks like this:

```
CREATE UNIQUE INDEX empno_cidx
  ON employees(empno)
  CLUSTER
```

When creating a clustering index, the CREATE INDEX statement's PCTFREE clause can be used to control how much space is reserved for future insert and update operations. A higher PCTFREE value (the default is 10 percent) can reduce the likelihood that index page splits will occur when records are added to an index.

Note: Over time, update operations can cause rows to change page locations, thereby reducing the degree of clustering that exists between an index and its data pages. Reorganizing a table (with the REORG utility) by the clustering index will return the index to its original level of clustering.

You can create any number of indexes for a table by using a wide variety of column combinations. However, as we saw in Chapter 4, "Working with Databases and Database Objects," every index comes at a price. Because indexes store key column and row pointer information, additional storage space is needed for each index used. Furthermore, write performance is negatively affected—every time a transaction performs an insert, update, or delete operation against a table with indexes, each index affected must be updated to reflect the changes made. Because of this, indexes should only be created when there is a clear performance advantage to having them.

Indexes are typically used to improve query performance. Therefore, tables that are used for data mining, business intelligence, business warehousing, and other applications that execute many (and often complex) queries but that rarely modify data are prime candidates for indexes. Conversely, tables in Online Transaction Processing (OLTP) environments or environments where data throughput is high should use indexes sparingly or avoid them altogether.

Altering Indexes

While existing tables can be modified significantly using the ALTER TABLE statement, the same cannot be said for indexes. If the key columns for an existing index need to be changed or a decision is made to convert an existing index to a clustering index, the index must be deleted (dropped) and a new index with the desired characteristics must be created.

However, there is one property that can be changed without requiring an index to be dropped and recreated. That property is the attribute that controls whether data for an index is compressed, and it can be changed by executing the ALTER INDEX statement. The syntax for this statement is:

```
ALTER INDEX [IndexName]
  COMPRESS [NO | YES]
```

where:

IndexName   Identifies, by name, the index whose compression attribute is to
                   be turned on or off

Thus, to enable compression for the index named EMPNO_IDX that was created earlier, you would execute an ALTER INDEX statement that looks like this:

```
ALTER INDEX empno_idx
  COMPRESS YES
```

A Closer Look at Triggers

In Chapter 4, "Working with Databases and Database Objects," we saw that a trigger is an object that is used to define a set of actions that are to be executed whenever a transaction performs an insert, update, or delete operation against a table or updatable view. Like constraints, triggers are often used to enforce data integrity and business rules. Unlike constraints, triggers can also be used to automatically update other tables, generate or transform values for inserted or updated rows, and invoke functions to perform tasks such as issuing errors or alerts.

Before you can create a trigger, you must identify the following components:

- **Subject table/view:** The table or view that the trigger is to be associated with
- **Trigger event:** An SQL operation that, when performed against the subject table or view, will cause the trigger to be activated (*fired*); the trigger event can be an insert operation, an update operation, a delete operation, or a merge operation that inserts, updates, or deletes data
- **Trigger activation time:** Indicates whether the trigger should be fired *before*, *after*, or *instead of* the trigger event (a BEFORE trigger is fired before the trigger event occurs and can see new data values that are about to be inserted into the subject table; an AFTER trigger is fired after the trigger event occurs and can see data values that have already been inserted into the subject table; and an INSTEAD OF trigger is executed against the subject view, in place of the trigger event)
- **Set of affected rows:** The rows of the subject table or view that are being added, updated, or removed
- **Triggered action:** An optional search condition and a set of SQL statements that are executed when the trigger is fired—if a search condition is specified, the SQL statements are executed only if the search condition evaluates to TRUE
- **Trigger granularity:** Specifies whether the triggered action is to be executed once, when the trigger event takes place, or once for every row that the trigger event affects

After the appropriate trigger components have been identified, a trigger can be created by executing the CREATE TRIGGER statement. The basic syntax for this statement is:

```
CREATE TRIGGER [TriggerName]
[NO CASCADE BEFORE | AFTER | INSTEAD OF]
[INSERT | UPDATE <OF [ColumnName], ... > | DELETE]
ON [TableName | ViewName]
<REFERENCING [Reference]>
FOR EACH [ROW | STATEMENT]
<WHEN ( [SearchCondition] )>
[TriggeredAction]
```

where:

TriggerName	Identifies the name to assign to the trigger that is to be created; the trigger name specified must be unique within the schema the trigger is to be defined in
ColumnName	Identifies, by name, one or more columns in the subject table or view whose values must be updated before the triggered action (*TriggeredAction*) will be performed
TableName	Identifies, by name, the subject table of the BEFORE or AFTER trigger that is to be created
ViewName	Identifies, by name, the subject view of the INSTEAD OF trigger that is to be created
Reference	Identifies one or more transition variables or transition tables that the triggered action (*TriggeredAction*) will use; the syntax used to create transition variables and transition tables is:

```
<OLD <AS> [CorrelationName]>
<NEW <AS> [CorrelationName]>
<OLD TABLE <AS> [Identifier]>
<NEW TABLE <AS> [Identifier]>
```

where:

CorrelationName	Identifies a shorthand name that can be used to reference a specific row in the subject table of the trigger, either before the triggered action altered the row (OLD <AS>) or after the triggered action modified it (NEW <AS>)

Identifier	Identifies a shorthand name that can be used to identify a temporary table that contains a set of rows found in the subject table of the trigger, either before the triggered action altered the rows (OLD TABLE <AS>) or after the triggered action modified them (NEW TABLE <AS>)
SearchCondition	Identifies a search condition that, when evaluated, will return TRUE, FALSE, or Unknown; this condition determines whether or not the triggered action (*TriggeredAction*) is to be performed
TriggeredAction	Identifies one or more SQL statements or SQL Procedural Language (SQL PL) statements that are to be executed when the trigger is fired; together, these statements act as a single dynamic compound SQL statement—if two or more statements are used, they should be enclosed with the keywords BEGIN ATOMIC and END, and each statement must be terminated with a semicolon (;)

Note: The following SQL and SQL PL statements can be used in the *TriggeredAction* of any type of trigger:

- DECLARE
- SET
- SELECT
- CALL
- IF
- FOR
- WHILE
- ITERATE
- LEAVE
- SIGNAL
- GET DIGNOSTIC

In addition, the following SQL statements can be used in AFTER and INSTEAD OF triggers (but not BEFORE triggers):

- INSERT
- UPDATE
- DELETE
- MERGE

As you can see from the CREATE TRIGGER statement syntax, SQL statements that are to be executed when a trigger is fired (that is, the triggered action) can reference specific values within the set of affected rows using what are known as *transition variables*. Transition variables inherit the names of the columns in the subject table and are defined with the REFERENCING [*Reference*] clause of the CREATE TRIGGER statement. The OLD <AS> keywords indicate that a particular transition variable refers to the original value (as it existed before the trigger event was executed), and the NEW <AS> keywords denote that the variable refers to the new value (after the trigger event has completed).

If it is necessary to access the entire set of affected rows, *transition tables* can be used in lieu of transition variables. Like transition variables, transition tables inherit the names of the columns of the subject table and are defined with the REFERENCING [*Reference*] clause. In this case, the OLD TABLE <AS> keywords indicate that the set of affected rows refer to the original records, whereas the NEW TABLE <AS> keywords denote that the set of affected rows refer to new records.

The type of SQL operation that causes a trigger to fire determines which transition variables and/or tables can be defined. For example, if the trigger event is an insert operation, only NEW transition variables and tables can be defined (because no original state of the record being inserted exists, there are no old values). If the trigger event is a delete operation, only OLD transition variables and tables can be defined (because no new values are available with delete operations). However, if the trigger event is an update operation, *both* OLD and NEW transition variables and tables can be defined. In addition, transition variables can only be specified for triggers whose granularity is FOR EACH ROW. Transition tables, however, can be specified for triggers whose granularity is FOR EACH ROW or FOR EACH STATEMENT.

Consequently, if you have a base table named EMPLOYEES that has the following characteristics:

Column Name	Data Type
EMPID	CHAR(3)
FIRSTNAME	VARCHAR(20)
LASTNAME	VARCHAR(20)
SALARY	DECIMAL(10, 2)
BONUS	DECIMAL(8, 2)

and you want to create a trigger that will recalculate an employee's annual bonus anytime his or her salary changes, you could execute a CREATE TRIGGER statement that looks something like this:

```
CREATE TRIGGER calc_bonus
  NO CASCADE BEFORE
  UPDATE OF salary
  ON employees
  REFERENCING NEW AS n
  FOR EACH ROW
  SET n.bonus = n.salary * .025
```

Earlier, we saw that there are essentially three different ways a trigger can be fired: before the trigger event takes place, after the trigger event completes, or in place of the trigger event. For this reason, triggers are often referred to as being BEFORE triggers, AFTER triggers, or INSTEAD OF triggers.

As the name implies, a BEFORE trigger is fired for every row in the set of affected rows *before* the trigger event takes place. Consequently, BEFORE triggers are often used to validate input data, to automatically generate values for newly inserted rows, and to prevent certain types of trigger events from being performed.

For example, to prevent users from changing the employee ID assigned to an individual after a record for that individual is stored in the EMPLOYEES table presented earlier, you might create a BEFORE trigger that enforces this behavior by executing a CREATE TRIGGER statement that looks something like this:

```
CREATE TRIGGER block_empid_updates
  NO CASCADE BEFORE
  UPDATE OF empid
  ON employees
  FOR EACH ROW
  SIGNAL SQLSTATE '75001'
  SET MESSAGE_TEXT = 'Updates of EMPID column not allowed!'
```

On the other hand, an AFTER trigger is fired *after* the trigger event has been successfully executed. Because of this, AFTER triggers are often used to insert, update, or delete data in the same or in other tables; to check data against other data values in the same or in other tables; or to invoke UDFs that perform nondatabase operations. For example, suppose you have a base table named SALES that has the following characteristics:

Column Name	Data Type
INVOICE	INTEGER
AMOUNT	DECIMAL(10, 2)
SALES_DATE	DATE
SHIP_DATE	DATE
BILL_DATE	DATE

Now, assume that business rules dictate that anytime a user inserts a record into the SALES table, the current date is to be recorded as the sales date, a shipping date is to be scheduled three days out, and billing is to occur 30 days from the date of the sale. You could create three AFTER triggers to enforce these business rules by executing a set of CREATE TRIGGER statements that look like this:

```
CREATE TRIGGER calc_sales_date
  AFTER
  INSERT ON sales
  REFERENCING NEW AS n
  FOR EACH ROW
  UPDATE sales SET sales_date = CURRENT DATE
    WHERE invoice = n.invoice

CREATE TRIGGER calc_ship_date
  AFTER
  INSERT ON sales
  REFERENCING NEW AS n
  FOR EACH ROW
```

Continued

```
   UPDATE sales SET ship_date = CURRENT DATE + 3 DAYS
     WHERE invoice = n.invoice

CREATE TRIGGER calc_bill_date
  AFTER
  INSERT ON sales
  REFERENCING NEW AS n
  FOR EACH ROW
  UPDATE sales SET bill_date = CURRENT DATE + 30 DAYS
     WHERE invoice = n.invoice
```

Notice that in this scenario, three triggers were created: one to generate a sales date, one to generate a shipping date, and one to generate a billing date. If necessary, several different triggers can be created for a single table. However, when multiple triggers are needed, the order in which they are defined can be important. That is because triggers are fired in the order in which they are created.

Thus, in the previous example, each time a new record is inserted into the SALES table, the CALC_SALES_DATE trigger will be fired first, followed by the CALC_SHIP_DATE trigger, followed by the CALC_BILL_DATE trigger. (It is easy to see the problems that could arise had these three triggers been defined in the opposite order.) If, for some reason, one trigger fails, the firing of the others will not be affected.

Unlike BEFORE and AFTER triggers, which are fired whenever a specific trigger event is performed against a subject table, INSTEAD OF triggers are fired only when specific trigger events are performed against a subject view. Consequently, INSTEAD OF triggers are often used to force applications to use views as the only interface for performing insert, update, delete, and query operations. However, to use a view in this manner, it must not have been defined with a WITH CHECK OPTION specified.

Thus, if you were to create an updatable view for the EMPLOYEES table presented earlier by executing a CREATE VIEW statement that looks like this:

```
CREATE VIEW emp_info AS
  SELECT * FROM employees
```

assuming all data entry is to be performed by using the EMP_INFO view just created, you can prevent users from changing the employee ID assigned to an individual after a record for that individual has been stored in the EMPLOYEES table by creating an INSTEAD OF trigger with a CREATE TRIGGER statement that looks something like this:

```
CREATE TRIGGER empv_update
  INSTEAD OF
  UPDATE ON emp_info
  REFERENCING NEW AS n OLD AS o
  FOR EACH ROW
  BEGIN ATOMIC
    VALUES(CASE WHEN n.empid = o.empid THEN 0
           ELSE RAISE_ERROR('75001', 'No EMPID changes!')
           END);
    UPDATE employees AS e
    SET (firstname, lastname, salary, bonus)
      = (n.firstname, n.lastname, n.salary, n.bonus)
    WHERE n.empid = e.empid;
  END
```

It is important to note that once a trigger is created, it cannot be altered. Therefore, if you create a trigger and later discover that you need to change its behavior, you must drop the existing trigger and then recreate it with the desired changes.

Data Concurrency

Fifteen percent (15%) of the *DB2 10.5 Fundamentals for LUW* certification exam (Exam 615) is designed to test your knowledge of the mechanisms DB2 uses to allow multiple users and applications to interact with a database simultaneously, without adversely affecting data consistency. The questions that make up this portion of the exam are designed to evaluate the following:

- Your ability to identify the appropriate isolation level to use for a given situation
- Your ability to identify the characteristics of DB2 locks
- Your ability to list objects that locks can be acquired for
- Your ability to identify factors that can influence locking

This chapter introduces you to the concept of data consistency and to the two important mechanisms DB2 uses to maintain data consistency in both single-user and multiuser database environments: *isolation levels* and *locks*. In this chapter, you will learn what isolation levels are, which isolation levels are available, and how to use isolation levels to keep transactions from interfering with each other in a multiuser environment. You will also discover how DB2 provides concurrency control through the use of locking, which types of locks are available, how to acquire locks, and which factors can influence locking performance.

Understanding Data Consistency

To understand how DB2 attempts to maintain data consistency in both single and multiuser environments, you must first know what data consistency is. In addition, you should be able to identify the types of events that can leave a database in an inconsistent state. So just what is data consistency? The best way to answer that question is by looking at an example.

Suppose a company that owns a chain of hardware stores uses a database to keep track of, among other things, the inventory at each store. Consequently, the database contains inventory tables for every store in the chain, and whenever a particular store receives or sells merchandise, its designated inventory table is updated. Now suppose a case of hammers is physically moved from one store (which has plenty of hammers in stock) to another (which has just run out).

To reflect this inventory move, a user must increase the hammer count value stored in the receiving store's inventory table and decrease the hammer count value stored in the donating store's table. If, however, a user raises the hammer count value in the receiving store's table, but fails to lower the value in the donating store's table, the data in the database will be inconsistent—the total hammer count for the entire chain is no longer accurate (nor is the hammer count for the donating store).

In single-user environments, a database can become inconsistent if a user fails to make all the necessary changes (as in the previous example), if the database system crashes while a user or application is in the middle of making modifications, or if an application terminates prematurely. In multiuser environments, inconsistency can also occur when several users or applications attempt to access the same data *at the same time*. For example, in the previous scenario, if one user is updating both stores' inventory tables to show that a case of hammers was physically moved from one store to another, and another user queries the database to obtain the hammer count value for the receiving store *before* the update has been committed, the query will erroneously indicate that no more hammers are available. (Reacting to this misinformation, the second user might then place an order for more hammers when no more hammers are needed.)

Transactions, Isolation Levels, and Locks

The primary mechanism that DB2 uses to keep data consistent is the *transaction*. In Chapter 5, "Working with DB2 Data Using SQL and XQuery," we saw that a transaction (also referred to as a *unit of work*) is a recoverable sequence of one or more SQL operations that are grouped as a single unit, usually within an application. The initiation and termination of a transaction defines points of consistency within a database; either the effects of all operations performed within a transaction are applied to the database and made permanent (committed), or they are backed out (rolled back) and the database is returned to its previous state.

In single-user environments, transactions are run serially and do not have to contend with other concurrently running transactions. But in multiuser environments, transactions are often run simultaneously. As a result, each transaction can potentially interfere with any other running transaction—the amount of interference allowed is controlled through the use of another mechanism, the *isolation level*.

Transactions that have the potential to interfere with one another are said to be *interleaved*, or *parallel*, whereas transactions that are completely isolated from one another are deemed *serializable*, which means that the results of running them simultaneously are the same as the results of running them serially (one after another). Ideally, every transaction should be serializable. Why?

Suppose a salesperson and an accountant are working with the same database simultaneously. Now assume the salesperson enters an order for Company X (to generate a quote) but does not commit the entry. At the same time, the accountant queries the database for a list of all unpaid orders, retrieves the new order for Company X, and generates a bill. Now imagine that the individual the salesperson is working with at Company X decides not to place the order. The salesperson rolls back the transaction since the order was not placed, and information about the order is removed from the database. However, one week later, Company X receives a bill for an order they did not place. Had the salesperson's transaction and the accountant's transaction been completely isolated from each other (that is, serialized), this situation would not have occurred— either the salesperson's transaction would have finished before the accountant's transaction began or vice versa. In either case, Company X would not have received a bill.

When transactions are not serializable, four types of phenomena can occur:

- **Lost updates:** Occurs when two transactions read the same data and both attempt to update that data at the same time, resulting in the loss of one of the updates—for example, Transaction 1 and Transaction 2 read the same row of data and calculate new values for that row based upon the values read; if Transaction 1 updates the row with its new value, and Transaction 2 then updates the same row, Transaction 1's update will be lost.
- **Dirty reads:** Occurs when a transaction reads data that has not yet been committed—for example, Transaction 1 modifies a row of data, and Transaction 2 reads the modified row before the change is committed; if Transaction 1 rolls back the change, Transaction 2 will have read data that never really existed.
- **Nonrepeatable reads:** Occurs when a transaction reads the same row of data twice and retrieves different results each time—for example, Transaction 1 reads a row of data, and then Transaction 2 modifies or deletes that row and commits the change; when Transaction 1 attempts to reread the row, it will retrieve different data values (if the row was updated) or discover that the row no longer exists (if the row was deleted).
- **Phantoms:** Occurs when a row of data matches some search criteria but is not seen initially—for example, Transaction 1 retrieves a set of rows that satisfies some search criteria, and Transaction 2 inserts a new row that matches the search criteria of Transaction 1's query; if Transaction 1 re-executes the query that produced the original set of rows, a different set of rows will be returned (the new row that Transaction 2 added will now be included in the set of rows produced).

Isolation Levels

Because different users and applications might attempt to access or modify data stored in a DB2 database at the same time, DB2 must be able to allow transactions to run simultaneously while ensuring that data integrity is never compromised. The simultaneous sharing of database resources by multiple users and applications is known as *concurrency*, and one way that DB2 enforces concurrency is through the use of isolation levels. As the name implies, isolation levels determine how DB2 *"isolates"* data that is accessed or modified by one transaction from other transactions that happen to be running at the same time. With DB2 10.5, the following isolation levels are recognized and supported:

- Repeatable Read
- Read Stability
- Cursor Stability
- Uncommitted Read

Table 7.1 shows the various phenomena that can occur when each of these isolation levels is used.

Table 7.1: DB2 isolation levels and the phenomena that can occur when each is used				
Isolation Level	**Phenomena**			
	Lost Updates	**Dirty Reads**	**Nonrepeatable Reads**	**Phantoms**
Repeatable Read	No	No	No	No
Read Stability	No	No	No	Yes
Cursor Stability	No	No	Yes	Yes
Uncommitted Read	No	Yes	Yes	Yes

The Repeatable Read (RR) isolation level

The Repeatable Read isolation level is the most restrictive isolation level available. It completely isolates the effects of one transaction from the effects of other concurrently running transactions. Thus, lost updates, dirty reads, nonrepeatable reads, and phantoms cannot occur.

With the Repeatable Read isolation level, every row that is referenced *in any manner* by the owning transaction is locked for the life of that transaction. (The transaction that has a resource associated with it is said to *hold* or *own* the lock on the resource.) Consequently, if the same query (SELECT statement) is issued multiple times within the same transaction, the result data sets produced are guaranteed to be identical. In fact, transactions running under the Repeatable Read isolation level can retrieve the same set of rows any number of times and perform any number of operations on them until terminated (by either a COMMIT or a ROLLBACK operation). However, other transactions are prohibited from performing insert, update, or delete operations that will alter rows that the owning transaction has accessed as long as that transaction remains active.

To ensure that other transactions do not adversely affect the data being accessed by a transaction running under the Repeatable Read isolation level, every row that the owning transaction references is locked—not just the rows that are actually retrieved or modified. Thus, if a transaction scans 1,000 rows to retrieve 10, locks are acquired and held on all 1,000 rows scanned—not on just the 10 rows retrieved.

•••

Note: With the Repeatable Read isolation level, if an entire table or view is scanned in response to a query, the entire table or all rows the view references are locked. This greatly reduces concurrency, especially when large tables and views are used.

•••

So how does this isolation level work in a real-world situation? Suppose you own a small motel and use a DB2 database to keep track of reservation and room rate information. You also have a Web-based application that allows individuals to reserve rooms on a first-come, first-served basis. If your reservation application runs under the Repeatable Read isolation level, a customer scanning the database for a list of available rooms for a given date range will prevent other customers from making or canceling reservations that would cause the list to change if it were to be generated again (by executing the same query—assuming, of course, that the query is executed from the same transaction).

Similarly, your motel's manager cannot change the room rate for any room records that were scanned in response to the first customer's query. However, other customers *can* make or cancel room reservations for rooms whose records were not scanned when the first customer's query was executed. Likewise, your manager can change room rates for any room whose record was not read when the list of available rooms was produced. (Anyone attempting to make or cancel room reservations or change room rates for rooms whose records were scanned in response to the first customer's query will be forced to wait until the first customer's transaction is terminated.) Figure 7.1 illustrates this behavior.

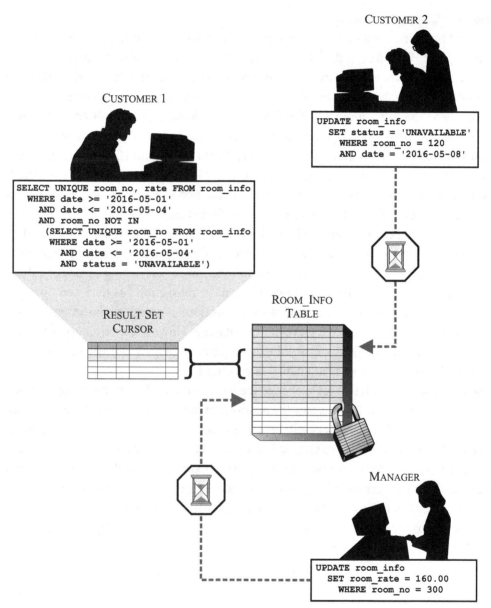

Figure 7.1: Example of how the Repeatable Read isolation level can affect application behavior

The Read Stability (RS) isolation level

The Read Stability isolation level is not quite as restrictive as the Repeatable Read isolation level. Therefore, it does not completely isolate one transaction from the effects of other concurrently running transactions. Specifically, when this isolation level is used, lost updates, dirty reads, and nonrepeatable reads cannot occur, but phantoms can and may be seen. That's because when the Read Stability isolation level is used, only rows that the owning transaction retrieves or modifies are locked. So, if a transaction scans 1,000 rows to retrieve 10, locks are acquired and held on just the 10 rows retrieved, not on the 1,000 rows that were scanned. Because fewer locks are acquired, more transactions can run concurrently. However, if the owning transaction executes the same query more than once, the result data set produced may be different each time.

As with the Repeatable Read isolation level, transactions running under the Read Stability isolation level can retrieve a set of rows and perform any number of operations on them. Other transactions, however, are prohibited from performing update and delete operations that will affect the set of rows the owning transaction has retrieved (for as long as the transaction remains active). But other transactions *can* perform insert operations against other tables or updatable views in the database. However, inserted rows that match the selection criteria of a query the owning transaction issued will appear as phantoms in any subsequent result data sets produced.

So how does this isolation level change the way your motel reservation application works? Now, when a customer scans the database to obtain a list of available rooms for a given date range, other customers will be able to make or cancel reservations that might cause the first customer's list to change if it were to be generated again (by executing the same query—assuming, of course, that the query is executed from the same transaction). Likewise, your manager can change the room rate for any room that did not appear in the first customer's list. Consequently, each time the first customer generates a list of available rooms for a given date range, the list produced may contain rooms and room rates not previously seen. Figure 7.2 illustrates this behavior.

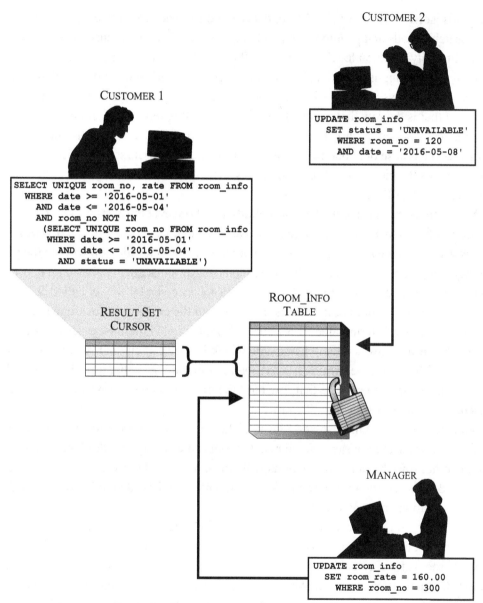

Figure 7.2: Example of how the Read Stability isolation level can affect application behavior

The Cursor Stability (CS) isolation level

The Cursor Stability isolation level is even more relaxed than the Read Stability isolation level in the way that it isolates the effects of concurrent transactions from each other.

When this isolation level is used, lost updates and dirty reads cannot occur; however, nonrepeatable reads and phantoms can and may be seen. That is because, when the Cursor Stability isolation level is used, only the row that the owning transaction is currently referencing is locked. (The moment a record is retrieved from a result data set, a pointer—known as a *cursor*—is positioned on the corresponding row in the underlying table, and that is the row that gets locked. This lock will remain in effect until the cursor is repositioned, usually by a FETCH operation, or until the owning transaction is terminated.) Because only one row-level lock is acquired, the Cursor Stability isolation level provides the highest level of concurrency available. Consequently, this is the isolation level that DB2 uses by default.

When a transaction using the Cursor Stability isolation level retrieves a row from a table (by means of a cursor), no other transaction is allowed to update or delete that row *as long as the cursor is positioned on it*. However, other transactions can add new rows to the table, and they can perform update and delete operations on rows that are positioned on either side of the cursor (locked row)—provided the row was not accessed by way of an index.

After the lock is acquired, it remains in effect until the cursor is repositioned or the owning transaction is terminated. If the cursor is repositioned, in most cases the lock held on the current row is released, and a new lock is acquired on the row the cursor is moved to. If, however, the owning transaction modifies any row that it retrieves, no other transaction can update or delete that row until the transaction ends—even if the cursor is subsequently moved off the modified row.

With the Cursor Stability isolation level, if the same query is executed two or more times within the same transaction, the results produced can vary. In addition, changes made to other rows by other transactions will not be seen until those changes have been committed. (This is true for transactions running under the Repeatable Read and Read Stability isolation levels as well.)

Once again, consider how this isolation level will affect the way your motel reservation application works. Now, when a customer scans the database for a list of available rooms for a given date range and then views information about the first room in the list, other customers can make or cancel reservations for any room *except* the room the first customer is currently looking at (for the date range specified). Likewise, your manager can change the room rate for any room *except* the room the customer is currently looking at (again, for the date range specified). When the first customer views information about the next room in the list, other customers, as well as the manager, can make changes to the record for the room the first customer was just looking at (provided the customer did not reserve that room). However, no one will be allowed to change the record for the room the first customer is viewing now. Figure 7.3 illustrates this behavior.

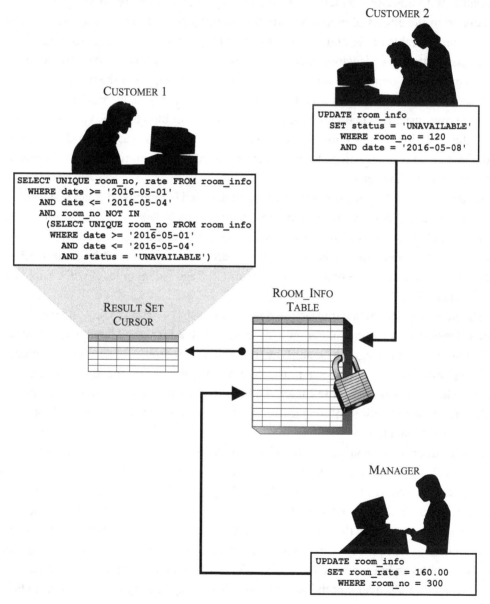

Figure 7.3: Example of how the Cursor Stability isolation level can affect application behavior

The Uncommitted Read (UR) isolation level

The Uncommitted Read isolation level is the least restrictive of all the isolation levels available. With this isolation level, the effects of one transaction are typically *not* isolated from the effects of other concurrently running transactions. Consequently, dirty reads, nonrepeatable reads, and phantoms can and often do occur. That's because when the Uncommitted Read isolation level is used, the rows that a transaction retrieves are locked only if that transaction attempts to modify the data stored in them. Or if another transaction attempts to drop or alter the underlying table the rows were retrieved from. Because rows usually remain unlocked when the Uncommitted Read isolation level is used, this isolation level is typically employed when transactions access read-only tables and views or when transactions for which the retrieval of uncommitted data will have no adverse effect are executed.

As the name implies, transactions running under the Uncommitted Read isolation level can see changes made to rows by other transactions *before those changes have been committed*. However, that is not the case when other transactions create tables, indexes, and views. In such situations, the transaction creating the objects must be committed *before* transactions running under the Uncommitted Read isolation level will be able to see or access them.

The same applies when a transaction deletes (or drops) existing tables, indexes, or views. Transactions running under the Uncommitted Read isolation level will not learn that these objects no longer exist until the transaction that dropped them is committed. (It is important to note that when a transaction running under the Uncommitted Read isolation level uses an updatable cursor, the transaction will behave as if it is running under the Cursor Stability isolation level, and the constraints of the Cursor Stability isolation level will apply.)

So how does the Uncommitted Read isolation level affect your motel reservation application? Now when a customer scans the database to obtain a list of available rooms for a given date range, other customers can make or cancel reservations for any room in the motel, including the room the first customer is currently looking at. Likewise, your manager can change the room rates for any room in the motel, over any date range. (Unfortunately, the first customer might be prevented from reserving a room that appears to have been taken but is actually available. Or that customer might reserve a room at one rate, only to discover that the original price has changed.) Figure 7.4 illustrates this behavior.

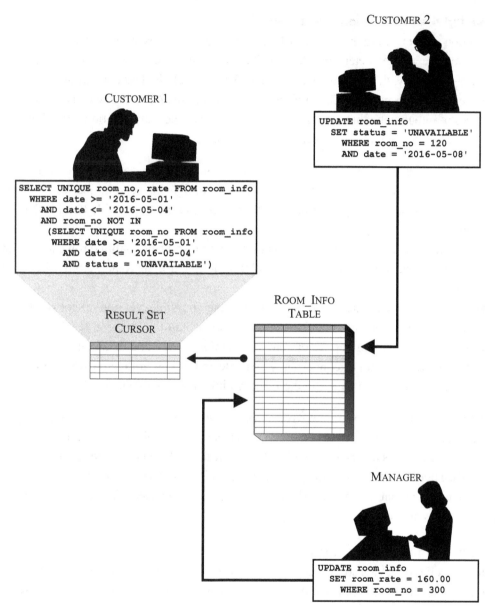

Figure 7.4: Example of how the Uncommitted Read isolation level can affect application behavior

Choosing the Proper Isolation Level

In addition to controlling the level at which DB2 provides transaction concurrency, the isolation level used determines how well concurrently running transactions will perform—typically, the more restrictive the isolation level, the less concurrency is possible. So how do you decide which isolation level to use? The best way is to identify the types of phenomena that are unacceptable, and then select an isolation level that will prevent those phenomena from occurring. For example:

- If you are executing large queries, and you want to prevent other concurrently running transactions from making changes that might cause your queries to return different results if they are run more than once, use the Repeatable Read isolation level.
- If you want some level of concurrency, yet you also want qualified rows to remain stable for the duration of an individual transaction, use the Read Stability isolation level.
- If you want the greatest amount of concurrency possible, yet you do not want queries to see uncommitted data, use the Cursor Stability isolation level.
- If you are executing queries on read-only tables, views, and databases, *or* you want the greatest amount of concurrency possible and it does not matter whether queries return uncommitted data, use the Uncommitted Read isolation level.

Keep in mind that choosing the wrong isolation level for a given situation can have a significant negative effect on both concurrency and performance (performance for some applications can be degraded as they wait for locks on resources to be released). Therefore, when deciding on an isolation level to use, consider your database environment as a whole. Then, make your decision according to the way most applications will need to interact with your data.

Specifying the Isolation Level to Use

Although isolation levels control concurrency at the transaction level, they are set at the application level (or sometimes at the SQL statement level). Therefore, in most cases, the isolation level that a particular application uses is applied to every transaction the application executes. (It is important to note that an application can be constructed in several parts, and that each part can be assigned a different isolation level. In this case, the isolation level that is assigned to a part determines which isolation level each transaction within that part will use.)

With Embedded SQL applications, the isolation level to use is specified at precompile time or when an application is bound to a database (if deferred binding is used). Here, the isolation level is set with the ISOLATION [RR | RS | CS | UR] option of the PRECOMPILE and BIND commands. With Call Level Interface (CLI) and Open Database Connectivity (ODBC) applications, the isolation level is set at application run time by calling the SQLSetConnectAttr() function with the SQL_ATTR_TXN_ISOLATION connection attribute specified. (Alternatively, the desired isolation level can be set by assigning a value to the TXNISOLATION keyword in the *db2cli.ini* configuration file. However, this approach does not provide the flexibility of using different isolation levels for different transactions that the first approach offers.) Finally, with Java Database Connectivity (JDBC) and SQL for Java (SQLJ) applications, the isolation level is set at application run time by calling the setTransactionIsolation() method that resides within DB2's java.sql connection interface.

As mentioned earlier, when the isolation level for a particular application is not explicitly set (by using one of the methods just outlined), DB2 uses the Cursor Stability isolation level by default. This holds true for DB2 commands, SQL statements, and scripts that are executed from the DB2 Command Line Processor (CLP), as well for Embedded SQL, CLI/ODBC, JDBC, and SQLJ applications. Therefore, not only can you control the isolation level that an application uses, but you can also control the isolation level that will be used when operations are performed from the DB2 CLP. Here, the isolation level used can be controlled by executing the CHANGE ISOLATION LEVEL command just before a connection to a database is established.

With DB2 Version 8.1 and later, it is also possible to override the default isolation level (or the isolation level specified for a particular application) when individual queries are executed. This is done by appending the WITH [RR | RS | CS | UR] clause to a SELECT statement—the clause itself indicates that the associated SELECT statement is to be executed using the Repeatable Read (RR), Read Stability (RS), Cursor Stability (CS), or Uncommitted Read (UR) isolation level. Thus, if you want to obtain a list of all employees who work in a specific department, *and* you want to run the query that will produce this list under the Repeatable Read isolation level, you can simply execute a SELECT statement that looks something like this:

```
SELECT lastname FROM employee WHERE workdept = 'E11'
  WITH RR
```

So if you have an application that needs to run in a less-restrictive isolation level the majority of the time (to support maximum concurrency), but that contains one or two queries that must not see certain types of phenomena, you can use a combination of application-level and SQL statement-level isolation levels to meet your objective.

Locks

The one commonality among the isolation levels just described (with the exception of Uncommitted Read) is that they all acquire one or more *locks*. But just what is a lock? A lock is a mechanism that is used to associate a data resource with a single transaction, for the sole purpose of controlling how other transactions interact with that resource while it is associated with the transaction that has it locked.

Essentially, locks in a database environment serve the same purpose as they do for a house or car: they determine who can and cannot gain access, in this case, to a particular resource, which can be one or more data partitions, table spaces, tables, or rows. DB2 imposes locks to prohibit other transactions from making data modifications that might adversely affect the owning transaction.

When an owning transaction is terminated (by a COMMIT or ROLLBACK operation), any changes that have been made to the locked resource are either made permanent or backed out, and all locks on the resource that were acquired on behalf of the owning transaction are released. Once unlocked, a resource can be relocked and manipulated by another transaction. Figure 7.5 illustrates the basic principles of transaction/resource locking.

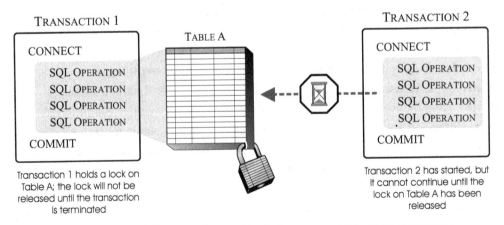

TRANSACTION 1

TABLE A

CONNECT

SQL OPERATION
SQL OPERATION
SQL OPERATION
SQL OPERATION

COMMIT

Transaction 1 holds a lock on
Table A; the lock will not be
released until the transaction
is terminated

TRANSACTION 2

CONNECT

SQL OPERATION
SQL OPERATION
SQL OPERATION
SQL OPERATION

COMMIT

Transaction 2 has started, but
it cannot continue until the
lock on Table A has been
released

Figure 7.5: How DB2 prevents uncontrolled concurrent access to a resource through the use of locks

Lock Attributes and Lock States

Locks used by DB2 have the following basic attributes:

- **Object:** Identifies the data resource that is being locked; DB2 implicitly acquires locks on data resources (specifically, data partitions, table spaces, base tables, and rows) whenever they are needed.
- **Size:** Identifies the physical size of the data resource that is being locked (in other words, how much data is being locked); a lock does not always have to control an entire data resource—for example, rather than giving a transaction exclusive control over an entire table, DB2 can elect to give a transaction exclusive control over just one or two rows within a table.
- **Duration** (or **Lock Count**): Identifies the length of time a lock is held; the isolation level used has a significant effect on the duration of a lock—for example, the lock acquired for a Repeatable Read transaction that accesses 500 rows is likely to have a long duration if all 500 rows are to be updated; on the other hand, the lock acquired for a Cursor Stability transaction is likely to have a much shorter duration.
- **State** (or **Mode**): Identifies the type of access that is allowed for both the lock owner and other concurrent users of the locked data resource. Table 7.2 shows the various lock states available (along with their effects) in order of increasing control over resources.

Table 7.2: Lock States (Modes) available with DB2 10.5			
Lock State (Mode)	**Applicable Objects**	**Lock Owner Access**	**Concurrent Transaction Access**
Intent None (IN)	Table spaces, blocks, tables, data partitions	Lock owner can read all data, including uncommitted data, stored in the locked resource; however, lock owner cannot modify data stored in the resource. Intent None locks are typically acquired for read-only transactions that have no intention of modifying data (thus, additional locks will not be acquired on the transaction's behalf).	Other transactions can read and modify data stored in the locked resource; however, they cannot delete data stored in the resource.
Intent Share (IS)	Table spaces, blocks, tables, data partitions	Lock owner can read all data (excluding uncommitted data) stored in the locked resource; however, lock owner cannot modify data stored in the resource. Intent Share locks are typically acquired for transactions that do not convey the intent to modify data (transactions that do not contain SELECT FOR UPDATE, UPDATE WHERE, or INSERT statements).	Other transactions can read and modify data stored in the locked resource.

Table 7.2: Lock States (Modes) available with DB2 10.5 (continued)			
Lock State (Mode)	**Applicable Objects**	**Lock Owner Access**	**Concurrent Transaction Access**
Intent Exclusive (IX)	Table spaces, blocks, tables, data partitions	Lock owner can read and modify data stored in the locked resource. Intent Exclusive locks are typically acquired for transactions that convey the intent to modify data (transactions that contain SELECT FOR UPDATE, UPDATE WHERE, or INSERT statements).	Other transactions can read and modify data stored in the locked resource.
Scan Share (NS)	Rows	Lock owner can read all data (excluding uncommitted data) stored in the locked resource; however, lock owner cannot modify data stored in the resource. Scan Share locks are typically acquired in place of a Share (S) lock for transactions that are running under the Read Stability or Cursor Stability isolation level.	Other transactions can read all data (excluding uncommitted data) stored in the locked resource; however, they cannot modify data stored in the resource.
Next Key Weak Exclusive (NW)	Rows	Lock owner can read all data (excluding uncommitted data) stored in the locked resource; however, lock owner cannot modify data stored in the resource. Next Key Weak Exclusive locks are typically acquired on the next available row in a table whenever a row is inserted into an index. This occurs only if the next row is currently locked by a scan that was performed under the Repeatable Read isolation level.	Other transactions can read all data (excluding uncommitted data) stored in the locked resource; however, they cannot modify data stored in the resource.
Share (S)	Blocks, tables, rows, data partitions	Lock owner can read all data (excluding uncommitted data) stored in the locked resource; however, lock owner cannot modify data stored in the resource. Share locks are typically acquired for transactions that do not convey the intent to modify data that are running under the Repeatable Read isolation level. (Transactions that contain SELECT FOR UPDATE, UPDATE WHERE, or INSERT statements convey the intent to modify data.)	Other transactions can read all data (excluding uncommitted data) stored in the locked resource; however, they cannot modify data stored in the resource.
Share With Intent Exclusive (SIX)	Blocks, tables, data partitions	Lock owner can read and modify data stored in the locked resource. Share With Intent Exclusive locks are typically acquired when a transaction holding a Share (S) lock on a resource attempts to acquire an Intent Exclusive (IX) lock on the same resource (or vice versa).	Other transactions can read all data (excluding uncommitted data) stored in the locked resource; however, they cannot modify data stored in the resource.

Table 7.2: Lock States (Modes) available with DB2 10.5 (continued)			
Lock State (Mode)	**Applicable Objects**	**Lock Owner Access**	**Concurrent Transaction Access**
Update (U)	Blocks, tables, rows, data partitions	Lock owner can modify all data (excluding uncommitted data) stored in the locked resource; however, lock owner cannot read data stored in the resource. Update locks are typically acquired for transactions that modify data with INSERT, UPDATE, or DELETE statements.	Other transactions can read all data (excluding uncommitted data) stored in the locked resource; however, they cannot modify data stored in the resource.
Exclusive (X)	Blocks, tables, rows, data partitions, buffer pools	Lock owner can both read and modify data stored in the locked resource. Exclusive locks are typically acquired for transactions that retrieve data with SELECT statements and then modify the data retrieved with INSERT, UPDATE, or DELETE statements. (Transactions that only retrieve data with SELECT statements do not require an Exclusive lock.)	Transactions using the Uncommitted Read isolation level can read all data, including uncommitted data, stored in the locked resource; however, they cannot modify data stored in the resource. All other transactions can neither read nor modify data stored in the locked resource.
Super Exclusive (Z)	Table spaces, blocks, tables, data partitions	Lock owner can read and modify data stored in the locked resource. Super Exclusive locks are typically acquired on a table whenever the lock owner attempts to alter the table, drop the table, create an index for the table, drop an index that has already been defined for the table, or reorganize the contents of the table (while the table is offline) by running the REORG utility.	Other transactions can neither read nor modify data stored in the locked resource.
Adapted from Table 1 under *Lock attributes* in the *IBM DB2 10.5 for Linux, UNIX, and Windows Knowledge Center*.			

How Locks Are Acquired

Except for occasions when the Uncommitted Read isolation level is used, it is never necessary for a transaction to explicitly request a lock. That is because DB2 automatically acquires locks as they are needed; once acquired, locks remain under DB2's control until they are released. By default, DB2 always attempts to acquire row-level locks. However, you can control whether DB2 will attempt to acquire row-level locks or table-level locks on behalf of transactions working with a specific table by executing a special form of the ALTER TABLE statement. This form of the ALTER TABLE statement has the following syntax:

```
ALTER TABLE [TableName] LOCKSIZE [ROW | TABLE]
```

where:

TableName   Identifies, by name, an existing table to lock at the locking level specified

For example, if the following SQL statement is executed:

```
ALTER TABLE employee LOCKSIZE ROW
```

DB2 will automatically acquire row-level locks for every transaction that accesses a table named EMPLOYEE. (This is the default behavior.) If the following SQL statement is executed instead:

```
ALTER TABLE employee LOCKSIZE TABLE
```

DB2 will attempt to acquire table-level locks for every transaction that accesses the EMPLOYEE table.

But what if you do not want every transaction that works with a particular table to acquire table-level locks? What if, instead, you want one or two specific transactions to acquire table-level locks, and all other transactions to acquire row-level locks when working with that table? In this case, you can simply leave the default locking behavior alone (so that row-level locking is applied) and use the LOCK TABLE statement to acquire a table-level lock on the table for select transactions. The syntax for the LOCK TABLE statement is:

```
LOCK TABLE [TableName] IN [SHARE | EXCLUSIVE] MODE
```

where:

TableName   Identifies, by name, the table to lock

As you can see, the LOCK TABLE statement allows a transaction to acquire a table-level lock on a particular table in one of two modes: SHARE or EXCLUSIVE. If a table is locked in SHARE mode, a table-level Share (S) lock is acquired on behalf of the requesting transaction, and other concurrent transactions can read, but not change, data stored in the locked table. If a table is locked in EXCLUSIVE mode, a table-level Exclusive (X) lock is acquired instead, and other concurrent transactions cannot perform any type of operation against the table as long as it remains locked.

For example, if the following SQL statement is executed:

```
LOCK TABLE employee IN SHARE MODE
```

a table-level Share (S) lock will be acquired on a table named EMPLOYEE on behalf of the current transaction (provided no other transaction holds a lock on this table), and any other concurrently running transactions will be allowed to read, but not change, data stored in the table.

On the other hand, if the following SQL statement is executed instead:

```
LOCK TABLE employee IN EXCLUSIVE MODE
```

a table-level Exclusive (X) lock will be acquired for the EMPLOYEE table, and no other transaction will be allowed to read or modify data stored in this table until the transaction that executed the LOCK TABLE statement is either committed or rolled back. Regardless of which type of table-level lock is acquired, when the transaction that obtained the lock is terminated, the lock is released automatically.

When deciding whether to use row-level locks or table-level locks, keep in mind that anytime a transaction holds a lock on a particular resource, other transactions can be denied access to that resource until the owning transaction is terminated. Therefore, row-level locks are usually better than table-level locks because they restrict access to a much smaller resource. However, because each lock acquired requires some amount of storage space (to hold) and some degree of processing time (to manage), there is usually considerably less overhead involved when a single table-level lock is used instead of multiple row-level locks.

To a certain extent, you can use the ALTER TABLE statement and the LOCK TABLE statement to control lock granularity (that is, whether row-level locking or table-level locking will be used) at both the global level (ALTER TABLE) and the transaction level (LOCK TABLE). So when is it more desirable to control granularity at the global level rather than at the transaction level? It all depends.

Suppose you have a read-only lookup table that multiple concurrent transactions must access. Forcing DB2 to acquire table-level Share (S) locks globally on behalf of each transaction that attempts to access this table might improve performance, because doing so will greatly reduce the locking overhead required. However, for a table that needs to be accessed frequently by read-only transactions and periodically by a single transaction that performs some type of maintenance, forcing DB2 to acquire a table-level Exclusive (X) lock only for the maintenance transaction is probably better than forcing DB2 to acquire a table-level Exclusive (X) lock for every transaction that attempts to access the table. In this case, if DB2 acquires a table-level Exclusive (X) lock at the instance level, the read-only transactions will be locked out of the table only when the maintenance transaction runs. In all other situations, these transactions will be able to access the table concurrently without requiring a lot of locking overhead.

Which Locks Are Acquired?

Although you can control whether DB2 will acquire row-level locks or table-level locks for a particular transaction, you cannot control what type of lock will be acquired. Instead, DB2 implicitly makes that decision by analyzing the transaction to determine the type of processing it has been designed to perform. To decide which particular type of lock a given situation needs, DB2 places all transactions into one of four categories:

- Read-Only
- Intent-to-Change
- Change
- Cursor-Controlled

The characteristics/data access methods used to assign transactions to these categories, along with the types of locks that are typically acquired for each, can be seen in Table 7.3.

Table 7.3: Types of transactions available and their associated locks		
Type of Transaction	**Description**	**Locks Typically Acquired**
Read-Only	Transactions that contain SELECT statements (which are intrinsically read-only), SELECT statements that have the FOR READ ONLY clause specified, or SQL statements that are ambiguous but are presumed to be read-only because of the BLOCKING option that was specified as part of the precompile and/or bind process	Intent Share (IS) and/or Share (S) locks
Intent-to-Change	Transactions that contain SELECT statements that have the FOR UPDATE clause specified, or SQL statements that are ambiguous but are presumed to be intended for change because of the way they are interpreted by the SQL precompiler	Intent Exclusive (IX), Share (S), Update (U), and Exclusive (X) locks
Change	Transactions that contain INSERT, UPDATE, or DELETE statements, but not UPDATE WHERE CURRENT OF or DELETE WHERE CURRENT OF statements	Intent Exclusive (IX) and/or Exclusive (X) locks
Cursor-Controlled	Transactions that contain UPDATE WHERE CURRENT OF or DELETE WHERE CURRENT OF statements	Intent Exclusive (IX) and/or Exclusive (X) locks

It is important to keep in mind that in some cases, a single transaction may consist of multiple transaction types. For example, a transaction that contains an SQL statement that performs an INSERT operation against a table using the results of a subquery consists of two different types of processing: Read-Only and Change. Here, locks needed for the resources referenced in the subquery are determined using the rules for Read-Only transactions, while the locks required for the target table of the INSERT operation are determined using the rules for Change transactions.

Lock Avoidance

Before DB2 Version 9.7, if the Cursor Stability isolation level was used and a row was locked on behalf of a transaction, DB2 would block attempts by other concurrently running transactions to modify the locked row. Furthermore, if the transaction holding the lock changed the locked row in any way, other SQL statements in concurrent transactions could not access the row (unless they were running under the Uncommitted Read isolation level) until the transaction that made the change was terminated. (In other words, writers would block readers, and in some situations readers could block writers.) In either case, concurrent transactions that needed to access a locked row were forced to wait for the lock to be released before they could continue processing. This, in turn, would often result in undesired behavior.

With DB2 Version 9.5 several lock avoidance techniques were introduced to help eliminate some of the locking overhead that is required for the Cursor Stability isolation level. Essentially, these techniques allow scan operations to execute without locking rows when the data and pages being accessed are known to have been committed. For example, consider the following query:

```
SELECT COUNT(*) FROM sales
```

Prior to DB2 Version 9.5, when such a query was executed, the first row in the table specified would be locked, a count would be taken, and the lock would be released. Then, the second row in the table would be locked, the count would be updated, and the lock would be released. And this process would continue until the query had counted all the rows in the table. With DB2 Version 9.5 and later, the same query will scan the table specified and count the rows, but intermittent locks are no longer acquired and released—provided DB2 can determine that the rows have been committed without having to acquire locks.

Essentially, lock avoidance allows DB2 to determine whether the data needed has been committed, and if that is indeed the case, locks are not acquired. With DB2 Versions 9.7 and later, lock avoidance works for any read-only SQL statement executed under the Cursor Stability isolation level that is using cursor blocking. (Cursor blocking is a technique that reduces overhead by having DB2 retrieve a block of rows, rather than a single row, in one operation.)

Currently Committed Semantics

With DB2 Version 9.7, a new implementation of the Cursor Stability isolation level was introduced that incorporates Currently Committed (CC) semantics to further prevent writers from blocking readers. The intent is to provide a Cursor Stability isolation level that avoids lock waits without violating ANSI standards for Cursor Stability isolation level semantics. (The following registry variables can be used to delay or avoid acquiring locks in certain circumstances:

- **DB2_SKIPINSERTED**: Allows Cursor Stability/Read Stability scans to skip uncommitted inserted rows

- **DB2_SKIPDELETED**: Allows Cursor Stability/Read Stability scans to skip uncommitted deleted rows and index keys
- **DB2_EVALUNCOMMITTED**: Allows Cursor Stability/Read Stability scans to apply and perform query predicate evaluation on uncommitted data; also permits such scans to skip uncommitted deleted rows—in effect, scans are treated as an Uncommitted Read operation until a qualifying row is found, at which time DB2 might acquire a lock to ensure that only committed data is processed or returned

However, the use of these registry variables violates the ANSI standard for Cursor Stability isolation level semantics.)

When the lock avoidance techniques that were introduced in DB2 9.5 are used, a read-only transaction operating under Currently Committed semantics will not acquire a lock as long as DB2 can determine that the data needed has been committed. (Transactions performing read and write operations avoid lock waits on uncommitted inserts, and transactions performing read-only operations end up trading a lock wait for a log read when they encounter uncommitted updates or deletes that have been performed by other concurrent transactions.)

If DB2 is unable to determine whether a row has been committed, it will try to acquire a lock on the row in question on behalf of the transaction—if a lock can be acquired, processing will continue using traditional Cursor Stability isolation level behavior. If, however, a lock cannot be acquired (because another transaction holds an Exclusive lock on the row), DB2 will examine the lock the other transaction is holding to obtain information about the row that contains the data needed. In this case, each lock can contain one of the following:

- **No information:** Indicates that the row is locked but nothing has been done to it (that is, no uncommitted changes are in-flight)
- **An Uncommitted Insert identifier:** Indicates that the row is a newly inserted row that has not yet been committed
- **Log information:** Indicates that the row contains uncommitted data; in this case, the log information identifies the log record that corresponds to the first time the row was modified by the transaction that currently holds the lock on the row

If the lock contains no information, the row is treated as if the desired lock were acquired. If the lock has an Uncommitted Insert identifier, the row is skipped because this identifier represents a row that has not yet been committed. And if the lock contains log information, this information is used to return the "currently committed" version of the row (that is, the row as it existed before changes were initiated) from a log record that is stored either in the log buffer or a transaction log file. (DB2 uses the Log Sequence Number, or LSN, to directly access the appropriate log record; all data row and index entries have a "flags" byte that contains a "Possibly UNCommitted"—or PUNC—bit. If the PUNC bit is not set, the data row/index entry is guaranteed to be committed. Otherwise, the commit status is unknown. Data pages contain a "pageLSN" that identifies the LSN of the log record that corresponds to the last modification made to the page. If the pageLSN is older than the database's "commitLSN" or a table's "readLSN", then the row/key is guaranteed to be committed. Otherwise, the commit status is unknown.)

Figure 7.6 illustrates how a SELECT statement running under the Cursor Stability isolation level with Currently Committed semantics enabled will retrieve records when another transaction is making changes to the records simultaneously. In this example, Transaction 1 executed three DML statements, which caused log information to be written to the log buffer and an uncommitted insert identifier to be written to the lock list for the SALES_REP table. When Transaction 2 queried the SALES_REP table, Currently Committed semantics allowed data for locked rows to be read from log records that contained information about previously committed transactions; the query did not return the record for the uncommitted insert.

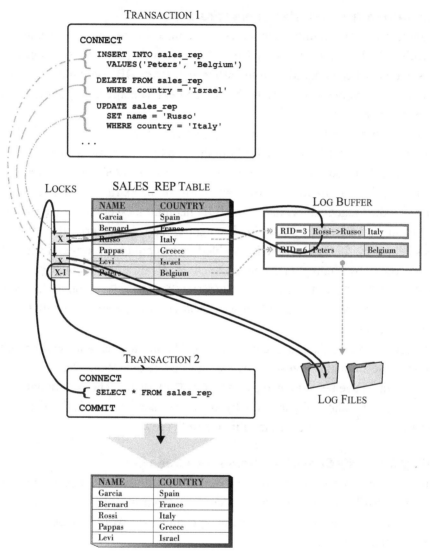

Figure 7.6: Example of how a query running under the Cursor Stability isolation level with Currently Committed semantics enabled will retrieve records

It is important to note that Currently Committed semantics can apply to SQL statements that are executed under both the Read Stability (RS) and the Cursor Stability (CS) isolation levels. However, under the Read Stability isolation level, Currently Committed semantics provides only DB2_SKIPINSERTED behavior, which is the capability to no longer incur lock waits for uncommitted inserted rows.

Enabling Currently Committed Semantics Behavior

By default, Currently Committed semantics are enabled for new databases that are created with DB2 9.7 and later. To use Currently Committed semantics for existing databases that have been upgraded from earlier releases of DB2, you must assign either the value ON or the value AVAILABLE to the *cur_commit* database configuration parameter of the converted database.

If the *cur_commit* database configuration parameter is set to ON, Currently Committed semantics are applied database-wide for both the Read Stability and Cursor Stability isolation levels. If this configuration parameter is set to AVAILABLE instead, DB2 will store the appropriate information in locks and perform the extra logging overhead needed (to ensure that the logged data contains the full uncommitted version of the row being changed) to support Currently Committed semantics. However, Currently Committed semantics behavior will then have to be enabled on an application-by-application basis. This is done either by binding an Embedded SQL application to the database using the CONCURRENTACCESSRESOLUTION USE CURRENTLY COMMITTED option, or by specifying the SQL_ATTR_CONCURRENT_ACCESS_RESOLUTION connection attribute with CLI/ODBC and Java applications.

It is important to note that the use of Currently Committed semantics will result in an increase in the amount of log space needed for update operations that are performed against tables that have been defined as DATA CAPTURE NONE. This additional space is used to log the first update of a data row by an active transaction; it is this data that is used to retrieve the currently committed image of the row.

Overriding Currently Committed Semantics Behavior

Just as it is possible to override the default isolation level used when select queries are executed, it is possible to override the behavior of Currently Committed semantics when certain queries are executed. This is done by appending the WAIT FOR OUTCOME clause to the SELECT statement used.

Thus, if the *cur_commit* database configuration parameter has been assigned the value ON or AVAILABLE, and you want to obtain information about all employees who work for the company and ensure that you will neither see uncommitted data nor retrieve versions of the data that existed before your query began, you could execute a SELECT statement that looks something like this:

```
SELECT * FROM employee WITH CS WAIT FOR OUTCOME
```

The WAIT FOR OUTCOME clause ensures that the query will wait for any concurrent transactions to commit or roll back their changes when data that is in the process of being updated or deleted is encountered. It is important to note that rows that are encountered that are in the process of being inserted are not skipped and that this clause can only be used when the Read Stability (RS) or Cursor Stability (CS) isolation level is in effect.

Locks and Performance

Because DB2 implicitly acquires locks as they are needed, aside from using the ALTER TABLE statement and the LOCK TABLE statement to force DB2 to acquire table-level locks, locking is pretty much out of your control. However, there are several factors that can influence how locking affects performance that you should be aware of. They are:

- Lock compatibility
- Lock conversion
- Lock escalation
- Lock waits and timeouts
- Deadlocks

Knowing what these items are and understanding how they affect performance can assist you in designing applications that work well in multiuser database environments.

Lock compatibility

If the state of a lock that one transaction places on a data resource is such that another transaction can place another lock on the same resource before the first lock is released, the locks are said to be *compatible*. And anytime a transaction holds a lock on a resource and another transaction attempts to acquire a lock on the same resource, DB2 will examine each lock's state to determine whether they are compatible. Table 7.4 contains a lock compatibility matrix that identifies which locks are compatible and which are not.

Table 7.4: Lock compatibility matrix										
	Lock Requested by Second Transaction									
Lock State	**IN**	**IS**	**NS**	**S**	**IX**	**SIX**	**U**	**X**	**Z**	**NW**
IN	Yes	Yes	Yes	Yes	Yes	Yes	Yes	Yes	No	Yes
IS	Yes	Yes	Yes	Yes	Yes	Yes	Yes	No	No	No
NS	Yes	Yes	Yes	Yes	No	No	Yes	No	No	Yes
S	Yes	Yes	Yes	Yes	No	No	Yes	No	No	No
IX	Yes	Yes	No	No	Yes	No	No	No	No	No
SIX	Yes	Yes	No	No	No	No	No	No	No	No
U	Yes	Yes	Yes	Yes	No	No	No	No	No	No
X	Yes	No	No	No	No	No	No	No	No	No
Z	No	No	No	No	No	No	No	No	No	No
NW	Yes	No	Yes	No	No	No	No	No	No	No

(Row label spanning left side: "Lock Held by First Transaction")

Yes	*Locks are compatible; therefore, the lock request is granted immediately.*
No	*Locks are not compatible; therefore, the requesting transaction must wait for the held lock to be released or for a lock timeout to occur before the lock request can be granted.*

Lock States:

IN	*Intent None*		*SIX*	*Share With Intent Exclusive*
IS	*Intent Share*		*U*	*Update*
NS	*Scan Share*		*X*	*Exclusive*
S	*Share*		*Z*	*Super Exclusive*
IX	*Intent Exclusive*		*NW*	*Next Key Weak Exclusive*

Adapted from Table 1 under **Lock type compatibility** in the IBM DB2 10.5 Knowledge Center (www-01.ibm. com/support/knowledgecenter/?lang=en#!/SSEPGG_10.5.0/com.ibm.db2.luw.admin.perf.doc/doc/r0005274. html).

Lock conversion

If a transaction that is holding a lock on a resource needs to acquire a more restrictive lock on that resource, rather than releasing the old lock and acquiring a new one, DB2 will attempt to change the state of the lock being held to the more restrictive state. The action of changing the state of an existing lock is known as *lock conversion*. Lock conversion occurs because a transaction is allowed to hold only one lock on any given resource at any one time. Figure 7.7 illustrates how lock conversion works.

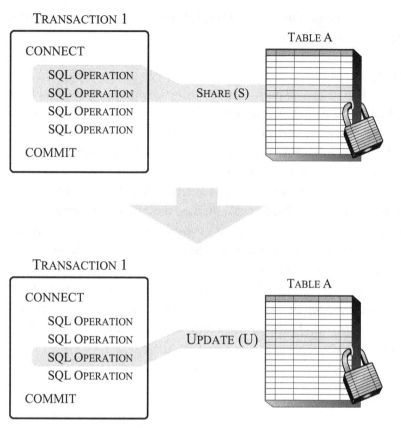

Figure 7.7: Lock conversion changing a lock being held—a Share (S) lock—to a more restrictive state—an Update (U) lock

Normally, lock conversion is performed on row-level locks, and the process is fairly straightforward. For example, if an Update (U) lock is held and an Exclusive (X) lock is needed, the Update (U) lock will be converted to an Exclusive (X) lock. However, that is not always the case when it comes to Share (S) and Intent Exclusive (IX) locks. Because neither lock is considered more restrictive than the other, if one of these locks is held and the other is requested, the lock that is held is converted to a Share With Intent Exclusive (SIX) lock.

With all other locks, the state of the current lock is changed to the lock state being requested—provided the requested lock state is more restrictive. (Lock conversion occurs only if the lock held can increase its restriction.) After a lock has been converted, it stays at the highest level attained until the transaction holding the lock is terminated, at which point the lock is released.

Lock escalation

When a connection to a database is first established, a specific amount of memory is set aside to hold a structure that DB2 uses to manage locks. This structure, known as the *lock list*, is where locks that are held by every active transaction are stored after they are acquired. (The *locklist* database configuration parameter is used to control the amount of memory that is set aside for the lock list.)

Because a limited amount of memory is available and because every active transaction must share this memory, DB2 imposes a limit on the amount of space each transaction can consume in the lock list. (This limit is controlled via the *maxlocks* database configuration parameter.) To prevent a database agent (that is working on behalf of a transaction) from exceeding its lock list space limits, a process known as *lock escalation* is performed whenever too many locks (regardless of their type) have been acquired on behalf of a single transaction. During lock escalation, space in the lock list is freed by replacing several row-level locks with a single table-level lock. Figure 7.8 shows how lock escalation works.

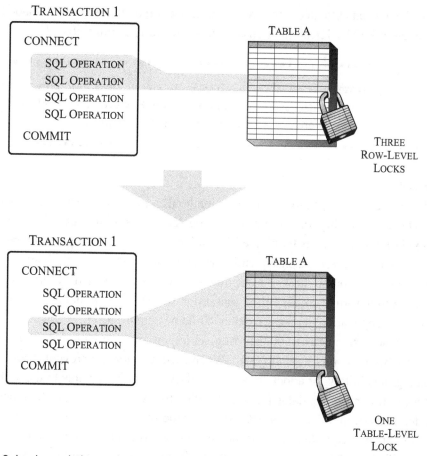

Figure 7.8: Lock escalation replaces several individual row-level locks with a single table-level lock.

So just how does lock escalation work? When a transaction requests a lock and a database's lock list is full or the number of locks held by the transaction is at the *maxlocks* percentage of the total lock list size, one of the tables associated with the transaction requesting the lock is selected, a table-level lock for that table is acquired on behalf of the transaction, and all row-level locks for that table are released to create space. The table-level lock is then added to the lock list, and if the lock list still lacks the storage space needed to acquire the requested lock, another table is selected and the process is repeated until enough free space is made available. Only then will the requested lock be acquired (at which point, the transaction will be allowed to continue). If, however, the lock list space needed is still unavailable (after all the transaction's row-level locks have been escalated), an error is generated, all database changes made by the transaction are rolled back, and the transaction is gracefully terminated.

Note: Use of the LOCK TABLE statement does not prevent normal lock escalation from occurring. However, it can reduce the frequency at which lock escalations take place.

Lock waits and timeouts

As you have already seen, anytime a transaction holds a lock on a particular resource, other concurrently running transactions can be denied access to that resource until the transaction holding the lock is terminated (in which case, all locks acquired on behalf of the transaction are released). Consequently, without some sort of lock timeout mechanism in place, one transaction might wait indefinitely for a lock that is held by another transaction. And unfortunately, if either transaction were to be terminated prematurely by another user or application, data consistency could be compromised.

To prevent such situations from occurring, an important feature known as *lock timeout detection* has been incorporated into DB2. When used, this feature prevents transactions from waiting indefinitely for a lock to be released. By assigning a value to the *locktimeout* parameter in the appropriate database configuration file, you can control when lock timeout detection occurs. This parameter specifies the amount of time that any transaction will wait to obtain a requested lock—if the desired lock is not acquired within the time interval specified, all database changes made by the transaction are rolled back, and the transaction is gracefully terminated.

Note: By default, the *locktimeout* configuration parameter is set to -1, which means that transactions will wait indefinitely to acquire the locks they need. However, in many cases, it is recommended that you change this value to something else.

Deadlocks

Often, the problem of one transaction waiting indefinitely for a lock can be avoided by using Currently Committed semantics and by defining a lock timeout period. However, that is not the case when lock contention results in a situation known as a *deadlock*. The best way to illustrate what a deadlock is and how it can occur is by looking at example.

Suppose Transaction 1 acquires an Exclusive (X) lock on Table A, and Transaction 2 acquires an Exclusive (X) lock on Table B. Now, suppose Transaction 1 attempts to acquire an Exclusive (X) lock on Table B, and Transaction 2 attempts to acquire an Exclusive (X) lock on Table A. You have already seen that processing by both transactions will be suspended until their second lock request is granted. However, neither lock request can be granted until one of the owning transactions releases the lock it currently holds (by performing a commit or rollback operation), and neither transaction can perform a commit or rollback operation because they both are waiting to acquire locks. As a result, a deadlock situation has occurred. Figure 7.9 illustrates this scenario.

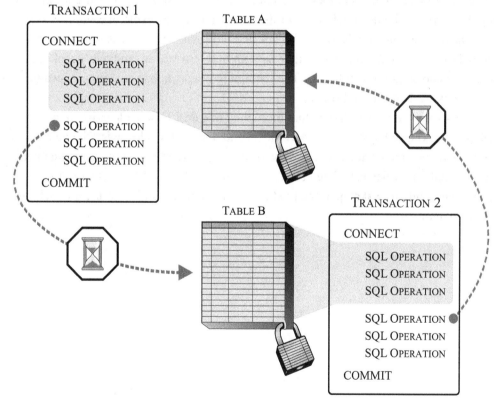

Figure 7.9: Example of a deadlock situation—Transaction 1 is waiting for Transaction 2 to release its lock on Table B, and Transaction 2 is waiting for Transaction 1 to release its lock on Table A; however, neither transaction can release its respective lock because each transaction is waiting to acquire the other lock it has requested.

A deadlock is more precisely referred to as a *deadlock cycle* because the transactions involved form a circle of wait states—each transaction in the circle waits for a lock held by another transaction in the circle to be released (see Figure 7.9). When a deadlock cycle occurs, all transactions involved will wait indefinitely for a lock unless some outside agent steps in to break the cycle. With DB2, this agent is a background process known as the *deadlock detector,* and its sole responsibility is to locate and resolve any deadlocks found in the locking subsystem.

Each database has its own deadlock detector, which is activated as part of the database initialization process. Once the deadlock detector is activated, it stays "asleep" most of the time but "wakes up" at preset intervals and examines the locking subsystem to determine whether a deadlock situation exists. Normally, the deadlock detector wakes up, finds that there are no deadlocks present in the locking subsystem, and goes back to sleep. However, if the deadlock detector discovers a deadlock cycle, it randomly selects one of the transactions involved to roll back and terminate. The transaction chosen (referred to as the *victim process*) is then sent an SQL error code, and every lock the transaction had acquired is released. The remaining transactions can then proceed because the deadlock cycle has been broken.

It is possible, but very unlikely, that more than one deadlock cycle exists in a database's locking subsystem. In the event several deadlock cycles exist, the detector locates each one and terminates one of the offending transactions in the same manner until all deadlock cycles have been broken. Eventually, the deadlock detector goes back to sleep, only to wake up at the next predefined interval and examine the locking subsystem again.

APPENDIX

DB2 10.5 Fundamentals for LUW Exam (Exam 615) Objectives

The *DB2 10.5 Fundamentals for LUW* exam (Exam 615) consists of 62 questions, and candidates have 90 minutes to complete the exam. A score of 61 percent or higher is required to pass.

The primary objectives the *DB2 10.5 Fundamentals for LUW* exam (Exam 615) is designed to cover are as follows:

Planning (16%)

- Knowledge of DB2 products (DB2 for LUW Editions and products—at a high level; when/why would you use each?)
- Knowledge of database workloads (OLTP vs. Data Warehouse; what is the appropriate product to use for each?)
- Knowledge of DB2 10.5 BLU Acceleration (i.e., the ability to configure a DB2 database for analytics; when BLU Acceleration should be used)
- Knowledge of Oracle compatibility features

Security (18%)

- Knowledge of restricting data access (authorities and privileges vs. views vs. RCAC vs. LBAC—at a high level; when is it appropriate to use each?)
- Knowledge of different authorities and privileges
- Given a DCL SQL statement, ability to identify results (GRANT, REVOKE, CONNECT statements)
- Knowledge of Roles and Trusted Contexts

Working with Databases and Database Objects (16%)

- Ability to create and connect to DB2 servers and databases
- Ability to identify DB2 objects
- Given a DDL SQL statement, knowledge to identify results (ability to create objects)
- Knowledge of different types of tables available (Base vs. MDC vs. ITC vs. RCT vs. MQT vs. Partitioned vs. Temporal—at a high level; when is it appropriate to use each type?)

Working with DB2 Data Using SQL and XQuery (23%)

- Ability to use SQL to SELECT data from tables
- Ability to use SQL to SORT or GROUP data
- Ability to use SQL to INSERT, UPDATE, or DELETE data
- Knowledge of transaction management (COMMIT, ROLLBACK, AUTOCOMMIT, and SAVEPOINTs)
- Ability to create and call an SQL stored procedure or a user-defined function (understanding of passing parameters and obtaining results)
- Knowledge of SQL compatibility enhancements
- Given an XQuery statement, knowledge to identify results

Working with DB2 Tables, Views, and Indexes (13%)

- Ability to demonstrate usage of DB2 data types (traditional data types, XML data types, Oracle compatibility data types)
- Ability to identify characteristics of a table, view or index

- Knowledge of temporary tables (how they are created and when they should be used)
- Knowledge of triggers (how they function; when they might be used)

Data Concurrency (15%)

- Ability to identify factors that influence locking
- Ability to list objects on which locks can be obtained (LOCK TABLE statement)
- Ability to identify characteristics of DB2 locks (common locks shared across platforms)
- Given a situation, ability to identify the isolation levels that should be used (knowledge of Currently Committed semantics)

B

Practice Questions

Welcome to the section that really makes this book unique. In my opinion, one of the best ways to prepare for the *DB2 10.5 Fundamentals for LUW* certification exam (Exam 615) is by answering practice questions that are similar to, and are presented in the same format as, the questions you will see when you take the actual exam. In this part of the book, you will find 125 practice questions, as well as comprehensive answers for each question. (It's not enough to know *which* answer is correct; it's also important to know *why* a particular answer is correct—and why the other choices are wrong!)

All the questions presented here were developed using copious notes that were taken during the exam development process. (As a member of the team that developed the *DB2 10.5 Fundamentals for LUW* certification exam, I had the opportunity to see every question that was created for this exam!) I trust you will find these practice questions helpful.

Roger E. Sanders

Planning

Question 1

Which two things can Data Studio be used for? (Choose two.)

☐ A. To perform instance and database administration tasks.

☐ B. To provide advice on how to change database configurations.

☐ C. To discover unwanted, unknown, and unacceptable access to data.

☐ D. To analyze and provide recommendations for tuning a single query.

☐ E. To identify, manage, and control database workloads to maximize server throughput.

Question 2

Which two DB2 editions provide both classic and adaptive compression functionality? (Choose two.)

☐ A. DB2 Express Server Edition

☐ B. DB2 Enterprise Server Edition

☐ C. DB2 Workgroup Server Edition

☐ D. DB2 Advanced Enterprise Server Edition

☐ E. DB2 Advanced Workgroup Server Edition

Question 3

Which two DB2 products provide native backup encryption functionality? (Choose two.)

☐ A. DB2 Express-C

☐ B. DB2 Express Server Edition

☐ C. IBM DB2 Encryption Offering

☐ D. DB2 Enterprise Server Edition

☐ E. IBM DB2 Performance Management Offering

Question 4

What is the Data Studio Web Console used for?

○ A. To monitor database health and availability.
○ B. To identify, manage, and control database workloads.
○ C. To offer advice on how to change database configurations.
○ D. To aid in data modeling, transformation, and DDL generation.

Question 5

Which product can NOT be used to provide workload management functionality to an existing DB2 Enterprise Server environment?

○ A. IBM Workload Manager
○ B. IBM DB2 Performance Management Offering
○ C. IBM InfoSphere Optim Configuration Manager
○ D. IBM DB2 BLU Acceleration In-Memory Offering

Question 6

Which enhancement was NOT added to DB2 pureScale in Version 10.5?

○ A. HADR support
○ B. Table space-level backup and restore
○ C. Random ordering for index key columns
○ D. In-place table REORGs for compressed tables

Question 7

When can it be beneficial to use row-organized tables?

○ A. When the majority of database workloads are analytical/OLAP in nature.
○ B. When the the majority of database workloads include queries that access more than 5% of the data and perform extensive scanning, grouping, and aggregation.
○ C. When the majority of workloads include a combination of analytic query processing and very selective data access, typically involving less than 2% of the data.
○ D. When the majority of database workloads are characterized by transactions that randomly access data, frequently perform insert or update activity, and execute queries that return small data sets.

Question 8

Which workload characteristics would most likely NOT be seen in a DB2 environment that uses the Database Partitioning Feature (DPF)?

○ A. Full-table scans and multiple table joins
○ B. Complex queries often involving aggregations
○ C. Analysis of historical data stored in multi-dimensional schemas
○ D. High throughput, measured in hundreds of transactions per minute

Question 9

Which statement about the DB2 pureScale feature is NOT TRUE?

○ A. The DB2 pureScale feature provides a database cluster solution for non-mainframe platforms.
○ B. The DB2 pureScale feature is best suited for Online Transaction Processing (OLTP) workloads.
○ C. The DB2 pureScale feature can only work with the General Parallel File System (GPFS).
○ D. The DB2 pureScale feature is only available as part of DB2 Advanced Enterprise Server Edition.

Question 10

If the following command executes successfully:

```
db2set DB2_WORKLOAD=ANALYTICS
```

Which statement is NOT TRUE?

- ○ A. The default page size for all newly created databases is 32 K.
- ○ B. The value ON is assigned to the AUTO_REORG database configuration parameter.
- ○ C. The value 4 is assigned to the DFT_EXTENT_SZ database configuration parameter.
- ○ D. The value AUTOMATIC is assigned to the INTRA_PARALLEL database manager configuration parameter.

Question 11

Which type of tables should be used when the majority of database workloads are transactional/OLTP in nature?

- ○ A. Row-organized tables
- ○ B. Column-organized tables
- ○ C. A combination of row-organized and column-organized tables
- ○ D. A combination of column-organized tables and synopsis tables

Question 12

Which two characteristics are part of BLU Acceleration? (Choose two.)

- ☐ A. "Always on" adaptive row compression
- ☐ B. Default and referential integrity informational constraints
- ☐ C. Scan-friendly memory caching that improves buffer pool utilization
- ☐ D. Automatic conversion of row-organized tables to column-organized tables
- ☐ E. Multiplied CPU power that uses Single Instruction Multiple Data (SIMD) instructions for many operations

Question 13

What should be used when the majority of database workloads are characterized by very selective data access (that is, queries that access less than 2% of the data)?

- ○ A. Row-organized tables
- ○ B. Column-organized tables
- ○ C. A combination of row-organized and column-organized tables
- ○ D. A combination of column-organized tables and synopsis tables

Question 14

If the DB2_WORKLOAD registry variable is assigned the value ANALYTICS, which configuration parameter is NOT assigned a value to establish an optimal configuration for analytic workloads?

- ○ A. DFT_DEGREE
- ○ B. PCKCACHESZ
- ○ C. UTIL_HEAP_SZ
- ○ D. SHEAPTHRES_SHR

Question 15

Which statement about the enhancements made to DB2's compatibility features in DB2 10.5 is NOT TRUE?

- ○ A. DB2's compatibility features can now be used with applications that were written for MongoDB.
- ○ B. TYPE declarations are now supported in functions, procedures, triggers, and anonymous blocks.
- ○ C. A pseudocolumn called ROWID that will return a unique identifier for every row found in a table is now available.
- ○ D. It is now possible to tell DB2 not to insert a key into an index object if all the columns in the key contain NULL values.

Question 16

Which two data types can NOT be used in PL/SQL statements when the database is a non-Unicode database? (Choose two.)

- ☐ A.   XML
- ☐ B.   NCLOB
- ☐ C.   DBCLOB
- ☐ D.   NUMBER
- ☐ E.   VARCHAR2

Question 17

Which statement about implicit casting is NOT TRUE?

- ○ A.   Implicit casting is used to perform comparisons or make assignments if two objects have mismatched data types.
- ○ B.   Implicit casting automatically converts data of one data type to another based on an implied set of conversion rules.
- ○ C.   Implicit casting is a way of assigning data values that do not have an associated DB2 built-in data type to a CHAR data type so they can be referenced in SQL statements.
- ○ D.   Implicit casting is an alternative way to parse character or graphic constants to support applications that expect these constants to be assigned the data types CHAR and GRAPHIC.

Security

Question 18

Which statement about the SERVER_ENCRYPT authentication type is TRUE?

- ○ A. When a remote database is cataloged in the system database directory, this is the default authentication type used.
- ○ B. With this type, authentication occurs at the server using the operating system's security facility; user IDs are encrypted at the client.
- ○ C. With this type, authentication is performed as a third-party service using conventional cryptography to create a shared secret key.
- ○ D. When a remote database is accessed from a client, this type is used to ensure user data is encrypted before it is sent from the server to the client.

Question 19

A company has the following requirements:

1. Employees can enter, review, and change information about their own sales.
2. District managers can see and change sales information, but only for employees that report to them.
3. Executives can only see sales information summaries for individual districts.

Which DB2 security mechanism can be used to meet the company's requirements?

- ○ A. Authentication
- ○ B. Security plug-in APIs
- ○ C. Authorities and privileges
- ○ D. Label-based access control

Question 20

Which two items does Label-Based Access Control (LBAC) rely on to control what data a user can access? (Choose two.)

☐ A. Security labels
☐ B. Column masks
☐ C. Security policies
☐ D. SQL search conditions
☐ E. SQL CASE expressions

Question 21

Which two items does Row and Column Access (RCAC) rely on to control what data a user is permitted to see? (Choose two.)

☐ A. Security labels
☐ B. Security policies
☐ C. Label components
☐ D. SQL search conditions
☐ E. SQL CASE expressions

Question 22

Which two authentication types can NOT be specified for a DB2 server? (Choose two.)

☐ A. SERVER
☐ B. LDAP_PLUGIN
☐ C. DATA_ENCRYPT
☐ D. KRB_CLIENT_ENCRYPT
☐ E. KRB_SERVER_ENCRYPT

Question 23

Which statement about authentication is TRUE?

○ A. Only one authentication type is allowed per database.
○ B. A user ID and password are required to authenticate a user.
○ C. User authentication is performed by a security facility that is part of DB2.
○ D. The authentication type for each instance determines what databases a user can access.

Question 24

Which two authorities are considered instance-level authorities? (Choose two.)

☐ A. SYSMON
☐ B. SECADM
☐ C. WLMADM
☐ D. SYSMAINT
☐ E. ACCESSCTRL

Question 25

Which operation is a user with SYSMAINT authority NOT allowed to perform?

○ A. Access user data.
○ B. Back up a database.
○ C. Connect to a database.
○ D. Force users off of a DB2 server.

Question 26

Which two authorities/privileges will NOT allow someone to insert data into a table with the IMPORT utility? (Choose two.)

☐   A.   LOAD
☐   B.   ALTER
☐   C.   INSERT
☐   D.   CONTROL
☐   E.   DATAACCESS

Question 27

Which authority/privilege must a user possess to create a view, as well as use the Export utility?

○   A.   LOAD
○   B.   ALTER
○   C.   SELECT
○   D.   UPDATE

Question 28

If the following SQL statement is executed:

```
GRANT UPDATE ON TABLE sales
   TO USER user1
   WITH GRANT OPTION
```

Which two things can user USER1 do? (Choose two.)

☐   A.   Remove records from the SALES table.
☐   B.   Modify records stored in the SALES table.
☐   C.   Give the ability to modify records stored in the SALES table to others.
☐   D.   Change information about the SALES table that is stored in the system catalog.
☐   E.   Give the ability to change information about the SALES table that is stored in the system catalog to others.

Question 29

A user named USER1 needs to revoke another user's ability to create tables in a database named MY_DB. Which two SQL statements will give user USER1 the authority needed to perform this task? (Choose two.)

☐ A. GRANT DBADM ON DATABASE TO user1
☐ B. GRANT SECADM ON DATABASE TO user1
☐ C. GRANT CONTROL ON DATABASE TO user1
☐ D. GRANT ACCESSCTRL ON DATABASE TO user1
☐ E. GRANT DATAACCESS ON DATABASE TO user1

Question 30

Which privilege must a user possess to run an embedded SQL application named GEN_PAYROLL that calls a package named CORP_PKG?

○ A. USE privilege on the CORP_PKG package
○ B. EXECUTE privilege on the CORP_PKG package
○ C. USE privilege on the GEN_PAYROLL stored procedure
○ D. EXECUTE privilege on the GEN_PAYROLL stored procedure

Question 31

Which authority/privilege must a user possess to assign a comment to a table?

○ A. ALTER
○ B. DBADM
○ C. UPDATE
○ D. SYSADM

Question 32

If the following SQL statement is executed:

```
REVOKE USE OF TABLESPACE mytbsp FROM user1
```

What will happen?

- ○ A. The ability to create tables in a table space named MYTBSP will be taken away from user USER1.
- ○ B. The ability to bind or rebind a package in a table space named MYTBSP will be taken away from user USER1.
- ○ C. The ability to retrieve data from a table or view stored in a table space named MYTBSP will be taken away from user USER1.
- ○ D. The ability to use XSR objects stored in a table space named MYTBSP will be taken away from user USER1.

Question 33

Which two attributes are NOT needed to define a trusted context? (Choose two.)

- ☐ A. A system authorization ID
- ☐ B. A data stream encryption value
- ☐ C. A system authorization password
- ☐ D. A Secure Sockets Layer (SSL) certificate
- ☐ E. The IP address or domain name of an incoming connection

Question 34

If the following statement is executed:

```
CREATE TRUSTED CONTEXT cntxt1
  BASED UPON CONNECTION USING SYSTEM AUTHID user1
  ATTRIBUTES (ADDRESS '192.168.1.100')
  WITH USE FOR user2 WITH AUTHENTICATION,
    user3 WITHOUT AUTHENTICATION
  ENABLE
```

Which of the following statements is NOT TRUE?

○ A. USER1 will inherit the privileges of USER2 and USER3.
○ B. USER1 will establish the trusted context connection used.
○ C. USER1 can switch to USER3 without providing a password.
○ D. USER1 can switch to USER2 if a correct password is provided.

Question 35

What item is used to group a collection of privileges together so they can be simultaneously granted to and revoked from multiple users, groups, or roles?

○ A. Role
○ B. Pool
○ C. Group
○ D. Schema

Question 36

Which two statements about trusted contexts are TRUE? (Choose two.)

☐ A. A trusted context can only be defined by someone with SYSADM or SECADM authority.

☐ B. A trusted context is a database object that defines a trust relationship for a connection between a database and an external entity such as an application server.

☐ C. After a trusted connection is established, if a switch request is made with an authorization ID that is not allowed on the connection, the connection is placed in the "Connection Pending" state.

☐ D. If WITH AUTHENTICATION is specified with a user ID at the time a trusted context is created, a password is required to switch from the current user (on a trusted connection) to the user ID specified.

☐ E. If a trusted context is assigned to a role, any authorization ID that uses the trusted context will acquire the authorities and privileges that have been assigned to the role; any authorities or privileges that have been granted to the authorization ID are ignored.

Question 37

Which statement about roles is NOT TRUE?

○ A. Only users with SECADM authority are allowed to create roles.

○ B. Any of the authorities and privileges available can be granted to a role.

○ C. Roles provide a way to control database access in a manner that mirrors the structure of an organization.

○ D. When one role is granted membership in another role, a role hierarchy is formed and cycles in the hierarchy are not allowed.

Working with Databases and Database Objects

Question 38

Which statement describes what pushdown analysis is?

- ○ A. The task of sending a query from a client to a server for processing.
- ○ B. The process of using SIMD instructions to perform the same operation on multiple data points simultaneously.
- ○ C. The process of breaking a query operation into several parts and running those parts, in parallel, across multiple CPU cores.
- ○ D. A task the DB2 optimizer performs to determine whether a particular federated operation can be conducted at a remote data source.

Question 39

A database administrator needs to catalog a remote server that hosts a database named PAYROLL. Assuming the following information is available:

Server address: 172:16:254:1
Port number: 52000
Instance name: db2inst1
Client node name: hrclient

Which command must be used to perform the desired task?

- ○ A. CATALOG TCPIP NODE db2inst1 REMOTE 172:16:254:1 PORT 52000
- ○ B. CATALOG TCPIP4 NODE hrclient REMOTE 172:16:254:1 SERVER 52000
- ○ C. CATALOG TCPIP4 NODE db2inst1 REMOTE 172:16:254:1 PORT 52000
- ○ D. CATALOG TCPIP6 NODE hrclient REMOTE 172:16:254:1 SERVER 52000

Question 40

Which two statements about Type 1 connections are TRUE? (Choose two.)

- ☐ A. Type 1 connections allow applications to be connected to only one database at a time.
- ☐ B. Type 1 connections allow applications to connect to and work with multiple DB2 databases simultaneously.
- ☐ C. With Type 1 connections, connecting to another application server will put the current connection into a dormant state.
- ☐ D. When Type 1 connections are used, the current unit of work must be committed or rolled back before a connection to another application server can be established.
- ☐ E. With Type 1 connections, connecting with a user ID and password will only be accepted when there is no current or dormant connection to the same named server.

Question 41

Which statement about Type 2 connections is TRUE?

- ○ A. Type 2 connections cannot be used with Embedded SQL applications.
- ○ B. Type 2 connections are used by default with DB2 for Linux, UNIX, and Windows.
- ○ C. Type 2 connections allow applications to be connected to only one database at a time.
- ○ D. Type 2 connections allow applications to connect to and work with multiple DB2 databases simultaneously.

Question 42

If the following SQL statement is executed:

```
CREATE DATABASE payroll RESTRICTIVE
```

Which two statements are TRUE? (Choose two.)

- ☐ A. The resulting database will have a page size of 4 KB.
- ☐ B. The resulting database will not be an automatic storage database.
- ☐ C. No database privileges will automatically be granted to the group PUBLIC.
- ☐ D. The resulting database will be assigned the comment "PAYROLL DATABASE."
- ☐ E. Users will not be able to create tables in the database that have names that start with the letters "SYS" or "DBM."

Question 43

What is a schema used for?

- ○ A. To provide an alternate name for a table or view.
- ○ B. To provide a logical grouping of database objects.
- ○ C. To generate a series of numbers, in ascending or descending order.
- ○ D. To provide an alternative way of describing data stored in one or more tables.

Question 44

In which two situations should an application-period temporal table be used? (Choose two.)

- ☐ A. When you want to keep track of historical versions of a table's rows.
- ☐ B. When you want to define specific time periods in which data is valid.
- ☐ C. When you want to cluster data according to the time in which rows are inserted.
- ☐ D. When you want to cluster data on more than one key or dimension, simultaneously.
- ☐ E. When you need to provide appropriate values for data, based on some application defined business time value.

Question 45

Which statement about indexes is NOT TRUE?

○ A. Before an index can be created, a table space and a table must exist.
○ B. Indexes provide a fast, efficient method for locating specific rows in a table.
○ C. When an index is created, metadata for the index is stored in the system catalog.
○ D. Indexes automatically provide both a logical and a physical ordering of the rows in a table.

Question 46

Which two database objects can NOT be explicitly created? (Choose two.)

☐ A. View
☐ B. Trigger
☐ C. Sequence
☐ D. Index node
☐ E. Package cache

Question 47

Which two statements about Materialized Query Tables (MQTs) are TRUE? (Choose two.)

☐ A. MQTs are used to improve the execution performance of qualified SELECT statements.
☐ B. MQTs are used to physically cluster data on more than one dimension, simultaneously.
☐ C. MQTs are normally populated with non-persistent data that is only available to a single application.
☐ D. MQTs cluster data using a virtual column that physically stores rows that are inserted at a similar time, together.
☐ E. MQTs are normally populated with data that consists of precomputed results that were obtained from one or more base tables.

Question 48

Which two objects are always enabled for compression, by default, when they are created? (Choose two.)

☐ A. Views
☐ B. Indexes
☐ C. Temporary tables
☐ D. Row-organized tables
☐ E. Column-organized tables

Question 49

If the following SQL statement is executed:

```
CREATE DISTINCT TYPE pound_sterling
  AS DECIMAL (10,2) WITH STRONG TYPE RULES
```

Which event will NOT happen?

○ A. A user-defined data type that can be used to store numerical data as British currency values will be created.
○ B. Six comparison functions will be created so that POUND_STERLING values can be compared to each other.
○ C. Two casting functions will be created so that POUND_STERLING values can be converted to DECIMAL values, and vice versa.
○ D. A compatibility function will be created so all of DB2's built-in functions that accept DECIMAL values as input can be used with POUND_STERLING data.

Question 50

Which two statements about shadow tables are TRUE? (Choose two.)

☐ A. Shadow tables are row-organized copies of column-organized tables that can include all columns or a subset of columns.

☐ B. Shadow tables are maintained by continuous replication, using a component of the InfoSphere Data Replication product.

☐ C. Shadow tables can be used to improve the performance of large analytical queries that are executed against an OLTP database.

☐ D. Shadow tables use a special algorithm to associate record key values that are similar to index key values with specific row locations.

☐ E. Shadow tables are automatically maintained, system-generated, tables that store metadata for associated user-defined, column-organized tables.

Question 51

Which statement about system-period temporal tables is NOT TRUE?

○ A. Every system-period temporal table must be associated with a history table.

○ B. A system-period temporal table keeps copies of deleted rows and original versions of updated rows.

○ C. System-period temporal tables provide users with the ability to retrieve data values that existed at any given point in time.

○ D. A primary key that prevents the overlapping of SYSTEM_TIME periods must be defined for every system-period temporal table created.

Question 52

Which statement about Multidimensional Clustering (MDC) tables is NOT TRUE?

- ○ A. MDC tables do not require frequent reorganization to maintain their clustering sequence.
- ○ B. The clustering index for an MDC table is larger than the clustering index for a base table.
- ○ C. MDC tables are primarily intended to be used with large tables in data warehouse and decision support environments.
- ○ D. When rows are deleted from an MDC table, free extents are created that can be reclaimed by executing the REORG command.

Question 53

Which statement about Materialized Query Tables (MQTs) is NOT TRUE?

- ○ A. MQTs have similar characteristics to MDC tables.
- ○ B. An MQT needs to have its data refreshed on a regular basis.
- ○ C. MQTs offer a powerful way to improve response time for complex queries.
- ○ D. MQTs are typically populated with precomputed results that have been obtained from one or more base tables.

Question 54

Which type of table utilizes block indexes?

- ○ A. Temporal tables
- ○ B. Range-clustered tables
- ○ C. Materialized query tables
- ○ D. Multidimensional clustering tables

Question 55

Which statement about range-partitioned tables is NOT TRUE?

○ A. Range-partitioned tables have no need for free space control records.
○ B. Range-partitioned tables improve performance by eliminating large amounts of I/O.
○ C. Range-partitioned tables allow maintenance operations to be performed at the partition level when each partition resides in a separate table space.
○ D. Range-partitioned tables use a data organization scheme in which data is divided across multiple storage objects, according to values found in one or more partitioning keys.

Question 56

Which statement about synopsis tables is TRUE?

○ A. Queries are automatically routed to synopsis tables according to results of a latency-based algorithm.
○ B. The only operations that can be performed against a synopsis table are SELECT and DELETE operations.
○ C. A synopsis table is used to store the minimum and maximum values for each column of a row-organized table.
○ D. The relationship between a user table and its synopsis table is recorded in the SYSCAT.TABDEP catalog view.

Question 57

Which two types of temporal tables can be used to store time-sensitive data?
(Choose two.)

☐ A. Bitemporal
☐ B. Time-period
☐ C. System-period
☐ D. Business-period
☐ E. Application-period

Working with DB2 Data Using SQL and XQuery

Question 58

A user wants to retrieve records from a table named SALES that meet the following criteria:

- The sales date (SALESDATE) is after June 1, 2016.
- The sales amount (AMT) is greater than $50,000.00.

Which SQL statement will produce the desired results?

○ A. SELECT * FROM sales
      WHERE (salesdate > '2016-06-01'
      AND amt > 50000)

○ B. SELECT * FROM sales
      WHERE (salesdate > '2016-06-01'
      AND amt > 50,000.00)

○ C. SELECT * FROM sales
      WHERE (salesdate > '2016-06-01'
      AND amt GREATER THAN 50000)

○ D. SELECT * FROM sales
      WHERE (salesdate > '2016-06-01'
      AND amt GREATER THAN 50,000.00)

Question 59

A database contains one table that holds employee records (named EMPLOYEES) and another table that contains department information (named DEPARTMENT). A user wants to produce a list of every employee who works for the company and the name of the department they work in; if the employee does not work for a particular department, their name should not appear in the list. In addition, any department that does not have employees assigned to it should appear in the list.

Which SQL statement will produce the desired list?

- A. SELECT employees.name, departments.deptname
    FROM employees
    INNER JOIN department ON
    employees.dept = departments.deptno
- B. SELECT employees.name, departments.deptname
    FROM employees
    INNER JOIN department ON
    departments.deptno = employees.dept
- C. SELECT employees.name, departments.deptname
    FROM employees
    LEFT OUTER JOIN departments ON
    employees.dept = departments.deptno
- D. SELECT employees.name, departments.deptname
    FROM employees
    RIGHT OUTER JOIN departments ON
    employees.dept = departments.deptno

Question 60

Which type of join will produce a result set that contains every row in one table that has a matching row in another table, plus every row in the second table that does not have a matching row in the first table?

- A. INNER JOIN
- B. LEFT OUTER JOIN
- C. RIGHT OUTER JOIN
- D. FULL OUTER JOIN

Question 61

Which operator is used to combine the result sets produced by two individual queries, and retain any duplicate records found?

○ A. UNION
○ B. EXCEPT
○ C. UNION ALL
○ D. EXCEPT ALL

Question 62

Which SQL statement will retrieve the minimum and maximum rainfall amounts (RAINFALL), for each month (MONTH), sorted by month, from a table named WEATHER?

○ A. SELECT month, MIN(rainfall), MAX(rainfall)
      FROM weather
      ORDER BY month
○ B. SELECT month, MIN(rainfall), MAX(rainfall)
      FROM weather
      GROUP BY rainfall
○ C. SELECT month, MIN(rainfall), MAX(rainfall)
      FROM weather
      SORT BY month
      ORDER BY month
○ D. SELECT month, MIN(rainfall), MAX(rainfall)
      FROM weather
      GROUP BY month
      ORDER BY month

Question 63

Which two data types can be used in an ORDER BY clause of a SELECT statement? (Choose two.)

- ☐ A. XML
- ☐ B. BLOB
- ☐ C. BIGINT
- ☐ D. DBCLOB
- ☐ E. TIMESTAMP

Question 64

A table named SALES has two columns: SALES_AMT and REGION_CD.

Which SELECT statement will retrieve the number of sales made in each region, ordered by the number of sales made?

- ○ A. SELECT sales_amt, COUNT(*)
       FROM sales
       ORDER BY 2
- ○ B. SELECT sales_amt, COUNT(*)
       FROM sales
       GROUP BY sales_amt
       ORDER BY 1
- ○ C. SELECT region_cd, COUNT(*)
       FROM sales
       GROUP BY region_cd
       ORDER BY COUNT(*)
- ○ D. SELECT region_cd, COUNT(*)
       FROM sales
       GROUP BY sales_amt
       ORDER BY COUNT(*)

Question 65

If the following SQL statement is executed:

```
SELECT state, city, SUM(cost) AS total_costs
  FROM expenses
  GROUP BY 1, 2
  ORDER BY total_sales
```

What will be the results?

- ○ A. Total costs, by state and city, will be retrieved from a table named EXPENSES and the results will be arranged in ascending order, by total costs.
- ○ B. Total costs, by state and city, will be retrieved from a table named EXPENSES and the results will be arranged in descending order, by total costs.
- ○ C. Total costs, state, and city, will be retrieved from a table named EXPENSES and the results will be arranged in ascending order, by state and city.
- ○ D. Total costs, state, and city, will be retrieved from a table named EXPENSES and the results will be arranged in descending order, by state, city, and total costs.

Question 66

Which statement about the ORDER BY clause is NOT TRUE?

- ○ A. If no sort order is specified with an ORDER BY clause, data is sorted in ascending order, by default.
- ○ B. An integer value representing a column's position, as it appears in the result data set produced, can be used with an ORDER BY clause.
- ○ C. The ORDER BY clause is frequently used to sort columns whose values are to be provided as input to aggregate functions like AVG() and SUM().
- ○ D. If a query with multiple sort specifications is executed, rows are ordered according to the first sort specification provided, then according to the second sort specification provided, and so on.

Question 67

Which two objects can NOT be the target of an INSERT statement? (Choose two.)

❒ A. A system catalog table
❒ B. A created global temporary table
❒ C. A declared global temporary table
❒ D. A user-maintained materialized query table
❒ E. A system-maintained materialized query table

Question 68

Which statement about identity columns is NOT TRUE?

○ A. If the CACHE 20 option is specified as part of an identity column's definition, 20 identity sequences will be generated at one time and kept in memory.
○ B. If an identity column is created with the GENERATED ALWAYS AS IDENTITY clause, an error will occur if a user attempts to insert a value into the column.
○ C. If an identity column is created with the GENERATED BY DEFAULT AS IDENTITY clause, an error will occur if a user attempts to insert a value into the column.
○ D. If the CYCLE option is specified as part of an identity column's definition, values will continue to be generated for the column after any minimum or maximum value specified has been reached.

Question 69

A table named TABLE_A contains 200 rows and a user wants to delete the last 10 rows from this table.

Which SQL statement will produce the desired results?

- ○ A. DELETE FROM
          (SELECT * FROM table_a
            ORDER BY col1 ASC
            FETCH FIRST 10 ROWS ONLY) AS result
- ○ B. DELETE FROM
          (SELECT * FROM table_a
            ORDER BY col1 DESC
            FETCH FIRST 10 ROWS ONLY) AS result
- ○ C. DELETE FROM
          (SELECT * FROM table_a
            ORDER BY col1 ASC
            FETCH LAST 10 ROWS ONLY) AS result
- ○ D. DELETE FROM
          (SELECT * FROM table_a
            ORDER BY col1 DESC
            FETCH LAST 10 ROWS ONLY) AS result

Question 70

When should the TRUNCATE statement be used?

- ○ A. When you want to delete all rows from a table without generating log records or firing triggers.
- ○ B. When you want to delete select rows from a table without generating log records or firing triggers.
- ○ C. When you want to delete all rows from a table and fire any delete triggers that have been defined for the table.
- ○ D. When you want to delete select rows from a table and fire any delete triggers that have been defined for the table.

Question 71

Which statement about delete operations is TRUE?

○ A. Positioned delete operations can work with multiple rows at one time.

○ B. If a WHERE clause is not specified with a DELETE statement, every record found in the table or view referenced will be deleted.

○ C. To perform a searched delete operation, a cursor must first be created, opened, and then positioned on the row that is to be deleted.

○ D. In some cases, the DELETE statement can be used to delete individual values from a table or view by replacing those values with NULL.

Question 72

Which two statements about transactions are TRUE? (Choose two.)

☐ A. The more SQL operations a single transaction performs, the easier it is to manage.

☐ B. Unless otherwise specified, INSERT, UPDATE, DELETE, and SELECT statements are not under transaction control.

☐ C. A transaction is a recoverable sequence of operations whose point of consistency can be obtained by querying the system catalog tables.

☐ D. A transaction is initiated the first time an SQL statement is executed after a database connection has been established or a running transaction has been terminated.

☐ E. If the DB2 Command Line Processor (CLP) is used to perform operations against a database and AUTOCOMMIT is turned ON, every SQL statement executed is implicitly committed.

Question 73

Which two statements about savepoints are NOT TRUE? (Choose two.)

☐ A. The CREATE SAVEPOINT statement is used to create a new savepoint.
☐ B. There is no limit on the number of savepoints that can be created within a single unit of work.
☐ C. The RELEASE SAVEPOINT statement is used to remove a savepoint that is no longer needed.
☐ D. The COMMIT FROM SAVEPOINT statement is used to commit a subset of database changes that have been made within a unit of work.
☐ E. The ROLLBACK TO SAVEPOINT statement is used to back out a subset of database changes that have been made within a unit of work.

Question 74

Which two SQL statements are NOT under transaction control, and therefore are not affected by the execution of a COMMIT or ROLLBACK statement? (Choose two.)

☐ A. ALTER
☐ B. COMMENT
☐ C. LOCK TABLE
☐ D. SET PASSTHRU
☐ E. SET CONNECTION

Question 75

An SQL function designed to convert Miles to Kilometers was created as follows:

```
CREATE FUNCTION mi_to_km (IN miles FLOAT)
   RETURNS FLOAT
   LANGUAGE SQL
   SPECIFIC convert_mtok
   READS SQL DATA
   RETURN FLOAT (miles * 1.60934)
```

How can this function be used to convert miles (MILES) values stored in a table named DISTANCES?

○ A. CALL mi_to_km (distances.miles)
○ B. CALL convert_mtok (distances.miles)
○ C. SELECT mi_to_km (miles) FROM distances
○ D. SELECT convert_mtok (miles) FROM distances

Question 76

If the following statement is executed:

```
CREATE PROCEDURE code.proc1(IN  p_arg1 INTEGER,
                           OUT p_arg2 INTEGER)
   BEGIN
     SET p_arg2 = p_arg1 * 2;
   END
```

Which statement(s) can NOT be used to execute the procedure named CODE. PROC1?

○ A. CALL code.proc1(?, ?)
○ B. CALL code.proc1(1, ?)
○ C. double result = 0; CALL code.proc1(1, :result);
○ D. DECLARE v_result INTEGER; CALL code.proc1(1, :v_result);

Question 77

Which two parameter modes can be used when creating a stored procedure? (Choose two.)

- ☐ A. IN
- ☐ B. TO
- ☐ C. OUT
- ☐ D. FROM
- ☐ E. TOFROM

Question 78

If the following SQL statement was used to create a user-defined function named STR_LEN:

```
CREATE FUNCTION str_len(IN string CHARACTER (10))
   RETURNS INTEGER
   RETURN LENGTH(string)
```

Which of the following statements will create a function whose signature does NOT match that of the STR_LEN function?

- ○ A. CREATE FUNCTION str_len(c1 CHAR(100))
- ○ B. CREATE FUNCTION str_len(c1 CHAR (10), i1 INT)
- ○ C. CREATE FUNCTION str_len(c1 CHAR(10) FOR BIT DATA)
- ○ D. CREATE FUNCTION str_len(c1 CHAR(100) FOR BIT DATA)

Question 79

Which statement about extended row size support is NOT TRUE?

- ○ A. Extended row size support enables users to create tables that have more columns than the maximum number of columns normally allowed.
- ○ B. Extended row size support simplifies the migration of tables (to DB2) that were created with another database vendor's product that have row sizes exceeding 32 KB.
- ○ C. Extended row size support enables tables that contain rows that exceed the maximum record length allowed by a particular table space to be constructed in that table space.
- ○ D. Extended row size support can help improve the performance of applications where the majority of data rows can fit on a smaller page but the table definition itself requires a larger page size.

Question 80

Which two things must happen before a row–organized table can take advantage of extended row size support? (Choose two.)

- ❏ A. The DB2_ROW_SIZE registry variable must be set to EXTENDED.
- ❏ B. A table must contain at least one column with a CHAR or GRAPHIC data type.
- ❏ C. The DB2_COMPATIBILITY_VECTOR registry variable must be set to ORA.
- ❏ D. The EXTENDED_ROW_SZ database configuration parameter must be set to ENABLE.
- ❏ E. A table must contain at least one column with a VARCHAR or VARGRAPHIC data type.

Question 81

Which SQL statement will create an index named UID_IDX for a table named
CUSTOMER that will NOT store entries in the index for records that have a NULL
value in the USER_ID column?

○ A. CREATE INDEX uid_idx ON customer (user_id)
        OMIT NULL KEYS
○ B. CREATE INDEX uid_idx ON customer (user_id)
        IGNORE NULL KEYS
○ C. CREATE INDEX uid_idx ON customer (user_id)
        PROHIBIT NULL KEYS
○ D. CREATE INDEX uid_idx ON customer (user_id)
        EXCLUDE NULL KEYS

Question 82

With DB2 10.5, columns that hold character data have a string unit attribute that
controls how the length of a data value for that column is determined. Which of these
string unit attributes can only be used with graphic string data types in a Unicode
database?

○ A. OCTETS
○ B. CODEUNITS8
○ C. CODEUNITS16
○ D. CODEUNITS32

Question 83

Given the following statements:

```
INSERT INTO customer VALUES (100,
'<customerinfo>
  <name>ACME Manufacturing</name>
  <addr country="United States">
      <street>25 Elm Street</street>
      <city>Raleigh</city>
      <state>North Carolina</state>
      <zip>27603</zip>
  </addr>
</customerinfo>');
```

If the following XQuery statement is executed:

```
XQUERY
for $info in db2-fn:xmlcolumn('CUSTOMER.CUSTINFO')/customerinfo
return $info/name
```

What will be the result?

○ A. ACME Manufacturing

○ B. <name>ACME Manufacturing</name>

○ C. <customerinfo>ACME Manufacturing</customerinfo>

○ D. <customerinfo><name>ACME
      Manufacturing</name></customerinfo>

Working with DB2 Tables, Views, and Indexes

Question 84

Which two data types can only be used in databases that are created after the DB2_
COMPATIBILITY_VECTOR registry variable has been set to ORA? (Choose two.)

❏ A. NUMBER

❏ B. VARCHAR

❏ C. VARCHAR2

❏ D. NVARCHAR

❏ E. CHARACTER VARYING

Question 85

Which statement about the TIMESTAMP data type is NOT TRUE?

- ○ A. TIMESTAMP values are stored as fixed-length character string values that are 32 characters in length.
- ○ B. By default, 6 digits (microseconds) are used to represent the fractional seconds portion of a TIMESTAMP value.
- ○ C. The TIMESTAMP data type is used to store six- or seven-part values that represent a specific calendar date and time.
- ○ D. The actual string format used to present a date or time value stored in a TIMESTAMP column is dependent upon the territory code that has been assigned to the database.

Question 86

When should the INTEGER data type be used?

- ○ A. When you need to store a 32-bit approximation of a real number.
- ○ B. When you need to store approximately 100,000 positive, whole numbers.
- ○ C. When you need to store data in a column that represents ID numbers that have a precision of five or fewer digits.
- ○ D. When you need to store data in a column that represents money and that accurately returns a two-position scale.

Question 87

Which statement about inline large object (LOB) data is NOT TRUE?

- ○ A. Inline LOB data is eligible for compression.
- ○ B. Inline LOBs improve the performance of queries that access LOB data.
- ○ C. When a table contains one or more inline LOB columns, more rows will fit on a page.
- ○ D. If inline LOBS are not used, LOB data values are stored in a location separate from the table row that references them.

Question 88

A database administrator wants to store commonly used state names (for example, 'Massachusetts', 'North Carolina', 'Rhode Island') in the minimum amount of space possible. What is the best data type to use?

- ○ A. CHAR(14)
- ○ B. CLOB(14)
- ○ C. NCHAR(254)
- ○ D. VARCHAR(254)

Question 89

Which data type should be used to store character string data in such a way that any comparisons of values that are made will be done so in binary format, irrespective of the database collating sequence used, and code page conversions will not take place when data is exchanged with other systems?

- ○ A. BLOB
- ○ B. VARCHAR
- ○ C. CLOB FOR BIT DATA
- ○ D. VARCHAR(200) FOR BIT DATA

Question 90

Which built-in data type can only be used in databases that have been configured for Oracle compatibility?

- ○ A. XML
- ○ B. DECIMAL
- ○ C. DECFLOAT
- ○ D. NVARCHAR2

Question 91

> Which type of constraint can be used to provide a method of ensuring a column's values are within a specific range?
>
> ○ A. Check
> ○ B. Unique
> ○ C. Referential
> ○ D. Informational

Question 92

> Which two statements about referential integrity constraints are TRUE? (Choose two.)
>
> ☐ A. A foreign key can reference multiple primary keys.
> ☐ B. A primary key can be referenced by only one foreign key.
> ☐ C. Primary keys and foreign keys are used to define relationships between two tables.
> ☐ D. A foreign key can be defined on an individual column or on a set of columns in a table.
> ☐ E. Foreign keys are enforced only during the execution of INSERT, UPDATE, DELETE, and SELECT statements.

Question 93

> Which two statements are TRUE regarding constraints? (Choose two.)
>
> ☐ A. A table can only have one unique key constraint.
> ☐ B. A table can have multiple primary key constraints.
> ☐ C. Unique constraints ensure that a column in a table will never contain duplicate values.
> ☐ D. Informational constraints tell DB2 what rules the data conforms to, but the rules are not enforced.
> ☐ E. Foreign key constraints are enforced on the values within the rows of a table, or between the rows of two tables, by a unique index on the foreign key.

Question 94

What type of constraint can be used to ensure that the value of one column in a table is never less than the value of another column in the same table?

   ○ A. A check constraint
   ○ B. A unique constraint
   ○ C. An informational constraint
   ○ D. A referential integrity constraint

Question 95

Which is NOT a reason to create an index?

   ○ A. To ensure data uniqueness
   ○ B. To improve query performance
   ○ C. To combine data from multiple tables
   ○ D. To provide a logical ordering of the rows in a table

Question 96

Which statement about indexes is NOT TRUE?

   ○ A. A row-organized table can have only one clustering index.
   ○ B. A column-organized table can have only one unique index.
   ○ C. If the INCLUDE clause is specified with the CREATE INDEX statement used, the UNIQUE clause must be provided.
   ○ D. The PCTFREE clause of the CREATE INDEX statement is used to control how much space is reserved for future insert and update operations.

Question 97

The following SQL statement was used to create a table named PARTS:

```
CREATE TABLE parts (
    part_no       VARCHAR(10),
    description   VARCHAR(80))
```

If values stored in the DESCRIPTION column are less than 36 characters in length, which SQL statement will successfully decrease the size of the DESCRIPTION column?

- ○ A. ALTER TABLE parts RESIZE COLUMN description 40
- ○ B. ALTER TABLE parts ADJUST COLUMN description
        VARCHAR(40)
- ○ C. ALTER TABLE parts ALTER COLUMN description
        SET DATA TYPE VARCHAR(40)
- ○ D. ALTER TABLE parts ALTER COLUMN description
        ALTER DATA TYPE VARCHAR(40)

Question 98

Which two operations can be performed by executing the ALTER INDEX statement? (Choose two.)

- ☐ A. Enable index compression
- ☐ B. Disable index compression
- ☐ C. Convert an index to a clustering index
- ☐ D. Add the ability to support reverse scans
- ☐ E. Remove the ability to support reverse scans

Question 99

Which two column attributes can NOT be defined using the CREATE TABLE
statement? (Choose two.)

☐ A. Column name
☐ B. Column alias
☐ C. Column schema
☐ D. Column data type
☐ E. Column check constraint

Question 100

A user wants to ensure that any rows that are inserted or updated with a view named
VIEW1 will conform to the view's definition. Which clause of the CREATE VIEW
statement can be used to accomplish this goal?

○ A. RESTRICT
○ B. CASCADE
○ C. WITH CHECK OPTION
○ D. WITH CONTROL OPTION

Question 101

Which statement about created global temporary tables is NOT TRUE?

○ A. Descriptions of created temporary tables are saved in the system catalog.
○ B. A user temporary table space must exist before created temporary tables can
be created.
○ C. The table description is not persistent beyond the life of the connection that
was used to create the table.
○ D. Each session that queries the table will only be able to retrieve the rows that
were inserted by that same session.

Question 102

When temporary tables that were created with the DECLARE GLOBAL TEMPORARY TABLE statement are used by applications that work with data in a database, which two statements are TRUE? (Choose two.)

☐ A. Indexes and SQL statements that modify data are not supported.
☐ B. Information about the temporary tables is saved in the system catalog.
☐ C. A user temporary table space had to exist before the tables could be created.
☐ D. Each connection that references a particular temporary table has its own unique instance of that table.
☐ E. In order to reference a particular temporary table in a SELECT statement, the table must be qualified with the schema name "SESSION".

Question 103

Which two statements about triggers are TRUE? (Choose two.)

☐ A. The triggered action (body) of a trigger cannot contain SQL Procedural Language (SQL PL) statements.
☐ B. Creating a trigger for a table that already has rows in it will cause the triggered action to be performed.
☐ C. Triggers are activated when an INSERT, UPDATE, or DELETE operation is performed on the subject table or view.
☐ D. When more than one trigger exists for a particular table, event, and activation time, they will be fired in the order in which they were created.
☐ E. When more than one trigger exists for a particular table, event, and activation time, triggers for INSERT operations will be fired first, followed by triggers for UPDATE operations, and then triggers for DELETE operations.

Question 104

Which two statements about BEFORE triggers are TRUE? (Choose two.)

- ☐ A. A BEFORE trigger can be used to automatically generate values for newly inserted rows.
- ☐ B. A BEFORE trigger can be used to insert, update, or delete data in the same or in different tables.
- ☐ C. A BEFORE trigger is fired for each row in the set of affected rows before the trigger event executes.
- ☐ D. A BEFORE trigger can be used to check data against other data values in the same or in different tables.
- ☐ E. A BEFORE trigger is fired for each row in the set of affected rows instead of executing the trigger event.

Question 105

Which two SQL statements can NOT be called in a BEFORE trigger? (Choose two.)

- ☐ A. SET
- ☐ B. CALL
- ☐ C. MERGE
- ☐ D. SELECT
- ☐ E. DELETE

Question 106

Which type of trigger is used to perform insert, update, and delete operations against complex views?

- ○ A. AFTER
- ○ B. BEFORE
- ○ C. BETWEEN
- ○ D. INSTEAD OF

Question 107

Which two events will cause a trigger to be fired (activated)? (Choose two.)

☐ A. Execution of an IMPORT command
☐ B. Execution of an UPDATE statement
☐ C. Execution of a TRUNCATE statement
☐ D. Execution of a LOAD ... REPLACE command
☐ E. Execution of an INSERT operation of a MERGE statement

Data Concurrency

Question 108

Which statement about lock conversion is TRUE?

○ A. Lock conversion is an event that occurs when several row-level locks are replaced with a single table-level lock.
○ B. Lock conversion is an event that occurs when a transaction waiting for a lock waits long enough to surpass the LOCKTIMEOUT period.
○ C. Lock conversion is an event that occurs when two applications lock data that is needed by the other, causing a situation in which neither application can continue executing.
○ D. Lock conversion is an event that occurs when a process accesses a data object upon which it already holds a lock, and the access mode desired requires a more restrictive lock.

Question 109

Which event will take place if the lock list runs out of space or the number of locks held by any one application reaches the MAXLOCKS percentage of the total lock list size?

○ A. Lock timeout
○ B. Lock exchange
○ C. Lock escalation
○ D. Lock conversion

Question 110

Which two statements about locking are TRUE? (Choose two.)

☐ A. Locks are used to enforce isolation levels.
☐ B. Declared temporary tables can be explicitly locked.
☐ C. Multiple locks can be acquired for a single resource.
☐ D. The type of lock used limits or prevents data access by concurrent application processes.
☐ E. The memory resources required to obtain and free locks can vary with the type of lock used.

Question 111

Which statement about lock timeouts is TRUE?

○ A. By default, transactions will wait 60 seconds to acquire the locks they need.
○ B. Use of the LOCK TABLE statement will prevent lock timeouts from occurring.
○ C. Lock timeouts can be avoided by using the Repeatable Read (RR) isolation level.
○ D. When seen in excessive numbers, lock timeouts can be as disruptive to a system as deadlocks.

Question 112

Which two data objects can be locked by the DB2 database manager? (Choose two.)

☐ A. Views
☐ B. Tables
☐ C. Indexes
☐ D. Buffer pools
☐ E. Table spaces

Question 113

If the following SQL statement is executed:

```
LOCK TABLE sales IN EXCLUSIVE MODE
```

Which statement is TRUE?

- ○ A. From now on, DB2 will attempt to acquire row-level Exclusive (X) locks for every transaction that accesses the SALES table.
- ○ B. From now on, DB2 will attempt to acquire table-level Exclusive (X) locks for every transaction that accesses the SALES table.
- ○ C. A table-level Exclusive (X) lock was acquired on the SALES table and concurrent transactions are allowed to perform both read and write operations against the table.
- ○ D. A table-level Exclusive (X) lock was acquired on the SALES table and concurrent transactions are prevented from performing both read and write operations against the table.

Question 114

If the ALTER TABLE ... LOCKSIZE TABLE statement is executed, which statement is NOT TRUE?

- ○ A. Concurrency may be improved.
- ○ B. Query performance may be improved.
- ○ C. Lock escalation will not be prevented.
- ○ D. Intent None (IN) locks can be acquired.

Question 115

Which command/statement is used to control the granularity of locks within a transaction?

- ○ A. db2set DB2_LOCK_TABLE=ON
- ○ B. LOCK TABLE ... IN SHARE MODE
- ○ C. ALTER TABLE ... LOCKSIZE TABLE
- ○ D. UPDATE DB CFG ... USING LOCKSIZE TABLE

Question 116

Which two are valid lock attributes? (Choose two.)

☐ A. Mode
☐ B. Object
☐ C. Activity
☐ D. Frequency
☐ E. Granularity

Question 117

Which statement about Exclusive (X) locks is TRUE?

○ A. They allow both the lock owner and concurrent applications to read and modify data in the locked object.
○ B. They allow both the lock owner and concurrent applications to read, but not modify data in the locked object.
○ C. They allow the lock owner to both read and update data in the locked object, but prevent concurrent applications that are not using the Uncommitted Read (UR) isolation level from accessing the locked data.
○ D. They allow the lock owner to modify, but not read data in the locked object; concurrent applications not using the Uncommitted Read (UR) isolation level can read, but not modify data in the locked object.

Question 118

In which two cases would a Super Exclusive (Z) lock NOT be acquired? (Choose two.)

☐ A. When a table is reorganized
☐ B. When a view on a table is created
☐ C. When a view on a table is altered
☐ D. When an index on a table is created
☐ E. When an index on a table is dropped

Question 119

Which two factors do NOT affect the mode and granularity of locks? (Choose two.)

☐ A. Lock list size
☐ B. Memory allocation
☐ C. Type of processing
☐ D. System architecture
☐ E. Data access method

Question 120

What is the primary reason for using Currently Committed semantics with the Cursor Stability (CS) isolation level?

○ A. To prevent read-only transactions from seeing uncommitted data, even when they are running under the Uncommitted Read (UR) isolation level.
○ B. To reduce the amount of log space needed to track data changes by automatically removing log records for transactions that have been committed.
○ C. To reduce lock contention by allowing read transactions to access the most recently committed data rather than having to wait for locks to be released.
○ D. To force DB2 to write all data changes to the database as soon as the DB2 database manager can make a determination that those changes will eventually be committed.

Question 121

Which isolation level offers the lowest level of data protection, but provides the greatest amount of concurrency?

○ A. Read Stability (RS)
○ B. Cursor Stability (CS)
○ C. Repeatable Read (RR)
○ D. Uncommitted Read (UR)

Question 122

> Which statement about Currently Committed semantics is NOT TRUE?
>
> ○ A. By default, Currently Committed semantics are enabled for new databases
>   that are created with DB2 9.7 and later.
> ○ B. Currently Committed semantics reduce lock contention by allowing read
>   transactions to access the most recently committed data rather than having
>   to wait for locks to be released.
> ○ C. If the CUR_COMMIT database configuration parameter is set to ON, Currently
>   Committed semantics are applied database-wide for both the Read Stability
>   and Cursor Stability isolation levels.
> ○ D. Currently Committed semantics reduce the amount of log space needed to
>   track data changes by forcing all data changes for a transaction to disk as
>   soon as DB2 can make a determination that those changes will eventually be
>   committed.

Question 123

> If a transaction updating rows in a table is still active, which statement is TRUE?
>
> ○ A. Only applications running under the Uncommitted Read (UR) isolation level
>   are allowed to retrieve the updated rows.
> ○ B. Only applications running under the Repeatable Read (RR) isolation level are
>   allowed to retrieve the updated rows.
> ○ C. Only applications running under the Read Stability (RS) or Cursor Stability
>   (CS) isolation level are allowed to retrieve the updated rows.
> ○ D. Only applications running under the Cursor Stability (CS) or Uncommitted
>   Read (UR) isolation level are allowed to retrieve the updated rows.

Question 124

Application APP_A would like to ensure that when a specific SELECT statement is executed, dirty reads, non-repeatable reads, and access to uncommitted data is not possible, but phantoms can and may be seen. Which SELECT statement will produce the desired results?

○ A. SELECT col1 FROM tab1 WITH RR
○ B. SELECT col1 FROM tab1 WITH RS
○ C. SELECT col1 FROM tab1 WITH CS
○ D. SELECT col1 FROM tab1 WITH UR

Question 125

How can the behavior of Currently Committed semantics be temporarily overwritten when a certain query is executed?

○ A. By assigning the value ON to the DB2_CUR_COMMIT registry variable.
○ B. By appending the clause WAIT FOR COMMIT to the SELECT statement used.
○ C. By appending the clause WAIT FOR OUTCOME to the SELECT statement used.
○ D. By assigning the value AUTOMATIC to the CUR_COMMIT database configuration parameter.

APPENDIX C

Answers to Practice Questions

Planning

Question 1

The correct answers are **A** and **D**. Data Studio is an Eclipse-based integrated development environment that can be used to perform instance and database administration; create, deploy, and debug data-centric Java applications; and analyze and provide query-tuning recommendations for one or more queries.

IBM InfoSphere Optim Configuration Manager provides advice on how to change database configurations (*Answer B*). The Audit Facility monitors data access and can help discover unwanted, unknown, and unacceptable access to data as well as keep historical records of activities performed on a database system (*Answer C*). And DB2 Workload Manager can help identify, manage, and control database workloads to maximize database server throughput and resource utilization (*Answer E*).

Question 2

The correct answers are **D** and **E**. The DB2 Storage Optimization Feature, a feature that helps decrease disk space utilization and storage requirements by transparently compressing data using classic row compression (where data is compressed at the table level), adaptive row compression (where data is compressed dynamically at the page level), or a combination of the two, is included with both DB2 Advanced Workgroup Server Edition and DB2 Advanced Enterprise Server Edition.

The DB2 Storage Optimization Feature does *not* come with DB2 Express Server Edition (*Answer A*), DB2 Enterprise Server Edition (*Answer B*), or DB2 Workgroup Server Edition (*Answer C*).

Question 3

The correct answers are **A** and **C**. Native encryption is included with DB2 Express-C, DB2 Advanced Workgroup Server Edition, and DB2 Advanced Enterprise Server Edition. IBM DB2 Encryption Offering is an add-on product that can provide native data encryption to DB2 Express Server Edition (*Answer B*), DB2 Workgroup Server Edition, and DB2 Enterprise Server Edition (*Answer D*).

IBM DB2 Performance Management Offering (*Answer E*) is a suite of tools that helps businesses monitor, manage, and improve database workload and application performance.

Question 4

The correct answer is **A**. IBM Data Studio consists of the *Data Studio client* and the *Data Studio Web console*. For most installations, the Data Studio client component is sufficient. However, to monitor database health and availability, as well as create and manage jobs, you also need the Data Studio Web console.

DB2 Workload Manager can help identify, manage, and control database workloads to maximize database server throughput and resource utilization (*Answer B*). IBM InfoSphere Optim Configuration Manager provides advice on how to change database configurations (*Answer C*). And, IBM InfoSphere Data Architect can be used for data modeling, transformation, and Data Definition Language (DDL) generation (*Answer D*).

Question 5

The correct answer is **C**. IBM InfoSphere Optim Configuration Manager provides advice on how to change database configurations; it also stores states and changes in a repository, making it possible to compare current and historical data, which can be helpful when trying to understand and resolve problems related to configuration changes.

IBM Workload Manager (*Answer A*) is a comprehensive workload management feature that can help identify, manage, and control database workloads to maximize database server throughput and resource utilization. IBM DB2 Performance Management Offering (*Answer B*) is a suite of tools that helps businesses monitor, manage, and improve database workload and application performance. And IBM DB2 BLU Acceleration In-Memory Offering (*Answer D*) provides workload management functionality for in-memory columnar processing.

Question 6

The correct answer is **B**. Table space-level backup and restore is *not* available with DB2 pureScale at this time.

In DB2 Version 10.5, the following enhancements were made to the DB2 pureScale Feature:

- HADR support (*Answer A*)
- The ability to add new members to an existing DB2 pureScale environment while the DB2 instance remains online and accessible
- The ability to apply FixPack updates to a DB2 pureScale environment while the DB2 instance remains available
- Support for in-place (online) table reorganization for tables that use adaptive compression (*Answer D*)
- The ability to perform extent reclamation operations on insert time clustering (ITC) tables
- The ability to use random ordering for index key columns (*Answer C*)
- The ability to isolate application workloads to one or more specific members that have been assigned to a member subset
- The ability to restore an offline database backup image that was taken on a DB2 Enterprise Server Edition instance to a DB2 pureScale instance (and vice versa)
- The ability to restore a database backup image taken on one DB2 pureScale instance to another DB2 pureScale instance that has a different topology
- The ability to restore table space backup images taken on one DB2 pureScale instance to a DB2 pureScale instance with a superset topology

Question 7

The correct answer is **D**. When the majority of database workloads are transactional in nature, it is recommended that traditional row-organized tables (with index access) be used. Workloads that are transactional in nature are typically characterized by transactions that randomly access data, frequently perform insert or update activity, and execute queries that return small data sets.

When the majority of database workloads are entirely analytical or OLAP in nature, the recommended approach is to put as many tables as possible into column-organized format (*Answer A*). Analytical and OLAP workloads are typically characterized by nonselective data access—usually involving more than 5% of the data—and extensive scanning, grouping, and aggregation (*Answer B*). For mixed workloads, which include a combination of analytic query processing and very selective data access (involving less than 2% of the data), it can be beneficial to use a mixture of row-organized and column-organized tables, as opposed to just one table type (*Answer C*).

Question 8

The correct answer is **D**. In an OLTP environment, high throughput, measured in hundreds of transactions per second, is required. And subsecond end-user response time is usually desired. Consequently, the DB2 pureScale Feature—*not the Data Partitioning Feature (DPF)*—is designed for OLTP workloads.

The Data Partitioning Feature, on the other hand, is designed primarily for large data warehouse environments; data warehousing involves storing and managing large volumes of data (often historical in nature) that is used primarily for analysis. As a result, data warehouse workloads often consist of full-table scans and multiple table joins (*Answer A*), complex queries involving aggregations (*Answer B*), and analysis of historical data stored in multi-dimensional schemas (*Answer C*).

Question 9

The correct answer is **D**. The DB2 pureScale Feature is included as part of DB2 Workgroup Server Edition, DB2 Enterprise Server Edition, DB2 Advanced Workgroup Server Edition, and DB2 Advanced Enterprise Server Edition.

The DB2 pureScale Feature leverages IBM System z Sysplex technology to bring active-active clustering services to DB2 for LUW database environments (*Answer A*). This technology enables a DB2 for LUW database to continuously process incoming requests, even if multiple system components fail simultaneously, which makes it ideal for OLTP workloads where high availability is crucial (*Answer B*). And, the DB2 pureScale Feature is based on a "shared data" architecture: the DB2 engine runs on multiple servers as data "members," each member has its own set of buffer pools and log files (which are accessible to the other members), and each member has equal, shared access to the database's underlying storage. IBM's General Parallel File System (GPFS) makes shared storage access possible (*Answer C*), and Cluster Caching Facility (CF) software provides global locking and buffer pool management and serves as the center of communication and coordination between all members.

Question 10

The correct answer is **D**. When the value ANALYTICS is assigned to the DB2_WORKLOAD registry variable, the *intra_parallel* database manager configuration parameter is set to YES. (The *intra_parallel* database manager configuration parameter can only be set to YES or NO—AUTOMATIC is not a valid setting.)

Additionally, when the value ANALYTICS is assigned to the DB2_WORKLOAD registry variable:

- The DFT_TABLE_ORG database configuration parameter is set to COLUMN.
- The DFT_DEGREE database configuration parameter is set to ANY.
- The PAGESIZE database configuration parameter is set to 32 K (*Answer A*).
- The DFT_EXTENT_SZ database configuration parameter is set to 4 (*Answer C*).
- The values of the SORTHEAP and SHEAPTHRES_SHR database configuration parameters are calculated and set specifically for an analytics workload.
- The UTIL_HEAP_SZ database configuration parameter is set to a value that takes into account the additional memory that is required to load data into column-organized tables.
- The AUTO_REORG database configuration parameter is set to ON (*Answer B*).
- A default space reclamation policy is installed and automatic table maintenance is configured so that empty extents for column-organized tables are automatically returned to table space storage for reuse.

Question 11

The correct answer is **A**. When the majority of database workloads are transactional in nature, it is recommended that traditional row-organized tables (with index access) be used.

When the majority of database workloads are entirely analytical or OLAP in nature, the recommended approach is to put as many tables as possible into column-organized format (*Answer B*). For mixed workloads, which include a combination of analytic query processing and very selective data access (involving less than 2% of the data), it can be beneficial to use a mixture of row-organized and column-organized tables, as opposed to just one table type (*Answer C*). And a synopsis table is a special internal table that is created automatically by DB2 and populated with metadata that describes the minimum and maximum range of the data values found in "chunks" of data; this metadata makes it possible to skip ranges of data that are not relevant to the current active query when column-organized tables are used (*Answer D*).

Question 12

The correct answers are **C** and **E**. DB2 10.5 with BLU Acceleration was designed around the following seven "big ideas":

1. Simple to implement and use

2. Compute-friendly approximate Huffman encoding and compression

3. Multiply the power of the CPU (by taking advantage of SIMD)

4. Column data store

5. Core-friendly parallelism

6. Scan-friendly memory caching that improves buffer pool utilization

7. Data skipping

Adaptive row compression is neither "always on" nor is it part of BLU Acceleration (*Answer A*); although referential integrity informational constraints have been available for quite some time, default informational constraints (*Answer B*) are not supported; and while the db2convert utility can be used to convert row-organized tables to column-organized tables, the conversion process is not done automatically (*Answer D*). Instead, the conversion must be done manually, on a table-by-table basis.

Question 13

The correct answer is **C**. For mixed workloads that include a combination of analytic query processing and very selective data access (involving less than 2% of the data), it can be beneficial to use a mixture of row-organized and column-organized tables, as opposed to just one table type.

When the majority of database workloads are transactional in nature, it is recommended that traditional row-organized tables (with index access) be used (*Answer A*). When the majority of database workloads are entirely analytical or OLAP in nature, the recommended approach is to put as many tables as possible into column-organized format (*Answer B*). And a synopsis table is a special internal table that is created automatically by DB2 and populated with metadata that describes the minimum and maximum range of the data values found in "chunks" of data; this metadata makes it possible to skip ranges of data that are not relevant to the current active query when column-organized tables are used (*Answer D*).

Question 14

The correct answer is B. A value is not assigned to the PCKCACHESZ database configuration parameter when the value ANALYTICS is assigned to the DB2_WORKLOAD registry variable.

Instead, when the value ANALYTICS is assigned to the DB2_WORKLOAD registry variable:

- The DFT_TABLE_ORG database configuration parameter is set to COLUMN.
- The DFT_DEGREE database configuration parameter is set to ANY (*Answer A*).
- The PAGESIZE database configuration parameter is set to 32 K.
- The DFT_EXTENT_SZ database configuration parameter is set to 4.
- The INTRA_PARALLEL database manager configuration parameter is set to YES.
- The values of the SORTHEAP and SHEAPTHRES_SHR (*Answer D*) database configuration parameters are calculated and set specifically for an analytics workload.
- The UTIL_HEAP_SZ (*Answer C*) database configuration parameter is set to a value that takes into account the additional memory that is required to load data into column-organized tables.
- The AUTO_REORG database configuration parameter is set to ON.
- A default space reclamation policy is installed and automatic table maintenance is configured so that empty extents for column-organized tables are automatically returned to table space storage for reuse.

Question 15

The correct answer is **A**. The compatibility features that are available in DB2 10.5 are designed to reduce the time and complexity of enabling applications that were written for **Oracle**, **Sybase**, and **MySQL** to run against a DB2 database. MongoDB is not supported.

In DB2 10.5, enhancements that were made to the compatibility features include:

- Implicit casting (weak typing)
- New built-in scalar functions
- Improvements to the TIMESTAMP_FORMAT and VARCHAR_FORMAT scalar functions
- The lifting of several SQL restrictions: specifically, the use of correlation names in subqueries and table functions is now optional; PL/SQL procedures, functions, triggers, and packages can now be created in a partitioned database environment; and TYPE declarations are now supported in a function, procedure, trigger, or anonymous block (*Answer B*)
- New synonyms for SQL syntax
- Global variable support

- An ARRAY collection data type
- Increased identifier length limits
- A pseudocolumn called ROWID that will return a unique identifier for every row found in a table (*Answer C*)
- Extended row size support
- NULL keys can be excluded from indexes (*Answer D*)
- New string unit attributes

Question 16

The correct answers are **A** and **B**. The compatibility features that are available in DB2 10.5 have the following restrictions:

- The NCLOB data type cannot be used in PL/SQL statements or contexts when the database is not defined as a Unicode database. (In Unicode databases, the NCLOB data type is mapped to a DB2 DBCLOB data type.)
- The XML data type is not supported.
- In a partitioned database environment, cursor variables cannot be accessed from remote nodes—they can only be accessed from the coordinator node.
- The use of nested type data types with PL/SQL package variables is not supported in autonomous routines.

The DBCLOB data type (*Answer C*), the NUMBER data type (*Answer D*), and the VARCHAR2 data type (*Answer E*) are supported.

Question 17

The correct answer is **C**. With DB2 10.5, implicit casting is *not* an alternative way of assigning data values that do not have an associated DB2 built-in data type to the CHAR data type.

Implicit casting is the automatic conversion of data of one data type to another based on an implied set of conversion rules (*Answer B*). If two objects have mismatched types, implicit casting is used to perform comparisons or make assignments, provided a reasonable interpretation of the data types can be made (*Answer A*). With DB2 10.5, implicit casting is an alternative way to parse character or graphic constants to support applications that expect these constants to be assigned the data types CHAR and GRAPHIC (*Answer D*).

Security

Question 18

The correct answer is **A**. When a remote database is cataloged in the system database directory, if a DB2 Connect remote client does not specify an authentication type, the client will try to connect using the SERVER_ENCRYPT authentication type first. If the server does not accept this authentication type, the client will try using an appropriate authentication type that is returned by the server.

When the SERVER_ENCRYPT authentication type is used, authentication occurs at the server workstation using the security facility that the server's operating system provides. However, the password supplied—*not the user ID (Answer B)*—by users wishing to access an instance or database is encrypted at the client workstation before it is sent to the server for validation.

When the KERBEROS authentication type is used, authentication occurs at the server workstation using a security facility that supports the Kerberos security protocol. This protocol performs authentication as a third-party service by using conventional cryptography to create a shared secret key—the key becomes the credentials used to verify the user's identity whenever local or network services are requested (*Answer C*).

When the DATA_ENCRYPT authentication type is used, authentication occurs at the server workstation using the SERVER_ENCRYPT authentication method and all user data is encrypted before it is passed from the client to the server (and vice versa) (*Answer D*).

Question 19

The correct answer is **D**. Label-based access control (LBAC) is a security feature that uses one or more security labels to control who has read access, who has write access, and who has both read and write access to individual rows and/or columns in a table.

The purpose of authentication is to verify that users really are who they say they are (*Answer A*). And if the GSSPLUGIN authentication type is used, authentication occurs at the server workstation using a Generic Security Service Application Program Interface (GSS-API) plug-in (*kind of Answer B*).

After a user has been authenticated and a connection to a database has been established, DB2 evaluates the set of authorities and privileges that have been assigned to the user to determine which operations, if any, he or she is allowed to perform (*Answer C*). Authorities convey the right to perform high-level administrative and maintenance/utility operations on an instance or a database. Privileges, on the other hand, convey the right to perform certain actions against specific database resources (such as tables, indexes, and views).

Question 20

The correct answers are **A** and **C**. Label-based access control (LBAC) is a security feature that uses one or more **security labels** to control who has read access, who has write access, and who has both read and write access to individual rows and/or columns in a table. LBAC is implemented by assigning unique labels to users and data and allowing access only when assigned labels match. To implement an LBAC solution, someone with SECADM authority must define the appropriate security label components, **security policies**, and security labels. Then, that individual must grant the proper security labels to the appropriate users. Finally, someone with LBAC credentials must create an LBAC-protected table or alter an existing table to add LBAC protection.

Row and Column Access Control (RCAC), on the other hand, secures data by stipulating rules and conditions under which a user, group, or role can access rows and columns of a table. Two sets of RCAC rules exist: row permissions and column masks (*Answer B*). Written in the form of a query, a row permission specifies the conditions under which a user, group, or role can access individual rows of data in a table (*Answer D*). Written in the form of an SQL CASE expression, a column mask indicates the conditions under which a user, group, or role can access values for a particular column (*Answer E*).

Question 21

The correct answers are **D** and **E**. Row and Column Access Control (RCAC) secures data by stipulating rules and conditions under which a user, group, or role can access rows and columns of a table. Two sets of RCAC rules exist: row permissions and column masks. Written in the form of a query, a row permission specifies the conditions under which a user, group, or role can access individual rows of data in a table (*Answer D*). Written in the form of an SQL CASE expression, a column mask indicates the conditions under which a user, group, or role can access values for a particular column (*Answer E*).

Label-based access control (LBAC) is a security feature that uses one or more security labels to control who has read access, who has write access, and who has both read and write access to individual rows and/or columns in a table. LBAC is implemented by assigning unique labels to users and data and allowing access only when assigned labels match. To implement an LBAC solution, someone with SECADM authority must define the appropriate security label components (*Answer C*), security policies (*Answer B*), and security labels (*Answer A*). Then, that individual must grant the proper security labels to the appropriate users. Finally, someone with LBAC credentials must create an LBAC-protected table or alter an existing table to add LBAC protection.

Question 22

The correct answers are **B** and **D**. There is no LDAP_PLUGIN or KRB_CLIENT_ENCRYPT authentication type.

Instead, the following authentication types are available with DB2 10.5 for LUW:

- CLIENT
- SERVER (*Answer A*)
- SERVER_ENCRYPT
- DATA_ENCRYPT (*Answer C*)
- DATA_ENCRYPT_CMP
- KERBEROS
- KRB_SERVER_ENCRYPT (*Answer E*)
- GSSPLUGIN
- GSS_SERVER_ENCRYPT

Question 23

The correct answer is **B**. Authentication is the first security portal most users must pass through on their way to gaining access to a DB2 instance or database. And in most cases, an external security facility that is <u>not</u> part of DB2 is used to perform this task (*Answer C*). This facility might be part of the operating system, or it can be a separate add-on product. In either case, the security facility used often must be presented with two specific pieces of information before a user can be authenticated: a unique *user ID* and a corresponding *password*.

On the server side, the authentication type is specified during the instance creation process; on the client side, the authentication type is stipulated when a remote database is cataloged. Only one authentication type is allowed per instance—*not per database* (*Answer A*). And after a user has been authenticated and an attachment to an instance (or a connection to a database) has been established, DB2 evaluates the set of authorities and privileges—*not the authentication type*—that have been assigned to the user to determine which operations, if any, he or she is allowed to perform (*Answer D*).

Question 24

The correct answers are **A** and **D**. System Administrator (SYSADM) authority, System Control (SYSCTRL) authority, System Maintenance (SYSMAINT) authority, and System Monitor (SYSMON) authority are instance-level authorities.

Database Administrator (DBADM) authority, Security Administrator (SECADM) authority (*Answer B*), Access Control (ACCESSCTRL) authority (*Answer E*), Data Access (DATAACCESS) authority, SQL Administrator (SQLADM) authority, and Workload Management Administrator (WLMADM) authority (*Answer C*) are database-level authorities.

Question 25

The correct answer is **A**. Users who receive System Maintenance (SYSMAINT) authority cannot access user data unless they have been explicitly granted the privileges needed to do so.

System Maintenance (SYSMAINT) authority provides select individuals with the ability to perform maintenance operations—such as forcing users off a server (*Answer D*) and backing up a database (*Answer B*)—on an instance and any databases that fall under that instance's control. SYSMAINT authority is intended to let special users maintain a database that contains sensitive data they most likely should not view or modify. And because a database connection is required to run some of DB2's maintenance utilities, users who have SYSMAINT authority for a particular instance automatically receive the privileges needed to connect to any database that falls under that instance's control (*Answer C*).

Question 26

The correct answers are **A** and **B**. LOAD authority allows a user to bulk-load data into one or more existing tables in a certain database. ALTER privilege allows a user to change a certain table's definition and/or the comment associated with the table, as well as create or drop a table constraint.

Because the Import utility populates a table by performing INSERT operations, an authority or privilege that allows an individual to add records to a table is required to use the Import utility. The INSERT table privilege allows a user to add data to a certain table (*Answer C*). The CONTROL table privilege provides a user with all of table privileges available—including the INSERT privilege (*Answer D*). And Data Access (DATAACCESS) authority provides select individuals with the ability to access and *modify* data stored in user tables, views, and materialized query tables (*Answer E*).

Question 27

The correct answer is **C**. The SELECT table privilege allows a user to retrieve data from a certain table, as well as create a view that references the table. And, because the Export utility retrieves data from a table before writing it to an external file, the SELECT privilege is needed to use the Export utility.

LOAD authority allows a user to bulk-load data into one or more existing tables in a certain database (*Answer A*). ALTER privilege allows a user to change a certain table's definition and/or the comment associated with the table, as well as create or drop a table constraint (*Answer B*). And UPDATE privilege allows a user to modify (change) data in a certain table (*Answer D*).

Question 28

The correct answers are **B** and **C**. UPDATE privilege allows a user to modify (change) data in a certain table. And if the WITH GRANT OPTION clause is specified with the GRANT statement used, the individual receiving the designated authorities or privileges will receive the ability to grant those authorities or privileges to others.

The DELETE table privilege allows a user to remove rows of data from the table or view within a federated data source that a certain nickname refers to (*Answer A*). The ALTER table privilege allows a user to change a certain table's definition and/or the comment associated with the table—a table's definition is stored in the system catalog (*Answer D* and *Answer E*).

Question 29

The correct answers are **B** and **D**. Security Administrator (SECADM) authority provides select individuals with, among other things, the ability to grant and revoke database-level authorities and privileges. Access Control (ACCESSCTRL) authority also provides select individuals with the ability to grant and revoke authorities and privileges.

Database Administrator (DBADM) authority provides select individuals with the ability to create database objects (such as tables, indexes, and views), issue database-specific DB2 commands, and execute built-in DB2 routines (*Answer A*). There is no CONTROL database authority (*Answer C*). And Data Access (DATAACCESS) authority provides select individuals with the ability to access and modify data stored in user tables, views, and materialized query tables, as well as execute plans, packages, functions, and stored procedures (*Answer E*).

Question 30

The correct answer is **B**. Package privileges control what users can and cannot do with a particular package. (A package is an object that contains information that DB2 uses to efficiently process SQL statements embedded in an application.) And the EXECUTE package privilege allows a user to execute or run a certain package.

While there is a USE table space privilege, there is no USE package privilege (*Answer A*). Nor are there stored procedure privileges (*Answer C* and *Answer D*). Instead, the routine privilege controls what users can and cannot do with a particular routine. (A routine can be a user-defined function, a stored procedure, or a method that different users can invoke.)

Question 31

The correct answer is **A**. The ALTER table privilege allows a user to change a certain table's definition and/or the comment associated with the table, as well as create or drop a table constraint.

Database Administrator (DBADM) authority provides select users with the ability to create database objects (such as tables, indexes, and views), issue database-specific DB2 commands, and execute built-in DB2 routines (*Answer B*). The UPDATE table privilege allows a user to modify data in a certain table (*Answer C*). And System Administrator (SYSADM) authority provides select individuals with the ability to run most DB2 utilities, execute most DB2 commands, and perform any SQL or XQuery operation that does not attempt to access data that is protected by Row and Column Access Control or Label-Based Access Control, as well as create databases and database objects (*Answer D*).

Question 32

The correct answer is **A**. The REVOKE statement can be used to remove any authorities and privileges that have been granted to a user, group, or role. And the USE table space privilege allows a user to create objects in a certain table space. So, when the following statement is executed:

```
REVOKE USE OF TABLESPACE mytbsp FROM user1
```

The ability to create tables in a table space named MYTBSP will be taken away from user USER1.

The BIND package privilege allows a user to bind or rebind (recreate) a certain package (*Answer B*). The SELECT table/view privilege allows a user to retrieve data from a certain table or view (*Answer C*). And the USAGE XML schema repository (XSR) object privilege allows a user to use a certain XSR object (*Answer D*).

Question 33

The correct answers are **C** and **D**. A system authorization password is not needed to define a trusted context. Neither is a Secure Sockets Layer (SSL) certificate.

However, the following information is required to create a trusted context:

- A system authorization ID that represents the authorization ID that an incoming connection must use to be considered "trusted" (*Answer A*).

- The IP address, domain name, or security zone name an incoming connection must originate from to be considered "trusted" (*Answer E*).

- A data stream encryption value that represents the level of encryption that an incoming connection (if any) must use to be considered "trusted" (*Answer B*).

Question 34

The correct answer is **A**. A trusted context does not enable one user to inherit privileges from another. So, in the example presented, user USER1 will *not* inherit the privileges of users USER2 and USER3.

Trusted contexts are created by executing the CREATE TRUSTED CONTEXT statement; when this statement is executed, if the WITH AUTHENTICATION clause is specified with the user ID identified, switching from the current user on a trusted connection to the identified user requires authentication (i.e., a password). If the WITHOUT AUTHENTICATION clause is specified, authentication is not required to switch to the user identified. So, if the following statement is executed:

```
CREATE TRUSTED CONTEXT cntxt1
   BASED UPON CONNECTION USING SYSTEM AUTHID user1
   ATTRIBUTES (ADDRESS '192.168.1.100')
   WITH USE FOR user2 WITH AUTHENTICATION,
      user3 WITHOUT AUTHENTICATION
   ENABLE
```

User USER1 will establish the trusted context connection used (*Answer B*). User USER1 can switch to user USER3 without providing a password (*Answer C*). And user USER1 can switch to user USER2 if a correct password is provided (*Answer D*).

Question 35

The correct answer is **A**. A role is a database entity that is used to group a combination of authorities and/or privileges together so they can be simultaneously granted to and revoked from multiple users, groups, or roles.

A buffer pool—which is the only kind of pool that is available with DB2—is an object that is used to cache table and index pages (*Answer B*). A group is an entity that is used to define a collection of users to which a combination of authorities and/or privileges can be granted or revoked (*Answer C*). And schemas provide a way to logically group objects in a database (*Answer D*).

Question 36

The correct answers are **B** and **D**. A trusted context is a database object that defines a trust relationship for a connection between a database and an external entity such as an application server. Trusted contexts are created by executing the CREATE TRUSTED CONTEXT statement;

when this statement is executed, if the WITH AUTHENTICATION clause is specified with the user ID identified, switching from the current user on a trusted connection to the identified user requires authentication (i.e., a password). If the WITHOUT AUTHENTICATION clause is specified, authentication is not required to switch to the user identified.

Trusted context objects can only be defined by someone with SECADM authority (*Answer A*). After an explicit trusted connection is established, an application can switch the connection's user to a different authorization ID—switching can occur with or without authenticating the new authorization ID, depending upon the definition of the trusted context object associated with the connection; if a switch request is made using an authorization ID that is not allowed, the explicit trusted connection is placed in an "unconnected" state (*Answer C*). And the authorization ID that uses a trusted context can inherit the privileges assigned to the associated role, *in addition to* the authorities and privileges that have already been granted to that authorization ID (*Answer E*).

Question 37

The correct answer is **B**. With the exception of SECADM authority, most of the authorities and privileges available can be granted to a role.

A role is a database entity that is used to group a combination of authorities and/or privileges together so they can be simultaneously granted or revoked; roles enable you to control database access in a manner that mirrors the structure of your organization (*Answer C*).

When one role is granted membership in another role, a role hierarchy is formed—in a role hierarchy, the role that is granted membership inherits the authorities and privileges that have been granted to the "parent" role. For example, if the role DOCTOR is granted to the role SURGEON, then the role SURGEON will inherit the authorities and privileges that have been granted to the role DOCTOR. When role hierarchies are formed, cycles are not allowed (*Answer D*). A cycle occurs if one role is granted to another role and then that other role is granted back to the original role. In other words, if the role DOCTOR is granted to the role SURGEON, the role SURGEON cannot be granted back to the role DOCTOR. Any attempt to create a cycle in a role hierarchy will result in an error.

Only users with SECADM authority are allowed to create roles (*Answer A*).

Working with Databases and Database Objects

Question 38

The correct answer is **D**. When queries are run against federated databases, the DB2 optimizer performs what is known as *pushdown analysis* to determine whether a particular operation (such as the execution of a system or user function) can be conducted at a remote data source.

An important feature of BLU Acceleration is its ability to exploit a leading-edge technology that is found in many of today's modern processors: Single-Instruction, Multiple-Data (SIMD) processing. SIMD instructions are low-level CPU instructions that enable an application to perform the same operation on multiple data points at the same time (*Answer B*). Core-friendly parallelism refers to

BLU Acceleration's ability to break an operation into several parts and running those parts, in parallel, across multiple CPU cores (*Answer C*). And in a basic DB2 client/server environment, each time a query is executed against a remote database stored on a server workstation, the statement itself is sent through a network from the client to the server for processing (*Answer A*). The database at the server then processes the query, and the results are returned, again through the network, to the client.

Question 39

The correct answer is **B**. The basic syntax for the CATALOG TCPIP NODE command is:

```
CATALOG [TCPIP | TCPIP4 | TCPIP6] NODE [NodeName]
REMOTE [IPAddress | HostName]
SERVER [ServiceName | PortNumber]
```

where:

NodeName	Identifies the alias to be assigned to the node to be cataloged; this is an arbitrary name created on the user's workstation and is used to identify the node
IPAddress	Identifies the IP address of the server where the remote database you want to communicate with resides
HostName	Identifies the host name, as it is known to the TCP/IP network; this is the name of the server where the remote database you want to communicate with resides
ServiceName	Identifies the service name that the DB2 instance on the server uses to communicate with
PortNumber	Identifies the port number that the DB2 instance on the server uses to communicate with

And since the server address 172:16:254:1 is an IPv4 address, the only CATALOG NODE statement that is valid is:

```
CATALOG TCPIP4 NODE hrclient
  REMOTE 172:16:254:1
  SERVER 52000
```

PORT is not a valid clause of the CATALOG NODE statement (*Answer A* and *Answer C*). And the server address 172:16:254:1 is not an IPv6 address (*Answer D*).

Question 40

The correct answers are **A** and **D**. Applications that interact with DB2 databases have the option of using two types of connection semantics: Type 1 and Type 2. And each connection type supports a very different connection behavior. For instance, Type 1 connections allow a transaction to be connected to only one database at a time.

Type 2 connections—*not Type 1 connections*—allow a single transaction to connect to and work with multiple databases simultaneously (*Answer B*). Also, when Type 2 connections are used, connecting to another application server will put the current connection into a dormant state (*Answer C*). And finally, when Type 2 connections are used, connecting with the USER...USING clause is only allowed when there is no dormant or current connection to the same named server (*Answer E*).

Question 41

The correct answer is **D**. Applications that interact with DB2 databases have the option of using two types of connection semantics: Type 1 and Type 2. And each connection type supports a very different connection behavior. For instance, Type 2 connections, allow a single transaction to connect to and work with multiple databases simultaneously.

With DB2 for Linux, UNIX, and Windows, when a database connection is established, Type 1 connections—*not Type 2 connections*—are used, by default (*Answer B*). The connection semantics that Embedded SQL applications use is controlled by SQL precompiler and Binder options. Thus, Type 2 connections *can* be used with Embedded SQL (*Answer A*). And Type 1 connections—*not Type 2 connections*—allow a transaction to be connected to only one database at a time (*Answer C*).

Question 42

The correct answers are **A** and **C**. When the simplest form of the CREATE DATABASE command is executed, the characteristics of the database produced are defined according to a set of predefined default values. For example, it will have a page size of 4 KB and it will be created on the default database path that is specified in the DFTDBPATH database manager configuration parameter. If the RESTRICTIVE clause is specified with the CREATE DATABASE command used, no authorities or privileges will automatically be granted to the group PUBLIC.

Unless the AUTOMATIC STORAGE NO clause is specified with the CREATE DATABASE command used, it is assumed that the database is to be an automatic storage database (*Answer B*). The WITH "PAYROLL DATABASE" clause would have to be specified with CREATE DATABASE command used to create a database that has the comment "PAYROLL DATABASE" associated with it (*Answer D*). And while database names cannot begin with the letter sequences "SYS," "DBM," or "IBM," there is no such restriction for table names (*Answer E*).

Question 43

The correct answer is **B**. Schemas provide a way to logically group objects in a database; they are used to organize data objects into sets.

An alias is an alternate name for a module, nickname, sequence, table, view, or other alias (*Answer A*). A sequence is an object that is used to generate a sequence of numbers, in either ascending or descending order (*Answer C*). And a view is an object that is used to provide an alternative way of describing data stored in one or more tables (*Answer D*).

Question 44

The correct answers are **B** and **E**. An application-period temporal table is a table that maintains "currently in effect" values of application data. Such tables let you manage time-sensitive data by defining specific time periods in which data values are considered valid. Application-period temporal tables are ideal when you need to provide appropriate values for data, based on some application defined business time value.

A system-period temporal table is a table that maintains historical versions of its rows (*Answer A*). Insert time clustering (ITC) tables are used to cluster data according to the time in which rows are inserted (*Answer C*). And multidimensional clustering (MDC) tables are used to physically cluster data on more than one key or dimension, simultaneously (*Answer D*).

Question 45

The correct answer is **D**. An index is an object that contains pointers to rows in a table that are logically ordered—*but not physically ordered*—according to the values of one or more columns (known as keys).

Before an index can be created, a table must exist (that the index will be created on) and a table space must exist (which is where the index will be created) (*Answer A*). Indexes provide a fast, efficient method for locating specific rows of data in large tables (*Answer B*). And when an index is first created, its characteristics (referred to as its metadata) are stored in one or more system catalog tables (*Answer C*).

Question 46

The correct answers are **D** and **E**. DB2 uses a B+ tree structure for index storage. The top level of this tree is known as the root node. The bottom level consists of leaf nodes that store index key values with pointers to the table rows that contain the corresponding data. And levels between the root and leaf node levels are known as intermediate nodes. None of these nodes can be explicitly created—instead, they are created, as needed, by the DB2 database manager. The package cache is a section of database shared memory that is used for caching static and dynamic SQL and XQuery statements. You can control the size of the package cache via the PCKCACHESZ database configuration parameter. However, DB2 is responsible for creating and maintaining this storage area.

Although servers, instances, and databases are the primary components that make up a DB2 database environment, many other different, but often related, objects exist. Some of the more common objects available that can be explicitly created include schemas, tables, views (*Answer A*), indexes, aliases, sequences (*Answer C*), triggers (*Answer B*), user-defined data types, user-defined functions, stored procedures, and packages.

Question 47

The correct answers are **A** and **E**. Materialized query tables (MQTs) derive their definitions from the results of a query (SELECT statement); their data consists of precomputed values taken from one or more tables the MQT is based upon. MQTs can greatly improve performance and response time for complex queries, particularly queries that aggregate data over one or more dimensions or that join data across multiple base tables.

Multidimensional clustering (MDC) tables—*not MQTs*—are physically clustered on more than one key or dimension, simultaneously (*Answer B*). Temporary tables are used to hold non-persistent data temporarily, on behalf of a single application (*Answer C*). And insert time clustering (ITC) tables cluster data using a virtual column that physically stores rows that are inserted at a similar time, together (*Answer D*).

Question 48

The correct answers are **C** and **E**. Temporary tables are automatically enabled for classic row compression at the time they are created. And a key feature of BLU Acceleration is that column-organized tables are compressed automatically, using a technique known as *approximate Huffman encoding* (which is sometimes referred to as *actionable compression*).

With the exception of temporary tables, before data in a row-organized table can be compressed, the table must first be "enabled" for compression (*Answer D*). Similarly, before data in an index can be compressed, it must be enabled for compression (*Answer B*). Views cannot be enabled for compression, nor can they be compressed (*Answer A*).

Question 49

The correct answer is **D**. Distinct types cannot be used as arguments for most built-in functions and built-in data types cannot be used in arguments or operands that expect distinct data types. Instead, user-defined functions (UDFs) that provide similar functionality must be developed if that capability is needed.

If the CREATE DISTINCT TYPE statement shown in the scenario presented is executed, a user-defined distinct data type that can be used to store numerical data as British currency will be created (*Answer A*). When a distinct data type is created, by default, six comparison functions (named =, <>, <, <=, >, and >=) are also created—provided the distinct type is not based on a LOB data type (*Answer B*). These functions let you compare two values of the distinct data type in the same manner that you can compare two values of a built-in data type. In addition, two casting functions are generated that allow data to be converted between a distinct type and the built-in data type that the distinct type is based on (*Answer C*).

Question 50

The correct answers are **B** and **C**. Shadow tables are implemented as materialized query tables (MQTs) that are maintained by replication; replication is performed by IBM InfoSphere Change

Data Capture for DB2 for Linux, UNIX, and Windows (InfoSphere CDC), which is a component of the InfoSphere Data Replication product. Shadow tables provide the performance benefits of BLU Acceleration to analytic queries that must be executed in online transaction processing (OLTP) environments.

A shadow table is a column-organized copy of a row-organized table—*not a row-organized copy of a column-organized table*—that contains all or a subset of the columns found in the row-organized table upon which it is based (*Answer A*). A range-clustered table (RCT) is a table that uses a special algorithm to associate record key values (which are similar to index key values) with specific locations of rows in the table (*Answer D*). And a synopsis table is a system-generated, automatically maintained, column-organized table that is used to store metadata for an associated user-defined, column-organized table (*Answer E*). A synopsis table contains the minimum and maximum values for each column in a column-organized table (across a range of rows)—DB2 uses those values to skip over data that is of no interest to a query during the evaluation of certain types of query predicates.

Question 51

The correct answer is **D**. A primary key that prevents the overlapping of SYSTEM_TIME periods does not have to be included in the definition for a system-period temporal table.

A system-period temporal table is a table that maintains historical versions of its rows. Such tables are used to automatically track and manage multiple versions of data values. For this reason, every system-period temporal table must be associated with a history table (*Answer A*)—anytime a row in a system-period temporal table is modified, DB2 automatically inserts a copy of the original row into the corresponding history table (*Answer B*). This storage of original data values enables you to retrieve data values that existed at any given point in time (*Answer C*).

Question 52

The correct answer is **B**. When an MDC table is created, a dimension block index is created automatically for each dimension specified. This index identifies the list of blocks available for a given key value and is used to quickly and efficiently access data along each of those dimensions. Dimension block indexes point to extents instead of individual rows and are much smaller—*not larger*—than regular indexes.

A multidimensional clustering (MDC) table is a special table that allows its data to be physically clustered on more than one key (dimension), simultaneously. In addition, an MDC table is able to maintain its clustering over the dimensions specified, automatically and continuously, eliminating the need to reorganize the table to maintain its clustering sequence (*Answer A*). Thus, MDC tables can significantly reduce maintenance overhead when clustering is desired. It is important to note, however, that deleted rows will result in free extents, which can only be reclaimed by executing the REORG command with the RECLAIM EXTENTS clause specified (*Answer D*). MDC tables are primarily intended to be used with large tables in data warehouse and decision support environments (*Answer C*).

Question 53

The correct answer is **A**. Insert time clustering (ITC) tables—*not Materialized query tables (MQTs)*—have similar characteristics to multidimensional clustering (MDC) tables; for example, ITC tables use block-based allocation and block indexes.

Materialized query tables (MQTs) are tables whose definition is based on the result of a query. MQTs can be thought of as a kind of materialized view because they are typically populated with precomputed results that have been obtained from one or more base tables (*Answer D*). MQT data is generated by executing the query upon which the MQT is based at regular intervals or at a user-controlled specific point in time (*Answer B*). And, MQTs offer a powerful way to improve response time for complex queries (*Answer C*).

Question 54

The correct answer is **D**. When a multidimensional clustering (MDC) table is created, a dimension block index is created automatically for each dimension specified. This index identifies the list of blocks available for a given key value and is used to quickly and efficiently access data along each of those dimensions. (Dimension block indexes point to extents instead of individual rows and are much smaller than regular indexes; therefore, they can be used to quickly access only those extents that contain specific dimension values.) If the table has more than one dimension, a composite block index containing all dimension key columns is created as well; this index is used to maintain the clustering of the data during insert and update operations, as well as to aid in query processing.

While temporal tables (*Answer A*), range-clustered tables (*Answer B*), and materialized query tables (*Answer C*) can have traditional indexes defined on them, they do not use dimension or composite block indexes.

Question 55

The correct answer is **A**. Range-clustered tables (RCTs)—*not range partitioned tables*—preallocate and reserve space for use at table creation time; therefore, they have no need for free space control records.

Partitioned tables (also known to as range-partitioned tables) are tables that use a data organization scheme in which data is divided across multiple storage objects, called data partitions or ranges, according to values found in one or more partitioning key columns (*Answer D*). When partitioned tables are used, table-level administration becomes more flexible because administrative tasks and maintenance operations can be performed on individual data partitions, as opposed to the entire partitioned table (*Answer C*). And, when resolving queries, one or more data partitions may be automatically eliminated based on the query predicates used, which can improve overall performance and eliminate large amounts of I/O (*Answer B*).

Question 56

The correct answer is **D**. Synopsis tables are created in the SYSIBM schema, and the relationship between a user-defined table and its associated synopsis table is recorded in the SYSCAT.TABDEP catalog view.

A synopsis table is a system-generated, automatically maintained, column-organized table that is used to store metadata for an associated user-defined, column-organized—*not row-organized*—table. The synopsis table for a user-defined table contains the minimum and maximum values for each column in that table, across a range of rows (*Answer C*). Because synopsis tables are generated and maintained by DB2, the only operation that can be performed against a synopsis table is a SELECT operation—DELETE operations are not allowed (*Answer B*). And when shadow tables—*not synopsis tables*—are used, queries are automatically routed to the source table or the shadow table according to the results of a latency-based algorithm that prevents shadow table access whenever replication latency exceeds a user-defined limit (*Answer A*).

Question 57

The correct answers are **A** and **E**. An application-period temporal table is a table that maintains "currently in effect" values of application data. Such tables let you manage time-sensitive data by defining the time periods in which specific data values are considered valid. Because a bitemporal table combines the historical tracking of a system-period temporal table with the time-specific data storage capabilities of an application-period temporal table, it too can be used to manage time-sensitive data by defining the time periods in which specific data values are considered valid.

A system-period temporal table (*Answer C*) is a table that maintains historical versions of its rows. There is no such thing as a time-period temporal table (*Answer B*). And while application-period temporal tables are created by executing a CREATE TABLE statement with the PERIOD BUSINESS_ TIME clause specified, such tables are not called business-period temporal tables (*Answer D*).

Working with DB2 Data Using SQL and XQuery

Question 58

The correct answer is **A**. The WHERE clause is used to tell DB2 how to select the rows that are to be returned in the result data set produced. When specified, this clause is followed by a search condition, which is a simple test that is applied to a row of data—if the test evaluates to TRUE, the row is returned in the result data set produced; if the test evaluates to FALSE or UNKNOWN, the row is ignored. By using parentheses and/or Boolean operators like AND and OR, it's possible to create a WHERE clause that is quite complex.

In the scenario presented, two different criteria are specified, which implies that the query must contain a WHERE clause that has a Boolean AND operator. And because the proper way to code the value $50,000.00 in a query is 50000—*not 50,000.00* (*Answer B* and *Answer D*), and the keywords

GREATER THAN are not valid comparison predicates (*Answer C* and *Answer D*), the only SQL statement shown that will meet the objective defined in the scenario presented is:

```
SELECT * FROM sales
  WHERE (salesdate > '2016-06-01'
    AND amt > 50000)
```

Question 59

The correct answer is **D**. When a right outer join operation is performed, rows that an inner join operation would have returned, together with rows stored in the rightmost table of the join operation (that is, the table listed last in the OUTER JOIN clause) that the inner join operation would have eliminated, are returned in the result data set produced. (In the scenario presented, the EMPLOYEE table is the leftmost table and the DEPARTMENT table is the rightmost table.)

When an inner join operation is performed (*Answer A* and *Answer B*), every row in one table that has matching values in one or more columns found in a row in another table are returned in the result data set produced—non-matching rows found in either table are excluded. When a left outer join operation is performed (*Answer C*), rows that an inner join operation would have returned, together with rows stored in the leftmost table of the join operation (that is, the table listed first in the OUTER JOIN clause) that the inner join operation would have eliminated, are returned in the result data set produced. Consequently, in the scenario presented, if a left outer join was used, the list produced would contain every employee who works for the company and the name of the department they work in; if an employee does not work for a particular department, their name will appear in the list as well. And any department that does not have employees would be excluded from the list produced.

Question 60

The correct answer is **C**. With a right outer join, rows that an inner join operation would have returned, together with rows stored in the rightmost table of the join operation (that is, the table listed last in the OUTER JOIN clause) that the inner join operation would have eliminated, are returned in the result data set produced.

With an inner join (*Answer A*), every row in one table that has matching values in one or more columns found in a row in another table are returned in the result data set produced—non-matching rows found in either table are excluded. With a left outer join (*Answer B*), rows that an inner join operation would have returned, together with rows stored in the leftmost table of the join operation (that is, the table listed first in the OUTER JOIN clause) that the inner join operation would have eliminated, are returned in the result data set produced. And, with a full outer join (*Answer D*), rows that an inner join operation would have returned, together with rows stored in both tables of the join operation that the inner join operation would have eliminated, are returned in the result data set produced.

Question 61

The correct answer is **C**. The UNION ALL set operator combines the result data sets produced by two individual queries, while retaining all duplicate records found.

The UNION set operator (*Answer A*) combines the result data sets produced by two individual queries and removes any duplicate rows found. The EXCEPT set operator (*Answer B*) combines the result data sets produced by two individual queries, removes all duplicate rows found, and then removes all records in the first result data set that have a matching record in the second result data set, leaving just the records not found in both result data sets. And the EXCEPT ALL set operator (*Answer D*) combines the result data sets produced by two individual queries (retaining all duplicate rows found), and removes all records in the first result data set that have a matching record in the second result data set, leaving the records not found in both result data sets.

Question 62

The correct answer is **D**. The GROUP BY clause is used to instruct DB2 on how to organize rows of data that are returned in a result data set; the ORDER BY clause is used to instruct DB2 on how to sort (order) the rows that are returned in a result data set. Therefore, in the scenario presented, the GROUP BY month clause will instruct DB2 to organize the data retrieved from the WEATHER table by month, and the ORDER BY month clause will then sort the organized records.

In the scenario presented, the GROUP BY clause—*not the ORDER BY clause* (*Answer A*)—is needed to organize the data retrieved from the WEATHER table by month. The ORDER BY clause will merely cause the data retrieved to be sorted by each column specified (in this case, in ascending order). A common mistake that is often made with the GROUP BY clause is the addition of non-aggregate columns to the list of columns that are supplied as the grouping expression—because grouping is performed by combining all the columns specified into a single concatenated key and breaking whenever that key value changes, extraneous columns can cause unexpected breaks to occur. (Such is the case with *Answer B*). The SELECT statement does not have a SORT BY clause (*Answer C*).

Question 63

The correct answers are **C** and **E**. Most numeric data types (including BIGINT), character string data types, and date/time data types (including TIMESTAMP) can be specified in an ORDER BY clause.

Columns that have a data type of BLOB (*Answer B*), CLOB, DBCLOB (*Answer D*), XML (*Answer A*), a structured data type, or a user-defined data type that is based on one of these data types cannot be specified in an ORDER BY clause.

Question 64

The correct answer is **C**. The GROUP BY clause is used to instruct DB2 on how to organize rows of data that are returned in a result data set; the ORDER BY clause is used to instruct DB2 on how to sort (order) the rows that are returned in a result data set. Therefore, in the scenario presented, the GROUP BY region_cd clause will instruct DB2 to organize the data retrieved from the SALES table by region, and the ORDER BY COUNT(*) clause will tell DB2 to order the data by the number of sales made (once it has been organized).

In the scenario presented, the ORDER BY COUNT(*) clause alone will not produce the desired results (*Answer A*)—instead, this clause will cause the data that was retrieved from the SALES table to be sorted, by sales amount, in ascending order. And the GROUP BY sales_amt clause (*Answer B* and *Answer D*) will cause the data retrieved to be organized by sales amount—not by region.

Question 65

The correct answer is **A**. The GROUP BY clause is used to instruct DB2 on how to organize rows of data that are returned in a result data set; the ORDER BY clause is used to instruct DB2 on how to sort (order) the rows that are returned. In the scenario presented, total costs, state, and city will be retrieved from a table named EXPENSES—SELECT state, city, SUM(cost) AS total_costs FROM expenses. Then, the results will be organized by state and city—GROUP BY 1, 2—and arranged in ascending order, by total costs—ORDER BY total_sales.

Because the DESC keyword was not specified with the ORDER BY clause used, the results of the query will not be arranged in descending order, by total costs (*Answer B* and *Answer D*). And to return total costs, state, and city, from a table named EXPENSES with the results arranged in ascending order, by state and city (*Answer C*) the SELECT statement used would need to look like this:

```
SELECT state, city, SUM(cost) AS total_costs
   FROM expenses
      ORDER BY 1, 2
```

Question 66

The correct answer is **C**. The GROUP BY clause—*not the ORDER BY clause*—is frequently used to sort columns whose values are to be provided as input to aggregate functions like AVG() and SUM().

The ORDER BY clause is used to instruct DB2 on how to sort (order) the rows that are returned in a result data set. When specified, this clause is followed by the name or an integer value representing the column's position, as it will appear in the result data set produced (*Answer B*) of one or more columns whose data values are to be sorted, followed by a keyword that indicates whether the data is to be sorted in ascending (ASC) or descending (DESC) order. If no sort order is specified, data is sorted in ascending order by default (*Answer A*). And when multiple columns are specified, the order in which the columns are listed determines the order in which the requested sorts are performed.

First, data is sorted for the first column specified, then the sorted data is sorted again for the next column specified, and so on until the data has been sorted for every column identified (*Answer D*).

Question 67

The correct answers are **A** and **E**. The basic syntax for the INSERT statement is:

```
INSERT INTO [TableName | ViewName]
  <([ColumnName], ...)>
VALUES ([Value | NULL | DEFAULT], ...)
```

where:

TableName	Identifies, by name, the table data is to be added to; this can be any type of table <u>except a system catalog table or a system-maintained materialized query table</u>
ViewName	Identifies, by name, the updatable view data is to be added to; this can be any type of view except a system catalog view or a read-only view that does not have a corresponding INSTEAD OF trigger associated with it
ColumnName	Identifies, by name, one or more columns that data values are to be assigned to
Value	Identifies one or more data values that are to be added to the table or updatable view specified

Aside from system catalog tables and system-maintained materialized query tables, the INSERT statement can be used to populate any table including a created global temporary table (*Answer B*), a declared global temporary table (*Answer C*), and a user-maintained materialized query table (*Answer D*).

Question 68

The correct answer is **C**. If an identity column is created with the GENERATED BY DEFAULT AS IDENTITY clause, when a user attempts to insert a record into the table, DB2 will generate a value for the identity column if no value is explicitly provided.

Identity columns are created by specifying the GENERATED...AS IDENTITY clause, along with one or more identity column attributes, as part of a column's definition. If an identity column is created with the GENERATED ALWAYS AS IDENTITY clause, an error will occur if a user attempts to insert a value into the column (*Answer B*). If the CYCLE option is specified as part of an identity column's definition, values will continue to be generated for the column after any minimum or maximum value specified has been reached (*Answer D*). And if specified, the CACHE 20 | NO CACHE | CACHE [CacheSize] option identifies the number of values of the identity sequence that are to be generated at one time and kept in memory (*Answer A*).

Question 69

The correct answer is **B**. The FETCH FIRST ... ROWS ONLY clause is used to limit the number of rows that are returned in a result data set. The ORDER BY clause is used to instruct DB2 on how to sort (order) the rows that are returned in a result data set—when specified, this clause is followed by the name (or position number) of one or more columns whose data values are to be sorted and a keyword that indicates whether the data is to be sorted in ascending (ASC) or descending (DESC) order. And a subselect can be used with a DELETE statement in place of the name of a table or view. Therefore, to achieve the desired objective, a delete operation must be performed on a subselect that uses the FETCH FIRST 10 ROWS ONLY clause and the ORDER BY clause to retrieve the last 10 rows in the table.

There is no FETCH LAST ... ROWS ONLY clause (*Answer C* and *Answer D*). And the ORDER BY clause used should instruct DB2 to sort the data for the table in descending—*not ascending* (*Answer A*)—order.

Question 70

The correct answer is **A**. Although the DELETE statement can be used to empty a table, such operations can have unwanted side effects. For example, the removal of every row in a table can cause a large number of log records to be generated, particularly if the table being emptied contains hundreds of thousands of rows. Similarly, if any DELETE triggers have been defined on the table being emptied, those triggers can be fired multiple times. A better alternative is to use the TRUNCATE statement to empty a table of its contents. Truncate operations do not generate transaction log records and they give you more control over any DELETE triggers that may have been defined.

A truncate operation will remove all rows from a table—*not just a few select rows* (*Answer B* and *Answer D*). And if the IGNORE DELETE TRIGGERS clause is specified with the TRUNCATE statement used, DELETE triggers that have been defined on the table will not be fired as the data in the table is deleted (*Answer C* and *Answer D*). If the RESTRICT WHEN DELETE TRIGGERS clause is used instead, DB2 will examine the system catalog to determine whether DELETE triggers on the table exist and if one or more triggers are found, the truncate operation will fail and an error will be returned.

Question 71

The correct answer is **B**. When the DELETE statement is used to remove records from a table, you should either provide an appropriate search criterion that can be used to locate one or more specific rows that are to be deleted (which is coded like the WHERE clause in a SELECT statement) or use the WHERE CURRENT OF [*CursorName*] clause. Otherwise, every row found in the table or updatable view referenced will be deleted.

Searched—*not positioned*—delete operations can work with multiple rows at one time (*Answer A*). To perform a positioned—*not searched*—delete operation, a cursor must first be created, opened, and then positioned on the row that is to be deleted (*Answer C*). And, while in some cases, the UPDATE statement can be used to delete individual values from a table or view by replacing those values with NULL, the DELETE statement can only be used to remove entire rows from a table (*Answer D*).

Question 72

The correct answers are **D** and **E**. A transaction (also known as a unit of work) is a sequence of one or more SQL operations that are grouped as a single unit, usually within an application process. The initiation and termination of a single transaction defines points of consistency within a database— normally, a transaction is initiated the first time an SQL statement is executed after a connection to a database has been established, or when a new SQL statement is executed after a running transaction has ended. Once transactions are initiated, they can be implicitly committed using a feature known as automatic commit (in which case, each executable SQL statement is treated as a single transaction, and changes made by that statement are automatically applied to the database unless the statement failed to execute successfully).

Transactions can also be explicitly terminated by executing either the COMMIT or the ROLLBACK statement. If the DB2 Command Line Processor (CLP) is used to perform operations against a database and AUTOCOMMIT is set to ON (which is the default behavior), every SQL statement executed is implicitly committed.

The system catalog is a set of special tables that contain information about everything that has been defined for a database system that is under DB2's control—it is not used to store points of consistency for individual transactions (*Answer C*). The longer a transaction is—that is, the more SQL operations a transaction performs—the more problematic it can be to manage (*Answer A*). This is especially true if multiple transactions must run concurrently. And the following SQL statements and operations are not under transaction control:

- SET CONNECTION
- SET SERVER OPTION
- SET PASSTHRU (although the session for submitting native SQL directly to an external data source that is opened by the execution of this statement is under transaction control)
- Assignments made to updatable special registers with the SET statement

INSERT, UPDATE, DELETE, and SELECT statements are not in this list and therefore *are* under transaction control (*Answer B*).

Question 73

The correct answers are **A** and **D**. Savepoints are created by executing the SAVEPOINT statement— *there is no CREATE SAVEPOINT statement*. And although the TO SAVEPOINT clause can be used with the ROLLBACK statement to back out a subset of database changes that have been made by a single transaction, the TO SAVEPOINT clause cannot be used with a COMMIT statement to apply a subset of database changes that have been made by a transaction to a database and make them permanent.

One or more savepoints can be used to break the work being done by a single large transaction into one or more smaller subsets. And you can create as many savepoints as you desire within a single transaction, provided you do not nest them (*Answer B*). The ROLLBACK TO SAVEPOINT statement is used to back out a subset of database changes that have been made within a unit of work (*Answer E*). And the RELEASE SAVEPOINT statement is used to remove a savepoint when it is no longer needed (*Answer C*).

Question 74

The correct answers are **D** and **E**. The following SQL statements and operations are not under transaction control, and therefore are not affected by the execution of a COMMIT or ROLLBACK statement:

- SET CONNECTION
- SET SERVER OPTION
- SET PASSTHRU (although the session for submitting native SQL directly to an external data source that is opened by the execution of this statement is under transaction control)
- Assignments made to updatable special registers with the SET statement

The ALTER (*Answer A*), COMMENT (*Answer B*), and LOCK TABLE (*Answer C*) statements are not in this list and therefore are under transaction control.

Question 75

The correct answer is **C**. The way in which a user-defined function (UDF) is invoked depends, in part, on what the UDF has been designed to do. Scalar UDFs are typically invoked as an expression in the select list of a query, whereas table functions are normally referenced in the FROM clause of a SELECT statement. In the scenario presented, the UDF named MI_TO_KM is a scalar function, therefore, it must be referenced in the select list of a query.

The CALL statement is used to invoke a stored procedure—not a UDF (*Answer A* and *Answer B*). And the specific name that is assigned to a UDF can be used to reference or delete (drop) the UDF, but not to invoke it (*Answer B* and *Answer D*).

Question 76

The correct answer is **A**. Once an SQL procedure has been created and registered with a database (via the CREATE PROCEDURE statement), it can be invoked by executing the CALL statement. And like other SQL statements that can be prepared and executed at runtime, CALL statements can contain parameter markers in place of constants and expressions. Parameter markers are represented by the question mark character (?) and indicate the position in an SQL statement where the current value of one or more host variables are to be substituted when the statement is executed. It is important to note, however, that when SQL statements are invoked from the DB2 Command Line

Processor (CLP), parameter markers can only be used for output parameters—the individual invoking the procedure is expected to supply values for any input parameters used. Therefore, since the first parameter in the SQL procedure named CODE.PROC1 is an input parameter, the statement CALL code.proc1(?, ?) will not execute.

The SQL procedure named CODE.PROC1() that was created in the scenario can be invoked by executing a CALL statement from the DB2 CLP that looks something like this: CALL code.proc1(1, ?) (*Answer B*). The same procedure can be invoked from an Embedded SQL application by executing a CALL statement that looks more like this CALL code.proc1(1, :result);. However, you would need to create a host variable named result first—this could be done by coding a statement that looks like this near the beginning of the application: double result = 0; (*Answer C*). And finally, the same SQL procedure could be invoked from within another SQL procedure by coding a DECLARE statement and a CALL statement within the body of the procedure that look something like this: DECLARE v_result INTEGER; CALL code.proc1(1, :v_result); (*Answer D*).

Question 77

The correct answers are **A** and **C**. The basic syntax for the CREATE PROCEDURE statement is:

```
CREATE PROCEDURE [ProcName]
  <([ParamType] [ParamName] [DataType], ...)>
  <LANGUAGE SQL>
  <DYNAMIC RESULT SETS [0 | NumRSets]>
  [SQLStmts])
```

where:

ProcName	Identifies the name to assign to the procedure that is to be created
ParamType	Indicates whether the parameter specified (in the *ParamName* parameter) is an input parameter (IN), an output parameter (OUT), or both an input and an output parameter (INOUT)
ParamName	Identifies the name to assign to one or more procedure parameters
DataType	Identifies the data type of the parameter specified
NumRSets	Identifies the number of result data sets the procedure returns (if any)
SQLStmts	Identifies one or more SQL statements (or SQL PL statements) that are to be executed when the function is invoked

TO (*Answer A*), FROM (*Answer D*), and TOFROM (*Answer E*) are not valid parameter modes.

Question 78

The correct answer is **B**. When a user-defined function (UDF) is created, the name (including the implicitly or explicitly provided qualifier), together with the number of parameters specified and the data type of each parameter make up what is know as the function's signature. The same name can be assigned to more than one function, but every function's signature must be unique—for the purpose of comparing function signatures, parameter names and data type length, precision, scale, and FOR BIT DATA attributes are ignored. The signatures of the two functions named STR_LEN are different because the numbers of input parameters used are not the same.

Because FOR BIT DATA attributes are ignored when comparing function signatures, the functions that have the same name and one input parameter with the CHAR data type and the FOR BIT DATA clause (*Answer C* and *Answer D*) have identical signatures. Similarly, because data type length is ignored when comparing signatures, the function that has the same name and one input parameter with the CHAR data type whose length is different (*Answer A*) has a matching function signature.

Question 79

The correct answer is **A**. While extended row size support enables users to create tables with more VARCHAR or VARGRAPHIC columns, its use does *not* change the maximum number of columns that are allowed. Instead, the ability to exceed the maximum record length for the page size used allows for more columns per row.

Extended row size support enables tables that contain rows that exceed the maximum record length allowed by a particular table space to be constructed in that table space (*Answer C*). Extended row size support simplifies the migration of tables (to DB2) that were created with another database vendor's product that have row sizes exceeding 32 KB (*Answer B*). And, extended row size support can help improve the performance of applications where the majority of data rows can fit on a smaller page but the table definition itself requires a larger page size (*Answer D*).

Question 80

The correct answers are **D** and **E**. With the exception of range-clustered tables (RCTs), any row–organized table can take advantage of extended row size support. However, to do so, the EXTENDED_ROW_SZ database configuration parameter must be set to ENABLE and the table must contain at least one column that uses the varying-length character string (VARCHAR) or the varying-length double-byte character string (VARGRAPHIC) data type.

There is no DB2_ROW_SIZE registry variable (*Answer A*). Whether a table contains at least one column with a CHAR or GRAPHIC data type makes no difference (*Answer B*). And while extended row size support helps Oracle users migrate their data to DB2, the DB2_COMPATIBILITY_VECTOR registry variable does not have be set to ORA (which will enable Oracle compatibility) before extended row size support can be used (*Answer C*).

Question 81

The correct answer is **D**. With DB2 10.5, the EXCLUDE NULL KEYS clause can be used with the CREATE INDEX statement to reduce the size of indexes whose data consists primarily of NULL values.

OMIT NULL KEYS (*Answer A*), IGNORE NULL KEYS (*Answer B*), and PROHIBIT NULL KEYS (*Answer C*) are not valid CREATE INDEX statement clauses.

Question 82

The correct answer is **C**. Starting with DB2 10.5, FixPack 4, columns that hold character data—that is, columns that have been defined as having a CHAR, VARCHAR, CLOB, GRAPHIC, VARGRAPHIC, or DBCLOB data type—have a special "string unit" attribute that controls how the length of a data value for that column is determined. This string unit attribute can be set to any of the following values:

- OCTETS
- CODEUNITS16
- CODEUNITS32

The CODEUNITS16 unit of length indicates that the units for the length attribute are Unicode UTF-16 code units (which are the same as double-byte). This unit of length can only be used with graphic string data types in a Unicode database.

The OCTETS unit of length (*Answer A*) indicates that the units for the length attribute are bytes and applies to all character string data types in a non-Unicode database. In a Unicode database, this unit of length can be explicitly specified, or it can be determined based on an environment setting. There is no CODEUNITS8 unit of length (*Answer B*). And the CODEUNITS32 unit of length (*Answer D*) indicates that the units for the length attribute are Unicode UTF-32 code units, which approximates counting in characters. The actual length of a data value is determined by counting the UTF-32 code units that would apply if the data were converted to UTF-32. As with CODEUNITS16, this unit of length can only be used in a Unicode database; however, its use is not limited to graphic string data types.

Question 83

The correct answer is **B**. The FLOWR XQuery expression is comparable to the SELECT-FROM-WHERE statement/clause combination available with SQL; the basic syntax for a FLOWR expression is:

```
XQUERY
    for $Variable1 IN Expression1
    let $Variable2 := Expression2
    where Expression3
    order by Expression4 [ASCENDING | DESCENDING]
    return Expression3
```

Consequently, the XQuery statement used in the scenario presented will return the expression "<name>ACME Manufacturing</name>". This expression is obtained by searching the XML data value stored in the CUSTINFO column of the table named CUSTOMER for the first opening tag found under the customerinfo root (outermost) element that is followed by a value.

Had the text() function been used with the XQuery statement used, the opening and closing tags for the name would have been removed and the value "ACME Manufacturing" would have been returned instead (*Answer A*). And because the customerinfo element is the root element of the XML data value presented, it is typically referenced in the for expression of the XQuery statement and is not returned as part of the return expression (*Answer C* and *Answer D*).

Working with DB2 Tables, Views, and Indexes

Question 84

The correct answers are **A** and **C**. When features that provide Oracle compatibility are explicitly enabled (by assigning the value ORA to the DB2_COMPATIBILITY_VECTOR registry variable), four additional Oracle-specific data types are made available for use. These data types are:

- DATE as TIMESTAMP(0)
- NUMBER
- VARCHAR2
- NVARCHAR2

The varying-length character string (VARCHAR or CHARACTER VARYING) data type (*Answer B* and *Answer E*) and the national varying-length character string (NVARCHAR) data type (*Answer D*) are built-in data types that can be used with non-Oracle–compatible DB2 databases.

Question 85

The correct answer is **A**. Externally, timestamp values appear to be fixed-length character string values that are up to 32 characters in length. However, the internal representation of a timestamp value requires between 7 and 13 bytes of storage.

The timestamp (TIMESTAMP) data type is used to store six- or seven-part values (year, month, day, hours, minutes, seconds, and microseconds) that represent a specific calendar date and time (*Answer C*). The range for the year portion is 0001 to 9999; the month portion is 1 to 12; the day portion is 1 to 28, 29, 30, or 31, depending upon the month value specified and whether the year specified is a leap year; the hours portion is 0 to 24; the minutes portion is 0 to 59; the seconds portion is 0 to 59; and the microseconds portion is 0 to 999,999,999,999—the number of digits used in the fractional seconds portion can be anywhere from 0 to 12; however, the default is 6 (*Answer B*). Because the representation of date and time values varies throughout the world, the actual string format used to present a date, time, or timestamp value is dependent upon the territory code that has been assigned to the database being used (*Answer D*).

Question 86

The correct answer is **B**. The integer (INTEGER or INT) data type is used to store numeric values that have a precision of 10 digits. The range for integer values is –2,147,483,648 to 2,147,483,647. Therefore, the integer data type would be a good choice for storing approximately 100,000 positive, whole numbers.

The small integer (SMALLINT) data type should be used when you need to store numeric values that have a precision of five or fewer digits (*Answer C*). The DECIMAL data type is ideal for storing numeric values that contain both whole and fractional parts separated by a decimal point—such as monetary values (*Answer D*). And the single-precision floating-point (FLOAT or REAL) data type should be used when you need to store a 32-bit approximation of a real number (*Answer A*).

Question 87

The correct answer is **C**. When a table contains one or more inline LOB columns, fewer—*not more*—rows will fit on a page.

When applications make extensive use of LOBs, and the LOB data they work with is relatively small—at most, just a few kilobytes—query performance can often be increased by storing the LOB data in the same data pages as the rest of a table's rows, rather than in a separate LOB storage object, which is where LOB data is stored by default (*Answer D*). Such LOBs are referred to as inline LOBs, and they are created by appending the INLINE LENGTH clause to a LOB column's definition. Inline LOBs improve the performance of queries that access LOB data because no additional I/O is needed to store and access this type of data (*Answer B*). Moreover, inline LOB data is eligible for compression, whereas traditional LOB data is not (*Answer A*).

Question 88

The correct answer is **A**. The fixed-length character string (CHARACTER or CHAR) data type is used to store character string values that are between 1 and 254 characters in length. And since most state names are less than 14 characters long, the CHAR(14) data type would be a good choice for storing commonly used state names like "Massachusetts", "North Carolina", and "Rhode Island" because only 14 bytes of storage space would be consumed for every value stored.

The character large object (CLOB) data type is used to store single-byte character set (SBCS) or multibyte character set (MBCS) character string values that are between 32,700 and 2,147,483,647 characters in length (*Answer B*). And while a CLOB(14) data value will require the same amount of storage space as a CHAR(14) data value, the CLOB data type is typically used for much larger data values. The national fixed-length character string (NCHAR) data type is used to store a sequence of bytes, up to 127 bytes in length, in a Unicode database that uses UTF-16BE encoding. So a NCHAR(254) data type cannot be created (*Answer C*). Finally, the varying-length character string (VARCHAR) data type is used to store character string values that are up to 32,672 characters in length. So while a VARCHAR(254) data type could be used to store commonly used names for states, it would be very inefficient to do so since 258 bytes of storage would be required for every value stored (*Answer D*).

Question 89

The correct answer is **D**. If the FOR BIT DATA option is used when a column with a character string data type (fixed-length character string or varying-length character string) is defined, data values stored in the column will be treated as binary data. This means that code page conversions are not performed if data in the column is exchanged between other systems, and that all comparisons are done in binary, regardless of the database collating sequence used.

The varying-length character string (VARCHAR) data type is used to store character string values; however, unless the FOR BIT DATA option is specified when a column is defined, the contents of a column with this data type will be treated as character data and code page conversions will be performed if data in the column is exchanged between other systems or if value comparisons are made (*Answer B*). The binary large object (BLOB) data type is used to store binary data values—not character string data values (*Answer A*). And while the character large object (CLOB) data type can be used to store character string values, the FOR BIT DATA option cannot be used with this data type (*Answer C*).

Question 90

The correct answer is **D**. When a database is configured for Oracle compatibility, four additional Oracle-specific data types are made available for use. These data types are:

- DATE as TIMESTAMP(0)
- NUMBER
- VARCHAR2
- NVARCHAR2

The decimal (DECIMAL) data type (*Answer B*), the decimal floating-point (DECFLOAT) data type (*Answer C*), and the Extensible Markup Language (XML) data type (*Answer A*) are built-in data types that can be used with non-Oracle compatible DB2 databases.

Question 91

The correct answer is **A**. A CHECK constraint is used to ensure that a particular column in a table is never assigned an unacceptable value; once a CHECK constraint has been defined for a particular column, any operation that attempts to place a value into that column that does not meet a specific set of criteria will fail. Consequently, a CHECK constraint is often used to ensure that a column's values fall within a specific range.

A UNIQUE constraint is used to ensure that values assigned to one or more columns of a table are always unique (*Answer B*). A referential integrity constraint is used to define a required relationship between select columns and tables (*Answer C*). And an informational constraint is used to make the DB2 optimizer aware of constraints that are being enforced at the application level so it can use this information to choose an optimal data access plan (*Answer D*).

Question 92

The correct answers are **C** and **D**. Referential integrity constraints are used to define required relationships between select columns and tables. Such relationships are established by comparing values that are to be added to one or more select columns (known as the foreign key) of a "child" table with values that currently exist for one or more columns (known as the parent key) of a corresponding "parent" table.

A foreign key can reference only one primary key—not multiple primary keys (*Answer A*). A primary key can be referenced by multiple foreign keys—not just one foreign key (*Answer B*). And referential integrity constraints are enforced only when INSERT, UPDATE, or DELETE statements are executed; they are not enforced when SELECT statements are executed (*Answer E*).

Question 93

The correct answers are **C** and **D**. A UNIQUE constraint is used to ensure that values assigned to one or more columns of a table are always unique. Informational constraints tell DB2 which business rules data conforms to; however, they not enforced. Instead, they are used to make the DB2 optimizer aware of constraints that are being enforced at the application level so it can take this information into account when choosing an optimal data access plan.

Only one primary key is allowed per table (*Answer B*); however, a single table can contain multiple UNIQUE constraints (*Answer A*). Referential integrity constraints are enforced by a unique index on the primary key of the parent table—not by a unique index on the foreign key (*Answer E*).

Question 94

The correct answer is **A**. A CHECK constraint is used to ensure that a particular column in a table is never assigned an unacceptable value; once a CHECK constraint has been defined for a particular column, any operation that attempts to place a value into that column that does not meet a specific set of criteria will fail. Consequently, a CHECK constraint can be used to ensure that the value of one column in a table is never less than the value of another column in the same table.

A UNIQUE constraint is used to ensure that values assigned to one or more columns of a table are always unique (*Answer B*). Informational constraints tell DB2 which business rules data conforms to; however, they not enforced (*Answer C*). Instead, they are used to make the DB2 optimizer aware of constraints that are being enforced at the application level so it can take this information into account when choosing an optimal data access plan. And referential integrity constraints are used to define required relationships between select columns and tables (*Answer D*).

Question 95

The correct answer is **C**. A view or a join operation—*not an index*—can be used to combine data from multiple tables.

Indexes are important because:

- They provide a fast, efficient method for locating specific rows of data in large tables (*Answer B*).

- They provide a logical ordering of the rows in a table (*Answer D*).

- They can enforce the uniqueness of records in a table (*Answer A*).

- They can force a table to use clustering storage, which causes the rows of a table to be physically arranged according to the ordering of their key column values.

Question 96

The correct answer is **B**. Column-organized tables do not need and cannot have *any* indexes defined on them.

The PCTFREE clause of the CREATE INDEX statement is used to control how much space is reserved for future insert and update operations (*Answer D*). If the INCLUDE clause is specified with the CREATE INDEX statement used, data from the secondary columns specified will be appended to the index's key values. In addition, the UNIQUE clause must also be provided (*Answer C*).

If the CLUSTER clause is specified with the CREATE INDEX statement used, the resulting index will be a clustering index, which is a special index that attempts to physically store records for a table on a page that contains other records with similar index key values. A clustering index usually increases performance by decreasing the amount of I/O that is needed to access data. However, a row-organized table can have only one clustering index (*Answer A*).

Question 97

The correct answer is **C**. Select properties of an existing table can be modified, and additional columns and/or constraints can be added or removed by executing the ALTER TABLE statement. For example, to change the data of a particular column in a table, you would execute an ALTER TABLE statement that looks something like this:

```
ALTER TABLE [TableName]
   ALTER COLUMN [ColumnName]
   SET DATA TYPE [DataType]
```

where:

TableName	Identifies, by name, the table whose definition is to be altered
ColumnName	Identifies, by name, the column whose data type is to be changed
DataType	Identifies the new data type that is to be assigned to the column

Thus, in the scenario presented, the following ALTER TABLE statement would be used to change the data type for the DESCRIPTION column in the PARTS table:

```
ALTER TABLE parts
  ALTER COLUMN description
  SET DATA TYPE VARCHAR(40)
```

The SET DATA TYPE clause—*not the ALTER DATA TYPE clause*—is used to change the data type (or the characteristics of the data type) that is assigned to a column in a table (*Answer D*). And there is no RESIZE COLUMN (*Answer A*) or ADJUST COLUMN (*Answer B*) clause for the ALTER TABLE statement.

Question 98

The correct answers are **A** and **B**. In most cases, if the properties of an existing index need to be changed, the index must be deleted (dropped) and a new index with the desired characteristics must be created. However, there is one property that can be changed without requiring an index to be dropped and recreated. That property is the attribute that controls whether an index is enabled or disabled for compression and it can be changed by executing the ALTER INDEX statement.

To convert an existing index to a clustering index (*Answer C*) or to make changes to an existing index such as adding the ability to support reverse scans (*Answer D*) or removing the ability to support reverse scans (*Answer E*), the existing index must be dropped and a new index with the desired characteristics must be created.

Question 99

The correct answers are B and C. Columns do not have aliases. And while tables are assigned to a specific schema at the time they are created, individual columns are not.

The basic syntax used to define a column element as part of a CREATE TABLE statement is:

```
[ColumnName] [DataType]
<NOT NULL>
<WITH DEFAULT <[DefaultValue] | NULL>>
<UConstraint>
<CConstraint>
<RIConstraint>
```

where:

ColumnName	Identifies the name to assign to the column (*Answer A*)
DataType	Identifies the data type to assign to the column (*Answer D*)
DefaultValue	Identifies the default value to provide for the column if no value for the column is supplied when a new record is inserted into the table
UConstraint	Identifies a UNIQUE or primary key constraint that is to be associated with the column

CConstraint	Identifies a CHECK constraint that is to be associated with the column (*Answer E*)
RIConstraint	Identifies a referential integrity constraint that is to be associated with the column

Question 100

The correct answer is **C**. If the WITH <LOCAL> CHECK OPTION clause is specified with the CREATE VIEW statement used, all insert and update operations that are performed against the resulting view will be checked to ensure that the rows being added or modified conform to the view's definition. Essentially, the WITH <LOCAL> CHECK OPTION clause guarantees that an insert or update operation performed against a view will not create a record that the view will never see.

RESTRICT (*Answer A*), CASCADE (*Answer B*), and WITH CONTROL OPTION (*Answer D*) are not valid clauses that can be used with the CREATE VIEW statement.

Question 101

The correct answer is **C**. With created global temporary tables, the table description is persistent and shareable across different connections. (With declared global temporary tables, the table description is not persistent beyond the life of the connection that was used to create it.)

A user temporary table space must exist before a created global temporary table or a declared global temporary table can be created (*Answer B*). Descriptions of created global temporary tables are saved in the system catalog, while descriptions of declared global temporary tables are not (*Answer A*). And each session that queries a created global temporary table will only be able to retrieve the rows that were inserted by that session (*Answer D*).

Question 102

The correct answers are **C** and **E**. A user temporary table space must exist before a created global temporary table (or a declared global temporary table) can be created. And, in order to reference a declared global temporary table in a SELECT statement, the table must be qualified with the schema name "SESSION".

With both declared global temporary tables and created global temporary tables, indexes and SQL statements that modify data (i.e., INSERT, UPDATE, and DELETE statements) *are* supported (*Answer A*). Descriptions of created global temporary tables are saved in the system catalog, while descriptions of declared global temporary tables are not (*Answer B*). And each connection that declares—*not references*—a declared global temporary table has its own unique instance of the table, and the instance is not persistent beyond the life of the connection (*Answer D*).

Question 103

The correct answers are **C** and **D**. A trigger is an object that is used to define a set of actions that are to be executed whenever a transaction performs an insert, update, or delete operation against a table or updatable view. If necessary, several different triggers can be created for a single table. However, when multiple triggers are needed, the order in which they are defined can be important. That's because when more than one trigger exists for a particular table, event, and activation time, they will be fired in the order in which they were created.

The triggered action (body) of a trigger is typically made up of SQL Procedural Language (SQL PL) statements (*Answer A*). When a trigger is created for a table that already has rows in it, it *will not* be fired immediately after it is created (*Answer B*). Instead, the trigger will be fired whenever a transaction performs an insert, update, or delete operation against the table. And when more than one trigger exists for a particular table, event, and activation time, they will be fired in the order in which they were created—not according to the type of event that causes them to be fired (*Answer E*).

Question 104

The correct answers are **A** and **C**. As the name implies, a BEFORE trigger is fired for every row in the set of affected rows before the trigger event takes place. Consequently, BEFORE triggers are often used to validate input data, to automatically generate values for newly inserted rows, and to prevent certain types of trigger events from being performed.

AFTER triggers—*not BEFORE triggers*— are often used to insert, update, or delete data in the same or in other tables (*Answer B*); to check data against other data values in the same or in other tables (*Answer D*); or to invoke user-defined functions (UDFs) that perform non-database operations. And INSTEAD OF triggers—*not BEFORE triggers*—are are fired when specific trigger events are performed against a subject view and their triggered actions are executed in place of the trigger event (*Answer E*).

Question 105

The correct answers are **C** and **E**. The following SQL and SQL Procedural Language (SQL PL) statements can be used in the triggered action of any type of trigger:

- DECLARE
- SET
- SELECT
- CALL
- IF
- FOR
- WHILE

- ITERATE
- LEAVE
- SIGNAL
- GET DIGNOSTIC

In addition, the following SQL statements can be used in AFTER and INSTEAD OF triggers (but not BEFORE triggers):

- INSERT
- UPDATE
- DELETE
- MERGE

Thus, the SET statement (*Answer A*), the CALL statement (*Answer B*), and the SELECT statement (*Answer D*) can be used in a BEFORE trigger.

Question 106

The correct answer is D. INSTEAD OF triggers are fired only when specific trigger events are performed against a subject view. Consequently, INSTEAD OF triggers are often used to force applications to use views as the only interface for performing insert, update, delete, and query operations.

BEFORE triggers (*Answer A*) and AFTER triggers (*Answer B*) are fired whenever a specific trigger event is performed against a subject table—*not a subject view*. And there is no such thing as a BETWEEN trigger (*Answer C*).

Question 107

The correct answers are **B** and **E**. A trigger is an object that is used to define a set of actions that are to be executed whenever a trigger event takes place; a trigger event can be an insert operation, an update operation, a delete operation, or a merge operation that inserts, updates, or deletes data.

The execution of the IMPORT command (*Answer A*), a TRUNCATE statement (*Answer C*), or the LOAD command with the REPLACE option specified (*Answer D*) will *not* cause a trigger to be fired.

Data Concurrency

Question 108

The correct answer is **D**. If a transaction that is holding a lock on a resource needs to acquire a more restrictive lock on that resource, rather than releasing the old lock and acquiring a new one, DB2 will attempt to change the state of the lock being held to the more restrictive state. The action of changing the state of an existing lock is known as *lock conversion*.

Lock escalation is an event that occurs when several row-level locks are replaced with a single table-level lock (*Answer A*). Lock wait is an event that occurs when a transaction waiting for a lock waits long enough to surpass the LOCKTIMEOUT period (*Answer B*). And a deadlock cycle is an event that occurs when two applications lock data that is needed by the other, causing a situation in which neither application can continue executing (*Answer C*).

Question 109

The correct answer is **C**. When a connection to a database is first established, a specific amount of memory is set aside to hold a structure that DB2 uses to manage locks. This structure, known as the *lock list*, is where locks that are held by every active transaction are stored after they are acquired. Because a limited amount of memory is available and because every active transaction must share this memory, DB2 imposes a limit on the amount of space each transaction is allowed to consume in the lock list. (This limit is controlled by the MAXLOCKS database configuration parameter.) To prevent a database agent (that is working on behalf of a transaction) from exceeding its lock list space limits, a process known as *lock escalation* is performed whenever too many locks have been acquired on behalf of a single transaction. During lock escalation, space in the lock list is freed by replacing several row-level locks with a single table-level lock.

Lock timeout (*Answer A*) refers to the amount of time that any transaction will wait to obtain a requested lock—if the desired lock is not acquired within the time interval specified, all database changes made by the transaction are rolled back, and the transaction is gracefully terminated. There is no such thing as "lock exchange" (*Answer B*). And lock conversion (*Answer D*) is an event that occurs when a transaction that is holding a lock on a resource needs a more restrictive lock and DB2 attempts to change the state of the lock being held to the more restrictive state.

Question 110

The correct answers are **A** and **D**. A lock is a mechanism that is used to associate a data resource with a single transaction, for the sole purpose of controlling how other transactions interact with that resource while it is associated with the transaction that has it locked. Locks are used to enforce isolation levels and the type of lock used can restrict or prohibit data access by concurrent transactions.

Locking and recovery do not apply to declared global temporary tables (*Answer B*). A transaction is allowed to hold only one lock on any given resource at any one time (*Answer C*). And while the memory resources available to store locks can affect the behavior of locking, the memory resources required to obtain and free locks does not vary with the type of lock used (*Answer E*).

Question 111

The correct answer is **D**. Anytime a transaction holds a lock on a particular resource, other concurrently running transactions can be denied access to that resource until the transaction holding the lock is terminated (in which case, all locks acquired on behalf of the transaction will be released). Consequently, without some sort of lock timeout mechanism in place, one transaction might wait indefinitely for a lock that is held by another transaction. Therefore, when seen in excessive numbers, lock timeouts can be as disruptive to a system as deadlocks.

By default, the LOCKTIMEOUT configuration parameter (which controls when lock timeout detection occurs) is set to –1, which means that transactions will wait indefinitely to acquire the locks they need (*Answer A*). Use of the LOCK TABLE statement will not prevent lock timeouts from occurring and may, in fact, cause them to occur more frequently (*Answer B*). And lock timeouts can be avoided by using the Uncommitted Read (UR)—*not the Repeatable Read (RR)*—isolation level; when this isolation level is used, the rows that a transaction retrieves are locked only if the transaction attempts to modify the data stored in them or if another transaction attempts to drop or alter the underlying table the rows were retrieved from (*Answer C*).

Question 112

The correct answers are **B** and **E**. DB2 implicitly acquires locks on the following data resources when needed: data partitions, table spaces, base tables, and rows.

DB2 does not acquire locks on views (*Answer A*), indexes (*Answer C*), or buffer pools (*Answer D*).

Question 113

The correct answer is **D**. If the following SQL statement is executed:

```
LOCK TABLE sales IN EXCLUSIVE MODE
```

a table-level Exclusive (X) lock will be acquired for the SALES table, and no other transaction will be allowed to read or modify data stored in this table until the transaction that executed the LOCK TABLE statement is either committed or rolled back.

If the statement ALTER TABLE sales LOCKSIZE ROW is executed, DB2 will always attempt to acquire row-level locks for every transaction that accesses the SALES table (*Answer A*). On the other hand, if the statement ALTER TABLE sales LOCKSIZE TABLE is executed, DB2 will always attempt to acquire table-level locks for every transaction that accesses the SALES table (*Answer B*).

When an Exclusive (X) lock is acquired, transactions using the Uncommitted Read (UR) isolation level can read all data, including uncommitted data, stored in the locked resource. However, they cannot modify data stored in the resource. All other transactions can neither read nor modify data stored in the locked resource (*Answer C*).

Question 114

The correct answer is **A**. If the following SQL statement is executed:

```
ALTER TABLE employees LOCKSIZE TABLE
```

DB2 will always attempt to acquire table-level locks for every transaction that accesses the EMPLOYEES table. However, any time a transaction holds a lock on a particular resource, other transactions can be denied access to that resource until the owning transaction is terminated.

Therefore, row-level locks are usually better than table-level locks because they restrict access to a much smaller resource, which in turn, allows more transactions to run concurrently. (Table-level locks limit concurrency; they don't improve it.)

Because each lock acquired requires some amount of storage space (to hold) and some degree of processing time (to manage), there is usually considerably less overhead involved when a single table-level lock is used instead of multiple row-level locks. So, in some cases, the use of table-level locks can improve query performance (*Answer B*). The use of table-level locks does not prevent lock escalation from occurring (*Answer C*). And the use of table-level locks does not prevent Intent None (IN) locks (or any other type of lock) from being acquired (*Answer D*).

Question 115

The correct answer is **B**. Both the ALTER TABLE statement and the LOCK TABLE statement can be used to control lock granularity (that is, whether row-level locking or table-level locking is used). However, only the LOCK TABLE statement can be used to control lock granularity at the transaction level (i.e., within a single transaction).

There is no DB2_LOCK_TABLE registry variable (*Answer A*), there is no LOCKSIZE database configuration parameter (*Answer D*), and the ALTER TABLE statement controls lock granularity at the global level—not within a single transaction (*Answer C*).

Question 116

The correct answers are **A** and **B**. Locks used by DB2 have the following basic attributes:

- Object
- Size
- Duration (or Lock Count)
- State (or Mode)

Activity (*Answer C*), Frequency (*Answer D*), and Granularity (*Answer E*) are not valid lock attributes.

Question 117

The correct answer is **C**. Exclusive (X) locks allow the lock owner to both read and update data in the locked object, but prevents concurrent applications that are not using the Uncommitted Read (UR) isolation level from accessing the locked data.

Intent Exclusive (IX) locks allow both the lock owner and concurrent applications to read and modify data in the locked object (*Answer A*). Share (S) locks allow both the lock owner and concurrent applications to read, but not modify data in the locked object (*Answer B*). And Update (U) locks allow the lock owner to modify, but not read data in the locked object; concurrent applications not using the Uncommitted Read (UR) isolation level, on the other hand, can read but not modify data in the locked object (*Answer D*).

Question 118

The correct answers are **B** and **C**. Super Exclusive (Z) locks are not acquired on a table when a view that utilizes the table is created or altered.

Instead, Super Exclusive locks are typically acquired on a table whenever the lock owner attempts to alter the table, drop the table, create an index for the table (*Answer D*), drop an index that has already been defined for the table (*Answer E*), or reorganize the contents of the table (while the table is offline) by running the REORG utility (*Answer A*).

Question 119

The correct answers are **B** and **D**. The system architecture used for a DB2 server and the amount of memory available, as well as how that memory is allocated, has no effect on lock granularity (that is, whether row-level locking or table-level locking is used).

When a connection to a database is first established, a specific amount of memory is set aside to hold a structure that DB2 uses to manage locks (known as the lock list). Because a limited amount of memory is available and because every active transaction must share this memory, DB2 imposes a limit on the amount of space each transaction can consume in the lock list—to prevent a transaction from exceeding lock list space limits space in the lock list can be freed by replacing several row-level locks with a single table-level lock (lock escalation). So, lock list size can affect lock mode and granularity (*Answer A*). And because the type of processing being performed can determine the type and number of locks that must be acquired, this can have an effect on lock mode and granularity as well (*Answer C*). Finally, the data access method used often determines the type and number of locks that are needed, so this metric can also have an effect on lock mode and granularity (*Answer E*).

Question 120

The correct answer is **C**. A read-only transaction operating under Currently Committed semantics will not acquire a lock as long as DB2 can determine that the data needed has been committed. (Transactions performing read and write operations avoid lock waits on uncommitted inserts, and transactions performing read-only operations end up trading a lock wait for a log read when they encounter uncommitted updates/deletes from concurrent transactions.)

Only transactions running under the Uncommitted Read (UR) isolation level are allowed to see uncommitted data—transactions running under any other isolation level cannot see uncommitted data and there is no mechanism that can be used to alter that behavior (*Answer A*). Likewise, there is no tool that can be used to force DB2 to write all data changes to the database as soon as the DB2 database manager can make a determination that those changes will eventually be committed (*Answer D*). Finally, the use of Currently Committed semantics will result in an increase—*not a decrease*—in the amount of log space needed (*Answer B*).

Question 121

The correct answer is **D**. As a general rule, the more restrictive the isolation level, the more data is protected. By the same token, the more restrictive the isolation level, the less concurrency is possible. Consequently, the Uncommitted Read (UR) isolation level offers the lowest level of data protection, but provides the greatest amount of concurrency.

The Repeatable Read (RR) isolation level (*Answer C*) offers the greatest level of data protection, but provides the least amount of concurrency. The Read Stability (RS) isolation level (*Answer A*) offers less protection than the Repeatable Read (RR) isolation level, but also provides more concurrency. And the Cursor Stability (CS) isolation level (*Answer B*) offers more concurrency than the Read Stability (RS) isolation level, but offers less data protection.

Question 122

The correct answer is **D**. The use of Currently Committed semantics will result in an increase—*not a decrease*—in the amount of log space needed; extra overhead is needed to ensure that logged data contains the full uncommitted version of any rows that are in the process of being changed. And there is no tool that can be used to force DB2 to write all data changes to the database as soon as the DB2 database manager can make a determination that those changes will eventually be committed.

Currently Committed semantics reduce lock contention by allowing read transactions to access the most recently committed data rather than having to wait for locks to be released (*Answer B*). By default, Currently Committed semantics are enabled for new databases that are created with DB2 9.7 and later (*Answer A*). To use Currently Committed semantics for existing databases that have been upgraded from earlier releases of DB2, you must assign either the value `ON` or the value `AVAILABLE` to the `CUR_COMMIT` database configuration parameter of the converted database. If the `CUR_COMMIT` database configuration parameter is set to `ON`, Currently Committed semantics are applied database-wide for both the Read Stability and Cursor Stability isolation levels (*Answer C*). If this configuration parameter is set to `AVAILABLE` instead, DB2 will store the appropriate information in locks and perform the extra logging overhead needed to support Currently Committed semantics. But, Currently Committed semantics behavior will then have to be enabled on an application-by-application basis.

Question 123

The correct answer is **A**. Transactions running under the Uncommitted Read isolation level can see changes made to rows by other transactions before those changes are committed. Therefore, only applications running under the Uncommitted Read (UR) isolation level are allowed to retrieve rows that have been updated by a transaction that is still active.

Applications running under the Repeatable Read (RR) isolation level (*Answer B*), the Read Stability (RS) isolation level (*Answer C*), or the Cursor Stability (CS) isolation level (*Answer C* and *Answer D*) can only see changes made to records after the changes have been committed.

Question 124

The correct answer is **B**. The Read Stability (RS) isolation level does not completely isolate one transaction from the effects of other concurrently running transactions. Consequently, when this isolation level is used, lost updates, dirty reads, and nonrepeatable reads cannot occur; however, phantoms can and may be seen. Access to uncommitted data is not allowed.

With DB2 Version 8.1 and later, it is possible to override the default isolation level (or the isolation level specified for a particular application) when individual queries are executed. This is done by appending the WITH [RR | RS | CS | UR] clause to the SELECT statement used. So, if you want to retrieve the data found in column COL1 of a table named TAB1, and you want to run the query under the Read Stability (RS) isolation level, you could do so by executing a SELECT statement that looks like this:

```
SELECT col1 FROM tab1 WITH RS
```

With the Repeatable Read (RR) isolation level (*Answer A*), access to uncommitted data is restricted; however, lost updates, dirty reads, nonrepeatable reads, and phantoms cannot occur. With the Cursor Stability (CS) isolation level (*Answer C*), access to uncommitted data is restricted; lost updates and dirty reads cannot occur, but nonrepeatable reads and phantoms can be seen. And with the Uncommitted Read (UR) isolation level (*Answer D*), dirty reads, nonrepeatable reads, and phantoms can and often do occur. However, access to uncommitted data is allowed.

Question 125

The correct answer is **C**. Just as it is possible to override the default isolation level used when select queries are executed, it is possible to temporarily override the behavior of Currently Committed semantics when certain queries are executed. This is done by appending the WAIT FOR OUTCOME clause to the SELECT statement used.

By default, Currently Committed semantics are enabled for new databases that are created with DB2 9.7 and later. To use Currently Committed semantics for existing databases that have been upgraded from earlier releases of DB2, you must assign either the value ON or the value AVAILABLE to the CUR_COMMIT database configuration parameter of the converted database. If the CUR_COMMIT database configuration parameter is set to ON, Currently Committed semantics are applied database-wide for both the Read Stability and Cursor Stability isolation levels. If this configuration parameter is set to AVAILABLE instead, DB2 will store the appropriate information in locks and perform the extra logging overhead needed to support Currently Committed semantics. But, Currently Committed semantics behavior will have to be enabled on an application-by-application basis (*Answer D*). There is no DB2_CUR COMMIT registry variable (*Answer A*). And the SELECT statement does not have a WAIT FOR COMMIT clause (*Answer B*).

Index

Boldface numbers indicate illustrations and tables.